MW01040775

Theory and History in International Relations

by Donald J. Puchala

ROUTLEDGE
NEW YORK AND LONDON

Published in 2003 by
Routledge
29 West 35th Street
New York, New York 10001
www.routledge-ny.com

Published in Great Britain by
Routledge
11 New Fetter Lane
London EC4P 4EE
www.routledge.co.uk

Copyright © 2003 by Routledge

Routledge is an imprint of the Taylor & Francis Group.

Printed in the United States of America on acid-free paper.

All rights reserved. No part of this book may be reprinted or reproduced or utilized in any form or by any electronic, mechanical, or other means, now known or hereafter invented, including photocopying and recording, or in any information storage or retrieval system, without permission in writing from the publishers.

10   9   8   7   6   5   4   3   2   1

Library of Congress Cataloging-in-Publication Data

Puchala, Donald James, 1939–
    Theory and history in international relations / Donald J. Puchala.
      p.   cm.
    Includes bibliographical references and index.
    ISBN 0-415-94535-6 (alk. paper)—ISBN 0-415-94536-4 (pbk. : alk. paper)
  1. International relations—Philosophy.   2. International relations—History.   I Title.

JZ1305.P83   2003
327.1'01—dc21
                                          2002037193

For
Jeanne,
Susan, Elizabeth, Madeline,
Alec, Max, and Annabella,
who deserve a better world.

CONTENTS

Acknowledgments

There are so many people who contributed to the conception and production of this book that I hardly know where to begin. Readers, however, will soon discover the tremendous intellectual debt that I owe to the generation of brilliant scholars who transformed the American study of international relations during the 1950s and 1960s. Foremost among these with regard to their influence on my thinking were Raymond Aron, Adda Bozeman, Karl Deutsch, William T. R. Fox, and Harold Lasswell. These scholars are no longer with us, but they are surely in my book. Very much with us, and also important contributors to my thinking about international relations, are my colleagues Roger Coate, Paula L'Écuyer, Paul Kattenburg, James Mittelman, Nicholas Onuf, Gregory Raymond, James Rosenau, and Mihály Simai. Morris Blachman had more than a small part in what became chapter 6. Richard Walker led me into a fascinating literature on T'ang Dynasty China, which in chapter 7 becomes part of my discussion about civilizations that do not clash. Ralph Mathisen knows more about ancient history than I can ever dream of knowing, so his comments on drafts of chapter 8 were invaluable. Harold French's commentaries on early versions of chapter 9 greatly enhanced my understanding of Hindu philosophy. Raymond Hopkins inspired my writing of chapter 10. Kenneth Thompson encouraged me to complete the intellectual odyssey that became chapter 5, and Ken was also one of the prepublication reviewers of my manuscript; his guidance was both welcome and most useful. Richard Mansbach also read my manuscript at prepublication. He improved it with his comments and then honored me by writing a most thoughtful foreword to the volume. Holli Buice prepared the bibliography, formatted the footnotes, and generally turned the congeries of pages into something resembling a manuscript. Sallie Buice protected my office door, which afforded me time to write, and the Walker Institute of International Studies generously financed those parts of my project that required financing. I finished the book during an academic sabbatical granted by the University of South Carolina's College of Liberal Arts, and for this leave time I am most grateful. Eric Nelson and his colleagues at Routledge were both very helpful and very patient. I also appreciate the cooperation of a number of publishers who granted me permission to reprint some of my writings that earlier appeared in academic journals or anthologies. Parts of chapter 2 originally appeared in the *Journal of International Affairs* and are reprinted with the consent of the editors. A version of chapter 3 and parts of chapter 11 appeared respectively in the *Mershon International Studies Review* and *International Studies Perspectives,* both published by Blackwell Publishers, Inc., and reprinted here with their permission. A version of chapter 4 appeared in *Ethics and International Affairs* and is reprinted here with the consent of the Carnegie Council on Ethics and International Affairs. Chapter 6 appears here with the permission of Addison Wesley Longman publishers. Chapters 7 and 8 are revised versions of articles published in *Global Society* and are reprinted here with the permission of the editors. An early version of chapter 9 appeared in the *Journal of Contemporary European Studies* and is included here with the permission of the editors. David Diop's poem "The Vultures" is excerpted here with the permission of Penguin Books, Ltd.

Foreword

RICHARD W. MANSBACH

It is rare to come across a book on theory that is so filled with common sense for the scholar and practitioner of international relations as is Donald Puchala's *Theory and History in International Relations*. Written by a wise and experienced theorist, it not only discusses what the title promises but also provides a panoramic sense of how the discipline has evolved—for better and worse—theoretically and methodologically. In doing so, it reminds international relations (IR) theorists of how much they have forgotten and, therefore, how much of what we think is new was there all the time in the work of earlier generations of scholars. In making his argument, Puchala shows that he is steeped in a wide variety of literatures and in refreshing fashion reminds us of the seminal contributions of some of the field's authentic intellectual heroes such as Adda Bozeman, Karl Deutsch, Harold Lasswell, Harold Sprout, and others. Their scholarly works endure and should not be ignored merely because of their dates of publication. The message for academics, especially younger ones, is that reinventing the wheel is hardly an optimal way to make progress.

In a word, *Theory and History in International Relations* is a splendid book and a major contribution to current debates over theory and method in global politics. Obviously some of the field's theorists and methodologists, especially those who still believe in the false promises of the field's "scientists," will disagree violently with Puchala's claims. But, then, this is a highly thematic piece of work that is likely to provoke healthy debate in the field.

An eloquently written volume of a series of the author's essays, the book is essentially a plea to scholars of global politics to turn away from the "manufacture" of data and narrow quantitative analysis and to return to systematic analysis of history to inform theory. It persuasively advances a definition of theory as informed "intuition" that, while affirming the use of modest empiricism, rejects the logical positivism of the so-called scientific revolution in the field. Although there are many books that deal with "method" or variants of "theory," few fit so well into and contribute so much to the revival of interest in history and historicism among IR theorists concerned with issues of change and continuity.

Theory and History is scholarship of the sort that we used to associate with those who regarded politics as a subject constructed from the stuff of life itself—philosophy, history, and the arts, as well as the social sciences. And the author draws on the natural and social sciences and from the humanities in persuasively arguing that IR theorists should rethink their enterprise. In this way, the essays stand in vivid contrast to the forgettable, often poorly written data-based syntheses that have cluttered the field in recent decades.

By now it be should clear that the *theoretical* achievements of our scientists were modest and that the widely advertised power of parsimony was greatly exaggerated. It should be equally clear that the much bruited claim of separating facts and values never really took place (despite the failure of many to acknowledge their normative premises) and seriously impeded our understanding of how and why things happen as they do in global politics. And, as Puchala's essays repeatedly remind us, skepticism toward undiluted positivism does not require that we reject empiricism or surrender to the narcissism and relativism of so much of postmodernism.

It is here that the critical role of history asserts itself, for the facts of the present only acquire meaning in light of the facts of the past. Although objectivity is elusive because historical interpretation is always contingent and the past acquires new meaning (inevitably biased) over time and place, the past is the soil from which our present emerges. In what follows, Puchala illustrates the search for meaning in a variety of interesting contexts, including the Cold War as a struggle between empires, the collision of civilizations, cultural encounters and colonies in the ancient world, and liberal approaches to the understanding of history and humanist/ethical contributions to the dialogue over theory. Anyone who has been involved in contemporary IR debates such as those that pit Francis Fukuyama and Samuel Huntington against each other will recognize the relevance of the problems that Puchala addresses.

Perhaps my fondness for this book is conditioned in part by recognition that at heart Puchala is a liberal like myself. History is, in Barbara Tuchman's words, "a distant mirror" of ourselves that reflects the importance of change in contrast to widely held assumptions about the permanence and universality of international phenomena. The problem of meaning in history emphasizes the impossibility of separating norms and values from actions and events. In this respect, chapter 9 in this book, concerning the search for universal normative principles in the context of three civilizations, is especially germane. As such, it provides a background for discussing human rights and, more generally, the normative underpinning of global politics from a historical perspective. Finally, acquaintance with history reveals how relatively unimportant are some of our debates, such as that over agent and structure. In history we quickly discover that both are always present in different weights, conditioning each other.

Still, while sharing Puchala's essential liberalism, I am probably less optimistic about the prospects for getting matters back in shape. Thus, where Puchala sees a genuine international relations "discipline," I see an absence of consensus as regards even basic concepts and a proliferation of isolated and isolating coteries of theorists who rarely speak to one another. Where Puchala optimistically sees a "distinctive and recognized body of theory," I see islets of theory with no mainland. Where he sees a possibility for recreating a mainstream by means of returning to history, I suspect that this will prove difficult owing to, among other things, the fact that very real rewards and penalties are at stake in our "theoretical" debates—rank, tenure, publications, and so forth. Furthermore, the nature of the beast with which we are wrestling makes it unlikely that we will get beyond the competing "stories" that we tell about the same phenomena, historical and otherwise.

This leads me to conclude by returning to IR's favorite historian, Thucydides. Realists and neorealists would have us believe that Thucydides' *History* tells the universal story of war as a consequence of the changing distribution of power. How much this underestimates the author: written in a tragic format, it confronts us with the antitheses of nobility in Pericles' *Funeral Oration* and the *Melian Dialogue*. Tragic fate brought on by hubris infuses the plague and the Sicilian expedition. Thucydides' *History* is hardly a work of "normal science," but then neither is Puchala's *Theory and History in International Relations*.

CHAPTER 1

Introduction

Reviewing Adda Bozeman's *Politics and Culture in International History* in 1961, Harold Lasswell welcomed the study as "sagacious, literate, luminous and opportune."[1] That same year, however, another reviewer, in the *American Political Science Review*, opined that in Bozeman's book "the American political scientist whose special interest is international relations will not find much that is centrally pertinent to his work."[2] This second reviewer's conclusion probably said more about American political science in 1961 than about Bozeman's study. Caught up in the aspiring scientism of their discipline, its ahistoricism and the attention-focusing environment of superpower competition, American political scientists in 1961 were preoccupied with coding and counting, correlating, minimaxing and modeling, and expecting that all of this, in addition to propelling scholarship forward, would somehow also lend the United States an advantage in competition with the Soviet Union. In this disciplinary context, Bozeman's examination of six thousand years of intercultural history might not have appeared centrally pertinent.

Yet it was by examining those six thousand years of peoples coming together that Bozeman was able to suggest in 1960 that the rivalry between the United States and the Soviet Union in the mid-twentieth century was a historical epiphenomenon. Though potentially apocalyptic, and therefore immediately important, the Cold War was not the most historically meaningful international phenomenon occurring at the time. There had been other cold wars in international history, indeed many of them, as well as countless "hot" wars, and other endless contests of power. But the strutting and fretting of states and their heroes through these episodes over millennia accomplished little more than to intermittently reconstruct political geography, desecrate a sizable proportion of humankind's artistic and architectural heritage, waste wealth, and extinguish hundreds of millions of lives.

A little more than a decade ago, an invitation to lecture on the topic "Culture and International Relations" afforded me opportunity to reread Bozeman's *Politics and Culture in International History*. Moving carefully through this remarkable work in the late 1980s, some twenty years after its publication, I noticed that time amplified its wisdom and fortified its conclusions. But the experience also raised questions about patterns and directions in international history. By the late 1980s, the Cold War was already fading from international history. But historically speaking, was this the end of something or the beginning? Had a grand cycle of power run its course, or was a new cycle starting—or does it really make any sense at all to think about international relations in terms of power cycles? Perhaps the Cold War had actually been an instance of great empires colliding. One empire collapsed; it imploded and then fragmented. Does this always happen when empires collide? Probably not, some would say, but then, why not? And what, in light of past experience, might happen to the empire left standing? Then again, in broader perspective, would it not be more meaningful to think of the entire last half of the twentieth century as an era of collapsing empires—first the Ottoman and the Austrian, later the British, the Dutch, the French, the Portuguese, the residual Spanish and the Russian—thus making *postimperial succession* the signal characteristic of our age? What exactly does this mean? Has it happened before? And what will follow? The period extending from roughly 500 to 1500 was also an era of postimperial succession, in this case the aftermath of Roman imperium, and after a great deal of rather painful shaking down, weeding out, sorting, and arranging, the durable European state system was the end result. Is this what usually happens during and after a period of postimperial succession?

Looked at somewhat differently, many aspects of the *modern* world were by the late 1980s beginning to look somewhat *medieval*. Structures and processes that identified twelfth-century international relations were reappearing in modern contexts. For one thing, ethnic frontiers in our contemporary world were beginning to obscure political frontiers—just, perhaps, as in medieval times: "-lands," "-marks," and "-stans" were better defined and sometimes politically more important than the "-doms" of the kings. Has it, for example, made much difference to the Kurdish peoples of recent decades as to where such places as Iraq, Iran, or Turkey begin and end, or to Pashtuns as to where Afghanistan ends and Pakistan begins? Is Serbia more usefully identified as the state pictured on political maps of the contemporary world, or as the place(s) where Serbs live? Might we say the same for Albania?

In some regions by the 1980s, intercommunal politics appeared to be superseding interstate politics, and sub- and suprastate ethnic interactions appeared to be conditioning, sometimes canceling, state-to-state transactions. Elsewhere, substate politics of other sorts appeared to be approximating interstate politics, as was also characteristic of the medieval world. By the 1980s, present-day warlords vied for and from their exclusive fiefdoms, tribes defended and extended tribal domains, and mafia strongmen fortified strongholds. Cities, too, appeared to be becoming increasingly autonomous as well as increasingly interlinked in commercial and communication networks, not entirely different from the networks of the Hanseatic league or medieval Venetian connections in the Mediterranean. States themselves were becoming highly varied in character, function, and capability. Only a very few could be considered actual states, and this too was reminiscent of medieval times. If such "medievalization" can be observed today, how is to be explained? More intriguing, is periodic medievalization a recurrent feature of international history? If so, what typically causes it and what typically comes after?

It also seemed in the late 1980s that the main axis of world politics had already shifted from East-West to North-South. As this shift was occurring, *interstate* relations remained vital, but *intercultural* relations became increasingly significant. Glimmerings of what we now call "the West and the rest" appeared. This is what Bozeman was writing about. But what exactly are intercultural relations? Are intercultural relations about power and domain, like interstate relations? Or are they about ideas contained in myths, creeds, philosophies, theologies, and ideologies? Are they benign or destructive, uplifting or regressive, pacific or violent? Intercultural relations have certainly been prominent at other times in history, as Greeks and Romans, Christians and Muslims, and Aztecs and Spaniards could surely attest. Yet what exactly does happen when cultures encounter one another, and what, if anything, does this have to do with interstate relations? Are the two kinds of encounters—intercultural and interstate—complementary, contradictory, or mostly exclusive, and, historically again, which have been more significant, consequential, or meaningful, and why?

Is *plus ça change, plus c'est le même chose* the leitmotif of international history, or is it simply *plus ça change, plus ça change*? One implication of the notion of "modernization" is that the present is different from the past and the future will likely be different from the present. Successive eras may differ in "evolutionary" ways—in which case, if we understand the mechanism of development, it may be possible to anticipate, perhaps even predict, the future. On the other hand, perhaps "revolutionary" change is what international history is really all about. Here, we probably can know a good deal more about the causes of revolutions, which are patterned and recurrent, than about their effects, which are manifold and varied. Regarding revolutions, therefore, it will always be easier to reflect than to project. So much more is this the case if change is at the same time directional and dialectical. Theses and antitheses always yield syntheses, although the latter are never predictable from either of the former. It is always possible, of course, that changes in the course of international history are both nonrecurrent and random, which would render the study of change most perplexing and attempts at theoretical understanding most frustrating.

Theory and History

This book is about international history, which I define *as the history of relations among states and peoples.* It has to do with encounters and their outcomes—that is, encounters among states and other organizations that interact across political and cultural boundaries and encounters among communities, ethnically, nationally, or civilizationally defined. Most of the essays that comprise the chapters of this book examine what happens when states and peoples come together in space and in time. Important parts of the ensuing discussions are also directed toward how we identify, describe, and explain what happens as a result of such encounters. It will become very clear in the pages that follow that I have great respect for the writings of historians. But I am not myself a historian, and I cannot claim to have uncovered anything from the records of the past of which historians are unaware. I am, rather, a scholar of international relations, and as such, what I mainly want to do in this book is to look at history through lenses crafted and polished by theorists in my discipline. I want to use international theory to interpret international history.

Theory and History in International Relations is not as much about historical *events* as it is about historical *patterns,* and identifying and explaining patterns is a theoretical undertaking. Using theory, however, is not the same thing as theorizing. The distinction is important: in this book I am primarily a consumer of theory, not a producer. Offering up new theoretical formulations is not what I intended when I began the research for this book, and though I make some generalizations about historical patterns in some later chapters, these were not the objects of my writing. Instead, *finding meaning in the history of international relations* is more what I had in mind. International relations theory is already rich in insights as a result of the contributions of many of my colleagues, past and present. Fine minds have long been at work describing and deciphering patterns of interstate and intercultural encounter, and the corpus of abstract thought about international relations is constantly expanding. The object of theorizing about human affairs is to fashion and hone intellectual tools that, when used, sharpen, deepen, and enrich our understanding of human affairs. Much of this book is about *using* such tools. Therefore, if readers are interested, as I am, in knowing more about how international relations theory illuminates international history they may find this book helpful.

The Nature and Uses of Theory in International Relations

Since a good deal is going to be said in this book about the nature of the body of abstract thought that I identify as international relations theory, only a very brief preview of what is to come need be entered here. First, international relations theory is not *scientific,* and this may be an attribute rather than a fault. Most of the corpus of thought identified as international relations theory satisfies few of the criteria of scientific theory. Little, for example, can be directly deduced from it, and even less can be predicted. It does not build from simple propositions to more complex ones, and on to "middle-level generalizations" waiting to be knit together by a social scientific Einstein into Hempelian unified theory.[3] For almost half a century, social scientists have been attempting to formulate scientific theories of international relations. As I shall try to make clear in later chapters, these efforts, if not misguided, have at least proven unsuccessful not only because the enigmas of the human condition are awesome, but also because the epistemological assumptions of the social scientists are questionable. The world may simply not be "grabbable" in the ways that social scientists have wanted to grab it. Searching for truth, furthermore, is an elusive quest under any circumstances, and limiting the search by privileging one methodology and disparaging all others renders the quest all the more unpromising.

In any event, most of the theory that today provides the intellectual superstructure for the study and understanding of international relations is not the result of the kind of scientific inquiry that most scientists would approve of. But while it fails deductively and predictively, it nevertheless offers a rich and exciting array of heuristics that can help us identify what happens "out there" in the phenomenal domain we call international relations. Our theories also excellently frame our ponderings about *how* and *why* what happens *happens*—which, of course, is what heuristics are supposed to do. International relations theory is an intellectual treasure trove of Weberian ideal types of phenomena, structures, processes, causes, effects, and outcomes. I shall treat it as such in this book.

What I also try to show in this book is that theory of the kind we have in our field is a most useful tool for historical interpretation. *Interpreting* international history means attributing significance to events, or, more broadly, attributing meaning to human experience. Significance may be wholly historical: all events are parts of patterns, and in the context of such patterns particular events may represent beginnings or endings, causes, consequences, or turning points. For example, they may mark the beginnings or ends of cycles or the beginnings or ends of progressions. They may also be symbols of continuity or change, the proofs of human sagacity, or the consequences of folly. Otherwise, significance may be political, economic, social, cultural, aesthetic, or moral. Theory can be a guide to interpreting happenings in all of these domains. A great deal of theorizing about international relations has focused on historical patterns. There are, for example, macropatterns of politics and economics—patterns of war and peace or of rise and decline and constancy and change; disheartening patterns of carnage, destruction, and inhumanity; and promising patterns of collective action in pursuit of beneficial goals. To the extent that theories of international relations can guide us to seek out and identify such patterns in history, they become intellectual tools. They facilitate interpretation by alerting interpreters to the broader contexts within which particular events or sequences are occurring. Particular historical events, even monumental ones, like the French Revolution or the Second World War, for example, are almost always manifestations of something larger in human experience or something deeper in the human condition. Theories can point us toward these more inclusive contexts.

Because theories are often normative as well as explanatory, they may also cue insights into the aesthetic and moral meaning of historical happenings. It is true that there is not very much theorizing in the discipline of international relations per se that can guide us toward interpreting aesthetic or moral significance. My disciplinary colleagues and I have perhaps paid too little attention to questions about how international relations "feel" or questions about the "rightness" and "wrongness" of perpetrations and outcomes. But writings within the discipline of international relations per se are not the only sources of international relations theory. Philosophers, artists, theologians, and, of course, historians all have reflected on relations between states and peoples. Their works are replete with insights. I highlight these later in this book, because they are centrally important, yet frequently overlooked. Social scientists are not the only ones who theorize about international relations.

History and Theory

While theorizing is not my main objective in this book, I nevertheless find it difficult to resist making generalizations about patterns I observe in international history. In this, I find myself in accord with a current trend in my discipline. There has been in recent years a resurgence of interest in international history among students of international relations. More accurately, the *renewed* interest is mainly among American students of international relations, because European colleagues have adhered rather consistently—and productively—to Hedley Bull and Adam Watson's affirmation that "our subject can be understood only in historical perspective."[4] Be this as it may, some of the renewed attention to history is in reaction to the substantive sterility of so-called formal theory fashionable today among American political scientists, and some of it follows from constructivism's increasing appeal and its emphasis on "historical specificity and contingency" in social structuring.[5] Some of the current interest in history is also related to the ending of the Cold War, which, as noted, has raised questions about the contest's world historical significance. In addition, there is now widespread recognition among scholars that too much of what has passed for theory in the field of international relations is actually an accumulation of generalizations about the politics of the European state system titularly confirmed by the Treaty of Westphalia in 1648.[6] There were, of course, international relations before 1648, and we are presently observing that international relations are continuing with vigor even though the Westphalian system has probably run its course. History remains the laboratory for the study of international relations, but this work space is actually a good deal larger than many theorists have been willing to recognize.[7]

In this book, my puttering in the laboratory of international history is largely guided by older traditions associated with comparative history and historical sociology. I look to identify regularities in the occurrence of human events, perhaps even to impose regularity upon such occurrences at levels of abstraction somewhat above the events themselves. There is at least the implicit expectation here that recognizing historical regularities and understanding their causes and effects can contribute to making better sense of human affairs. This enterprise is akin on the one hand to what Stanley Hoffmann (and others) have identified as *comparative history,* where the analyst initially conducts an inventory—a Weberian search for ideal types, if you will—of *kinds of things that happen* in international history.[8] Understanding international relations amounts in good measure to understanding *outcomes* in relations among states and peoples—that is, things that happen. There is of course continual novelty in international outcomes through time, but there is also continual recurrence. *Certain kinds of events happen again and again.* And as they happen recurrently, studying their recurrence in varying historical contexts can add to an understanding of why and how they occur.[9]

Closely related to the notion of comparative history is the methodology of *historical sociology.* Here we are not talking about historical sociology as the sociology of history or the evolution of society through time, as offered in the very thoughtful works of Michael Mann, Charles Tilly, and others from whom we can learn a great deal.[10] Instead, historical sociology as described by Raymond Aron is closer to what I believe I am doing. This is a method that involves (1) posing more or less general questions about kinds of happenings in human affairs, (2) seeking answers in varying historical contexts, (3) formulating generalizations on the basis of such answers, and (4) further examining the generalizations in additional historical contexts, refining or abandoning them as the case might be.[11] The procedures are inductive and interpretative. As Hoffman notes, "We must proceed inductively, before we reach any conclusions about general trends [or recurrent outcomes] manifest throughout history."[12] But we also must proceed with a certain amount of humility. Because of its distance from us, international history cannot be accessed with anything approaching certainty. Therefore, as Bull reminds us, "general propositions about this subject must . . . derive from a scientifically imperfect process of perception or intuition."[13]

I do not believe that my examination of international history has yielded any remarkably innovative theoretical insights, although I do in this book pay somewhat more attention to non-Westphalian contexts than has been customary in my discipline. I also ask and try to answer somewhat broader and deeper questions about intercultural relations than are normally taken up in so-called mainstream literatures in my discipline, and I concern myself with intra-, inter-, and postimperial affairs that, while not entirely ignored, are nevertheless often overlooked in contemporary writings. I make generalizations, but I offer no new theories. These can emerge only from much more exhaustive research than this book's essays represent.

The Discipline of International Relations

This book contains a good deal of commentary on the discipline of international relations. The reason, I suppose, that I make a case for the identity, integrity, and autonomy of this discipline is because many of my colleagues don't, and the case therefore needs to made. Relations between states and peoples constitute a distinct realm of human affairs. Studying these relations in all of their aspects and manifestations commands the attentions and shapes the careers of a distinct, distinctively trained, mutually conversant, constantly interacting, and professionally organized community of scholars. These students of international relations contribute to a distinct literature contained in an enormous collection of specialized journals, monographs, and books typically housed in distinct sections of great libraries. They also provide professional training aimed at intergenerationally reproducing their scholarly community, and any number of major universities around the world offer advanced degrees in international relations to certify professional qualifications. Most important, international relations flourishes intellectually as a result of having formulated a distinct and recognized body of theory that describes and explains phenomena in the relations of states and peoples that are of preeminent interest to students of the discipline. It is true that much of international relations theory is eclectically cobbled from a variety of sources. The theoretical frameworks and contents of several chapters in this book reflect such cobbling. But eclecticism can enrich thought, and it certainly enriches thinking about relations between states and peoples. Its sources notwithstanding, the distinctiveness of international relations theory lies in the fact that it is centrally useful to students of international relations and only marginally useful to others, just as the theories that intellectually frame other disciplines are centrally useful there and only marginally useful to international relations.

There is a tendency, especially in American academia, to define international relations as a subfield of another discipline. Political scientists, for example, are prone to define everything nonpolitical out of international relations. They then equate "international politics" with "international relations" and relegate the subject to the status of a subfield within their discipline. Several other disciplines also claim "international" subfields. This is perfectly reasonable because there are international aspects to their respective subject matters. But international relations theory informs little of the work that goes on in these fields, and equally little work there is directed toward improving upon, expanding, or refining international relations theory. Why should it? The concerns of other disciplines are their own. International relations theory defines the concerns of the discipline of international relations. Improving international relations theory is an important objective of the discipline of international relations. International relations is not a field; it is a discipline.

Theory and History in International Relations

Ten essays compose this book, as chapters 2–11, and they were written over the course of an extended decade, roughly between 1989 and 2001. Several were previously published in somewhat different forms. All were edited and revised to suit the purposes of this book, although, except when absolutely necessary, I did not try to update the essays historically. In places, therefore, the texts tap into the very turbulent real world of the 1990s as well as the equally turbulent, yet often quite unreal, academic world of the same era. All of the essays are variations on themes of history and theory, international relations as a realm of human activity and as an academic discipline.

There is no compelling logic behind the sequencing of the ten essays. Each piece can stand alone as an inquiry into an aspect of either international history or international relations theory. Readers therefore might like to look upon the essay collection as I do—that is, as a series of reports on experiments in hermeneutics, historiography, induction, deduction, reflection, and prognostication conducted in the spacious laboratory of international history. Some of my experiments were probably more successful than others, although each one was for me something of an intellectual adventure. On the other hand, the whole of this collection of essays is somewhat greater than the sum of its parts inasmuch as an important purpose of this book is to define an epistemological domain and then to demonstrate the efficacy of working within it. I thought it reasonable therefore to place epistemological and methodological issues at the head of the agenda, to then proceed through the interplay of theory and history, and at the end to reflect on the state of my discipline today, or perhaps better said, to reflect on where I stand with respect to my discipline.

Chapter 2, "International Relations Theory in Perspective," is in part autobiographical since I was very much caught up in the intellectual ferment that is now referred to as "the second great debate" among scholars in international relations. This one featured "scientists" and "traditionalists"; neither viewpoint triumphed. Triumph never happens in our debates about international relations. Debating continues even now, and some say that a third great debate is presently in full swing. Such disciplinary divides are distracting, yet they are also useful because they force participants—and onlookers—to reconsider first assumptions about directions and modes of inquiry. I found opportunity, not so much in the course of the second great debate, but rather in retrospect, to reflect on the nature and sources of international relations theory, which was mostly what the debate was about, and also what chapter 2 is predominantly about. This chapter establishes themes and sets tones for the rest of volume.

Chapter 3, "The Pragmatics of International History," in some ways extends the arguments offered in the previous chapter, but its main thrust is an attempt to epistemologically ground the interpretative methodologies that I use throughout the rest of the book. I am not confident that this attempt fully succeeds, but what does come through in the chapter is that interpretative methodologies are neither more nor less well-grounded epistemologically than other methodologies. There are no privileged pathways to the truth. Instead, there are numerous avenues of enlightenment. These days, in the discipline of international relations, it is rather fashionable to criticize postmodernists for having tossed truth into the dustbin by declaring it unattainable.[14] Chapter 3 hints that this may not be the whole story, as some of the more moderate proponents of postmodernism exert a liberating influence on scholarship by essentially, and refreshingly, taking epistemological questions off of our intellectual agenda.

Chapter 4, "International Theory and Cyclical History," is an interpretative essay that uses international relations theory to identify patterns in international history. Cyclical patterns are this chapter's main focus, and international relations theory calls our attention to several. There are, for example, cycles of power, imperial cycles, cycles of ideological diffusion and dissolution, and cycles of civilizational eminence and decline. There are also important theoretical literatures describing and explaining each. Chapter 4 uses theory heuristically: it examines manifestations of several of the cyclical historical patterns in twentieth-century international relations, and in terms of these it speculates about the future.

Chapter 5, "The Tragedy of War and the Search for Meaning in International History," highlights historical continuity in international relations. Conflict and war, pillage, plunder, and the recurrent and apparently limitless destruction of human lives and livelihoods are, sadly, constants in international history. The narrative of carnage is not difficult to document, and while it is important that the story be told, more central to this essay is *the meaning of the story*. To interpret meaning I turn to the insights of students of comparative literature, and then to literature itself to elaborate a vision of tragedy. I then use it to illuminate international history. Sources of international relations theory need not be sought only in the social sciences, and I believe that chapter 5 shows this. The chapter is not a diatribe against war, but rather an acknowledgment of an abiding fatalism in the human condition.

Chapter 6, "The Dancing Dinosaurs of the Cold War," was originally written in collaboration with my colleague Morris Blachman. It was substantially overhauled for inclusion in this book, but Blachman's contribution remains central to the essay and his name should therefore remain associated with it. The piece takes up and elaborates themes introduced in chapter 4—that is, what happens when great empires encounter one another in space and time? The answer, of course, is that a great deal happens in such contexts and the implications are manifold. Interimperial relations, as it turns out, tend to influence intraimperial relations, and vice versa. Blachman and I apply to the contest between the Soviet Union and the United States what we think we have come to understand theoretically about the international history of empires. Historically, the most recent Cold War was neither a unique nor even an extraordinary instance of imperial competition. Chapter 6 is of substantive interest because it approaches the Cold War era from a rather unusual perspective. Yet the more important point of our exercise is to underline that there are recurrent patterns in imperial experience.

Chapter 7, "International Encounters of Another Kind," is another elaboration on themes introduced in chapter 4. It is also one of the places in the book where I shift from using international relations theory to attempting to extend it. Collisions of great civilizations in international history are complex intercultural phenomena. They have been of considerable interest to historians, but until very recently, they have not attracted very much attention among social scientists. Nor, until very recently, have such major intercultural encounters led to very much theorizing. All of this symbolically changed with the publication of Samuel Huntington's "The Clash of Civilizations?" in 1993, and then later his book, *The Clash of Civilizations and the Remaking of World Order*.[15] But as much as anything else, the controversies surrounding Huntington's work reminded students of international relations that "culture" as a political determinant could be ignored no longer. Chapter 7 is not about Huntington or "the West and the rest," but instead about what happens more generally and recurrently when great civilizations encounter one another. The essay is an experiment in comparative history and historical sociology that I look upon as at least partially successful.

Chapter 8, "Colonization and Culture in the Ancient World," is about "the West and the rest"—but only in a very roundabout way. Methodologically, this essay is another experiment in comparative history and historical sociology, and it is also another attempt at theoretical generalization. Mainly, though, the analysis follows upon and elaborates some of the notions concerning intercultural international relations that were introduced in chapter 7. In chapter 8, I ask and answer, in a preliminary way, questions about the intercultural affects of colonization. What happens when culture encounters culture in colonial situations? The laboratory for this particular experiment is the ancient world, Egypt and Iran in the aftermath of the conquests of Alexander the Great. Intercultural interactions in the lands of the eastern Mediterranean during the last three centuries before the birth of Christ were complex; their results were manifold, and culture and politics were integrally intertwined. As it turns out, there is a good deal that can be gleaned from the history of this first extensive European colonization of non-European lands that contributes to our better understanding of the cultural results of the second extensive European colonization of non-European lands that ended only a few decades ago.

Chapter 9, "Myth, History, and Morality," takes a somewhat different look at intercultural relations. The international history with which we are most familiar is the story of how human beings arrayed on opposite sides of political or cultural frontiers have treated one another. By and large, they have usually not treated one another very kindly. Yet, there is also a parallel history of writing and thinking about how human beings *ought* to treat one another, and especially about how neighbors and strangers ought to treat one another. Chapter 9 traces the "ethics of the other" through the moral philosophies of three venerable civilizations: the Western, the Hindu, and the Confucian. The analysis underlines the importance of myths in human affairs and identifies complementary moral myths across cultures. At first glance, this esoteric foray into ethics and comparative religion may appear somewhat irrelevant to both the themes of this book and the problems of the world. However, it is not very difficult to recognize that claims concerning moral universalism, rivaled by affirmations of moral relativism, are at the heart of present-day, highly politicized controversies about human rights. At least in this subject area, ethical theory is of considerable practical importance. It ought therefore to be considered an integral and important dimension of international relations theory.

Chapter 10, "Liberal Theory and Linear History," is the sequel to chapter 4's concerns with cycles in international history. It asks whether international history is in any sense directional. Is it perhaps teleological? Is it at least progressive? Present-day liberal theories in international relations hint at all of these linear historical possibilities, the preponderance of which points to a benign future of peace and well-being. Westerners in particular—inheritors of the Enlightenment—can accept that the idea of progressive history is plausible. Or at least to many of us it is not entirely outlandish. But where, with regard to such positive anticipations, does fond hope end and serious scholarship begin? Focusing on liberal international theory, chapter 10 examines both the controversial idea of linear history and the mechanisms that may account for historical directionality. It also introduces the possibility that international history may indeed be directional, but degenerative instead of progressive. The "end of [international] history" could be no world at all.

Chapter 11, "Beyond the Divided Discipline," brings this book full circle. It closes on a note that recalls its opening here in chapter 1 and connects with the materials and discussion in chapter 2. "Beyond the Divided Discipline" was written almost a decade after "International Relations Theory in Perspective." The world dramatically changed during these ten years, but the discipline of international relations hardly changed at all. Great debate continues in full swing; it is healthy if it has the effect either of separating intellectual chaff from wheat, or of yielding convergence or consensus. Academic debates seldom result in either of these, leastwise methodological and epistemological debates about the study of international relations. In an ironic way the seemingly perennial intellectual conflict within our discipline reflects the endless political conflict in the world we study. Chapter 11 offers a review and evaluation of the current state of the discipline of international relations. The commentary is notably biased because it emerges from my own experience. This experience may have been peculiar, although I think not entirely so, because concerns about intellectual intolerance, disappointment over increasing factionalism, questioning regarding the value in sacrificing richness in the interest of theoretical parsimony, and dismay over the closing out of humanistic approaches and insights are rather widespread in our profession today. Having said all of this, the main message of chapter 11 is its call for less debate and more dialogue about an ever-changing, highly complex, and very dangerous realm of human affairs that continues to defy satisfactory understanding.

CHAPTER **2**

International Relations Theory
in Perspective

When in 1967 the Department of Public Law and Government at Columbia University voted to change its name to the Department of Political Science, I enthusiastically joined the majority. Several of my more senior colleagues, William T. R. Fox among them, questioned this change of academic symbolism. They argued, wrongly I thought at the time, that inserting the designation "science" into the department's title signaled a veering toward a philosophy of knowledge that had not yet adequately proven its efficacy in the study of human affairs. "Public law" and "government" were, after all, only objects of study, while "political science" was a prescribed way to study, and there was some risk, my senior colleagues explained, in favoring, even by a choice of symbols, one pathway to understanding over others. But as Bertrand Russell had poetically underlined quite some time earlier, that which "presents itself as empiricism is sure of widespread acceptance, not on its merits, but because empiricism is the fashion."[1] And so, political science was embraced by Columbia University.

As it turned out, the name change failed to elevate the Columbia department in Albert Somit's prestige rankings. Most of the department's members were insufficiently avant-garde and not especially "scientific" in their methods of scholarship, and these were the keys to high ranking on Somit's list.[2] Actually, most of the members of the Columbia department were specialists in international relations and remained largely unbothered by the "scientific revolution" in political science. One result of the agnosticism of these scholars regarding science as applied to the study of human affairs was that they missed most of what Fred Warner Neal and Bruce D. Hamlett described as the "enthusiastic, well financed, faddist, nationally oriented" academic circus that was the field of international relations in the United States during the 1960s and '70s.[3]

The more significant result of ignoring the scientific revolution was that the Columbia specialists in international relations produced, or had a hand in producing, several of the most highly respected, and still widely read, contemporary works in the theory of international relations. These included, among others, Kenneth Waltz's *Man, the State and War,* Hedley Bull's *The Anarchical Society,* Louis Henkin's *How Nations Behave,* and Raymond Aron's *Peace and War.*[4] At the time, the other large island of relative indifference toward scientism in international relations (or "behavioralism," as the movement was alternatively designated) was Harvard University. There Stanley Hoffmann held court, Samuel Huntington was newly arrived (from Columbia), Joseph Nye held an assistant professorship, Steven Krasner held a degree, and Robert Keohane held a return ticket. The stature of this Harvard cast in the field of contemporary international relations theory needs no reiteration here.

Being indifferent to scientism is not the same as disparaging science. Each of the scholars I have mentioned probably identifies himself as a social scientist and, indeed, the theoretical work of each qualifies as social science. But very few of what I would consider to be the most insightful works of contemporary international relations theory seem to have resulted from commitments to epistemologies of logical positivism, operationalism, or empirical verifiability that rest at the philosophical core of behavioralism. If there are epistemological commitments underlying the theoretical accomplishments of thinkers like Raymond Aron, Hedley Bull, Ernst Haas, Stanley Hoffmann, Robert Keohane, Hans Morgenthau, Joseph Nye, Kenneth Thompson, and Kenneth Waltz; more recently Peter Katzenstein and Stephen Krasner; and most recently Yale Ferguson, Richard Mansbach, and Alexander Wendt, they would seem to be to either a traditional kind of empiricism, reminiscent of David Hume or John Locke, or something akin to Kantian transcendentalism, about which more will be said later.

It needs to be acknowledged here, however, that important contributions to the theory of international relations have also been made by scholars centrally identified with both scientism and behavioralism. Karl Deutsch, Morton Kaplan, and Harold Lasswell are certainly prominent among these. But, as I will attempt to show below, the greatest theoretical contributions were made by these scholars not when they were performing as positivists but when they were thinking as metaphysicians.

The thesis of this essay is that striving for enhanced theoretical understanding in the discipline of international relations has not been entirely the "elusive quest" portrayed by Ferguson and Mansbach, although one can sympathize with their consternation and accept much of what they offer to account for it.[5] To the extent that there has been an elusive quest, it has taken the form of a two-decade detour (heralded as a shortcut to enlightenment) through pseudoscience. This way turned out to be fraught with quicksands that swallowed most of the unwitting intellectual pilgrims. However, not everyone took the detour. Some travelers found their way back, and our theoretical understanding of international relations is presently the better for this.

The Twenty-Year Detour

Michael Haas's fine 1970 essay "International Relations Theory" captured the exuberance of the behavioral revolutionaries then emerging from Yale University, the University of Michigan, Northwestern University, and elsewhere. These scholars were well armed—that is, statistically trained, computer literate, and Hempel-Popper primed—to transform international relations into a true science. "Although advocates of earlier emphases are still active," Haas asserts with some confidence, "the behaviorist school is certainly the most important source of innovation today." "The behaviorist," he explains, "defines knowledge as the sum of all tested propositions." Haas expected that "in years to come it will be imperative to link theory and research much more intimately in order for the field of international relations as a whole to yield tested propositions that may be pyramided into the edifice of a theoretical science.... Since a strictly empirical science would only consist of almanacs of raw data or isolated findings, in a theoretical science there must be an analytical structure capable of generalizing beyond data to predict relationships within as yet unexperienced situations."[6] Oran Young agreed, writing that "one important conception of theory focuses on highly and deductively interdependent propositions dealing with specified classes of phenomena."[7] At the time, I also shared this vision of international relations as a deductive science. For there it was: an edifice of ever-broadening and deepening knowledge about international relations, built up in pyramid fashion, tested proposition added onto tested proposition until the masses of verified facts amounted to umbrella statements about particular realms of international behavior as, for example, crisis behavior, escalation, or integration. Such umbrella statements would constitute "middle-gauge" theories, and these would then be heaped and summed to ultimately arrive at a general theory of international relations. From such a general theory—indeed, even from the middle-gauge levels of the propositional pyramid—it would be possible to explain particular events by deducing (albeit probabilistically) from discovered laws of human behavior. Knowing such laws would also make it possible to predict future happenings within statistically determined intervals of confidence.

Nor was there much doubt in the ranks of the aspiring scientists of international relations that these propositional pyramids could be built, because systematic, replicable observations were the handles, as one young scholar put it to me, for "grabbing the world where it is grabbable." Many, like J. David Singer and Charles McClelland, for example, believed that social reality was almost universally "grabbable" and that data could be generated, or "made" as was said in the vernacular of the time, that would render observable just about anything that the social scientist needed to observe.[8] Nor were the scientists of international relations predisposed to forgo opportunities that the new room-sized computers presented for the systematic storage, rapid retrieval, and statistical and visual scrutiny of data.

The "scientific revolution" in the discipline of international relations began in the early 1960s. It was in full swing by 1968 when it was highlighted by the publication of Singer's *Quantitative International Politics*.[9] Yet by the mid-1980s, Ferguson and Mansbach observe, "the scientific revolution" had been "all but abandoned as a goal" because among other things it had "precious few results to show for decades of work and countless dollars spent."[10] Even a most sympathetic reviewer of the behaviorist literature in international relations would have to share this view, particularly regarding the scientists' early aspirations for building propositional pyramids into empirical theories.

Still, proponents of scientism in international relations continue to ply their trade. Interestingly, the intellectual genre, while largely ignored in the United Kingdom and France, has caught on in Germany and Scandinavia as well as in Eastern Europe and in Russia, where "science" imparts elevated academic stature. However, in the United States, today's proponents of scientism in international relations are mostly the second- and third-generation students of the early enthusiasts. They organize panels at meetings of the International Studies Association, talk about such things as the promise of new databases, pitfalls in coding the *New York Times*, and finally settling the debate between Waltz and Deutsch and Singer about stability and polarity (which took place in 1964!). They cite one another profusely in their books and journal articles, but they tend to be cited less and less frequently outside of their intellectual subculture. Their attentive readership in publications such as the *Journal of Conflict Resolution* has also fallen off noticeably. These are, alas, the orphans of the scientific revolution in international relations.

What Went Wrong? The Critics and Their Claims

From the beginning, scientism as applied to the study of international relations raised hackles. Over time, the crescendo of criticism rose in direct proportion to the revolution's failure to revolutionize knowledge in the discipline. The behaviorists were labeled "number crunchers." They were accused of being uninterested in philosophy and unmindful of history, which in Parkinson's estimation is "the greatest potential danger to the field of study of international relations."[11] When they ventured to make policy prescriptions on the basis of their work, as the Peace Researchers sometimes did, they were panned for being irresponsible, and when they abstained from policy involvement they were pilloried for being irrelevant.[12] Some outspoken critics, like Hedley Bull, argued that the behavioralists could not answer any questions about international relations that were worth asking. "If by a scientific theory of international relations," Bull wrote in 1975, "we mean one which is . . . strictly empirically verifiable, then in my view no strictly scientific theory can come to grips with the central issues of the subject . . . which concern the value premises of international conduct."[13]

In the midst of this came Oran Young's harsh review of Bruce Russett's *International Regions and the International System.* Young memorably referred to Russett as the "industrious tailor to a naked emperor," and criticized him for "purist induction," which meant running everything against everything else in the hopes that something interesting might emerge.[14] *International Regions,* frankly, was not one of Russett's better efforts, but neither was it the worst case of purist induction then running rampant in the literature. "There is, in much of this," Neal and Hamlett summarize for the critics, "a commendable effort to be objective. . . . But the result seems to be more one of avoiding the real problems of international relations-theory at the expense of philosophy, data collection at the expense of analysis, quantification at the expense of meaning. While the objective is to be scientific, what is achieved is often merely technical."[15]

I have allowed several of the critics of scientism as applied to international relations to speak here for themselves, partly to convey the spirit of the antibehavioral attack, and partly to signal its superficiality. There was nothing fundamental in the criticism, nothing, that is, that could not be responded to by telling the critics that they simply did not understand what science as applied to international relations entailed. In fact, criticism had the effect of encouraging the behavioralists to work harder and plow deeper into the intellectual fields they had chosen to till. For one thing, the behaviorists were not without a philosophy. They espoused logical positivism and it carried great authority among scientists. Second, the behaviorists were not ignoring history—they were coding it! Instead of "crunching numbers" they were comparing sampled social-political reality to established, inter-pretable, intuitively meaningful statistical models. Correlation and regression models, even when reduced to rudimentary linear and bivariate forms, are not outlandish departures from the common sense of how things go together in the world. Rather than engaging in "purist induction," most of the more sophisticated behavioralist scholars, like Singer, were in fact trying to build the propositional pyramids of progressively higher-level theory that was their scientific goal. Many behavioralist scholars are still trying to do this.

Deeper Issues of Epistemology

I, however, am no longer looking to build an empirical theory of international relations by testing and heaping propositions or by otherwise working methodically from the parts to the whole of the social-political realities in which I am interested. This is because I am now reasonably convinced that no general theory will, or even can, emerge from such a piecemeal theory-building effort. Theories, scientific or otherwise, are simply not born by cobbling wholes from parts.[16]

Behavioralism in international relations has not been overwhelmed by its critics; it has instead hit an epistemological iceberg that has been floating in its intellectual waters since the beginning. In the rush to "go scientific" in the early 1960s, practitioners of behavioralist international relations rather uncritically adopted from political science the logical positivistic epistemology that political science, in its haste to move away from public law and government, had rather uncritically adopted from sociology. How critical or uncritical the sociologists were is not clear to me, though it is most likely that they adopted their logical positivism from psychology, which in its ambitions to be a true science of the mind embraced positivism to ape the natural sciences, where the sense-dependent, observation-bound pathway to knowledge was apparently producing exhilarating results.

Simply and briefly put, the positivist believes that knowledge about the world can only be gained from sensory experience, that complex ideas (or facts) about the world are arrived at by combining simpler ideas, but that all complex ideas ultimately can be traced back to component simpler ideas acquired by sensory experience. What the positivist does not believe is also significant. He does not believe that alternative pathways to knowledge— that is, ways other than through sensory experience and the amalgamation of simple experience-born facts, are possible or indeed necessary. He does not therefore believe in metaphysics, or knowledge of reality gained through reasoning, contemplation, or intuition (or in religion, which instills knowledge through revelation). Seeing, for the positivist, is believing, and that which cannot be observed (or otherwise sensed) cannot be real. In Susanne Langer's phrasing,

> The only philosophy that rose directly out of a contemplation of science is positivism, and it is probably the least interesting of all doctrines, an appeal to common sense against the difficulties of establishing metaphysical or logical first principles.
>
> Positivism, the scientists' metaphysic, entertains no doubts and raises no epistemological problems; its belief in the veracity of sense is implicit and dogmatic knowledge from sensory experience was deemed the only knowledge that carried any affidavit of truth; for truth became identified, for all vigorous modern minds, with empirical fact. And so, scientific culture succeeded....An undisputed empiricism—not skeptical, but positivistic—became its official metaphysical creed, experiment its avowed method, a vast hoard of "data" its capital, and correct prediction of future occurrences its proof.[17]

It was this positivism that behavioral international relations bought wholesale in the 1960s, without acknowledging—possibly without recognizing—that positivism's entire epistemological edifice was at that very time being challenged by the work of important figures in the field of the philosophy of knowledge such as Ernst Cassirer, Paul Feyerabend, Thomas Kuhn, Susanne Langer, and Hilary Putnam.[18] In fact, as Harold Morick explains in his introduction to the 1980 volume *Challenges to Empiricism*, "one of the main themes of philosophy and theory of science in the last 20 years is the critical assessment of the foundations of contemporary empiricism."[19] Positivism's orthodoxy was shaken by a variety of pulls from those who made a profession of studying pathways to the truth. Langer raised practical questions: In what sense could science claim to be building knowledge from sensory experience, when most of the phenomena being studied were not being experienced? Were not the findings of science revealed as "readings" on instruments rather than as sensed objects? If so, are our "sense data" not actually symbols of objects, and do we therefore need an epistemology based on the meaning of symbols rather than on the interpretation of sensed objects?[20] Other critics challenged the positivists' notion of generalization via induction: Does observation lead to theoretical intuition through the amalgamation of simple understandings into complex ideas and ultimately into laws, or does prior intuition inspire and organize observation? To the extent that the latter is the case, what are the sources of prior intuition? Need intuitions come from prior observations, or can physical and human reality be known through reason and introspection much in the way that the ethereal realm of mathematics is accessed? Reflecting on the development of natural science, Feyerabend, for example, emphasizes that "progress was often made by following theory, not observation, and by rearranging our observational world in conformance with theoretical assumptions." Further noting that "in the struggle for better knowledge theory and observation enter on an equal footing," Feyerabend concludes that, "empiricism, insofar as it goes beyond the invitation not to forget considering observations, is . . . an unreasonable doctrine, not in agreement with scientific practice."[21]

There is more. Most fundamental, and most damaging to logical positivism, is the question of whether there is an unobservable reality, natural, social or otherwise, that is nonetheless knowable. Philosophers of every age, beginning perhaps with Plato, have of course believed in the unobservable but knowable, or in its linguistic variant the knowable but verbally unexplainable (due to the constraints of the discursive nature of human languages). What intrigues me, and what might bother positivists practicing in the social sciences that wish to think about it, is that many of the central concepts of our human-oriented disciplines denote unobservables, which we nevertheless hope are knowable. "State " "society," "international system," "international interdependence," "global economy," "world revolution," "security community," and the like are bread-and-butter notions for those of us who make a profession trying to say intelligent things about world affairs. Yet none of these are observable as wholes, and they never will be. This is quite a different problem from much that has been encountered in the natural sciences, where initial unobservables like atomic particles, chromosomes, genes, moons around Neptune, and chemical reactions at the molecular level frequently become observable as observational techniques are improved. By contrast, social wholes are not likely to become more empirically accessible once we have figured out better ways to look at them. Of course, natural science, in its theoretically most ambitious endeavors (like the quest for a unified theory in physics), is also dealing with unobservables; here problems of "knowability" are similar to those facing social scientists. But social scientists tend to run into unobservability at much lower levels of abstraction.

Logical positivism as applied to international relations could resolve the problem of unobservable wholes if it could assure us that the nature of unobservable wholes could be induced from the nature of observable parts, and that the wholes are in no sense greater than or different from the sum of their respective parts. Frankly, I am skeptical on both of these counts. One can accept that in physics and chemistry, where elements and reactions seem to be universally invariant, it is possible to infer something about the universe by observing happenings on Earth or in other parts of the cosmos. One can even suppose that in archaeology or paleontology the nature of wholes can be induced from the study of parts, though within limits, as we cannot really be certain what a brontosaurus looked like. And surely, the limits of parts-and-wholes inferences must be even greater regarding social structures and processes where there is apparently great variability across time and space, because unlike the physical universe or the dead and fixed worlds of archaeology and paleontology, social wholes change their nature. There is also always considerable uncertainty about whether parts observed are actually elements of the wholes inferred. Some philosophers, like Langer, whose work I find to be extremely insightful, tell us that our attempts to infer or otherwise know about social wholes from observed parts have been futile and therefore probably misguided from the start. Langer writes, "The physical sciences found their stride without much hesitation; psychology and sociology tried hard and seriously to 'catch the tune and keep the step,' but with mathematical laws they were never really handy. Psychologists have probably spent almost as much time avowing their empiricism, their factual premises, their experimental techniques, as . . . making general inductions. They still tell us that their lack of laws and calculable results is due to the fact that psychology is but young. When physics was as old as psychology is now, it was a definite systematic body of highly general facts, and the possibilities of its future expansion were clearly visible."[22]

Other philosophers, like Cassirer, tell us that the problem is that we cannot simply combine observation-generated facts together to get at the nature of the unobservable social wholes because the formulas for making the combinations are not to be found in the facts themselves. Notes Cassirer, "Our technical instruments for observation and experimentation have been immensely improved, and our analyses have become sharper and more penetrating. We appear, nevertheless, not yet to have found a method for the mastery and organization of this material. . . . Our wealth of facts is not necessarily a wealth of thoughts. Unless we succeed in finding a clue . . . to lead us out of this labyrinth, we can have no real insight into the general character of human culture; we shall remain lost in a mass of disconnected and disintegrated data which seem to lack all of conceptual unity."[23]

Most dramatically, philosophers like Louis Arnaud Reid warn us that we should not seek knowledge about unobservable wholes by trying to sum up observation-generated facts, because such knowledge would be false, since the wholes are different from the sums of their parts. Reid writes, "It is the old difficulty of the wood and the trees. The man who trusts in propositions alone to bring him truth may completely miss, in his preoccupation with parts, the significance of the whole, particularly if that whole is of a higher sort than one of mere aggregation. Propositions can only be summed and synthesized into syllogisms, and the man who takes them for more than they are worth is likely to take reality as a mere heap or the mere syllogistic synthesis which it is not. This is often admitted, and the need of imagination, of a wholeness of outlook for the man of science, is frequently pointed out."[24]

The scientific revolution in international relations is not over for everybody. Indeed, it cannot be ended or superseded until the behaviorists and their critics resist attributions like "number crunchers" and "traditionalists" and center their debate on the epistemological issues that separate them. These issues are absolutely fundamental. Until this dialogue about philosophies of knowledge takes place, the proponents of the alternative epistemological schools will continue to talk past one another, or as is more the present case, they will simply not talk to each other at all.

For me, however, the scientific revolution is over. To be sure, I continue to be inspired by and try to emulate the careful designs and rigorous approaches to research problems that the behavioralists favor. I also appreciate quantitative efforts to describe those aspects of international relations that can be quantitatively described. Nevertheless, I can no longer picture myself positivistically proposition-testing my way to international relations theory.

The Metaphysicians among Us

Whatever form the quest for theory in international relations may have taken during the last five decades, the actual development of theory has been rather impressive. As noted, the most notable theoretical accomplishments have, on the whole, been made by those who did not take the detour toward scientism. To evaluate and appreciate this theoretical development, one must step away from logical positivism, because by positivism's gauge very few "empirically verified," general propositions have been discovered. Moreover, using anything that has been discovered as a starting point for deductions down to and through lower levels of generality remains fraught with considerable intellectual danger. Robert Keohane worries about this; he writes, "If we took literally (science philosopher Imre Lakatos's) requirements... all actual theories of international politics... would fail the test."[25] This is true: the abstract formulations we call "theories" of international relations, are, scientifically speaking, nothing of the sort. However, there may not be as much cause for concern in this as Keohane believes there is, because neither empirical verifiability in a strict sense nor prediction by rigorous deduction are actually what theorizing in international relations has been about.

The value of international relations theory should really not be assessed in terms of satisfying the requirements of natural science. Successful theorists of international relations are those who have tried to gain knowledge of the "unobservable wholes" of human affairs, and who have done this innovatively and convincingly enough to compel us to take them seriously. They can be considered successful because their work has been either plausible, provocative, or elegant enough to capture our attention, to inspire our careful criticism, to fire our imagination and to influence our research. Those generally recognized as leading theorists of international relations today have earned their stature through accomplishments in holistic image-building—feats of imagination, if you will—and not necessarily by exhibiting extraordinary prowess at working systematically through empirical problems. The theorists are first and foremost conceptualizers, symbolizers, synthesizers, and abstract organizers. Kenneth Boulding would call them experts in eiconics.[26] What they have been doing as theorists is painting for us in their writings bold-stroked, broad-brushed pictures of social reality and telling us that the real world is like their pictures. This world may be empirically unobservable, except in a partial and piecemeal way, and its wholeness may be different from or greater than the sum of its parts, but the theorists suggest that they know what it looks like in its wholeness.

If the theorists were as straightforward as they could be, and not as sensitive as they are about being branded "unscientific," they might explain that they believe their pictured worlds to be real because they emerged from human intuition, and relying on human intuition is a fully legitimate thing to do. It is an avenue to knowledge. "Great discoveries," Morton Kaplan explained in 1969, "when they do not occur accidentally or as a consequence of trial-and-error procedures, are the product of scientific intuition."[27] Indeed, intuition is the basic stuff from which metaphysics are made, if we appreciate that metaphysics properly deal with the nature of unobservable reality and not with the mystical matters that common parlance has attributed to this branch of philosophy. There is then more to *knowing* than empirically *seeing,* and it is in this alternative epistemological realm—call it imagining, image-making, symbolization, or eiconics—that all abstract theorists, including the leading theorists of international relations, operate.[28] This realm of the symbolic, incidentally, is also where artists dwell philosophically. Conceivably, aesthetic criteria could be brought into the evaluation of the "pictures" that the abstract theorists verbally paint.[29] However, at this point let us not require that good international relations theory must be "beautiful"; "insightful" will do.

Some Big Pictures

What has been impressive in the development of theory in the field of international relations has been the flow of alternative images of reality projected by the theorists. Admittedly, those who have been looking for a cumulatively broadening and deepening understanding of international relations, or something akin to physicists' Unified Theory, would be understandably less impressed with this flow of varying images than those, like me, who choose to experience the abstract theoretical literature somewhat in the way one might experience a gallery full of fine art. If the works are worthy of inclusion in the collection, they probably all capture the truth in some manner, or at least they captured something that was true when they were composed. Each work, however, delivers a different intellectual experience, and the greater the variety of such experiences contained in the collection, the greater the overall value of the collection.[30] International relations theory has its old masters, like Thucydides and Machiavelli, its established contemporaries like Yale Ferguson, Ernst Haas, Samuel Huntington, Robert Keohane, Richard Mansbach, Joseph Nye, John Ruggie, and Oran Young; and even an avant-garde corps, like Fritz Kratochwil, Nicholas Onuf, Andrew Schmookler, and Alexander Wendt. The venerable James Rosenau has memorable pieces in every collection.

Lest the reader here suspect that I have been terminally stricken with the "humanist's disease," let me point out that the clash of alternative theories has always been an integral part of the advancement of knowledge. "You can be a good empiricist," epistemologist Feyerabend instructs, "only if you are prepared to work with many alternative theories rather than with a single point of view." This plurality of theories must not be regarded as a preliminary stage of knowledge which will at some time in the future be replaced with the One True Theory. Theoretical pluralism is assumed to be an essential feature of all knowledge that claims to be objective."[31]

The intellectual danger is actually in diminishing theoretical pluralism, where single, privileged perspectives can degenerate into dogmas, much as political realism did during the first decades after World War II. Once these systems of thought have answered all of the questions that they initially raised, they create the illusion that there are no further questions to be asked. With regard to social theory, there is the additional danger that dogmatized thought systems could become political ideologies, as happened with the sociopathological "isms" of the twentieth century. These were snatched by later-generation political fanatics from the lively pluralism of nineteenth-century political thought and used, in the guise of utopian schemes, to justify some of history's grandest-scale atrocities.[32] So-called liberal economic theory and dependency theory are today almost fully dogmatized and the realities they purport to explain are crying out for alternative, innovative theoretical treatments.

It is both impossible and unnecessary to move through the entire gallery of images of the world that contemporary theorists of international relations have projected. Let me, however, highlight a few that I find especially insightful, or that seemed to me to be particularly innovative and insightful during their heydays at the center of disciplinary attention. Some of the "still lifes" in the gallery of theories are intriguing. The realists are most prominent among theorists who have given us images of the structure of the international system. Some, like Hans Morgenthau and Kenneth Waltz, organize their anarchical worlds of states in terms of distributions of power and explain why, because of inherent equilibrating tendencies, these distributions tend to be relatively resistant to short-term change.[33] Nowhere, in all of the theoretical literature, for example, is the balance of power more elegantly presented than in part 4 of Morgenthau's *Politics among Nations*.

Raymond Aron, in structuring his imagined world, adds a distribution of political ideologies to the distribution of power and invites us then to envisage various combinations of power polarity and ideological heterogeneity in a variety of differently structured international systems.[34] Morton Kaplan nurtures the image of anarchy, as he finds no "international political system" in his imagined world. But his anarchically interacting states or "national actors" are themselves rather intriguingly structured as hierarchies of nested systems and subsystems, all of these operating similarly and repetitively—homeostatically and antientropically—to maintain their structural integrities.[35] Kaplan's *System and Process in International Politics* was rather harshly criticized for its portrayal of unreal worlds in the form of mythical models, but what the critics frequently missed was the extent to which, at a more abstract level, the image of linked systems and subsystems taps insightfully into social-political reality and in fact explains a good deal of behavior at the different intersystemic nodes.

Anarchy is a lesser leitmotiv in Hedley Bull's picture of the international system inasmuch as he identifies, in addition to distributions of power and political fragmentation, an international society in the form of transactions and connections among peoples and normative bonds among governments. An edifice of internationally acknowledged laws and rules tends to constrain extreme manifestations of anarchy, so that international relations play out not in a Hobbesian state of nature but in more or less ordered society of states.[36] In their *Power and Interdependence*, which remains, in my estimation, one of the most innovative contributions to contemporary theory in international relations, Keohane and Nye imagine a world beyond anarchy. They add a variety of nonstates to the inventory of structural elements in the international system, insert degrees of interdependence into the ordering of relationships among their elements, build in a more prevalent implicit and explicit institutional structure in the form of regimes, and posit a pattern of structural variation according to issues or the substantive promptings to interaction.[37] These authors' ability to paint both power and order into their picture of international relations in the second half of the twentieth century was a theoretical accomplishment of major import. Then there are Samuel Huntington's cultural tectonics that describe a world fragmented along the fault lines of major civilizations.[38] Interestingly, the farther we creep into the twenty-first century the more provocative becomes Huntington's picture.There are of course many more pictures of international structure contained in the theoretical literature of international relations—Immanuel Wallerstein's, Richard Mansbach and John Vasquez's, and John Burton's, for example—but again, there is no need here to be comprehensive as the main point is that the theorists are first and foremost image makers, and exciting images of the structure of the international system have flowed in some profusion.

The moving pictures are also fascinating. Since explaining systemic and intrasystemic changes have remained among the perplexing puzzles of our discipline, any number of theorists of contemporary international relations have directed their image making toward the dynamics of international politics or international political economy. Harold Lasswell, always well ahead of his time, makes a major effort to explain change in his *World Politics and Personal Insecurity*.[39] Here he offers an involved moving picture of simultaneous ideological and power polarization at the international level. He invites his readers to watch as international polarization and ideological differentiation first feed, and then feed upon, the anxieties of the human beings, until tensions are ultimately released in the catharsis of the Great War. Raymond Aron paints a remarkably similar picture in his intriguing discussion of "the dialectics of peace and war," except that he adds additional dynamics to explain relationships among technological change, socioeconomic structural change, and differential changes in the international capabilities of states.[40]

Robert Gilpin pictures a dynamic, homeostatic linking of national wealth, national power, and international aggrandizement that, for benefiting states, tends to generate exponential ascents toward hegemony.[41] But the same dynamic also works in reverse: at a point near an ascending state's logistic plateau, the marginal power costs of maintaining international position begin to outweigh the marginal benefits, and accelerating exhaustion, exploited by ambitious and marauding rivals, sets in. From a systemic perspective, Gilpin gives us an elegant version of historically familiar cycles of the rise and fall of power. Paul Kennedy sees the same cycle(s), but sets them in contexts of innovating technologies, developing economies, and strengthening states.[42]

Andrew Schmookler, in his amazingly erudite volume *The Parable of the Tribes,* offers an alternative image of the dynamics of national aggrandizement stemming from imperatives to maximize societal power in the interest of successful selection in the course of social evolution.[43] Altogether different kinds of international dynamics are pictured by Karl Deutsch and his colleagues, as they show peoples evolving toward peaceful coexistence and commingling through communication, social learning, and shifting political allegiances.[44] Different kinds of international dynamics are also displayed in the writings of David Mitrany, where international cooperation begets greater international cooperation; in the work of Amitai Etzioni, where international transactions beget international management; in the work of Keohane and Nye, where international interdependence begets international rules; and in the respective works of Oran Young and Marvin Soroos, where global problems beget global governance.[45] Again, many other theorists' images of the dynamics of international relations—those of Ernst Haas, Edward Morse, A. F. K. Organski, or Karl Polyani, for example—could be displayed here, but the point is made. Unless the theorists paint their holistic pictures for us, our worldviews, as Andrew Schmookler tells his readers, would tend "to be myopically mired in the magnifying-glass stage" where "the parts are delineated in excruciating detail ... [but] the whole is left for some invisible hand to assemble or is regarded as no more than the sum of its parts."[46]

The Origins of the Art

To me it is not entirely clear what the actual epistemological principles are that explain theorizing about international relations, except that they are not principles of logical positivism. Nor are they principles of pure rationalism, where adherents aver that reality can be known through powers of human reason uncomplemented by sensory experience.[47] Pure rationalists in the form of game theorists and kindred deductive model builders continue to ply their trade in the field of international relations theory, and in fact in recent years there has been a resurgence of such efforts. The undertakings of the new generation modelers, however, are no more convincing than those of the game theorists of the 1960s, who, like Arthur Burns, Morton Kaplan, Duncan Luce and Howard Raiffa, and Anatol Rapoport, subsequently and progressively modified their enthusiasms for deductively generated mathematical models as vehicles for understanding international relations.[48] The criticisms and self-criticisms of the deductive modelers from within the genre have dealt largely with uncertainties involved in assigning values to variables (like utilities in game matrices) a priori. Values and priorities tend to vary between individuals and across groups as well as across time and space, so that what is rational for all players in a given game can never be posited with certainty. This makes the assigning of utilities a wholly speculative undertaking, and it makes the dynamics of the game indeterminate unless the identities of particular human players are stipulated and their motives examined. Once this is done, however, the model loses its generality and deductive interest.

From outside the genre the fundamental difficulty has been one of accepting that real-world outcomes could ever be deduced from abstractly modeled relationships, or, as Rapoport notes, mathematical decision theory has been used as "a prop for *rationalizing* decisions arrived at by processes far from rational," and "in this role rational decision theory can become a source of dangerous fixations and delusions."[49] Again, as Philip Green expressed it, "this [game-theoretic] definition of rational behavior ... does not at first glance have any real-world relevance. Purely instrumental choice unhindered either by emotional or ideological blocks on the one hand, or by ignorance on the other, exists only in the abstract theory of games."[50]

Most of the theorists who have painted appealing and useful holistic pictures of the structure and functioning of the international system have not been very explicit about the epistemological origins of their images. Many have not been at all self-conscious concerning epistemological matters; most have contended that they have been operating as scientists and have left it at that. Raymond Aron endorsed a philosophy of knowledge based on empirical generalization from historical experience that he called "historical sociology" and Stanley Hoffmann accepted its tenets.[51] In his criticisms of the behavioralists, Bull made clear that he too believed that holistic pictures could be painted on the basis of empirical generalizations from history. Kaplan contended that he was working deductively from the tenets of general systems theory, but I am inclined to agree with the critics who argued that Kaplan's three "real-looking" models—the balance of power and loose and tight bipolarity—were actually empirical generalizations from nineteenth-century European and twentieth-century international history, respectively, and the rest of the models were variations on these.

Overall, it would appear that the holistic "pictures" of the theorists emerge from combinations of experience—vicarious experience, for the most part—and reasoning. Experience acquired by watching the world in various ways, particularly by reading history, produces countless perceptions to which the human mind adds form, order, relationship, and cause and effect so as to transform the perceptions into cognitions in the nature of images and symbols. "There is such a thing as a sense of realities and possibilities of social activity, which can be developed from a study of the proper sort of history," historian Joseph Strayer suggests. "It is in acquiring, or seeking to acquire, this sense of social realities," he says, "that the historian ceases to be a scientist and becomes an artist."[52]

I like to call the product of such a process of generalizing imaginatively from long and varied experience not art, but intuition. Immanuel Kant has called it *transcendental logic*. "Our cognition," he writes, "has, on the part of the mind, two sources. Of these the first is the receptivity of impressions, and the second the spontaneity of notions.... The first receives the crude appearances of sense, and the second works them up into the finished perception of the object.... Thoughts, without a content of perceptions, are void; perceptions without the focus of notions, are blind."[53]

Langer calls the same process *symbolization or ideation,* and in slight contrast to Kant locates it prior to thought in the procedural chain of human understanding, saying that "it is not the essential act of thought that is symbolization, but an act essential to thought and prior to it."[54] To think about the world, we must first symbolize our raw impressions of it. We must symbolize in order to, as Cassirer would have it, transform our "wealth of facts" into a "wealth of thoughts," and we must symbolize the world in order to organize our empirical inquiries about it. *Rather than emerging from empirical inquiry, theory, generated by intuition as here defined, launches it.* Successful theorists of international relations are first and foremost masters of such intuition.

What about Validity?

Since, as Bull notes, "the general propositions about this subject ... derive from a scientifically imperfect process of perception and intuition," he concludes that "these general propositions cannot be accorded anything more than tentative and inconclusive status."[55] Positivistically speaking, Bull is correct. Ultimately, there is no way to empirically ascertain the validity of the images of reality that theorists of international relations have conceived and projected. It should be borne in mind, however, that there are respectable epistemological traditions that do not insist that truth can be ascertained only through empirical verification. As emphasized above, positivistic approaches to verification will not work because the wholes are unobservable, and investigating the parts separately simply will not do.

More practically speaking, with regard to theorizing about the world in real time (which many theorists usefully do), realities in international relations do not last long enough to mount comprehensive, systematic, and effective empirical assaults on them. This is especially the case where such efforts are conceived and designed to involve operationalizing, coding, and testing all of the propositions the various theories propound or all of the aspects of the various theoretical pictures verbally painted to describe and explain contemporaneous international relations. Before we really got going empirically on "hegemonic stability," for example, the world had moved "beyond hegemony." Before that, "protracted conflict" turned into "multipolar equilibrium." Before our eyes in the 1980s we witnessed "the decline of the major powers" just as we had begun digging empirically into the nature and attributes of "the superpowers." And, when we finally got some theoretical handles on "Westphalian world politics," we were informed by the course of world events that that we were likely moving into an era of "nonterritorial" or newly "medieval" happenings.[56]

International reality is a moving target that theorists track reasonably well. But the dynamism befuddles empiricists who wish to be simultaneously absolutely right and absolutely relevant. Naturally, these reservations do not apply with regard to the empirical examination of immediate and distant eras past, but even here we run into the "wholes/parts" problem. There are no conceivable "grand experiments" that will, at a stroke, render true or false, adequate or wanting, the holistic thought systems of social theorists in the way that, for example, Sir Arthur Stanley Eddington's 1919 "light deflection" and William Wallace Campell's 1922 "red shift" experiments unseated Newtonian physics and enthroned Einstein's theory of relativity.[57] To the extent that social science lacks philosophical justification for inducing wholes from parts, and given that probabilism will not do because meaningful sampling from indefinable populations is impossible, the ultimate empirical validity of the theorists' big pictures must remain elusive. But again, positivistically *unverifiable* does not necessarily mean *untrue*.

As long as any positivistic juices continue to trickle within us, we will probably continue to worry about empirical verification and resist evaluating our theories in purely pragmatic terms. Perhaps there is something to be learned from our colleagues in the discipline of history who tend on the whole to be a good deal more modest about the status of their generalizations about and interpretations of human affairs.[58] They do not seek deductive laws, and they no longer seek teleological meanings, but they do look for generalizations about individual and collective behavior, about plausible causes and plausible effects, to help explain the chronologies they observe.

Contrasting historians' and scientists' uses of generalizations, philosopher of history W. B. Gallie observes that applying generalizations to history is "basically different from applying them with a view to deducing, and in particular predicting, some future event." This use of generalizations, that is, the scientific use, Gallie continues, "enables us to anticipate and even dispense with observation," since we need only to deduce happenings from general propositions and rest reasonably assured that they will occur as anticipated. But for the historian, the whole purpose of making generalizations "is to render possible, or set in motion again, certain kinds of 'progressive observation'" that locate events within the "still developing whole" to which they belong.[59] In other words, the use of theory is to facilitate the interpretation of history. Functionally speaking, this is precisely the role that theory plays in the understanding of international relations: it helps us follow events by setting them within the contexts of wholes of which they are parts. It does not, because it cannot in the absence of laws (probabilistic or otherwise) invite us to deduce, and it does not permit us to predict. Rather, theory helps us to understand events because it gives them context and meaning in terms of higher abstractions.

Perhaps, then, we need not ask so emphatically whether a theory is scientific, but whether it is useful. Does it give plausible meaning to events as they occur around us and perhaps as they have occurred in the past? Does it especially give new meaning to events that have confused us, or identify new events that have eluded us? Does it order, or at least suggest an order to, our experiences? Does it cue us to ask questions that we are not otherwise prompted to ask, and does it direct our search for answers to places where we are not otherwise predisposed to search? And we should also ask those among us who are the agents that make international events occur whether the pictures painted by theorists of international relations improve their understanding of the realities surrounding them. Does this understanding ease the process of actually coping with international realities? The ultimate goal of international relations theory should be to enable respondents to give positive answers to these questions.

CHAPTER 3

The Pragmatics of
International History

One of the more welcome recent developments in the American study of international relations is that Adda Bozeman's *Politics and Culture in International History* is back in print.[1] Scholars are rereading and increasingly citing it, along with Hedley Bull and Adam Watson's *The Expansion of International Society*, Watson's *The Evolution of International Society*; other works from the British school, Edward Said's *Culture and Imperialism*; Francis Fukuyama's *The End of History and the Last Man*, Michael Doyle's *Empires*, and articles published in *Ethics and International Affairs*, an important journal focused on historical, cultural, and normative issues.[2] Students of international relations have also rediscovered the metahistorical writings of William McNeill.[3] They are studying the sociohistorical work of Fernand Braudel and other writings of the Annales school, and they are showing considerable interest in Paul Kennedy's contributions at the interface between history and theory.[4] There is even today some modest new attention being paid to Arnold Toynbee.[5] All of this suggests a growing interest in the history of international relations, a core subject in the curricula of European universities, but one that is seldom taught in the United States. Broadly construed, the history of international relations is the history of relations among states and peoples, which appropriately defines the subject as the history of interacting cultures.

Some of this emergent interest in the history of international relations stems from the growing appreciation that mainstream American scholarship in international relations has for too long confined itself mainly to the workings of the Westphalian state system. The concern is that generalizations derived from the study of this modern European mode of interstate interaction might have limited meaning across the chronological length and cultural breadth of the human behavioral field we define as international relations.[6] Interest in the history of international relations has also been aroused by the recognition that human evolution has been as dramatically affected by interactions among peoples across cultural divides as by interactions among states across political divides.[7] Intercultural relations among peoples have historically occurred within many contexts that were not state systems at all, and scholars of international relations have not intensively studied these contexts. There is also the awareness that the global distribution of wealth is decisively affected by the workings of a capitalist world economy that evolved historically and whose future might be better anticipated if its past were better understood.[8]

Some of the turning toward history among scholars of international relations is also driven by frustrations with the intellectual sterility of many present-day theoretical renderings. Just as Hayden White argues that "the contemporary historian has to establish the value of the study of the past, not as an end in itself, but as a way of providing perspectives on the present that contribute to the solution of problems peculiar to our own time," students of international relations are turning to interpreting the past in order to better understand the present.[9] Many are doing this because other approaches—for example, those that emphasize high abstraction and mathematical formalism—have yielded relatively little that contributes to the solution of problems, either practical, ethical, or intellectual, peculiar to our own time. Disappointed by the unproductiveness of formalistic modes of analysis, Yale Ferguson and Richard Mansbach, in the conclusion to their study of international relation's elusive quest for disciplinary grounding, invited a reconsideration of humanistic approaches.[10] Their invitation is beginning to be taken seriously.

The Question of Epistemology

While there is undoubtedly enlightenment to be gained from examining the historical record of human experience, there are epistemological problems connected with humanistic approaches for which, frankly, there are no wholly satisfactory solutions. However, there are also epistemological problems connected with scientific approaches to the study of human experience that render these neither obvious nor preferable alternatives to the ways of the humanists. The purpose of this essay is to examine some of these epistemological problems connected with the study of the history of international relations. My thesis is that the degree to which one becomes intellectually uncomfortable about the dubiousness of claims about truth, or about ways to come upon it emanating from one approach or another, depends ultimately upon what one demands of the truth. There is the danger, already present in poststructuralist and postmodernist critiques of the bases of our knowledge, that we could allow epistemological solipsism to immobilize our intellectual efforts.[11] But there is also the promise in several of these recent works, and in some rediscovered older ones as well, that we may be finally prepared to allow truth to be useful instead of controversial. This, at least, is the conclusion toward which this essay is driving.

Interpreting History

Humanistic pathways to knowledge in history, as well as in literature, religion, and art, lead to representations of reality mediated through subjective interpretations. These are usually composed from unspecified combinations of empirical observations, lived experience, intuitions, and imagination. Alternatively, interpretations may be composed hermeneutically by moving transsubjectively via textual analysis into the mind(s) of human beings whose thoughts and actions constitute social reality.[12] Here, more simply, the artist interprets reality and embodies it in the artifact, and then the analyst accesses the embodied reality by hermeneutically interpreting the artifact. Any of these interpretations may be valid, and the arrived-at representations of reality may be quite accurate, for who would deny humans the ability to intuit the truth? But on what basis or by what logic may we accept or reject the validity of proffered interpretations? This is the humanities' epistemological dilemma. With regard to history in particular, we can observe, with some sympathy, historiography's two-century-long, unsuccessful effort to ground itself epistemologically by finding a logic that would justify truth claims associated with interpretations.[13]

The historian's epistemological problems with interpretation are compounded for the student of international relations because the typical uses to which our discipline puts the examination of history smack of what the historical profession unkindly calls *historicism*. Students of international relations study history mainly to abet their theorizing. They seek bases for generalization by conceptually constructing and reconstructing history, by identifying and naming perceptibly recurrent patterns of events, and by then doing the same with regard to the causes of the patterns they identify. They look for temporal and spatial discontinuities in patterns of occurrence in order to delimit the spaces within which their generalizations can apply. They test, and if necessary modify, existing generalizations by examining anticipated and observed patterns of occurrence. Some seek "laws" of historical development by trying to explain seemingly invariant very-long-term empirical trends.[14]

All of this, Hayden White says, is historicism, and historians tend to treat it as intellectually suspect.[15] White notes, "Discussions of historicism sometimes proceed on the assumption that it consists of a discernable and unjustifiable distortion of a properly 'historical' way of representing reality. Thus, for example, there are those who speak of the particularizing interest of the historian as against the generalizing interest of the historicist. Again, the historian is supposed to be interested in elaborating points of view rather than constructing theories, as the historicist wishes to do. Next, the historian is supposed to favor a narrativist, the historicist an analytical mode of representation. And finally, while the historian studies the past for its own sake . . . the historicist wants to use his knowledge of the past to illuminate the problems of his present or, worse, to predict the path of history's future development."[16]

White's own conclusion is that all historians are at the same time historicists because they metaphorically emplot the stories they tell. But this is a very sophisticated argument that, while persuasive, still leaves untouched the basis of many historians' distaste for historicism, which is that historicism rests on an even weaker epistemological footing than conventional historiography because the subjective interpretation involved is much more ambitious. The conventional historian interpretatively fills gaps created by incomplete documentation concerning events, whereas the historicist attempts to attribute structure and process to epochs, to impute latent driving forces, to detect algorithms in patterns of recurrent events, to sort events into categories and kinds of happening, and to otherwise move analysis onto a surreal plain, apparently, but not always demonstrably, anchored to the empirical one. What logic or formula justifies truth claims associated with such grand interpretative efforts?

Historians furthermore suspect historicists of selecting evidence to satisfy abstract explanations rather than actually discovering patterns amid the confounding complexities of historical reality. Patterns emerge by "leaving out" contradictory occurrences, and the richness of the record is often such that almost any pattern can be constituted from selected drawings upon it. To the extent that the historicist chooses to enter into prediction by allowing imputed historical patterns to run on into the future, he can be criticized for speculating about the future on the basis of speculations about the past. And when the historicist happens to be a student of international relations examining the past for theoretical edification, interpretative problems are compounded by the fact that documentary sources are most often texts written by historians, so that the most that can result are interpretations of interpretations.

The Same Old German Quarrels

Scientific approaches to the study of human affairs, like scientific approaches more generally, aspire, through rigorous procedure, careful empiricism, and precise neutral vocabulary to eliminate subjective interpretation from the representation of reality. International history can be studied scientifically, although there must admittedly be a good deal of technical slippage in the empirical phases of the scientific procedure because the "objects to be observed" no longer exit. More important, however, is that attempts to study history scientifically, or even to assert that it can be done, have traditionally ignited heated epistemological controversies.[17]

The *Methodenstreite* that especially agitated German scholars during the last half of the nineteenth century and the first decades of the twentieth were confrontations between scholars who insisted that the human sciences, or *Geisteswissenschaften,* were not amenable to scientific treatment, and others who contended that because human beings were as "natural" as rocks and stars they too could be studied scientifically.[18] For example, the noted nineteenth-century positivist historian Hyppolyte Taine asserted that "cultural science is nothing other than a form of applied botany."[19] But those who leaned toward Geisteswissenschaft argued that the empirical methods of the scientists could probe no deeper than surface appearances and therefore never reach the essences of human motivations. Nor could such approaches apprehend structures that explain behavior or forces that drive history. Others questioned the nomological goals of the scientific project either by contending, as did Friedrich Nietzsche that there are no laws of human behavior since all social reality is contingent, or by arguing, after David Hume, that inductions from empirical observations could never yield laws. "Hume's problem," notes Wesley Salmon, "has proved astonishingly recalcitrant."[20] Even today it remains bothersome for social scientists bent upon nomological discovery, because Hume argued that since empirical inductions can be based only upon observations of the past, generalizations from them can have no predictive value because "the future might be radically unlike the past."[21]

For their part during the Methodenstreite, proponents of science, or *Naturwissenschaft,* not only argued that human beings and societies were explainable on the basis of deductions from "laws" of human behavior, but also that by their methods scientists were uniquely able to "objectively" identify and validate such laws. These positivists looked askance at the subjectivity and nonempirical predilections of the students of *Geisteswissenschaft.* They balked at the intrusion of values into research, and cautioned that "theory" arrived at nonscientifically was indistinguishable from ideology.

Richard Rorty nicely summarizes the battle of approaches in his *Philosophy and the Mirror of Nature;* he writes, "The traditional quarrel about the 'philosophy of the social sciences' has proceeded generally as follows. One side [Geisteswissenschaft] has said that 'explanation' (subsumption under predicative laws, roughly) presupposes, and cannot replace, 'understanding.' The other side [Naturwissenschaft] has said that understanding is the ability to explain, that what their opponents call 'understanding' is merely the primitive stage of groping around for explanatory hypotheses. Both sides are quite right."[22]

The Methodenstreite should have ended with Max Weber, who at the turn of the twentieth century rather sensibly argued that there probably are laws of human behavior to be discovered and that they can and should be called upon to help explain historical events or the course of history itself. But, for the historian, analyzing history in terms of such laws is insufficient because one cannot readily move from general causes to concrete events, since concrete events have concrete causes.[23] Furthermore, although Weber does not use the term historicist, his implication is that patterns in history, such as those the historicist seeks, are much more the products of conceptualization than of observation and that historicism therefore necessarily involves subjective imagining. In rather lyrical prose at one point in his essay on "'Objectivity' in Social Science and Social Policy," Weber explains that "the fate of an epoch which has eaten of the tree of knowledge is that it must know that we cannot learn the meaning of the world from the results of its analysis, be it ever so perfect; it must rather be in a position to create this meaning itself. It must recognize that general views of life and the universe can never be the products of increasing empirical knowledge."[24] Methodologically, Weber acknowledges that the student of history works both "by means of comprehensive historical induction " and "according to our subjective experience."[25] Weber maintains that scientific and humanistic approaches are in fact different. But his attempt to affirm the legitimacy of both as approaches to the study of history, to explain their complementarities, and to limit both to particular spheres of usefulness should have signaled an armistice among epistemological warriors.

Yet of course it didn't. The "positivist dispute" reopened in postwar Germany, where Theodor Adorno, Max Horkheimer, Jürgen Habermas, and others of the Frankfurt school reinitiated the critique of positivism as an approach to the study of human society. Many of the traditional arguments were restated: empirical procedures cannot apprehend latent social structures that condition human behavior;[26] "positivism will only allow appearance to be valid, whilst dialectics [which the Frankfurt school endorsed as a superior alternative] will not allow itself to be robbed of the distinction between essence and appearance";[27] operational procedures methodologically restrict both the questions that can be asked and the answers that can be found.[28] Thus, according to Habermas, "The analytical-empirical

modes of procedure tolerate only one type of experience which they themselves define. Only the controlled observation of physical behavior, which
is set up in an isolated field under reproducible conditions by subjects in-
terchangeable at will, seems to permit intersubjectively valid judgments of
perception. These represent the experiential basis upon which theories must
rest if the deductively acquired hypotheses are to be not only logically correct but also empirically convincing. Empirical sciences in the strict sense
insist that all discussable statements should be checked, at least indirectly, by
means of this very narrowly channeled experience."[29] The Frankfurt group
and their followers were answered by Karl Popper, Hans Albert, and others
who contended that the limitations of positivism were exaggerated and that
the "dialectical" positions of Adorno, Habermas, and company were imprecise, subjective, and ideological. Albert, for example, took Habermas to
task for being wrongly preoccupied with "the Hegelian inheritance preserved in Marxism. . . . It is well known that the dialectical concept of total-
ity . . . constantly recurs in theoreticians who follow in Hegel's footsteps. . . . It
is therefore all the more regrettable that Habermas makes no attempt to provide a more precise clarification of this concept, which he strongly emphasizes and frequently uses. He merely says of it that it is to be understood 'in
the strictly dialectical sense.'"[30] According to Albert, then, Habermas was
both ideological and imprecise, and this kind of ethereal fuzziness could
not be the grounding for a science of man. By the 1970s, the "positivist
dispute" in sociology in Germany had become the "traditionalism versus
scientism" dispute in American social science. It deeply divided students of
international relations, and it continues today.[31]

Escaping from Interpretation?

Proponents of scientific and humanistic approaches to the study of human
affairs continue to do battle. Ironically, these contestants seem intent upon
proceeding in their present-day rendering of *Methodenstreit* apparently
oblivious to the fact that many contemporary philosophers have long since
abandoned the "positivist dispute." Indeed some, like Richard Rorty have
made strong cases for abandoning epistemology altogether.[32]

The thrust of a good deal of recent philosophic musing about the origins
of knowledge—scientific, humanistic, or otherwise—is that there are no
unimpeachable groundings for anything we might like to define as "truth,"
particularly when truth is conceived of as observational or propositional
correspondence with something we define as "reality."[33] In this context,
the main reason why scientific approaches are not superior alternatives
to humanistic approaches with regard to the study of history is that in a
number of epistemologically problematic aspects scientific approaches share

the weaknesses of humanistic ones. As White notes, "It now seems fairly clear that the nineteenth-century belief in the radical dissimilarity of art to science was a consequence of a misunderstanding fostered by the romantic artist's fear of science and the positivistic scientist's ignorance of art. . . . But modern criticism—mostly as a result of advances made by psychologists in the investigation of the human synthesizing faculties—has achieved a clearer understanding of the operations by which the artist expresses his vision of the world and the scientist frames his hypotheses about it."[34]

The critique of science as applied to the study of human affairs has come full circle since the nineteenth century. As White indicates, the traditional critique of science by humanists was that human affairs were qualitatively different from natural phenomena, and to therefore seek to explain them on the basis of general and invariant "laws" of nature was misguided. The natural sciences had to be separated from the human sciences because their subjects were different, and their respective modes of analysis—objective/empirical on the one hand, and subjective/interpretative on the other—were mutually exclusive.[35] Today, critics contend that science—and particularly social science—as an approach to knowledge is not sufficiently distinct from other approaches to warrant any privileged epistemological position. The problem with science, then, is not that it is so different from the humanities as to raise questions about its applicability to the study of human affairs, but that it is so much like the humanities that it suffers from their epistemological vulnerabilities.

Interpretation, for example, enters at both ends of the scientific enterprise: at the beginning, when the scientist constructs her hypotheses, which involves a good deal more than a "primitive stage of groping around," and at the end, when she reports the meanings of her findings or discusses "causes" that, after all, can only be attributed. While White would label these first and last stages of the scientific procedure the *poetic* or *metaphorical* phases, we need only go so far as to call them *interpretative* phases. Initially, the "reality" to be observed is constituted by the researcher (or by a predecessor who offered a "theory" for testing or application). Such "reality" appears first as an array of conceptual categories, or symbols usually in the form of words, and their stipulated interrelations, and then again later as an array of operational indicators of the presence, absence, magnitude, stability, change, and so on of the conceptually constituted objects. Therefore, in studying history the scientifically oriented scholar begins by conceptually creating the "reality" that she aims to study, and then "observes" it by assuming that it is mirrored by perceptible facts, which she also constitutes.[36] What is a "fact" outside of a conceptual context, and why then may we not say that the context constitutes the fact? Of course, the historian also constitutes her "reality," though usually less self-consciously, or at least less abashedly since her discipline allows her to interpret. But as she is most often interested in particularity, she conceptually constitutes "events," whereas the scientifically oriented scholar interested in generality, conceptually constitutes kinds of events and kinds of actors acting in kinds of ways under kinds of conditions. The point here is that the variety of "realities" conceivable is rather large. All of them can be tested empirically, and a good many of them, operationalized creatively, can be engineered to test valid. Even in the natural sciences there are a number of conceivable "universes," and evidentiary bases can be identified that would affirm the existence of most of them. Whether any of the conceptualized "universes"—physical or social—*mirror nature* may not be an answerable question.[37] It may not even be an important question unless we insist that validity or truth must lie either in the relationship between our sensory perceptions (i.e., our empirical faculties) and reality or in the relationship between our words (i.e., our propositions) and reality. More about this later.

The scientist may or may not want to say anything about the significance of her observations, generalizations, or conclusions, or to otherwise comment on their meaning. Yet, it is difficult to imagination that the social scientist cum historicist can avoid commenting on meaning, because it is difficult to imagine that her seeking after patterns in the record of human experience is either purposeless or engaged only for its own sake. Max Weber presented a most reasonable exposition of the normative and cultural contexts that invariably found and surround scholarly inquiry;[38] his argument need not be repeated here, though it should be taken seriously by anyone concerned about "value-free" research. What needs to be underlined, following Weber, is that whenever a scholar says of her findings "this means..." or "this is important or significant because..." she has at that point crossed over from explanation to interpretation. At that point, whatever epistemological security the scientific method may have offered falls away, and the humanist's interpretative dilemma becomes the scientist's interpretative dilemma. If the scholar hedges and says "this *may* mean..." or "this *may* be significant, but these are only hypotheses and they have to be scientifically tested" she opens the way to a possible infinite regress that produces neither meaning nor significance but rather a never-ending sequence of operationalizations and empirical tests. If she claims that her finding is significant because it either corresponds to or falsifies existing theory, her immediate scientific aim might thereby be satisfied, but then she can rightly be asked, What is significant about the existing theory?

Attributing cause has similar implications. Causes must be attributed because they cannot be observed. It is possible to empirically observe all manner of associations among events. Such associations—for example, contingency, covariation, and correlation—can be statistically observed with considerable precision (as long as we bear in mind that we are here "observing" central tendencies and dispersions in distributions of events and their interrelations, and not the particular juxtapositions of any tangible occurrences). But, when the scholar concludes *cause* regarding observed associations he has again crossed over from observation to interpretation because he cannot "see" events acting causally upon each other. What he can see is that the arrangement of events in time either satisfies one of the algorithms of causal analysis, such as priority/posteriority, or that such arrangements meet the requirements of being a particular case of a more general situation (or "law" of human behavior) wherein one set of events nearly always (i.e., probablistically) follows after another. To attribute cause outside the realm of everyday common sense, and especially in the ethers of constituted reality where the historicist wanders, is to take an interpretative leap. "Necessity," Hume has summarized, "is something that exists in the mind, not in objects."[39] Attributing cause is always rendered uncertain by the recognition that there may be several plausible explanations for any observed relationship, particularly among historical events. Or, the observed relationships may be entirely contingent.[40] To remain "closer to the data" by avoiding causal interpretations is to perpetually beg the question "Why?" regarding empirically associated events. To respond scientifically that answers to "Why?" questions can only be hypotheses that must be operationalized and tested is again to invite infinite regress.

The Disappearance of Solid Grounding

To argue as I have that there is no way around having to deal with the question of interpretation and truth claims associated with it renders the social sciences and humanities similarly problematical. But, recognizing that all of the human sciences are epistemologically vulnerable because interpretation cannot be kept out does not get us very far beyond Weber, the "positivist dispute" or traditionalist positions in the scienticism versus traditionalism debates.

The contemporary critique of theories of knowledge, however, is both broader and deeper than that offered in the contexts of the old disputes. At present, several leading figures in the postmodernist movement, as well as a number of widely read contributors to the discussion of the philosophy of science, have innovatively reopened debate about the so-called correspondence theory of truth, upon which modern empiricism is grounded. George Marcus and Michael Fischer call this the "crisis of representation" that "arises from uncertainty about adequate means of describing social reality."[41] Although it assumes a variety of forms, the crux of the critics' argument is that it is futile to assume not only that "reality" is accessible to sensory perception, but also to assume that such perceptions and inductions about them can be reported in language that speaks truthfully about reality. Summarizing the postmodernist position with regard to the correspondence theory, Seyla Benhabib writes that,

> modern epistemologists agreed that the task of knowledge, whatever its origins, was to build an adequate representation of things.... [T]he classical episteme of representation presupposed a spectator conception of the knowing self, a designative theory of meaning, and a denotative theory of language.
> ... [T]hree directions of critique of the classical episteme, leading to its eventual rejection, formed themselves.... [T]he first can be described as the critique of the modern epistemic subject, the second as the critique of the modern epistemic object, and the third as the critique of the modern concept of the sign.[42]

It has therefore become dubious to define truth as correspondence to reality, or as accurate mirroring. Acknowledging this does not destroy the idea of truth or its practical and moral usefulness, as I will attempt show. It merely brings into question one version of truth, though admittedly it is the version that has grounded Naturwissenschaft in both its physical and social projects.

Much of the criticism of correspondence theory has come from philosophers interested in language and its contribution to human distinctiveness. For example, one feature of Michel Foucault's critique of the human sciences—which for him include the social sciences and history indistinguishably lumped together, and all fraudulent—is that they are essentially rhetorical renderings wherein the vocabularies of their respective discourses may cohere internally. But these syntactical coherences can have little to do with the events of the world, because among these events, Foucault contends, there is no coherence. Foucault's aim, notes White, "is to return consciousness to an apprehension of the world as it might have existed before human consciousness appeared in it, a world of things which is neither orderly nor disorderly but which simply *is* what it *appears to be*. Far from believing that things have an intrinsic order, Foucault does not even honor the thing called order."[43] For Foucault then, ordering pursuits, of the kind that historicists especially engage, where it is assumed that the order of words somehow represents the order of things, cannot be more than exercises in "wording" whose purpose is "to live in books."[44] One does not have to accept Foucault's contention that "ordering pursuits" in the human sciences are useless, for to do so would be to undermine both historicism and what the social scientist terms "theorizing." Still, it is possible to agree with Foucault that these pursuits are essentially exercises in "wording" rather than reliable mirrorings of an essentially inaccessible reality.

Yet defining the human sciences as "wording strategies" is only one aspect of Foucault's critique. The deeper problem is with the words themselves, which, Foucault argues, are opaque: they do not represent reality (or anything else their speakers would wish them to represent) because their meanings are imprecise, ever changing, context dependent, intersubjectively untranslatable, culture laden and value laden. For Foucault words are *things* like other things that one could study and write narratives about. They have histories, implications, consequences, and attributes, though being able to serve as reliable instruments of representation is not among these attributes because things cannot neutrally and transparently represent other things. It is as if, for example, we had a deck of playing cards and we let each stand for a historical phenomenon—aces for revolutions, kings for wars, queens for arms races, and so on. We could load the cards with all of the known attributes of the phenomena that they represent, but they would nevertheless also retain their attributes as playing cards—shape, picture, color—and these would invariably show through to add to, detract from, or otherwise confuse their signifying functions. Summarizing Foucault, White explains that "what modern linguistic theory demonstrates is that words . . . will always obscure as much as they reveal about the objects they are meant to signify, and that, therefore, any system of thought raised on the hope of contriving a value-neutral system of representation is fated to dissolution."[45] Students of the human sciences are compelled to describe their observations and report their findings in conventional discursive language, and in narrative form, because no other mode of presentation is available (unless we take seriously the possibility of reducing social scientific signing to mathematical expressions). Therefore, even the empirical core of the scientific procedure becomes a fundamentally interpretative and tropic exercise because it is built from words.[46] Prose readily becomes poetry because words always connote more than they denote. Of course, this is also the case with regard to the historian's reporting of history, though again this is precisely the point that critics of scientific and historicist approaches are trying to make. Neither social science nor history ought to look for epistemological grounding in a correspondence theory of truth.

Writers such as Thomas Kuhn, Richard Rorty, and Wilfrid Sellars come at the correspondence theory of truth and modern empiricism from a somewhat different perspective, though they end up about where Foucault does. Kuhn's main thesis in *The Structure of Scientific Revolutions* is by now well known.[47] The history of scientific inquiry is discontinuous, since recurrent paradigmatic shifts diachronically sort scientists into mutually incommensurable communities of discourse. During the most dramatic paradigmatic shifts, prevailing and all-encompassing ways of looking at the world are discarded and replaced by alternate all-encompassing ways of looking at the world. Old conceptual schemes are swapped for new ones. What is of partic-ular interest here concerning Kuhnian paradigmatic shifts is that they imply that what is accepted as true, or *reflective of reality,* at any given time is con-ditioned by the conceptual framework within which the truth is pursued.[48] Not only does the conceptual framework impose a narrative vocabulary for reporting the truth, but it also imposes an operational vocabulary for finding and verifying it. Again, facts are only facts because the conceptual scheme privileges certain varieties of observations.

It is also crucially important to bear constantly in mind that *conceptual frameworks change,* and truth claims and their justifications change along with them. This caused little concern for William James, who was not un-comfortable admitting that "we have to live today by what truth we can get today, and be ready tomorrow to call it falsehood."[49] But, constantly changing conceptual frameworks lead Richard Rorty to wonder, "What if all the theoretical entities postulated by one generation . . . invariably 'don't exist' from the standpoint of later science?—this is, of course, one form of the old skeptical 'argument from error'—or how do you know you aren't in error *now?* But it is the form in which the argument from error is a *serious* worry for many people today."[50] On the other hand, many who continue to believe that social science can achieve a mirroring of reality contend that Kuhnian scientific revolutions are in fact progressive, and that after each revolutionary turn the mirror gets clearer. This is because Kuhn explains that scientific revolutions are precipitated by anomalies which prevailing conceptual frameworks cannot address. To the extent that new frameworks can both address these anomalies and accommodate all that was contained and explained within older frameworks, they may be welcomed as dialectical scientific steps forward.

However, with regard to the human sciences at least, Foucault casts con-siderable doubt on the notion of scientific progress, dialectical or otherwise. Foucault's *Order of Things* is an intellectual history of the human sciences from the sixteenth to the twentieth century, wherein he identifies discon-tinuous "epistemic fields" that appear to be analogous to Kuhn's scientific paradigms. Each of Foucault's fields is essentially unrelated to the one it displaced. It does not take shape in response to anomalies unmanageable under prevailing conceptual schemes, but because students of the human sciences in given epochs and those who consume their intellectual products eventually lose interest in the questions traditionally asked, the objects tradi-tionally studied, and the discourses traditionally composing their narratives. Inquiry within the respective epistemic fields sooner or later exhausts itself with most of its intellectual promise unfulfilled. It fades, and is displaced by an incommensurably new epistemic field. Notes White, "The . . . epochs which Foucault discerns in the chronicle of the human sciences . . . represent discrete colonizations of the order of things by fundamentally different linguistic protocols, each of which remained imprisoned within its own peculiar wager on the adequacy of its 'wording' strategy.... But when a given set of human sciences has run the course of its cycle, then this set is not so much overturned as simply *displaced* by another one...."[51]

Foucault traces the emergence and displacement of epistemic fields in the human sciences by focusing upon the treatment of life, labor, and language through time. What emerges is the constantly changing meaning of these terms, along with changing questions about them, with the result that "each of the epochs... appears to be locked within a specific mode of discourse, which at once provides its access to 'reality' and delimits the horizon of what can possibly appear as real."[52] What is important in Foucault's critique for the argument being made in this essay is that "reality," as well as the reporting of "truths" about it, apparently change diachronically from epistemic field to epistemic field. Therefore, movement through the history of the human sciences does not appear to be a dialectical course of clearer and clearer mirroring, or progressively greater approximation to some knowable reality. It is rather a chronicle of exhausted projects and changing interests.

Saying what appears to be the same thing, but with emphasis shifted from the discursive character of the sciences to their social contexts, Rorty observes that truth claims are as much justified by their correspondence to culture as by their correspondence with "reality." Starting from the question "How do our peers know which of our assertions to take our word for?" Rorty notes that at the level of common sense and everyday occurrence claims about truth are most often evaluated in terms of correspondence with lived experience, in terms of the authority of the speakers and in terms of the language of presentation.[53] Then, drawing upon Sellars's *Science, Perception and Reality,* Rorty goes on to introduce the notion of "epistemological behaviorism," the standpoint of which is that acceptance by peers is not only the justification for everyday truth, but for scientific truth as well. Truth is behavioristic in the sense that it is a product of conversation among peers conducted in a mutually understood language with particular and observed rules of usage and syntax. But truth is also holistic in the sense that it is a product of the total social, cultural, and historical context within which it is spoken. It cannot be "true" outside of its context, because it will not be culturally understood or socially accepted there. In the same way, propositions from outside a cultural context cannot be accepted as "true" within it: "We can only come under epistemic rules," and therefore become entitled to speak the truth, "when we have entered the community where the game governed by these rules is played."[54] There is nothing conspiratorial about the peer group acting as gatekeeper for the truth. This is the normal state of human affairs, in response to which Rorty explains that "we will be holistic not because we have a taste for wholes, any more than we are behavioristic because of a distaste for 'ghostly entities,' but simply because justification has always *been* behavioristic and holistic."[55] Not surprisingly, epistemological behaviorism leads, for Rorty, to "the crucial premise ... that we understand knowledge when we understand the social justification of belief, and thus we have no need to view it as accuracy of representation."[56] Reality becomes what scientific communities accept it to be, and the mirror of nature is replaced by the consensus of peers, or, as James was fond of saying, reality is what it is known as.[57]

It goes without saying that the contemporary assault on the correspondence theory of truth is controversial. To accept this critique of the foundations of empirical science is to destroy not only many of the moorings of much of our social-scientifically accumulated knowledge, but also much of our confidence in our ability to continue to accumulate knowledge systematically. Even to take the critique seriously, without necessarily accepting it, is to rattle us with doubt, as it becomes more difficult to distinguish between what we *know* and what we *believe.* Our inabilities to epistemologically ground interpretations become more discomforting as more and more of our knowledge has to be redefined as interpretation.

To the contemporary assault on the correspondence theory of truth we can respond in three ways. First, we can reject the claims of the critics, cling to the well-established empirical tradition in our human sciences and continue our efforts toward arriving at clearer and clearer representations of reality in our mirror of nature. Taking this conservative tack is dubious, I would argue, on account of the slim promise that social science will ever generate a mathematical or otherwise neutral reporting language on the one hand, and the postmodernist critique of the opaqueness of discursive language on the other. This critique is persuasive: we live in a social universe of discourses that constitute disparate realities, and our words will probably never give us access to an "objective" reality. Second, we can accept the claims of the postmodernist critics and acquiesce in the relativism and solipsism toward which their arguments lead. Moving in this direction is tantamount to negating scholarship, for how are we ever to apprehend what the world was like before human consciousness stepped in to order it? Some postmodernists would welcome this, though it tends to contradict not only the course of human biological evolution that yielded the mind, but also the course of human cultural evolution which, over time, has seen this mind ever so much more creatively used.[58] Third, we can redefine "truth" in a manner that acknowledges the fallibility of the correspondence theory but still renders truth attainable and usable. It is in this third direction that I want to move in the concluding section of this essay.

Pragmatics and Truth

It is sometimes the case that looking forward requires looking backward. James, writing at the turn of the twentieth century, added two elements to the discussion of the foundations of knowledge that turn out to be significant for the case that I am trying to make here. First, he abandoned the vocabulary of "truth claims" and spoke instead of "belief-assertions." This was not a dramatic reformulation for James because for him "to justify a belief" still meant to cognitively verify that what was believed in fact existed.[59] However, separating *beliefs* from *truths* becomes important in light of the postmodernist critique of science—outlined in the last section—that casts doubt upon our ability to establish and/or communicate objective truths. Second, James adds as a requirement for truth (or justified belief) that an idea must "work." Or, more colorfully, a true idea must have "cash value." This requirement supplies the pragmatic dimension of truth, which distinguishes James's formulation. It means that for an idea to be pragmatically true it must contribute in some manner to the believer's better adapting to reality. "What meaning indeed can an idea's truth have save its power of adapting us either mentally or physically to a reality?"[60] Truth, pragmatically defined, has instrumental value.

Those familiar with the philosophical debates that followed James's lectures on pragmatism at Harvard and Columbia Universities in 1906 and 1907, respectively, will recognize that the notion of the instrumental value of truth provoked great controversy. To avoid reopening the debates here, because they are not pertinent to this analysis, let it be noted that (1) James did not abandon the correspondence theory of truth because what he termed "cognitive agreement" with reality was very much a requirement of any idea's being true (although reality was experientially constructed and ever changing) and (2) James asserted that "pragmatic truth" *was not all truth.* "Working" was an added condition of the kind of truth that James reckoned was most meaningful in human experience. It is entirely possible in James's thinking to have useless truths that do not lead to better adaptations to reality, but these were not of interest to him.[61]

The pathway to justifying the interpretative practices of the human sciences leads from William James to the postmodernists, or more specifically, from James to Rorty. Whereas James adhered to the idea of a cognitively approachable reality and was methodologically an empiricist, Rorty dismisses the notion of a cognitively approachable reality, or at least a communicable one, and is methodologically a hermeneuticist. What is common to the two thinkers, writing almost three-quarters of a century apart, is their affinity for the pragmatic dimension of belief. Because we must conceptually construct our own reality, which in human affairs may be the only reality there is, and because we can never validate these conceptual constructions objectively since neither our language nor our confinement within epistemic fields will permit this, our conceptualizing can yield heuristics only, and our knowledge must take the form of *beliefs,* not truths. In these contexts what must distinguish between acceptable beliefs and unacceptable ones, or between interesting and uninteresting ones, is pragmatic usefulness.

Agreeing with James, let me suggest that a belief is useful to the extent that it meets a practical or intellectual need created by the circumstances surrounding the community of holders. "Pragmatic truth," according to James, "is not a property of ideas or statements but of the circumstances and events in which an idea or statement contributes to an action with a beneficial or satisfactory outcome."[62] The theorist's theories, the historicist's interpretations, the Weberian's ideal types are useful, and therefore *pragmatically true,* to the extent that they contribute to our abilities to deal with elements of our circumstances that we find problematic.[63] A pragmatic truth is an element of a coping strategy. Moreover, pragmatic truth is not a figment of the method by which it is established. Neither rigorous scientific procedures, nor hermeneutic interpretations, nor poetic imagination necessarily lead to useful beliefs, *though any or all of them certainly may lead to such beliefs.* There is a relationship between interpretation in the human sciences and problem solving in the experiential world, and pragmatically true beliefs facilitate problem solving. Such beliefs in the form of interpretations of the record of human experience are what the historicist seeks, because his purpose is present-day problem solving. Such beliefs are also what the theorist of international relations records because his purpose is picturing a world that "makes sense" to those who wish to understand it. Theorists also seek to depict a world that can be coped with in the sense that living in it and responding to it will result in as few surprises as possible. James would say that since what we call theories cannot be *true* in any objective sense, they ought to be evaluated in terms of their usefulness in helping us adapt to the social contexts in which we find ourselves. A useful theory has "cash value," and in the literature of international relations there are several such theories.

Interpreting the History of International Relations

I noted at the beginning of this essay that the attempt to justify truth claims associated with interpretations has not been wholly satisfactory. Certainly, if one maintains that truth must be defined as a correspondence to reality and that knowledge must mirror nature, then very little displayed here could have been persuasive. But, on the other hand, if one can entertain the notion that there is no "objective reality" to correspond to, that what we term reality is a construction of subjective or epistemic fancy, and that the ordering is ours and not nature's, then the definitions and standards for truth have to change. Under such conditions, pragmatic truth may have some appeal, and interpretations may then be evaluated not only from the standpoint of how they are arrived at but out of concern for whether they "work." If some of us in international relations are going to remain intent upon becoming historicists, if identifying patterns in relations among states and peoples is our preoccupation, then we are also going to have to become interpreters (or hermeneuticists) and pragmatists. We are going to have to accept that our standards of epistemological justification will not satisfy our positivist colleagues, nor will theirs satisfy us for many of the reasons reviewed in this essay. There is, of course, always room for intellectual conversation between discourses. But this means that all must accept that there is no privileged pathway to understanding international relations, or, for that matter, anything else.

CHAPTER **4**

International Theory and Cyclical History

"Most of the significant philosophies of history," Pitirim Sorokin observed, "and most of the intelligible interpretations of historical events...have...appeared either in periods of serious crisis, catastrophe, and transitional disintegration, or immediately before or after such periods."[1] The twentieth century was an age of continuing crisis in world politics. In terms of lives sacrificed to political idols, the century immediately past, by almost every interpretation, was a profound catastrophe.[2] The century's last decade was indeed a time of transitional disintegration. Transition continues in our time, disintegration perhaps as well.

Somewhat contrary to Sorokin's generalization, and with Francis Fukuyama's provocative efforts notwithstanding, the waning years of the twentieth century did not invite extensive philosophizing about history.[3] Nor did the end of one millennium and the beginning of another provoke much macrohistorical reflection, this despite the fact that "intelligible interpretations of historical events" are these days much in demand. The primary aim of this essay, therefore, is to speak to our understandable hankering to know where we are in history, or, more specifically, where we are in the history of international relations. A further objective here is to use the literatures of philosophical history and international relations theory prognostically to address the problem of conflict and cooperation in the post–Cold War world.

International Relations

If we were to define "international relations" too narrowly, many of the more interesting aspects of historical change would escape our attention. In this analysis therefore international relations are broadly defined as *interactions among states and peoples.* Later attempts to historically locate the present and forecast the future build from the notion that one way to conceptualize human experience is to see it as continuous communication across political, territorial, communal, and cultural frontiers—the sum total of which we can call "international relations."

International relations among modern states date roughly from the seventeenth century—that is, from the inception of the Westphalian state system. But, while patterns and outcomes in relations among states in this rather recently evolved Europe-centered system are the subjects of most of the generalizations today contained in international relations theory, relations among *states per se* date from the third millennium B.C.E. with the emergence of the city-state empires of Ancient Mesopotamia.[4] It is quite possible then that observed patterns in the four-hundred-year-old Westphalian system might actually be deviations from more prevalent patterns etched into the nearly six thousand years of interstate relations.[5] As a result, our intelligible interpretations of historical events at the beginning of the twenty-first century might find meaning either in terms of the history of the modern state system or in terms of the longer history of interstate relations per se, or both.

Then again, the most significant elements of historical meaning in today's international relations may derive less from international relations defined as relations among states, and more from international relations defined as relations among peoples. The grandest events—both heroic and tragic, stemming from interactions among human communities—may not come from interactions among states at all but from interactions between civilizations. Such intercultural outcomes are often millennial in duration, demiglobal in impact and fundamental to the extent that they can alter human character itself. This was certainly Arnold Toynbee's conclusion; it is one of the compelling themes of Adda Bozeman's *Politics and Culture in International History;* and it is the essence of F. S. C. Northrop's *Meeting of East and West.*[6] To these and many other interpreters, states repeatedly play through their political games—making and breaking alliances, fighting wars, gaining and losing power, prestige and wealth, and wreaking havoc with people's lives—but all this with only ephemeral effect. Meanwhile, the lasting impacts of international relations are those that emerge from the coming together of cultures. Kenneth Thompson instructs that analysts of the history of international relations ought to explore intercultural relations "as thoroughly and carefully" as interstate relations.[7] His advice is well given, although it has not been particularly well taken by American students of international relations.

Some Comparative Heuristics

By the standards of positivistic science, there exist no *theories* of the history of international relations. The prodigious efforts of generations of scholars have revealed no laws of human affairs in this domain of inquiry, and indeed there may not be any.[8] What scholarship has usefully produced, however, in the manner of Weberian *Gedankenbilder,* is a variety of appealing and intriguing heuristic models of historical processes that can educate our thinking about where we have come from and where we might be going in international relations.[9]

There are two major categories of historical process models: the linear and the cyclical. Some students have concluded that relations among states and peoples have been historically evolving in manners such that successive epochs are qualitatively different. These analysts contend that international history does not repeat itself. International history, they say, is directional and perhaps even teleological. On the other hand, the greatest number of scholars contributing to Western literatures has concluded that conditions, modes, and outcomes in relations among states and peoples have been historically recurrent. International history is cyclical. Human experiences do repeat themselves: actors, ideas, and technologies change from epoch to epoch, but patterns and phases of international political and cultural interaction relentlessly repeat.

Linear Process Models

It naturally makes a good deal of difference whether one informs one's interpretations and prognostications with linear or cyclical heuristics. Regrettably for humankind, most of the more benign linear models, which interpret the history of international relations as building incrementally toward increasing civility, harmony, and order, almost all ran empirically aground in the twentieth century. In different but equally revealing ways during the interwar period, for example, both E. H. Carr and Karl Polanyi exposed the whimsicalities of nineteenth-century Western thinking about "progress" toward a harmonious world.[10] The sober data of political and economic reality, they pointed out, simply did not fit the progressive evolutionary model. Neither has the Marxist mapping of the historical road to utopia proven accurate, not only because the partially constructed promised land turned out to be hell for its inhabitants, but also because most of what was theoretically supposed to happen during the worldwide proletarian revolution never happened and presumably never will. More recently, Hedley Bull and Adam Watson's contention in *The Expansion of International Society* that international relations have been becoming more orderly since the sixteenth century because a normative underpinning for an international society has emerged is intriguing. It is supported by some evidence and plausible to the extent that we can accept that Western-fashioned rules of the international game will remain in effect even after Western civilization loses its luster. Still, there is sufficient intellectual counterpoint in the Bull and Watson volume itself—for example, in the chapters by James Piscatori, Elie Kedourie, and Adda Bozeman, as well as strong refutation in some of Bozeman's other work, to render the editors' progressive evolutionary contention no more than a hypothesis.[11] Since the eighteenth-century Enlightenment not a few Westerners have been convinced that a noble, yet historically extraordinary, cluster of European ideas about individualism, property, constrained government, and democracy was destined to diffuse worldwide and to universally and uniformly influence institutions and behavior.[12] In this progressive tradition, Francis Fukuyama's setting of the "end of [unpleasant] history" near the turn of the twenty-first century looks a bit like Woodrow Wilson's setting it near the end of the 1920s, or Alfred, Lord Tennyson's imagining it at "Locksley Hall" in 1842.[13] I am going to return to Francis Fukuyama and visions of a liberal world in chapter 9; so let us therefore not dismiss the idea of progressive international history just yet.

Most of the apocalyptic historical models with implications for international relations that emerged from Judeo-Christian tradition involve divine intervention into and ultimate judgment of human affairs.[14] They are difficult to deal with in the context of an essay such as this, and they suffer, in any event, both operationally and empirically. Andrew Schmookler's ominous interpretations, however, assume a history that is biologically and culturally, rather than supernaturally, driven, and his *Parable of the Tribes* should therefore be taken seriously.[15] Schmookler suggests that both biological and cultural evolution select for organisms or organizations that structure themselves to maximize predatory power. The millennial trend toward territorially larger, organizationally more efficient, militarily more destructive, economically more acquisitive, and externally more predatory states fits Schmookler's evolutionary model. It predicts either world domination by a sole surviving predator, or the destruction of human civilization in a nuclear war.[16]

Cyclical Process Models

Of course, political realism also predicts either world domination or world destruction, because even well-crafted balances of power sometimes break down, would-be imperialists sometimes get unleashed, and big wars must sometimes be fought for power-balancing purposes. Implicit in political realism, therefore, is the greater-than-zero probability that some future round of power balancing will cause the "great power war" that will annihilate all of us. But until that happens, say the realists, international relations will pass through continuing, roughly analogous, cycles.

The historic pattern of the "rise and fall of the great powers" has been so extensively explored in the literature of international relations that little elaboration is necessary here.[17] The pattern has also been so frequently identified and extensively documented by historians that we can be reasonably confident that it exists and will recur unless the future brings dramatic changes in the factors that cause it. State systems tend toward hierarchy: differential changes in the components of power, both tangible and intangible, including such factors as internal political stability, lend differential competitive advantage to different states. Some are therefore able to elevate their demands for rewards from the system and rise to positions of hegemony, while others are forced to trim their demands and may eventually sink into obscurity. The costs and strains of maintaining hegemony, and advantages to others in not having to bear these, eventually force the hegemons into decline and open the way to recycling the pattern of rising and falling power.

In important contributions to the literature of power cycles, Robert Gilpin and Paul Kennedy have added important analyses concerning interrelationships between the economic capabilities of states and political-competitive endurance.[18] Additional insights concerning political-economic processes are to be found in careful readings of Fernand Braudel's *The Perspective of the World* and Immanuel Wallerstein's *The Capitalist World-Economy,* where both scholars, using different analytical tools and conceptual vocabularies, reveal that not only is political-military ascendance abetted by world market dominance, as we might expect, but aggressive and consistent state intervention into the market is required if political-military as well as economic ascendance are to be maintained.[19] World economic "playing fields" are always tilted to the advantage of dominant political actors, *because these actors do everything they possibly can to tilt them!* There are, then, in historical cycles of rising and declining power concurrent cycles of relative political-military ability to affect competitive economic advantage. The contemporary significance of this observation will become apparent later in this essay.

The rise and decline of great empires is not exactly the same thing as the rise and fall of great powers, although in the Westphalian state system great powers also often have been the core states of great empires. It has also been true in the modern state system that the rise of great powers has frequently been linked with imperial success, and that the decline of great powers has frequently been linked with imperial troubles. But the rise and decline of empires as a process in the history of international relations predates the modern state system by approximately four thousand years if Sumer actually declined in 2300 B.C.E., and this process has distinctive characteristics of its own.[20] It could very well be the most frequently recurrent cyclical process in the history of international relations.

Empires are the core states of imperial systems, which also contain varying numbers of subordinate states whose autonomy is constrained in such manner that they may not act contrary to the interests of the core, and they are usually compelled to act in support of the interests of the core.[21] Empires constrain the autonomy of subordinate units in various direct and indirect ways, although all amount in effect to controlling the recruitment and tenure of subordinate-unit elites. Empires are inherently politically unstable because subordinate units almost always prefer greater autonomy, and counterelites in such units almost always act, upon opportunity, to obtain greater autonomy. In this sense, empires do not *fall*; they rather *fall apart*, usually very slowly, though sometimes remarkably quickly.

It is a pity that Harold Lasswell did some of his most insightful work about two decades before his discipline was ready to receive it. His *World Politics and Personal Insecurity* was not very well received in 1935, and when political science finally got to it in the 1960s the attraction was Lasswell's pre-behavioralism and not his philosophical historicism.[22] Lasswell's image of international relations is essentially a people(s)-to-people(s) picture—interacting "sentiment areas," he calls them—and what passes between peoples are political-philosophical and economic-philosophical ideas, or *ideologies*. Flows of ideologies via international relations are historically patterned. Clusters of ideas are conceived or assembled at particular places and times, and they then diffuse outward across societies until they reach the cultural or historical limits of their appeal. By the time that any given ideology has run its course, or sometimes in direct response to its diffusion, another ideology is conceived and it too begins diffusing outward from a new political-philosophical center. Lasswell called this process of ideological diffusion via international relations "world revolution."[23] Lasswellian world revolutions have usually occurred over centuries; modern mass communications may speed them; there is always one going on.

Several of the major contributors to the literature of philosophical history have observed that there is always more going on in relations among peoples than political-ideological diffusion. International relations is cross-cultural communication in the broadest sense, and one of the most pronounced and profound processes in the history of international relations is the diffusion of ascendant cultures outward from centers of civilization where they are born. A "culture" in the sense used here is a distinctive way of life that includes distinctive patterns of nonhereditary behavior, distinctive social institutions, and a distinctive weltanschauung founded in distinctive philosophical and religious beliefs.[24] Every epoch of history has witnessed the emergence of powerful cultures with attributes that make them attractive to alien others. Powerful cultures often also have messianic ingredients that turn their adherents into aggressive proselytizers.[25]

Historically, cultural diffusion has also been a cyclical phenomenon. For reasons whose discovery has been at the heart of the philosophical historical puzzle, great civilizations also rise and decline, and during phases of decline they lose their external influence and are displaced, albeit never completely, in areas of former dominance either by resurgent provincialisms or by the magnetism or messianic force of other, newly ascendant cultures. This was the story of the Hellenistic culture that flowered from 400 to 200 B.C.E.; the Byzantine culture that reached ascendance about the tenth century; the Arab-Islamic culture that spread through North Africa, southern Europe, and the Near East and reached zenith between the seventh and eighth centuries; Turkish culture at its prime in Suleiman's sixteenth-century Ottoman Empire, and the Chinese culture at apogee during the fourteenth- through seventeenth-century Ming Dynasty. This may well be the story of Western culture between the eighteenth and the twenty-first centuries. More about this shortly.

The purpose of heuristics is to aid in discovery by alerting analysts as to what to look for. Their purpose here is to offer some insights into plausible patterns of outcomes in early twenty-first-century international relations. Table 4.1 summarizes some of the patterns we might look for in assessing how the long- and short-term past became the present, and how the present might become the future.

International Relations in the Post–Cold War World

Naturally, if the twenty-first century is to be wholly novel, models derived from the history of international relations will be poor guides to the future. However, at almost any point in the past, an analyst's best prediction for the future of international relations would have been to foresee a rerunning of one or more of the cycles described in table 4.1. Contrariwise, consistently less accurate predictions would have followed from projecting dramatic departures from the cycles. Obviously, the implicit assumption in such analyses was that the causal factors and relationships driving the cycles had not changed. This assumption is explicitly made here, and the hypothesis that founds the analysis below is that not only some, but all of the historical cycles in table 4.1 are currently rerunning and will affect international relations in the early-twenty-first century. Not one, but many

Table 4.1. Plausible Patterns of Change in the History of International Relations

MODE OF INTERACTION	MODEL	DESCRIPTION/ EVIDENCE
State to state	Cyclical: rise and fall of the great powers	Hierarchy of great powers changes as some gain power and stature, relatively or absolutely, while others decline; tensions between tendencies toward hegemony and tendencies toward balanced power.
State to state	Cyclical: rise and decline of the great empires	The progressive establishment of dominance-subordination relationships between core and peripheral states; eventual fragmentation as peripheral states exploit opportunities for greater autonomy.
People to people	Cyclical: Lasswellian "world revolutions"	The diffusion outward of political and economic ideologies from revolutionary core areas; eventual truncation, followed by new diffusion of another ideology.
People to people	Cyclical: cultural diffusion	The outward diffusion of total ways of life from centers of advanced civilization, followed eventually by cultural rejection and displacement by older or newer ways of life.

courses of events are in train, and there is good possibility that several of them will amplify each other.

A Power Transition

The last power transition in international relations is well documented. The hundred years' war, which lasted roughly from 1850 to 1950, was fought to decide whether the powerful Germany that emerged from unification by "blood and iron" and the powerful Japan that emerged from the Meiji Restoration would or could be properly admitted to the great power hierarchy. Ultimately, neither was admitted; both were destroyed, but in the process so too was the hierarchy of world power that had been in place since the sixteenth century. The most notable casualties of the struggle, besides Germany and Japan, were Austria-Hungary and the Ottoman Empire, which disappeared; France, which never recovered from World War I; and Great Britain, whose incapacities for sustained ascendance were written into economic statistics as early as the 1890s.[26]

The long struggle for mastery in Europe and in the Pacific propelled to mid-twentieth-century centrality the one country that had long remained at the periphery of the contest. After World War II, and particularly with the dawn of the nuclear era, the preponderance of economic and military power in the world was concentrated in the United States. Mid-twentieth-century America also nearly monopolized what Joseph Nye refers to as "soft power," or influence attributable to trust and moral leadership.[27] By hindsight, we know now that from the 1950s to the 1990s American hegemony was more pronounced, and Soviet power less countervailing, than the Cold War atmosphere suggested, and the United States was much more secure than American statesmen supposed.[28] The post–World War II period could have been a *pax Americana*. Instead it was an era of incessant warfare, with Americans doing a good deal of the fighting in pursuit of objectives other than global pacification.

The historical model of rising and falling power suggests that American hegemony could diminish and disappear in the decades ahead. The conditional here applies to the *when* and not to the *whether* of American decline. Forty years at the pinnacle of power is, historically, a rather brief ascendance, and American decline is not likely to be precipitous. Yet, Joseph Nye's argument notwithstanding, there were by the 1990s numerous indications that U.S. power was slipping both relatively and absolutely, and that others' power was increasing, thus suggesting that another historic power transition is likely in train. Whatever the merits of particular policies in given situations, a good deal of American "soft power" was squandered during the Cold War by an interventionist strategy that was frequently insensitive to others' national and cultural aspirations and a unilateralist diplomacy that has unnecessarily disregarded world opinion.[29] Soft power was also dissipated in a series of unilateral economic moves, beginning with the Nixon shocks that undermined the world monetary system in the 1970s, and the monetary policies of the Reagan administration, which appeared to be oblivious to international interdependence and which meted penalties to foreigners accordingly. The relative indifference of the United States toward the United Nations from the 1970s onward has further damaged the American image and adversely affected Washington's international influence.

To the extent that economic capability remains the foundation of national power, the United States remains impressively capable. After a wrenching, but mostly successful, restructuring of its economy during the 1990s, the United States emerged positioned to take advantage both of the dawning postindustrial age and the economically globalizing world. Nevertheless, the United States is unlikely—perhaps ever again—to enjoy the singular world economic ascendance that characterized its position from roughly 1950 to 1970. Other countries have also been accumulating capacities to act internationally. Economically dynamic, technologically advanced Japan began in the mid-1980s to convert some of its wealth into political power by increasing and diversifying its development assistance and overseas investment programs; elevating its visibility in important multilateral institutions; pressing to move Japanese nationals into high executive positions in international organizations; participating physically in international peacekeeping operations like those in Namibia, Cambodia, and Afghanistan; and increasing defense spending.[30] At the same time, Europe, in the form of the European Union, appears, after several decades of economic accomplishment, to be on the threshold of a new political-military assertiveness.[31] Reunified Germany, with the Eastern *Lander* nearly fully reintegrated, is increasingly capable of motoring Europe in directions set by collectively defined interests or of reinserting itself independently into a multipolar world power structure. Though its development is uneven and everywhere constrained by limited infrastructure and population pressure, the People's Republic of China is nonetheless becoming wealthy. Its government—historically status-conscious, under pressure from liberalizing forces within, and perceptibly under siege from ideologically alien forces without—appears both increasingly impelled and increasingly able to convert new wealth into enhanced political-military power. As Paul Kennedy has concluded regarding China, "it is only a matter of time."[32] Some say that it is also only a matter of time before Russia resurges.[33]

Other alterations of the world power structure, such as Indian ascendance, are more difficult to anticipate because means and/or motivations for converting increased wealth into externally projectable power are less discernable. It is reasonably apparent, if the cyclical pattern of rising and falling power holds up, that the middle decades of the twenty-first century will see a resetting of the international balance of power in a world beyond American hegemony. This resetting will partially refocus both international conflict and cooperation in ways discussed later in this analysis.

The End of Empire

It is surprising that more scholarship in the field of international relations has not been directed toward examining the coming apart of empires, particularly since present-day scholars have been eyewitnesses to the disintegration of several great empires. The Dutch East Indian empire did not survive World War II; the British and French empires came apart in pieces between the late 1940s and the 1970s; what was left of the Portuguese empire in Africa came undone in 1975. But, as the European empires that were assembled over five centuries collapsed, two others, also built over a long period of time, prospered.

At the pinnacle of its ascendance—let us say just before the Sino-Soviet schism in 1961—the Russian continental empire stretched longitudinally from the western frontier of the German Democratic Republic to the Pacific Ocean. It encompassed most of the Eurasian landmass, including the Baltic States, truncated Germany, Poland, Czechoslovakia, Hungary, Romania, Bulgaria, and Albania in the West, and Mainland China, Mongolia, North Korea, and North Vietnam in the East. Extracontinentally, Soviet suzerainty extended to Cuba, for a short while to Afghanistan, and possibly to South Yemen, Angola, and Ethiopia. The Soviet Empire was the successor to the Russian Empire of the Tsars, and the revolution of 1917 hardly affected the course of Russian empire building. The beginning was an "insignificant *ostrog* [block house] built in the first half of the twelfth century, on an insignificant river by an insignificant princeling."[34]

Paralleling the growth of the Russian empire in the East was the American empire in the West. At the height of its imperium in 1959, just before the first challenges of Charles de Gaulle and the Cuban Revolution, the United States was the core state of an imperial system that included all of North America, all of Central America, virtually all of South America, the Western Alliance states of Europe, plus Iran, Japan, South Korea, the Republic of China on Taiwan, the Philippines, Israel, a scattering of Pacific islands, and a cluster of Caribbean islands. This sprawling empire had taken more than two centuries to build. The core state began with a strip of territory along the Atlantic coast of North America together with some initially unenforceable claims to lands west of the Appalachian Mountains. But even at the beginning, the first president of the United States predicted that "there will assuredly come a day, when this country will have some weight in the scale of empires."[35] That day came in the twentieth century.

Though the political styles of the two imperial core states were somewhat different and their respective philosophical appeals for legitimacy were dramatically different, both were expansionist, both enforced hierarchical intraimperial relations, and both maintained their dominance within by controlling the recruitment of elites in peripheral states. Both also restricted the autonomy of peripheral states, particularly in issue areas involving interimperial relations. The interimperial relations of Russia and the United States highlighted the international politics of the post–World War II era.

As noted, empires typically come apart from the outside inward: peripheral states grasp for greater autonomy when central control falters. Control falters when power diminishes and/or legitimacy fails (or when imperial will lapses). Readers need hardly be told that the Russian empire manifestly began disintegrating in the late 1980s for reasons of diminished power, failed legitimacy, and flagging imperial will. This disintegration may continue. Less precipitously, but just as assuredly, the American empire is presently also disintegrating, and the process is being hastened by the passing of East-West ideological rivalry, which legitimated American hegemony. Assertions of United States "leadership" attract fewer and fewer "followers" these days, largely for reasons of diminished legitimacy. Washington is no longer as able as in the past to install and sustain peripheral elites of its choosing. Instead, there are today tendencies even in allied and friendly countries, like Japan, Korea, the Philippines, Mexico, and even Germany, for example, for politicians to capitalize on anti-Americanism in order to acquire office. Practically speaking, what is left of the United States global empire is a continuing omnipresence in Central American and Caribbean affairs. But while the American capacity to maintain its empire has diminished it is not clear that the American imperial will has waned.[36]

Nor is it clear who the twenty-first century's empire builders will be. For cultural reasons discussed below, it is likely that the next imperial core state(s) will be non-Western. Both China and Japan have imperial histories, and both have increasing capabilities and heightening aspirations in Asia. India has hegemonic aspirations in the Indian Ocean region, and Iran, Syria, and Egypt are all potential cores of an Islamic empire, though it is not likely that the rest of the world would look away long enough to allow Islamic empire-building to gather any momentum. Much will depend on the course of economic development in the decades ahead and on the ideologies that would-be imperialists call upon to legitimize their political and economic expansion. To expect that there will be no new drives toward empire in the twenty-first century would be to discount four thousand years of international history.

World Revolution

By one interpretation we might conclude that a Lasswellian world revolutionary cycle has just run its course. The diffusion outward of Marxism-Leninism from the Soviet core area was nearly global: professedly Marxist elites displaced non-Marxists in dozens of states; Marxist symbols and vocabularies proliferated widely, as did Leninist parties, organizations, and political styles.[37] But, by the early 1990s Marxism-Leninism reached the limits of its appeal, as even the stalwarts discovered that neither the predictions nor the prescriptions of the ideology practically equipped adherents to deal with social, economic, or political realities. The Marxist-Leninist world revolution was therefore truncated: Marxist symbols were discredited; Marxist elites were displaced; Leninist organizations were disbanded and Leninist political styles were eschewed. The new outward-diffusing ideology became Western, democratic, free-market liberalism, and by the 1990s a renewed liberal world revolution was under way.

Less conventionally, but probably more accurately in historical perspective, the world's flirtation with Marxism-Leninism should be interpreted as a brief but intense challenge to Western liberalism, and the menaces of fascism and Nazism during the two decades preceding World War II were briefer challenges still, but also very intense.[38] The Lasswellian world revolutionary ideology of modern times all along, therefore, has been Western liberalism itself, and not its intermittent challengers, all of which legitimated politico-cultural and institutional retrogressions to medieval or oriental despotism. Liberalism, built around a value cluster of individuality, liberty, property, political equality, and limited government, has been diffusing outward from England, France, and the United States since the eighteenth century.

Born in the politically radical intellectual confluence of the eighteenth-century Enlightenment, liberalism has been in the expansive, outward-diffusing phase of its historical cycle for the past three centuries. Its legitimating symbols—"constitution," "parliament," "representative government," "popular sovereignty," "individual liberty," "rule of law," "rights of man"—have been displacing the legitimating symbols of authoritarianism, monarchism, despotism, and the ancien régime. The legitimacy of its prescribed methods of elite recruitment via free elections has been displacing traditionally accepted (and expected) admixtures of ascription, conspiracy, mob endorsement, and brute force. The legitimacy of liberalism's preferred political styles—dialogue, debate, deliberation, compromise, majoritarianism—has been displacing traditionally accepted (and expected) decision making by cabal and rule by executive decree. It is true that the diffusion of liberal government has lagged well behind the diffusion of liberal ideas over the past three centuries. But Lasswellian world revolutions are about ideas, and the spreading appeal of liberal ideas has been such that even blatantly illiberal regimes almost everywhere have found it necessary to disguise themselves in liberal masks.

The question for our time is how much longer the outward-diffusing phase of the liberal world revolutionary cycle will last. Just after the end of the Second World War, historian Hans Kohn, who wrote extensively on the diffusion of Western ideas, foresaw continuing movement toward the universalization of liberal political ideas. Interpreting the historical meaning of this great war, Kohn observed that Western civilization had "proven its power of resistance against fanatic ideologies." He concluded that "there is the possibility that in the second half of the twentieth century the Western spirit of tolerance and compromise, of self-criticism and fair-minded objectivity, of reasonableness and individualism may spread again."[39]

But, Kohn also had some reservations. It is possible to argue, he noted, "that this tremendous effort of the last century... has left Western Civilization fatigued and exhausted. ... Twentieth century man has become less confident than his nineteenth century ancestor was. He has witnessed the dark powers of history in his own experience. Things which seemed to belong to the past have reappeared: fanatical faith, infallible leaders, slavery and massacres, the uprooting of whole populations, ruthlessness and barbarism."[40]

Though the evidence is mixed, and even though the West today enthusiastically advocates Western-styled democracy for all, there are reasons why we might prudently wonder whether the outward diffusion of eighteenth-century Western liberal ideas is over or will be soon. Lasswell concluded that world revolutions fizzle out short of universalization, or "truncate," for at least three reasons: (1) outward-diffusing ideologies lose their appeal when they lose their practical usefulness as interpreters of reality; (2) outward-diffusing ideologies lose their appeal when they cannot be culturally assimilated; and (3) outward diffusion is halted when ideologies are overpowered by alternative formulations of sociopolitical meaning.[41]

In the first instance with regard to Western liberalism, the kinds of political institutions prescribed and legitimated by it are proving increasingly cumbersome, inefficient, and inept in the face of early twenty-first century societal complexities, and the ideas and principles underpinning them may be losing their appeal. Pluralism tends toward immobilism; parliaments tend toward political gridlock; elections fail to recruit capable leaders; electoral imperatives frequently forbid hard or wise policy choices; majoritarianism founders when majorities persistently fail to materialize, and it perverts when it abuses minorities. The political institutions sprung from Western liberalism tend to function satisfactorily under noncrisis conditions, which probably will not be the modal conditions of politics, particularly non-Western politics, for several decades into our new century.

It is also the case that "[t]hings which seemed to belong to the past, have [most assuredly] reappeared," and some of these things are culturally incompatible with liberal principles or the institutions and political styles that follow from them. The integral nationalism that has reappeared in the Balkans, Central Europe, the former USSR and elsewhere, as well as the tribalism rampant in Somalia, South and Central Africa, Nigeria, Sri Lanka, Afghanistan, Pakistan, and elsewhere, are not hospitable to Western liberalism. The leaders of these ethnic communities seek to minimize differentiation within, while maximizing autonomy without; there is here little room or justification for a politics of compromise. Nor, of course, are the religious fundamentalisms of the Islamic world, or religious fundamentalism more generally, compatible with Western liberalism, or indeed even with rudimentary political pluralism. Lest it be forgotten, the gerontocracy that rules over the 1.2 billion people residing in the People's Republic of China finds nothing particularly attractive about liberalism, and those who are most likely to succeed the old men are not liberals either.[42] Elsewhere in East Asia, those who are enthusiastically endorsing "Asian values" are also enthusiastically rejecting Western ones.

Western liberalism has never been without rivals, though today there are no apparent alternative political philosophies in the world that have much potential to diffuse transculturally. Still, the Lasswellian model of world revolution alerts us to the probability that new ideologies will emerge in the years ahead. The most likely diffusion path for a new ideology in the next few decades would be through the mobilized and currently alienated populations of the non-Western world who are seeking philosophical formulas for material betterment and spiritual exhilaration, or seeking images that otherwise give meaning to non-Western conditions in our time.[43] For many of these communities liberalism rings hollow for reasons already noted, nationalism either never took hold or proved a false prophecy, anti-imperialism is wearing thin as injustices suffered a half century or more ago no longer explain current conditions and religion fails to resolve problems that are distinctly secular. Millions of thinking people in the third world today are in search of an ideology that will lend meaning and inspiration to their political lives. We would do well, therefore, to monitor the political and political-economic thinking emerging from China as the Beijing regime seeks legitimation for its experiments with a quarter of mankind. It would appear that Chinese political theory is moving ever farther from the principles of Maoism, and indeed from those of communism as well, toward a form of developmentalistic authoritarianism.[44] When credited by actual accomplishments in economic development, such a set of ideas about appropriate principles and institutions for moving from poverty to wealth and from weakness to power in non-Western milieus could be readily exportable.

The Decline of the West

Much that has already been said about the probable truncation of Western liberalism may be generalized for the state of Western civilization. As analytical obsession with the American-Soviet rivalry of the last half century diminishes and historical perspectives are adjusted, the Cold War becomes an episode in Westphalian interstate relations, not entirely unlike the sixteenth-century rivalry between Spain and France, the eighteenth-century rivalry between England and France or the nineteenth- and twentieth-century rivalry between England and Germany.[45] What is easily overlooked is that while the interstate politics of the Westphalian system were being played out, a much broader, and perhaps historically more significant, episode in intercultural relations was unfolding. Western civilization was maturing, blossoming, and diffusing outward from Europe to all other regions of the world.[46]

K. N. Panikkar dates the beginning of the global diffusion of Western civilization from 1498, when Vasco da Gama arrived in Calicut and opened the Portuguese phase of European penetration in Asia.[47] We might as easily date it from 1492, when Columbus sailed into the Caribbean to begin the Spanish phase of European penetration in the Americas. Between the end of the fifteenth century and the middle of the twentieth, Westerners exported, and non-Westerners imported, both by choice and under duress, a total way of social, economic, technological, political, philosophical, and religious life. In the process, non-Western cultures were technologically superseded and intellectually and spiritually suppressed to the point that by the middle of the nineteenth century it appeared to some that humanity was well on its way to cultural homogenization under Western tutelage.

Nevertheless, the judgment of a number of cultural historians is that, in the twentieth century at least, Western civilization has lapsed into decline.[48] One need not agree with Oswald Spengler that the West, having exhausted its creativity in the eighteenth century, has been in decline for the past two hundred years. Yet, it is reasonably clear that, except in realms of applied science and pop culture (whose influence should not be underestimated), Western cultural forms, ideas, and institutions have been for some time either losing their appeal or confronting non-Western forms, ideas, and institutions that are equally appealing. Part of the explanation why Western culture is no longer diffusing within the non-Western world as readily as it was a century ago is that the West no longer controls all the channels nor monopolizes the means of intercultural transmission such as direct rule over aliens, relatively uncontested access to alien societies, unique physical presence in extra-European regions, unchallengeable economic and military superiority and corps of dedicated proselytizers. Nor are Western forms, ideas, and institutions as welcome in the non-Western world as they were a century ago, and where they *are* admitted they exist side by side with resilient non-Western forms. The carnage of the two world wars of the twentieth century did much to destroy the notion that Western culture somehow represented an elevated form of human civilization. Similarly, the spread of industrialism in the twentieth century, particularly to postrevolutionary Russia and Japan, demonstrated that producing material abundance was not culture bound, and neither was technological innovativeness. Perhaps most telling of all was the spreading realization on the part of non-Westerners that assimilation to Western culture was ultimately impossible because the inherent racism that is part of this culture rendered assimilation unacceptable even to those who promoted it.

In fact, the last fifty years have been witness to the vigorous reassertion of "non-Westernness" in a variety of cultural dimensions.[49] This reassertion is politically symbolized and epitomized in the drama of decolonization and the ensuing north-south debates over the principles and institutions of a "new world order." Culturally it is to be found in the thinking and behavior contained in anti-imperialism and third-world nationalisms where non-Western spiritualism is set against Western materialism, non-Western mysticism against Western rationalism, non-Western intuitiveness against Western empiricism, non-Western collectivism against Western individualism, and non-Western authoritarianism against Western pluralism.[50]

Christopher Dawson and others have argued that the non-Westernism that is being asserted in Asia and Africa today is more than a revival of traditional ideas and ways, since too much has changed over the last five hundred years to allow this.[51] It is, rather, a variety of cultural hybrids made up of traditional philosophical and religious elements and borrowings from the West. Dawson notes, "Oriental nationalism does not mean, as one might suppose, a reaction in defense of traditional oriental culture; on the contrary it means the adoption or appropriation by Eastern peoples of Western culture.... [But] beneath the surface of oriental nationalist movements ... there are age-old differences of culture and religion and race which exercise a profound unconscious influence on the thought and behavior of the masses."[52] One common, and fundamental, ingredient in cultural non-Westernisms today is a profound resentment against the West. Writes the Senegalese poet David Diop,

> In those days
> When civilization kicked us in the face
> When holy water slapped our cringing brows
> The vultures built in the shadow of their talons
> The bloodstained monument of tutelage
> In those days
> There was painful laughter on the metallic hell of the roads
> And the monotonous rhythm of the paternoster
> Drowned the howling on the plantations
> O the bitter memories of extorted kisses
> Of promises broken at the point of a gun
> Of foreigners who did not seem human
> Who knew all the books but did not know love[53]

Asian and African encounters with the West over the past five centuries are not pleasantly recalled, and as long as painful images of the European-,

Caucasian-, Christian-dominant, colonial past remain components of non-Western identity there can be no global culture. There will be no dominant civilization in the early-twenty-first century: West and non-West will likely linger at an intercultural impasse.

The Outline of Contemporary International History

As we are not dealing with theories but heuristics, we cannot make predictions—but we can talk about plausibilities. First, it is plausible to assume that several simultaneously occurring processes characteristic of the history of international relations have produced the events that compose international relations at present. It is also plausible to assume that these processes will continue to effect events in the future. Making such assumptions yields the summaries contained in table 4.2.

Far from being at the "end of history" and on the threshold of the universalization of Western values and institutions, we may be on the threshold of the end of the era of Western world supremacy. It certainly appears that American primacy will be challenged. Its power could well be neutralized by some of its closest Cold War allies, its suzerainty even in the Western Hemisphere could be progressively weakened, and its values could be rejected, along with Western values more generally, as the utility of liberalism and the appeals of Western civilization ebb. By contrast, international history in the twenty-first century could find its mainstreams in the non-Western world, and more specifically in East Asia, where power and ideas appear to be converging. Naturally, all of this has to be phrased in the conditional, because the international relations of the decades immediately ahead will be shaped by what could be a major confrontation between the forces of the status quo and the would-be inheritors of a new twenty-first-century world order. Neither the United States nor Western civilization are likely to be eclipsed without a struggle because, historically, decisive transitions in international relations never occur without contest.

Conflict and Cooperation in the Post–Cold War World

To the extent that the history of international relations is cyclical, and to the added extent that the cycles are presently phased as suggested in table 4.2, lines of potential conflict in post–Cold War international relations are discernible. There is likely to be a contest for position in the hierarchy of powers, a contest over the remaining integrity of the Russian and American empires, a contest between Western liberalism and its critics and a contest between Western civilization and its challengers. Since all of these world-historical contests are long-term by definition, we need not expect, or look

Table 4.2. Plausible Changes in Twenty-First Century International Relations

MODE OF INTERACTION	MODEL	DESCRIPTION/ EVIDENCE	PLAUSIBLE FUTURE OUTCOMES
State to state	Cyclical: rise and fall of the great powers	Hierarchy of great powers changes as some gain power and stature, relatively or absolutely, while others decline; tensions between tendencies toward hegemony and tendencies toward balanced power.	Paramount position of the United States disappears; China, Japan, and Europe rise.
State to state	Cyclical: rise and decline of the great empires	The progressive establishment of dominant-subordinate relationships between core and peripheral states; eventual fragmentation as peripheral states exploit opportunities for greater autonomy.	Continuing fragmentation of the former Soviet empire as weakness of core compounds; and fragmentation of American empire, particularly as "soft power" ebbs.
People to people	Cyclical: Lasswellian "world revolutions"	The diffusion outward of political and economic ideologies from revolutionary core areas; eventual truncation, followed by new diffusion of another ideology.	The truncation of Western liberalism; eventual conceptualization, probably in Asia, of a twenty-first-century creed that will diffuse outward first in the non-Western world.
People to people	Cyclical: cultural diffusion	The outward diffusion of total ways of life from centers of advanced civilization, followed eventually by cultural rejection and displacement by older or newer ways of life.	Fading appeal of Western civilization; rising appeal of non-Western forms, ideas, and institutions; no global homogenization of culture.

for, definitive outcomes in decades immediately ahead. Lines of contention and directions of movement, however, should be identifiable.

The contest for power position will be engaged primarily by the United States, which will struggle to salvage and preserve all it can of its Cold War–era primacy, and aspirants who will press to turn new wealth into new political stature and influence, as well as into more wealth. Participants in the unseating of the United States should include Japan, the European Union or Germany, and most assuredly China. The contest should be largely economic in content, with all governments intervening vigorously and continually to manipulate the world market to their producers', consumers', and traders' advantage. One outcome of the struggle for power will be the opportunity to define the normative content of the issue-area regimes that will order early-twenty-first-century international relations, and practically speaking, to run the international organizational system. Another result, should China or Japan emerge paramount, for example, might be the opportunity to formulate and diffuse a new political ideology and thus open a new cycle in world revolution. Then again, doing well in the contest for power might conceivably whet someone's imperial appetite.

If the imperial decline of Russia and the United States is true to historical form, the early years of the twenty-first century should see the former hegemons struggling to preserve whatever remains of their former intraimperial relations. They may even attempt to reassert their suzerainty. The former peripheral states of the respective empires will be pressing ever more emphatically to maximize their autonomy and to remove residual dependencies. With regard to Russia, relations are likely to be strained between Moscow and the newly independent states emerged from the former Soviet Union, as Russians find it difficult to treat former subjects as autonomous neighbors, and as these neighbors insist ever more emphatically that their independence must be respected. The United States will have similar problems adjusting to the dissolution of the Western bloc. The North Atlantic Treaty Organization will either fail to survive the period of post–Cold War adjustment or rediscover itself as something other than an instrument for the exercise of American hegemony. We might also expect considerable friction between Washington and Western Hemispheric neighbors as these latter press to expand their autonomy. There is also evidence these days that the United States, tethered by a political culture that lacks a sense of the general will, risks tearing itself apart internally. Tensions within what remains of the Cold War empires may provoke military interventions to preserve the status quo, as well as armed rebellions against peripheral-state governments that refuse to challenge the lingering imperial relationship. The great European overseas empires are gone forever.

Western liberalism in the decades ahead is likely to be challenged by a number of "isms" of regional or provincial ilk. Ideological contest will likely take the form of liberalism pushing outward from the Western world and invariably being confronted by countervailing, powerful illiberal political creeds. Nationalisms, new and old—possibly including German nationalism—that now appear to be firing political emotions may well gain rather than lose appeal in the years ahead. What the West today labels "Islamic fundamentalism" is neither strictly Islamic, because of its utter intolerance, nor fundamentalist, because it finds little support either literally or interpretatively in the Qu'ran. It is, rather, a modern political legitimation for totalitarian statism facilitated by the manipulation of religious symbols. It is nonetheless a powerful ideological force within regions where Islamic symbols have sacred meaning. Chinese "communism" is now almost totally disconnected from its Marxist utopian pedigree, but in prevailing practice it may embody the first promising formula for state-led, third-world development. It rejects Western liberalism and, if conceptualized, could emerge as the twenty-first-century focal point of world ideological contest.

The philosophical bases of the Western way of life may be waning in outward appeal, but they are still staunchly upheld in the West. Moreover, many Westerners, and particularly Americans, Britons, and Frenchmen, remain convinced that what is good for them must also be good for all of mankind. Therefore, vigorous efforts to export and universalize Western values and institutions will continue. Westerners will continue to declare their obligations to "lead"; they will continue to champion "democracy," "human rights," "private property," "free markets," and "the rule of law" as they define them. They will seek to maintain executive positions and policy-making monopolies in as many international organizations as possible, and they will resist structural, substantive, or normative innovations or reforms in the international organizational system that threaten the Western-centric status quo. More broadly, Westerners will continue to export secularism, materialism, individualism, rationalism, empiricism, pragmatism, and modernism defined as becoming "like the West." Set against this will be an accelerating revival of non-Western cultural forms suppressed during the era of Western dominance, a mounting critique of Western institutions, styles, and values centered in accusations of hypocrisy and spiritual sterility, and a countervailing projection of spiritualism, collectivism, and modernism defined as enriching the quality of life produced by purging Western ways. In international relations much of the West/non-West contest is likely to take place within international organizations, which will not work very well because of the intercultural contradictions, but where the allocation of leadership positions and the normative content of resolutions will index the course of the contest between civilizations.

Unfortunately, areas of potential cooperation in the post–Cold War era are less discernible, unless cooperation is minimally defined as keeping conflict from getting out of hand. Realistically speaking, hedging against worst-case outcomes by deterring and halting grand aggressors—otherwise frustrating self-interested but system-destructive behavior, alleviating great human suffering, and codifying order under given status quos—has been most of what the history of international cooperation has been about. Such efforts at international cooperation will likely continue. However, erecting a new normative and legal international order in the decades immediately ahead is likely to be most difficult because the dawning era of contested power, contested political-philosophical foundations, and contested cultural values and institutions is not likely to be the time when mankind will finally constructively coalesce to solve common problems.

CHAPTER 5

The Tragedy of War and the Search for Meaning in International History

Pablo Picasso's *Guernica* hangs massively in Madrid's Paseo del Prado, offering there a permanent, Cubist testimony to the horrors of war. *Guernica*, as every fledgling art student surely knows, was painted in 1937 to memorialize the bombing of the Basque town of Guernica by fascist air forces during the Spanish Civil War. As there were no republican soldiers in Guernica at the time of the attack, the victims were civilians—old men, women, and children. This Picasso symbolically depicts the omnipresence of death, the suffering of the survivors, and the physical destruction of the city. Yet depiction is not what *Guernica* is about, because Picasso's object in creating his masterpiece was to find *meaning* in the horrific events of April 1937. For Picasso in this particular instance, as for other artists working in their preferred media, finding and conveying meaning becomes tantamount to *explaining*. For Picasso, perhaps, and certainly for countless interpreters, *Guernica* explains by giving meaning to the Spanish Civil War, to Spain itself, and to war itself, even to the human condition overall.[1] This work of art may also capture something of the meaning of international history, the subject of this essay.

Cause versus Meaning in International History

International history is the record of interactions among states and peoples. Adda Bozeman may have introduced the notion of international history in her classic *Politics and Culture in International History.* In any event, I use *international history* here much in the same way that Bozeman does.[2] It is the record of things that have happened when states and peoples encountered one another in times past. International history can be scrutinized chronologically, in the manner of conventional historiography, or topically, in the way that Jacob Burckhardt looked into the civilization of the Italian Renaissance, or phenomenologically, as Bozeman approached it and as most social scientists prefer.[3] This essay is about the phenomenon of war, a familiar recurrence in international history, but it is not about the *causes of war,* which have so excited the interests of social scientists, beginning perhaps with Thucydides. The causes of war have fascinated countless modern contributors like Raymond Aron, Robert Gilpin, Stanley Hoffmann, Lewis Fry Richardson, J. David Singer, Pitirim Sorokin, Kenneth Waltz, and Quincy Wright, to name but a few.[4] Because of these intellectual efforts well invested, a good deal is known about the causes of war—war in general, kinds of war in particular, and specific wars specifically. The *meaning* of war, however, has been of less concern to social scientists, in part perhaps because ascertaining meaning both eludes positivism's logic and lends itself rather poorly to empiricism's methodological repertoire.

On the other hand, ascertaining meaning, or better said, attributing meaning, is the ken of artists, poets, dramatists, novelists, and those historians who lean toward the artistic side of their professional calling. Picasso's *Guernica;* the etchings and paintings of Francisco Goya; the seventeenth-century engravings of Jacques Callot, Hans Ulrich Franck, Rudolf Meyer, and Christian Richter; Homer's *Iliad;* Lev Tolstoy's *War and Peace;* Erich Maria Remarque's *Im Westen nichts neues;* Jean Giraudoux's *La guerre de Troie n'aura pas lieu;* Kurt Vonnegut's *Slaughterhouse Five;* Vera Brittan's *Testament of Youth;* Steven Pressfield's *Gates of Fire;* Dimitri Shostakovich's *Leningrad Symphony* and his *Eighth Symphony;* and many other works of art attribute meaning to war—personal meaning, societal meaning, mythical meaning, and ethical meaning. In the same manner, interpretations that attribute *historical meaning* enrich the writings of many noted historians, as, for example, in the closing paragraphs of C. V. Wedgewood's classic study of the Thirty Years' War, in which she tells her readers that the war "solved no problem. Its effects, both immediate and indirect, were either negative or disastrous. Morally subversive, economically destructive, socially degrading, confused in its causes, devious in its course, futile in its result ... [t]he overwhelming majority in Europe, the overwhelming majority in Germany, wanted no war.... The decision was made without thought of them." To this Wedgewood adds, "After the expenditure of so much human life to so little purpose, men might have grasped the essential futility of putting the beliefs of the mind to the judgment of the sword. Instead, they rejected religion as an object to fight for and found others."[5]

There is also the famous passage in Polybius's *Histories* where Roman Consul Scipio Aemilianus, who commanded the burning of Carthage, reflects on the meaning of the great city's destruction. Here, it may well have been Polybius rather than Scipio who was actually reflecting, but the famed Greek historian nevertheless recalls,

> At the sight of the city utterly perishing amidst the flames, Scipio burst into tears and stood reflecting on the inevitable change which awaits cities, nations, and dynasties, one and all, as it does every one of us men.... And unintentionally or purposefully he quoted—the words perhaps escaping him unconsciously—The day shall come when holy Troy shall fall and Priam, lord of spears and Priam's folk.
> (Homer, *Il.* 6, 448)

> And on my asking him boldly (for I had been his tutor) what he meant by these words, he did not name Rome distinctly, but was evidently fearing for her, from his sight of the mutability of human affairs.... [6]

Whereas artists attribute meaning, audiences, readers, critics, and scholars search for it in their works. Meaning is always contained in texts, but texts may be of many kinds. Conventionally, we think of texts as documents—that is, synthetically connected, grammatically structured, discursively moving, punctuated arrangements of words. Here, the meaning is in the words and their arrangement. Poems are arrangements of words, symbols, tropes, meters, and rhymes, usually moving discursively and usually punctuated. Artists' canvases are composed of nondiscursive collections of forms, symbols, and colors arranged in bounded space, and sculptures and architectural works are aggregations of forms set in unbounded space. All of these are also texts; they embody meaning implanted by their authors and interpretable by readers. Seeking meaning by interpreting texts is a hermeneutic exercise, explicated in fascinating manner by Hans-Georg Gadamer in his *Truth and Method.*[7] The hermeneutic process is aimed at discovering meaning by interrogating texts—that is, by asking why they are composed as they are. "The movement of understanding," Gadamer explains, "is constantly from the whole to the part and back to the whole.... The harmony of all the details with the whole is the criterion for correct understanding."[8] In effect, the interpreter tests, and tests again, for a best fit between a hypothesized whole (the meaning) and observed parts (words, lines, forms, or symbols) until consistency and coherence emerge.

Building upon foundations laid in the late nineteenth century by Wilhelm Dilthey, some contemporary historiographers suggest that human experience is also a text, or perhaps a catalog of texts, all with embedded meaning accessible through hermeneutic interpretation.[9] Among these historiographers, I find Hayden White and his work to be particularly intriguing, although, as he himself is well aware, his thinking is likely better accepted among students of comparative literature than among his colleagues in history. Nevertheless, I shall try to show that White's insights are directly applicable to international history and the study of war. In his book *Metahistory,* White speaks of "historical fields," by which he means temporally and/or episodically delimited theaters of human experience.[10] Such fields may be expansive, extending to the universal history of humankind, or they may be narrowed to the span of a day or less. They may frame macro-events, like the French Revolution, or micro-happenings like the storming of the Bastille on the afternoon of July 14, 1789. Historical fields are texts; figuratively speaking, they are what historians *read.* While White is not entirely clear as to what we may expect to find within an historical field, or read in the text as it were, let us suppose that these particular kinds of texts consist at least of arrangements of people, human collectivities, motivations and aspirations, actions, emotions, and fates. Hermeneutics here consist of interrogating the texts to discern why they are composed as they are. What motivations, aspirations, actions, emotions, and fates associated with what particular people or collectivities populating the historical field are displayed, and why are these manifested components of the text arranged in the way(s) they are? Via interpretation, historians as chroniclers and recorders transform their readings of historical fields into stories—that is, narratives or supertexts—about *what happened.* Historians as *analysts* transform their readings into stories that purport to be explanations of how and/or why what happened in fact happened, sometimes imputing causes.[11] Historians as artists transform their readings of historical fields into stories about the meaning of what happened. White writes that "questions about the connections between events which make them elements of a *followable* story should be distinguished from questions that ask 'what does it all add up to?' or 'what is the point of it all?' These kinds of questions have to do with the structure of the *entire set of events.*"[12] Such questions also probe for meaning.

Although admittedly derivative of the work of literary scholar Northrop Frye, one of Hayden White's most important contributions to the interpretation of historical meaning is to be found in his discussion of "emplotment," which is best elaborated in his essay on "Interpretation in History."[13] "By an extension of Frye's ideas," White writes, "it can be argued that interpretation in history consists of the provisions of a plot structure for a sequence of events so that their nature as a comprehensible process is revealed by their figuration as a *story of a particular kind*."[14] From this, White derives his notion of "metahistory," which he identifies as "pre-generic plot structures" or "archetypal story-forms that define the modalities of a given culture's literary endowment." And, he argues, "Historians, no less than poets, can be said to gain 'explanatory affect'—over and above whatever formal explanations they may offer of specific historical events—by building into their narratives patterns of meaning similar to those more explicitly provided by the literary art of cultures to which they belong."[15] This formulation is analogous to R. G. Collingwood's discussion of what he calls "the historical imagination," or "*a priori* imagination" wherein he speaks of implicit similarities between literary and historical storytelling, which both find their coherence in plot structures. Each of them, novelist and historian, Collingwood observes, "makes it his business to construct a picture which is partly a narrative of events, partly a description of situations" and "each aims at making his picture a coherent whole," by, in effect, adding a plot.[16] For White, "in historical narrative, story is to plot as the exposition of 'what happened' in the past is to the synoptic characterization of what the whole sequence of events contained in the narrative might 'mean' or 'signify.'"[17]

The thrust of White's theory, impressively tested on the works of Jacob Burckhardt, Benedetto Croce, G. W. F. Hegel, Karl Marx, Jules Michelet, Friedrich Nietzsche, Leopold von Ranke, and Alexis de Tocqueville, in *Metahistory*, is that the literary endowments of particular cultures allow for a variety of story forms. But these varieties are finite and culture-bound. Meaning is conveyed through story forms, and within given cultures only certain kinds of stories have commonly apprehended meanings. In our culture—Western culture—four story forms or modes of emplotment are distinct, recurrent, and commonly apprehended: romance, tragedy, comedy, and satire.[18] "Romance is fundamentally a drama of self-identification symbolized by the hero's transcendence of the world of experience, his victory over it and his final liberation from it—the sort of drama associated with the Grail legend or the story of the resurrection of Christ in Christian mythology," notes White.[19] Comedy and tragedy are both dramas of conflict, the difference being that comedic plots play out to reconciliation, while tragic plots drive toward destruction. Redemption is sometimes an aspect of the tragic finale; but it need not be. Satire plots narratives of irony, where humans, by their limitations, repeatedly fall short of nobility or ideal goodness. There is much more to the working out of White's notions of emplotment, and much more to the derivation of his theory of meaning from Piaget's psychology and from tropic analysis in linguistics.[20] But, going deeper at this point would be to digress from the main purpose of this essay, which is to bring these historiographical and literary considerations to bear on the meaning of war in international history. To summarize, then, in White's words, "the historian must draw upon a fund of culturally provided *mythoi* in order to constitute the facts as figuring a story of a particular kind, just as he must appeal to that same fund of *mythoi* in the minds of his readers to endow his account of the past with the odor of meaning or significance."[21]

Reading the Texts of War

Nationalistic historians writing in a traditional genre of their profession frequently glorify war, particularly wars won against archenemies. Even wars lost can be taken as the beginning or end of important chapters in the national narrative. By telling such stories, William McNeill argues, nationalistic historians create "mythistories" that bolster national identities but also disparage human universals.[22] McNeill finds national mythistories objectionable, and I take a similarly dim view concerning the glorification of war. The real stuff of such violent encounters in human history most often resembles the description offered by the eleventh-century Arab historian Imad Addin when he recorded the fall of Tiberias during the Third Crusade. "The plain," according to Imad Addin, "was covered with prisoners and corpses. . . . The dead were scattered over the mountains and valleys, lying immobile on their sides. . . . the perfume of victory was thick with the stench of them. I passed by them and saw the limbs of the fallen cast naked on the battlefield, scattered in pieces over the site of the encounter, lacerated and disjointed, with heads cracked open, throats split, spines broken, necks shattered, feet in pieces, noses mutilated, extremities torn off, members dismembered, parts shredded, eyes gouged out, stomachs disemboweled, hair colored with blood."[23] And the carnage is almost never limited to battlefields or the killing to combatants only. For example, the Thirty Years' War, John Weltman notes, "devastated the territory in which it was fought. Parts of Germany were almost depopulated. Some estimates say half or more of the German population may have been lost. While most of the major governments intentionally got themselves into the war, the fighting quickly went beyond their control. Armed bands rampaged across the countryside, usually wreaking far more havoc on the civilian populations than they did upon opposing armies."[24]

More revealing were the observations of William Crowne, an English emissary who crossed Germany from west to east in 1636. Geoffrey Parker recounts Crowne's experiences, writing, "On the local level . . . the war never seemed to stop. Large armies starved and small ones were beaten, but nothing could check the marauding of garrison commanders and freebooters. . . . devastation was apparent everywhere. They found the entire territory between Mainz and Frankfurt to be desolate, with the people of Mainz so weak from hunger that they could not even crawl to receive the alms that the travelers distributed. . . . Beyond Nuremberg, as far as the Danube, there was again total devastation: the English party came across one village that had been pillaged eighteen times in two years, even twice in one day. In several other places there was no one left to tell what had happened. . . . No one was safe from attack."[25]

Then, there is Parker's account of the destruction of Magdeburg in 1631, which was captured by Habsburg armies on May 20. "The entire city," Parker notes, "was promptly sacked by the enraged soldiery, who had suffered terrible privations in the siege trenches. A large part of the population was massacred, and even more perished in the fire which broke out soon after capture. . . . There was nothing special about the level of brutality at Magdeburg—to sack a town that resisted was standard practice during the war—but the scale of the slaughter was unusual. A village or market town plundered or burnt was one thing; the annihilation of a city of 20,000 . . . was quite another."[26]

Tales of cities destroyed and civilians massacred are countless across the history of war. In ancient times, for example, we hear of Troy, Melos, and Carthage. As Alan Lloyd writes of Carthage, "According to Appian, the Roman general remained in personal command, without sleep, through the entire attack . . . Carthaginian fury was matched by Roman savagery. In the buildings, the attackers slaughtered everyone they came across, tossing many of the disarmed to troops below, who impaled them on raised pikes. Dead and dying citizens were used to fill ditches across which advanced Scipio's transport. . . . Everywhere, bodies festooned the tortured city: young and old, male and female, sprawled on footways, protruding amid crumbled masonry and charred beams. . . . Carthage was lost."[27]

During The Hundred Years' War, which was a supposedly chivalrous affair, extreme carnage on the battlefield resulted from first English and then also French reliance on the long bow. Murdering and robbing the wounded left on the field were common practices, and non-noble prisoners were similarly dealt with. Farms and towns in the paths of both advancing and retreating armies were plundered and burned, and sieges frequently ended in massacres. Sieges were also frequently accompanied by turning out *les bouches inutiles*—the useless mouths—from besieged cities, which set old men, women, and children at the mercy of attacking armies. Sometimes these innocents were allowed to pass through the military lines, but at other times, as at Rouen in 1418, this did not happen:

> By the end of July 1418, Henry [Henry V of England] had the city of Rouen completely surrounded. . . . [I]n early December 1418 . . . the

defenders attempted to reduce the demands on their ever-declining food stocks by expelling 12,000 people—the so-called *bouches inutiles*—useless mouths—from the city. Henry refused to let these people pass through the lines, and many of them, old men, women and children, perished in the winter chill, starving and helpless, between the walls and the tents of the besiegers. The scenes of suffering were recorded by an Englishman, John Paige: "Here and there were children of two or three, begging for bread and starving, their parents dead. . . . a woman was clutching her dead baby to her breast, and a child was sucking the breast of its dead mother. There were ten or twelve to every one alive, many dying quietly and lying down between the lines as though asleep."[28]

The horrors of war, including the massacre of civilians, are not the characteristics of past eras only. Barbarism is timeless and chivalrous warfare is a myth. There never has been much distinction between combatants and noncombatants, as attacking armies have always made war on civilians. Hostilities driven by noxious ideologies, recurrent from ancient times to the present day, have exacted particularly heavy tolls in civilian suffering. To the costs in lives, livelihoods, and property tallied across the history of war, we must also add the less quantifiable, but still momentous, costs in anguish, loss, tension, fear, and terror experienced by combatants and civilians alike as personal lives as well as all forms of human attachment are jeopardized and often destroyed. Again from the records of the Thirty Years' War comes the autobiography of Johann Valetin Andreä, a Lutheran cleric from Swabia. Geoffrey Parker records that in 1639 Andreä "wrote despondently that of his 1,046 communicants in 1630 only 338 remained. 'Just in the last five years . . . 518 of them have been killed by various misfortunes.' Among these, he noted five intimate and thirty-three other friends, twenty relatives and forty-one clerical colleagues. 'I have to weep for them', he continued, 'because I remain here so impotent and alone. Out of my whole life I am left with scarcely fifteen persons alive with whom I can claim some trace of friendship.'"[29]

Anguish is timeless. When John Keegen delivered the BBC's Reith Lectures in 1998, he devoted most of his first lecture to the costs of war, and opened his reflections on the emotional costs of war with an ironic metaphor about telegrams, writing, "The telegraph boy on his bicycle, pedaling the suburban street and symbol to the Victorians of a new and benevolent technological advance, became for parents and wives during both world wars literally an omen of terror—for it was by telegram that the awful flimsy form beginning 'We regret to inform you that' was brought to front doors, a trigger for the articulation of the constant unspoken prayer, 'Let him pass by, let him stop at another house, let it not be us.' In Britain during the first world war that prayer was not answered several million times. ..."[30]

Even today, students of international relations continue to puzzle over Harold Lasswell's *World Politics and Personal Insecurity*, frequently failing to find in it either world politics *or* personal insecurity.[31] But only slightly obscured by Lasswell's rather arcane vocabulary is the central message of his work: world politics is an omnipresent source of personal insecurity because at any given moment hostilities between states and peoples can break out and intervene most destructively into otherwise commonplace lives. Because the dread of war is constant, personal insecurity is an inherent aspect of the human condition.

Let us update our list of cities destroyed and civilians massacred: Coventry, Dresden, Nanking, Rotterdam, Stalingrad, Tokyo, Warsaw— surely Nanking. Despite the controversy surrounding Iris Chang's *The Rape of Nanking*, there ought to be no dispute about the fact that an ignoble episode in human affairs unfolded during the six weeks following the Japanese storming of the city in December 1937.[32] Over 300,000 people were killed, mainly civilians, many of them tortured. Twenty thousand Chinese women were raped. Most of these were then murdered. On December 17, 1937, a *New York Times* reporter who witnessed the initial phases of the sack of Nanking filed a dispatch from aboard the USS *Oahu*, then moored in Shanghai's harbor. "Through wholesale atrocities and vandalism at Nanking," the story began,

> the Japanese Army has thrown away a rare opportunity to gain the respect and confidence of the Chinese inhabitants and of foreign opinion there. ...
>
> The killing of civilians was widespread. Foreigners who traveled widely through the city Wednesday [December 16] found civilian dead on every street.
>
> Policemen and firemen were special objects of attack. Many victims were bayoneted and some of the wounds were barbarously cruel. ...
>
> The Japanese looting amounted almost to plundering the entire city. Nearly every building was entered by Japanese soldiers, often under the eyes of their officers, and the men took whatever they wanted. ...
>
> The mass executions of war prisoners added to the horrors the Japanese brought to Nanking. After killing the Chinese soldiers who threw down their arms and surrendered, the Japanese combed the city for men in civilian garb who were suspected of being former soldiers. ...

> The Japanese appear to want the horrors to remain as long as possible, to impress on the Chinese the terrible results of resisting Japan.[33]

Before the Japanese occupation of China ended in 1945, an estimated thirteen million Chinese civilians died. If anything, the carnage and inhumanities connected with war have increased in the industrial age, with the twentieth century exacting the greatest tolls of all. Altogether, the First World War "killed at least ten million people in battle, most of them young or very young, and millions more died from war-related causes. The Second World War killed fifty million, of whom fewer than half were servicemen in uniform. Yugoslavia, for example, lost ten percent of its population, of which but a fraction belonged to the Royal Yugoslav Army; the rest died as a result of deprivation, reprisal or internecine massacre."[34] At the very end of the Second World War two more cities destroyed—Hiroshima and Nagasaki—were added to the ever-lengthening list. The nuclear age opened on August 6, 1945, when the military forces of the United States dropped an atomic bomb on the city of Hiroshima. In an instant, 300,000 people, nearly all of them civilians, were killed, injured, or missing, and 90 percent of the city was leveled. Three days later, another atomic bomb was dropped on the city of Nagasaki, this one killing or wounding 75,000 people and obliterating a third of the city.

Total war, wherein entire populations are pitted against one another with little distinction drawn between combatants and civilians, is reputedly a phenomenon of modern times. Perhaps so, and even more so perhaps as we enter the twenty-first century, where interstate warfare appears to be giving way to internecine warfare. In the civil wars of our time, military professionalism has diminished and international legal constraints are frequently ignored. In situations reduced to Hobbesian wars of all against all civilians are both victims and perpetrators as neighbors slaughter one another.[35] Whether all against all, some against all or some against some, warfare has always been Hobbesian in character to the extent that it has been "nasty" and "brutish." It has also been deadly, destructive, atrocious, and anguishing.

Tragic Visions

Students of international history are likely to find little about war that might render resulting narratives romantic, comedic, or satirical. Some might say that epics have been made from the stuff of violent encounters among states and peoples, but those who see things this way often turn out to be overly taken by national egoism, or overawed by heroism and generalship, or myopic regarding suffering, death, and destruction. *Tragedy* emplots the history of war. Conventionally understood, tragedy is a literary plot, yet I am certainly not the first to assert that history too unfolds in a tragic way. But those who make such assertions more often than not use the term *tragic* in the general, adjectival sense, meaning "sorrowful," "regrettable," or "disastrous." These writers also frequently employ "tragedy" using the genitive case, to denote the sorrowful, regrettable, or disastrous condition or fate of something, as, for example, in *The Tragedy of the Commons*. Emplotment is sometimes implied in such usages, but the particular *kind of tragedy* playing out is seldom elucidated.

There are several different kinds of tragic plots. There is also a seemingly perennial debate among literary scholars concerning the nature of tragedy, which John Kekes wisely advises nonprofessionals to stay out of.[36] Europeans and Americans are most familiar with the great Shakespearean unfoldings, where a tragic hero is overwhelmed by a situation that is at least partly of his or her own making. The situation, the hero's inability to deal with it, and his or her ultimate undoing follow from a shortcoming or flaw in an otherwise noble character—Hamlet's rancor, Lear's naiveté, Lady Macbeth's ambition. Some of the typical Aeschylean and Sophoclean tragic plots similarly cast humans as victims of their own shortcomings, as with Oedipus's inability to leave well enough alone concerning his family history, or Orestes's overriding passion for justice. Otherwise, in Greek tragedies truer to Homeric form, humans are cast as playthings of the gods; with their options limited and their fates often predetermined. The *Oresteia*—that is, the trilogy overall—has such a plot, as certainly does Aeschylus's *Prometheus Bound*. Then, of course, there is the *Iliad* itself, wherein "Zeus the father took his golden scales/ In them he put two fates of death that cuts down all men/ One for the Trojans, tamers of horses, one for the bronze-sheathed Greeks."[37]

Yale University's noted literary scholar Richard Sewall celebrates the tragic hero. His ordeal, suffering, determination to stand against overwhelming odds and predetermined defeat, and even the hero's ultimate destruction, all instruct about human nobility. This, for Sewall, is what tragedy is about: "In the man of action, the tragic vision impels him to fight against his destiny, kick it against the pricks, and state his case before God or his fellows. In the artist, the tragic vision impels him, in his fictions, toward what Jaspers calls 'boundary situations,' man at the limits of his sovereignty—Job on the ashheap, Prometheus on the crag, the outcast Oedipus, Lear on the heath, Ahab on his lonely quarterdeck. Here, with all the protective covering stripped off, the hero faces as if all over again the existential question—Job's question, 'What is man?' or Lear's 'Is man nothing but this?'"[38]

And for the Canadian interpreter Ekbert Faas, tragedy is similarly edifying. Faas links tragedy to the "assumption that suffering and death, however, terrifyingly, have a function in an ultimately purposive scheme of things. . . . Tragedy, in both its Greek and its Christian variants, implies a teleology of either progressive-minded or eschatological orientation in which even suffering and evil in some way perform a meaningful function"[39]

Yet this is not what tragedy is entirely about, and sometimes it is not at all what tragedy is about. Tragic emplotment requires neither a tragic hero, nor an edifying denouement. It need not instruct about the human condition, but merely display it. Tragedy need be neither about the nobility of the human, nor about the malevolence of deities. If anything, it is about the indifference of the deities, or if one prefers, about a cosmos in which there is neither benignity nor malevolence, neither justice nor injustice. Tragedy is about pain, suffering, death, and destruction, and in the end about the contingency of the human condition, which always subjects individual and collective aspirations for good lives to elements beyond anyone's control.

Tragedy is centrally about evil. What distinguishes it from other dramatic forms "is its peculiar and intense preoccupation with *evil* in the universe."[40] The evil in play is a Schopenhauerian form involving "the scornful mastery of chance, and the irretrievable fall of the innocent," wherein, in the context of Arthur Schopenhauer's pessimism, "lies a significant hint of the nature of the world of existence."[41] But evil is not a metaphysical presence, a satanic will, a force from the dark side, or any other kind of supernatural agent or willfulness. It is, rather, an *occurrence,* something that happens to persons and people when outside agents enter uninvited to disrupt and destroy their lives. Following the insightful thinking of John Kekes, we may conceive of evil as the infliction of "undeserved harm." "The agents in tragic situations, and often others who depend on them," Kekes writes, "suffer evil, understood as undeserved harm. The harm may be totally undeserved, or it may be grossly disproportional to what is merited by the agents' life and conduct. Moreover, the evil is serious. It is often irremediable, like dishonor or mutilation, and it leaves a lasting mark on the agents or on others whose welfare the agents are committed to protecting. One consequence of the serious evil is that the agents can no longer pursue their projects. And since the projects were essential to their conceptions of a good life, the harm they suffer causes the failure or the radical disorientation of their aspirations because it goes so deep that it basically alters them. Having experienced what they had, they cannot just pick up the pieces and carry on."[42]

The perpetrators of evil may be either natural forces like flood, famine, and pestilence, or human agents—more pertinent to this essay's discussion—that are able to exact their tolls because of what Kekes identifies as "the conditions of life." Among these, he emphasizes "the contingency of human existence," "the moral indifference of nature," and "the presence of destructiveness in human motivation."[43] Humans exist in environments where much that happens, and happens to them, is beyond their control. This is especially true for individuals, but also the case regarding collectivities, even very large ones. For all moral purposes, moreover, humans are essentially alone in the universe: "There is no cosmic justice: the good may suffer."[44] The bad may also triumph. Nor is there any Hegelian progression toward perfection that, despite contradictions along the way, will eventuate in universal rectitude. Humans are also capable of unleashing phenomenal destructiveness and have proclivities to do so under permissive conditions. Stripping away civilizing constraints, as Sigmund Freud explained, exposes a primal bestiality in human nature—Joseph Conrad's "heart of darkness," perhaps—that makes barbarism and destructiveness not only possible, but almost predictable.[45]

These more somber, less heroic, and less redeeming tragic plots—let us call them *dark tragedies*—have excited the sensitivities of many artists. Conrad's *Heart of Darkness,* a classic example, is an ominous tale about what happens to a highly civilized, cultured European, who is physically and emotionally displaced into an environment where the constraints of civilization are no longer compelling. Transported into the central African jungle, the heart of darkness, the character Kurtz descends into brutality and bestiality and becomes a perpetrator of evil among the very natives he at first sought to enlighten. In recording Kurtz's descent, Conrad answers Job's question "What is man?" by revealing the human capacity for destructiveness. William Shakespeare's *Othello,* to take another example, is plotted differently from his other great tragedies because in this play there is no redemption or heroic self-realization, not even any just punishment for unspeakable villainy. Othello and Desdemona are entirely innocent, yet they lose their lives because of what Kekes identifies as the "motiveless malignity of Iago."[46] Michael Cassio, similarly innocent, almost loses his life as well, and in the grander playing out of the drama, Othello's entire world is totally rent asunder by Iago's malevolence. Just as evil prevails in *Othello,* so does it also prevail in Eugene O'Neill's *Mourning Becomes Electra.* In O'Neill's twentieth-century reinterpretation of Aeschylus's *Oresteia,* the dramatist remains true to Aeschylus almost until the very end. But O'Neill then changes the ending to eliminate the justice bestowed by the gods at the end of the Greek play. No such thing happens in the O'Neill version, where many lives have been destroyed—some of them entirely innocent like Peter's and Hazel's—yet there is no indication that any of the suffering has been worthwhile, that any justice has been meted, that any evil has been overcome. Lavinia, O'Neill's Electra, wreaks havoc with the lives of those around her throughout the last two plays in the trilogy. At the end, shoulders square, standing erect, she enters the Mannon house—her house—"closing the door behind her."[47]

Among the Greeks, the tragic vision of Euripides perhaps comes closest to an apodixis of evil as here defined. Euripides' *Medea* is a drama about a woman's fury that once unleashed enters and destroys the lives of everyone around her including her own children, who were certainly victims of undeserved harm. Euripides' Medea is much like O'Neill's Lavinia—or perhaps vice versa would be more accurate. Revealingly, at the end, after wreaking her destruction, Medea departs the scene of her perpetrated carnage, unscathed and unpunished. Jason, whose family she murdered, calls for "justice that avenges murder," and asks Zeus and the gods to invoke their powers in the interest of that justice. But the gods pay Jason no heed.[48] Euripides' *The Trojan Women* is even truer to the plot of rampaging evil and lives undeservedly destroyed. It also approaches the integral connection between tragedy and war. The play is about the fates of the women of Troy—Hecuba, the former queen; her daughter, the prophetess Cassandra; and the wives of Troy's fallen heroes. The women's world is already largely destroyed when the drama begins. They wait before their burning city, either to be assigned to Greek captains as slaves or concubines or to be put to death. Their anguish deepens as each learns of fates more horrible than could have been imagined. Appeals to the gods are voiced throughout the play, but no one's prayers are answered. The profound point of Euripides' dramatization is that the Trojan women, and certainly their children, were innocent. They neither caused the Trojan War, nor started it, nor fought it. They deserved no harm. Yet they suffered egregiously under circumstances utterly beyond their control. War had permitted the perpetration of evil, and as the prescient Cassandra observed, it was not only Trojan women's lives that were destroyed. We read, "Then after they [the Greeks] had come to the banks of the Scamander, they met their deaths.... Those that Ares took never saw their children; no wives' hands wrapped them in their cerements; they lie in a foreign land. And back home the misery was no less: widows dying lonely, old men left childless in their halls, the sons they reared serving others, none to visit their graves and make them blood offerings. This is the praise the expedition has earned.... Of their crimes it is better to say nothing; may my muse never lend her voice to sing of evil things."[49]

Christopher Marlowe tells a similar story of war and tragedy in his two-part drama *Tamburlaine the Great*. At first reading, and perhaps even in watching, the play appears rather pedestrian. Sequences of action are monotonously repeated: word arrives in a particular city that the armies of Tamburlaine are approaching; confident kings and captains dismiss the threat from "this shepherd's son" from central Asia; Tamburlaine attacks, sacks, and destroys the vanquished city and kills or enslaves the population. He then moves toward his next target for conquest; word arrives of his approach; the sequence repeats. Wherein lies the tragedy? In this: Tamburlaine himself is the source of evil. He swoops into people's lives—surely uninvited and unwelcome—like a tempest out of the desert, with no better motive than to conquer for conquest's sake, and he destroys everything in his path. His armies rob, rape, ravage, murder, and enslave, over and over and over again. Marlowe's imagery likens Tamburlaine to a fury, a kind of the Greco-Roman she-demon, and Tamburlaine describes himself as a "scourge." The play is also replete with imagery to suggest that Marlowe saw Tamburlaine as an emissary of the devil. Revealingly, at the end of part 2, Tamburlaine dies placidly in bed of natural causes. Not only is there no retribution for the pain and suffering that Tamburlaine inflicted, but his quiet passing signals that no earthly power ever succeeded in stopping him; no human force could control him. *Tamberlaine the Great* is anything but a pedestrian play. Its plot is an archetype for dark tragedy, a drama about evil triumphant. In the poet's vision, moreover, *Tamberlaine* again connects tragedy and war.

So does Picasso's *Guernica*. The eye-capturing focal point of *Guernica* is the intruding figure of the light bearer. This stylized female enters the painting—enters Guernica, that is—from the upper right, and "flies or suddenly swoops down into the scene."[50] The buildings of Guernica burn behind her, and before her are strewn the symbolic consequences of the air raid, among these the women in agony, one probably in death throes, the dead child, the contorted and wounded horse, and the fallen warrior. The light bearer, then, is the apparent perpetrator of the carnage displayed in *Guernica*, "the initiator of a chain of action that runs across the canvas."[51] Some interpreters believe that Picasso intended the light bearer to be a fury or Erinnye—that is, a demonic female from ancient mythology who in Greek lore was a servant of Persephone, goddess of the underworld. Others postulate that the light bearer may represent Lucifer (Latin: "bearer of light"), the personification of evil in Judeo-Christian mythology, or Phosphor ("bringer of light") from Greek mythology, who is also the embodiment of evil. By these interpretations, *Guernica* becomes a narrative plotted as dark tragedy: a story about the city of Guernica, about the intrusion from without of agents of destruction, about the harsh meting of undeserved harm, about the suffering and death of innocents caught up in the situation beyond their control—about war.

The great tragic writers, writes Ernst Cassirer, "do not entertain us with detached scenes from the spectacles of life. Taken in themselves these scenes are but fugitive shadows. But suddenly we begin to see behind these shadows and to envisage a new reality."[52] The text of war in human history should be plotted as dark tragedy; Euripidean tragedy; Marlowesque tragedy; Conradian tragedy; tragedy of situation; tragedy that is inherent in the contingent, destructive, and unredeeming conditions of life. The texts of all of the wars discussed in this essay—the Trojan, the Peloponnesian, the Punic, the Hundred Years' War, the Thirty Years' War, World Wars I and II, as well as countless others—read like dark tragedies. All of the elements are there: suffering and death are the leitmotivs. Harm befalls many who least deserve to be harmed, and those who perhaps deserve punishment for villainy often evade it. War enters common people's lives uninvited, often unexpected and surely unwelcome, but innocents seldom have any control over the situations that destroy them. Those whose lives are churned in the maelstroms may appeal to their gods, but there is no evidence that anyone listens.

From plot emerges meaning. In the first instance, the meaning is moral. War as dark tragedy strips away the veneers of civility that raise us up out of the Hobbesian state of nature. Historically, John Keegen laments, "war has been a dirty business."[53] Indeed, war transports us back into environments where the mores of civilized living no longer apply, and where evil is therefore unconstrained. Evil therefore occurs, and evil frequently triumphs. Once begun in any given war, the meting of undeserved harm tends to escalate, slaughter to avenge slaughter, massacre in retribution for massacre, city in exchange for city. What people would never do to their neighbors when the rules of morality apply they readily do during wartime when the rules are suspended. In dark tragedies, there are no moral rules. Evil runs rampant.

The Meaning of Meaninglessness

There is yet another tragic plot that reveals something more about the meaning of war in international history. Some say that the texts of human history can be most readily and most often read as narratives about *meaninglessness.* This is not to say that history itself is meaningless, but rather to observe that fleetingness, futility, and failure are recurrent results of human projects. Or, in their broader contexts, particular events or episodes turn out to make little difference historically inasmuch as nothing of special historical significance changes because these events occurred. The insignificance—that is, the meaninglessness of most events—is in itself part of the meaning of history. Simone Weil captures this in her commentary on the *Iliad,* where she observes that "the auditors of the *Iliad* knew that the death of Hector would be but a brief joy to Achilles, and the death of Achilles but a brief joy to the Trojans, and the destruction of Troy but a brief joy to the Achaians."[54] Percy Bysshe Shelley similarly captures the meaninglessness of historic events in the irony of his poignant poem *Ozymandias,* as, of course, does Shakespeare when he allows the despondent Macbeth to recognize that life "is a tale / Told by an idiot, full of sound and fury, / Signifying nothing."[55]

However, futility and insignificance are not yet tragedy. What makes tragedies from historically insignificant human undertakings is their cost. When set against the meaninglessness of outcomes, the greater the toll in anguish, physical suffering, lives, and livelihoods the deeper the tragedy. *Historical meaninglessness deepens dark tragedy.* This was surely Euripides' insight, expressed as that of Cassandra, who briefly, but significantly, emerges from delirium in *The Trojan Women* to observe that "for the sake of one woman and one woman's passion, the Greeks went chasing after Helen and perished in their thousands."[56] Helen was repatriated (and later assumedly stoned to death). But here, Euripides asks, were the costs of the Trojan War worth the result? It should be remembered that *The Trojan Women* was staged in ancient Athens in 415 B.C.E. This was just after the Athenian slaughter of the Melesians and in midst of preparations for the expedition to Sicily, about which, because of their victory at Melos, the Athenians were enthusiastic.[57] Could it be, asks Euripides' translator Moses Hadas, that such "a passionate and poetic expression of the horror and futility and degradation of war" was "desperately urgent in its particular setting?"[58]

Aside from *King John*, Shakespeare's histories deal with the struggle for the English crown that went on from the close of the fourteenth to the end of the fifteenth century. In a modern reinterpretation of these historical plays, the three parts of *Henry IV, Richard II,* and *Richard III* in particular, the Polish literary scholar Jan Kott argues eloquently that tragedy should indeed be plotted as *historical meaninglessness at great cost.* For Kott, the vision of tragedy takes shape not by dealing with "the king plays" separately, but rather from examining their progression. "Each of these great historical tragedies," Kott explains,

> begins with a struggle for the throne, or for its consolidation. Each ends with the monarch's death and a new coronation. In each of the Histories the legitimate ruler drags behind him a long chain of crimes. He has rejected feudal lords who helped him to reach for the crown; he murders, first, his enemies, then his former allies; he executes possible successors and pretenders to the crown. But he has not been able to execute them all. From banishment a young prince returns—the son, grandson, or brother of those murdered—to defend the violated law. The rejected lords gather round him, he personifies the hope for new order and justice. But every step to power continues to be marked by murder, violence, treachery. And so, when the new prince finds himself near the throne, he drags behind him a chain of crimes as long as that of the until now legitimate ruler. When he assumes the crown, he will be just as hated as his predecessor. He has killed enemies, now he will kill former allies. And a new pretender appears in the name of violated justice. The wheel has turned full circle. A new chapter opens. A new historical tragedy.[59]

What the king plays signify is "that history has no meaning and stands still, or constantly repeats its cruel cycle."[60] A monotonous mechanism grinds on from kingship to kingship, altering very little in English history save the names of monarchs, who could as well remain nameless. The tally of murdered nobles mounts, but neither their numbers nor their identities are of historical import. The size of the residue of suffering and bereavement grows, but who remembers? "The flattering index of a direful pageant," Shakespeare has his anguished Queen Margaret say, "one heav'd a high to be hurl'd down below."[61] Neither Kott nor even Shakespeare pays much heed to the continuous, bloody civil warfare that surrounded the monotonous course of monarchial succession. Yet, here too we must recognize that men were fighting and dying, destruction was being wreaked, and innocents were likely caught up in the carnage and chaos—and all of this to what end? History "deprived of the goal towards which it is supposed to be moving— progress, the millennium, or the last judgment—can be apprehended only as process whose sole meaning is its meaninglessness."[62]

Whether life imitates art or art mirrors life is unimportant; tragic plots are common to both. Not all wars can be judged historically insignificant, but it is certainly true that most wars have been inconsequential in any macro-historical sense. They have altered little that is fundamental to or character-istic of their eras. Most often they have simply sown the seeds for succeeding wars. Historically, most wars have been fought for either domain, power, or booty—that is, to control territory or people, to command the deference or oblige the subservience of others, or to rob neighbors near and far. Where aggressors have succeeded, the greatest number of wars have resulted in po-litical borders moved and jurisdictions adjusted, sometimes by only a few kilometers, and sometimes more extensively. Relationships of dominance and subordination between states and peoples have also been altered by war, and successful aggressors have always been able to rob their victims. Notably, most of these outcomes eventually have proven impermanent, as borders get readjusted, the victimized and vanquished reverse their roles, and the plundered become the plunderers. In broadest context and with preciously few exceptions, successful aggression and resultant wars have sel-dom altered either the course or the pattern of international history. Names have changed and political maps have changed, but international history has not; its patterns and processes relentlessly play out—tragically. Where aggressors have failed in their objectives, little has resulted from war except death and destruction. Again, this is not to say that *all* wars have been histor-ically insignificant, nor is it to imply that self-defense is unjustified. People are obliged to fight because aggressors assault their fundamental values. To the extent that the Second World War was successfully fought to stop the maniacal Adolf Hitler, it perhaps had to be fought. But the outcome of the war preserved rather than changed the course and pattern of international history. There were other maniacal Hitlers in the past, and there will likely be new ones in the future.

The Peloponnesian War decided the rivalry between Athens and Sparta, but it neither ended the chronic warfare among the Greek cities nor even guaranteed Spartan ascendancy.[63] It certainly brought no peace to ancient Greece, but instead fit well the historical pattern of unending internecine violence. Rome's obliteration of Carthage gave the Romans the western Mediterranean, but the end of the Roman-Carthaginian rivalry amounted to little more than yet another extension of the Roman Empire. It occurred at approximately the same time that Rome was overrunning Macedonia, completing its domination of Greece and extending itself across the Iberian Peninsula. The Punic Wars, in broader context, were but episodes in the continuous warfare that characterized the entire Roman era. They changed no historical patterns and marked no real turning point. The first Punic War affirmed the prevailing pattern of Roman imperialism, while the second was an instance of the Carthaginians unsuccessfully attempting to limit the scope of Roman hegemony. Hannibal invaded Italy, wreaked havoc, occupied some territory, and, sixteen years and tens of thousands of lives later, was forced to withdraw with little to show for the expedition. The Third Punic War, which resulted in the obliteration of Carthage, was unnecessary in terms of strategy or Roman interest. Demagogy, rancor, and revenge drove the huge bloodletting. For its part, the Hundred Years' War was one of Western history's most senseless. It was about contested, personal claims to territories in France, the province of Aquitaine in particular, and it was fought over who in the feudal scheme of things owed homage to whom. It went on for one hundred years because many of those later involved had conflicting interpretations of how it began and no one knew how to stop it. It petered out rather than ended when royalty on both sides finally tired of fighting. If anything, the Hundred Years' War institutionalized the Anglo-French rivalry, which was to persist for five hundred more years, through dozens of further wars and at the cost of ten of thousands of French and British lives.

The Thirty Years' War rivaled the Hundred Years' War for historical meaninglessness. It was partly about religious differences, which exchanged massacres could hardly resolve; partly about grandeur and imperial domain, as were most of the wars of medieval Europe; and partly about plunder, which appeared the prevalent motive among those actually doing the fighting. Students of international relations tend to read epoch-ending significance into the Treaty of Westphalia, signed at the termination of the Thirty Years' War. But historians of the period are less generous; as C. V. Wedgwood notes, "The Peace of Westphalia was like most peace treaties, a rearrangment of the European map ready for the next war. . . . The Peace has been described as marking an epoch in European history, and it is commonly taken to do so. It is supposed to divide the period of religious wars from that of national wars, the ideological wars from wars of mere aggression. But the demarcation is as artificial as such arbitrary divisions commonly are. Aggression, dynastic ambition and fanaticism are all alike present in the hazy background behind the actual reality of war, and the last wars of religion merged insensibly into the pseudo-national wars of the future." From this, Wedgwood concludes that The Thirty Years' War "is the outstanding example in European history of meaningless conflict."[64]

There is little controversy over the meaninglessness of World War I. It was the war that few expected and certainly the kind of war that few anticipated. Its immediate causes were petty; its underlying causes were true to historic patterns; its outcome settled almost nothing, and the flawed Peace of Versailles planted the seeds for World War II. The Second World War was something of a crusade against evil, and therefore not completely senseless if judged morally (and if the obliteration of cities is removed from moral consideration). But, again, its outcome altered little in the relentless cycling of international history. The names attached to power changed, maps were redrawn, and enmities and amities were redefined, but all of this was in apparent preparation for the next war. The results of the Second World War contributed to the ensuing Cold War, which was anything but "cold" in places like Korea, Burma, Vietnam, Nicaragua, El Salvador, Angola, and Ethiopia.

The Tragedy of War and the Discovery of Meaning in International History

Is the story of war in international history tragic? Yes, of course. Is it dark tragedy? Indeed it is. When the historical meaninglessness of war is set against the monumental costs wars have inflicted upon humankind, the tragic emplotment clearly emerges. When the record of innocents slaughtered, cities burned, countrysides plundered, and evil unleashed is pondered, the tragedy darkens ominously. Social scientists have made a profession of counting wars, counting deaths, and otherwise measuring war-related destruction, and while different tallies result from different studies, the total numbers are all astonishingly enormous. How many battlefield casualties were there over the length of the record? Hundreds of millions, even by conservative reckoning. How many civilian deaths were there, and how many cities sacked, farms burned, women raped, children orphaned? We don't really know: the records are poor. Such things are difficult to count. But let us assume that here again, the numbers are enormous. They have to be. How much terror, anguish, loneliness, and bereavement? How is this even to be measured?

Dark tragedy is a defining aspect of human existence, and war is the dark tragedy of international history. The plot is the meaning. Aristotle associated tragedy with *katharsis*, a beneficial process of learning through suffering. The purpose of tragedy as a dramatic form, Aristotle reasoned, is to provoke *katharsis* vicariously in those who witness the play—in other words, to ignite insight into human nature and human affairs. Read as tragedy, the record of war in international history surely does this. But, we wonder, why does so little learning result? Concluding her study of the Thirty Years' War, Wedgwood says of the contenders, "They wanted peace and they fought for thirty years to be sure of it. They did not learn then, and have not since, that war breeds only war."[65] The number of acts in this tragedy of international history is seemingly infinite.

CHAPTER **6**

The Dancing Dinosaurs
of the Cold War

Written in collaboration with MORRIS J. BLACHMAN

When Charles Dickens composed his ever-popular novella A *Christmas Carol,* he assured his readers at the very outset that "Marley was dead." If the fact of Marley's demise were not understood and accepted from the beginning, the rest of Dickens's recounting could have no impact. Dickens's little work about ghosts and history is a fairy tale; this essay about empires and history is not. Let us nonetheless begin in Dickensian fashion by assuring our readers that the United States and the Soviet Union were empires. The United States is still an empire, albeit a diminished one. But during the years of the Cold War, upon which this essay focuses, the American and Soviet empires had their respective heydays. They looked like empires and behaved like empires, and they can therefore be studied as empires. If these propositions are not understood and accepted from the start, then our analysis will have little meaning.

Writing in *Foreign Affairs* in 1988, Marshall Shulman characterized the American-Soviet relationship of that time as a "dance of the dinosaurs" that had lost both meaning and relevance because international history was passing the Cold War by. Nevertheless, the superpower rivalry continued to endanger our planet and neither "partner" knew how to end it. "Both the Soviet Union and the United States," Shulman wrote, "have been so constrained by parochial domestic interests and weighed down by outworn ideologies that they have been unable to summon up a competent and enlightened management of their affairs reasonably proportionate to their respective common problems."[1] Yet, writing about the same time, John Lewis Gaddis observed that one of the remarkable facts about the American-Soviet Cold War was that at the level of superpower-to-superpower relations it remained "cold" for nearly fifty years. Gaddis interpreted the Cold War as a "long peace" in major-power relations, and challenged researchers to explain this.[2] The fact of this long peace must be appreciated, because alternatives to superpower peace in the nuclear age are dreadful beyond contemplation. Yet in broad and analytically appropriate historical perspective, this particular long peace may have been neither extraordinary in its occurrence or duration nor especially difficult to fathom.

To take Cold War history as somehow exceptional is to assume, perhaps unwittingly, that international relations after World War II should have evolved in ways characteristic of traditional relations among European states, where major-power warfare, via mass military border crossings and direct assaults, was almost incessant. For more than a millennium of European history, peace was only the short period of recovery after the last war and preparation for the next. Obviously, what we saw in Soviet-American relations after 1945 did not resemble traditional international relations among European states.[3] Instead, it was a return to, or at least an analogue of, a more deeply seated and older pattern of international relations characteristic of the uneasy coexistence of great empires. Much of the history of international relations is in fact the story of the rivalries of great empires such as the Babylonian and the Egyptian, the Ptolemaic and the Seleucid, the Roman and the Parthian, the Han and the Hsiung-nu, the Byzantine and the Arab, the Ottoman and the Habsburg, and the British and the Russian. From this perspective, Soviet-American relations during the Cold War, though conditioned by modern technologies, institutions, and ideologies, were not altogether exceptional.

Empire As a Concept

Because of the connotations associated with the term *imperialism* in the rhetorics of former east-west and contemporary north-south politics, some tend to look upon empires as illegitimate forms of political organization, indeed even as "evil" forms. All varieties of behavior associated with establishing, maintaining, and extending empires have come to be associated with political villainy. Contrariwise, behavior directed toward undoing empires, and the perpetrators of such, have come to be associated with political progress. Of course, empires and imperialism have not always been derogatorily regarded, but the times when the symbolism of empire connoted glory, order, justice, and even goodness are probably long past.[4] For political reasons, imperial statesmen have frequently found it opportune to deny the existence of their own empires. They have found it similarly expedient to attribute the villainies of imperialism to their international rivals and adversaries.

Walter Lippmann asked Americans to recognize the reality of their empire as early as 1927, writing, "All the world thinks of the United States today as an empire, except the people of the United States. We shrink from the word 'empire,' and insist that it should not be used to describe the dominion we exercise.... We feel that there ought to be some other name for the civilizing work which we do so reluctantly in these backward countries. We do not feel ourselves to be imperialists as we understand that word ... We have learned to think of empires as troublesome and as immoral, and to admit that we have an empire still seems to most Americans like admitting that they have gone out into a wicked world and there lost their political chastity."[5]

What is unfortunate in all of this is that the notion of "empire" has been so politicized that it has been stripped of much of its usefulness as an analytical concept. Yet there is no good substitute for the concept, and there is no way to get around the fact that international politics during the Cold War were dominated by the internal and external affairs of two very extensive and preponderantly powerful empires, the United States of America and the Union of Soviet Socialist Republics.[6] George Liska is one of the very few non-Marxist Western scholars who has made effective analytical use of the concept of empire, and he is also one of the rather small number of American scholars who have disregarded the taboo against labeling the United States an empire. Liska's gumption yielded considerable insight. For him (and for the purposes of this chapter) an empire is

> a state exceeding other states in size, scope, salience and sense of task. In size of territory and material resources, an imperial state is substantially larger than the mean or norm prevailing in the existing system. The scope of its interests and involvements is coterminous with the boundaries of the system itself, rather than with a narrower security zone or habitat; the involvement is implemented directly, or indirectly through client states. The salience of an imperial state consists in the fact that no other state can ignore it and that all other states—consciously or half-consciously, gladly or reluctantly—assess their position, role, and prospects more in relation to it than to closer neighbors or to local conflicts. Finally, the sense of task which distinguishes the imperial state is typically that of creating and then maintaining, a world order the conditions and principles of which would harmonize the particular interests of the imperial state with the interests of the commonweal.[7]

For clarity we need add to Liska's definition of empire that a *state* is a governing organization, distinguishable from the society it governs, and that no personification of the state is necessary.[8] States "perceive," "sense," "intend," and "pursue" via the persons and personalities of those who direct them. Empires are the *core states* of imperial systems, and *imperial systems* are composed of such core states plus *client states* that are either directly or indirectly governed by them. *Governing* in an imperial system means controlling from the core in such a manner that subordinate states are continually obliged to support the preferences of the core state. Governing in imperial systems need not imply subjugating, though subjugation is often involved. In historic eras when great empires were the principal actors in international relations, there were two primary modes of international relations: intraimperial relations between core states and their client states, and interimperial relations between the core states themselves.

By the standards of size, scope, salience, and sense of task that Liska's definition establishes, the United States and the USSR qualify as empires in the second half of the twentieth century. As they reached their prime in the two decades after 1945, they were continental in size and accordingly endowed in natural resources, very large in population, economically advanced, and readily capable of maintaining order within the societies they controlled as well as of projecting rather awesome power beyond their borders. Their interests had become avowedly global; they pursued them in virtually every country on every continent. Nor could their interests, if they chose to be interested, ever be ignored, whatever the substantive context. Each aspired to create a global environment supportive of its interests and values by seeking directly or indirectly to determine the composition of other states' governing elites or by otherwise constraining others' political decision making in ways that constantly produced outcomes acceptable to the core.

That each of these superpowers evolved a "sense of task" in expanding its political and ideological domain, or in frustrating the expansionist aspirations of the other had a great deal to do with the prevailing rivalry between them. That each also remained committed to the global vision symbolized in its political ideology thus transformed rivalry into crusade. Clashing ideologies created the cacophonous tune to which the dinosaurs danced. The onset of the Cold War, Christer Jönsson explains, "revealed and crystallized the similarities of the two 'social myths' at the same time as it blinded the two sides to these similarities." He notes,

> For the United States and the Soviet Union alike, the enemies thus identified were not really states, but "conspiracies disguised as states."
> ... Both sides thus found themselves fighting "isms" rather than nations and inferring the intentions of the adversary not so much from what they *did* as from what they were (imperialists/communists).

> ... The mutual identification of an ideological enemy... [helped
> unleash] the missionary zeal of both foreign policy ideologies. Having
> long articulated what they were fighting for, both now had a clearer
> vision of what they were fighting "against."... The enemy... revealed
> concretely the face of "sin."[9]

Two Twentieth-Century Empires

As outlined in chapter 4, by 1959 the United States had consolidated an imperial system that was global in its expanse. The United States was the core
state, and the empire encompassed all of North America, most of Central
and South America, the NATO allies of Western Europe, and far-flung client
states including Iran, Israel, Japan, South Korea, Taiwan, the Philippines, and
a scattering of smaller island countries in the Pacific and the Caribbean. The
American empire had taken more than two hundred years to build, but even
at the beginning, while the United States amounted only to a narrow strip of
territory along the Atlantic seaboard of North America, George Washington
envisaged that "there will assuredly come a day, when this country will have
some weight in the scale of Empires," and some among his contemporaries forecast that "we cannot but anticipate the period, as not far distant,
when the American Empire will comprehend millions of souls, west of the
Mississippi."[10] Alexander Hamilton is known to have had designs on the
Caribbean, and Thomas Jefferson confided to James Monroe in 1801 that
"it is impossible not to look forward to distant times, when our rapid mul-
tiplication will expand it [the United States] beyond those limits, and cover
the whole northern if not the southern continent, with people speaking the
same language, governed in similar forms, and by similar laws."[11]

Via diplomacy and conquest, the United States pursued its "manifest
destiny" through the nineteenth century, and politically assembled, piece by
piece, the continental core state of its eventual global empire. Meanwhile,
the ascendancy of the central government over the provincial governments,
which had far-reaching implications for the accretion of state power, was
firmly established between 1861 and 1865.

At the turn of the twentieth century, the United States flirted with colonialism, actually acquired a few overseas possessions, but ultimately found
such European-styled imperial arrangements to be rather cumbersome and
distasteful. For the most part, the American overseas empire was constructed
and maintained through indirect governance: countries and peoples were
brought under American dominion via Washington's abilities to keep
sympathetic elites in ascendance and friendly governments constantly in
power. This was accomplished by economically subsidizing friends abroad,
educating succeeding foreign elite generations at American institutions,

guaranteeing governments' internal security and peoples' external security, arming pro-American forces and factions, and occasionally intervening covertly or overtly to prop up friendly governments or remove dubious ones. The most frequent results of such American practices were predictable flows of supportive policies from politically and economically beholden client governments.

During the first half of the twentieth century, American suzerainty encompassed the Western Hemisphere and the Pacific possessions. After the Second World War it was extended to Western Europe and to the several other anticommunist outposts of the U.S. alliance system. American economic and military assistance continued to keep friendly governments in power in the post–World War II era, but the United States also maintained its ascendance by legitimizing it through moral leadership, thus capitalizing on residual "soft power."[12] Challenge from within the empire was improbable as long as Washington could be perceived as promoting or protecting broadly appealing values.

"Washington was the center of the system," Susan Strange observed in a 1983 essay, "a kind of keep in the baronial capital of capitalism, from which radiated military, monetary, commercial and technological as well as purely political channels carrying the values of American polity, economy, and society down through the hierarchy of allies and friends, classes and cultural cousins, out to the ends of the earth. The new kind of global empire, under the protection of American nuclear power, did not need territorial expansion. It could be achieved by a combination of military alliances and a world economy opened to trade, investment and information."[13]

At its fullest extent, attained about 1960, the Russian empire enveloped most of the Eurasian landmass. Its European frontier was at the western border of the German Democratic Republic and the eastern frontier was the Pacific coast of China. A substantial part of this vast domain was of course the Soviet core state itself, but the cluster of clients was impressive—East Germany, six other countries in Central Europe, the Baltic states, China, Mongolia, North Korea, and North Vietnam. Beyond Eurasia there were Fidel Castro's Cuba, for a time a fledgling communist regime in Afghanistan, and also for a time dependent regimes in Yemen, Angola, and Ethiopia. The Soviet Empire was the successor to the Russian Empire of the Tsars, and while the Bolshevik revolution in 1917 dramatically altered polity and economy in Russia, it did nothing to dampen the Russian empire-building impulse.

As noted in chapter 4, the beginning of all this, in the words of G. Vernadsky, was an "insignificant *ostrog* [block-house] built in the first half of the twelfth century, on an insignificant river by an insignificant princeling [which] became, in the course of time, the pivot of an empire extending into two, and even three continents."[14] This twelfth-century minor fortification was destined to become the city of Moscow, and its hinterland, the Duchy of Muscovy, was to become the core of an ever-expanding Slav empire originally peopled by a Nordic tribe identified as the Rus. Ivan the Great, who ruled Muscovy from 1462 to 1505, is widely credited with consolidating the first centralized Russian state in what is today the Moscow area in the northwest-ern part of present-day Russia. Ivan and his immediate successors extended Russia outward by absorbing weaker neighboring Slav principalities and by confronting the more powerful forces of medieval Lithuania, Poland, and Sweden. Later, Ivan the Terrible, circa 1584, pushed east and southeast to the northern shores of the Caspian Sea, finally breaking the power of the Mongols of the Golden Horde, who had since the thirteenth century occu-pied regions in what are today the Ukraine and the former Soviet territories in central Asia. Interaction with the Mongols, Lionel Kochan and Richard Abraham observe, "provided future Russian rulers with a model: a state with universalist aspirations, subordinating everything to efficiency in matters of military administration and relying on a class of serving men bound to serve their khan with absolute obedience."[15]

After the Russians, expanding eastward, crossed the Ural Mountains into Siberia in the 1580s, it took them only another century to annex the vast expanse of central Asia. By the end of the reign of Peter I in 1725, tsarist hegemony extended to the Pacific Ocean. Meanwhile, Russian successes in the Great Northern War between 1706 and 1718 added territory in the Baltic region at Sweden's expense, and later, the three partitions of Poland dur-ing the reign of Catherine the Great added to the Russian empire in the west. The tsars of the nineteenth century focused most of their expansion-istic attentions southward and pushed, between 1801 and 1881, through Georgia, Azerbaijan, Turkistan, and Kazakhstan to the northern frontiers of Persia and Afghanistan. The last decades of the nineteenth century found the tsars consolidating and extending their domain along their Pacific coast.

The Treaty of Brest-Litvosk in 1918 extricated Russia, by then recon-stituted as the Soviet Union, from World War I, but it cost the Russians dearly in terms of territory in the Baltic region to the west, and in the Black Sea area. However, the Red Army retook most of this territory during the revolutionary wars in the early 1920s. Estonia, Latvia, and Lithuania were annexed again to the Soviet Union as a result of the Molotov-Ribbentrop Pact of August, 1939; some Finnish territories were annexed to the USSR as a result of the Russo-Finnish Wars of 1940 and 1944; and most of Eastern Europe occupied by the Soviet Union in 1945 became thereafter the new western cordon of the Soviet Empire. With the success of its revolution in 1949, the Chinese Communist Party initially accepted the tutelage of the Soviet Union and thus became a part of the latter's imperial system. Most of the communist parties in power elsewhere in the world were more or less obliged to do likewise.

Since the Russian empire was largely territorially contiguous, the tsarist and Soviet governments opted mainly for direct rule via annexation to the core state and administrative subordination to Moscow. The territories and peoples added to the empire after World War II were, however, governed less directly by keeping local communist parties, whose leaders were strictly beholden to Moscow, in power. Rather, generous Soviet economic and military assistance helped client communist governments to keep societies in the subordinate states under close control. In several countries in Eastern Europe, communist parties' political monopolies were also buttressed by large contingents of permanently stationed Red Army troops. Legitimacy was never a major contributing element in Moscow's indirect rule over client states, though during the height of the Cold War the degree to which legitimacy abetted the government in the core state should not be underestimated.

Intra- and Interimperial Relations

The point in going to some length to demonstrate that the United States and the Soviet Union fit the model as empires is to open the way to explaining that they behaved in the post–World War II era as great empires have typically behaved in the past. We say "typically" because we are looking at the broad patterning of relations between great empires. As in any historical analogy there are notable features of the phenomena being compared that are similar. But there are also some that are different. As the differences become more prominent and the similarities recede, the utility of the comparison wanes. On the other hand, where the similarities persist over long historical stretches, they can be of great value to assist in our understanding.

If we choose as our historical analogues the celebrated rivalries between the Romans and Parthians (170 B.C.E.–224 C.E.), and the Romans/Byzantines and the Sassanian Persians (224–642), the Byzantines and Arabs (632–1100), the Ottomans and the Austrians (1539–1914), and the Ottomans and the Russians (1686–1917), we can begin to construct a rough model of international relations under conditions of imperial rivalry. For one thing, simply looking at the dates suggests that historical imperial rivalries continued over long stretches of time—centuries, usually. As great imperial rivals were typically powerful, durable, and capable of repeatedly regenerating from within, contests between them tended to be very long and often inconclusive. Imperial rivalries typically have been trials of slow attrition that have led in the past less often to victory or supremacy and more often to mutual exhaustion and/or inabilities to cope with challenges from newly rising and more vigorous rivals.

Second, warfare between the great imperial rivals of the past was continuous, but it was most often geographically confined to regions of interimperial intersection—that is, to the *marches,* where rival imperial armies literally marched back and forth for centuries. Although continuous, warfare in the marches, costly as it was in lives and treasure, was also typically indecisive. By the same token, core state–to–core state onslaughts were rare, capital cities were seldom attacked and taken, and total triumphs or knockout blows were seldom registered. Oddly, while the inconclusive skirmishing in the marches continued, people living in certain core states and capital cities might have easily perceived themselves in the midst of periods of long peace. But conditions undoubtedly must have appeared very different to the unfortunate souls inhabiting the borderlands. Among the historic cases listed above, only Constantinople succumbed as a result of direct assault by rival imperial armies. The main reasons for the continuous interimperial warfare were successive political rulers' quests for glory, military leaders' need for employment, and economic rewards anticipated from plunder and territorial acquisition. Religious zeal sometimes also played a part. As time went on, in many cases revanchist motives, drives for revenge, and repayment for defeats and indignities suffered in earlier battles became important motives for launching succeeding ones. In this way, the constant interimperial conflicts came, in effect, to feed upon themselves. The primary reason that the interimperial wars were usually inconclusive, as well as the reason core states and capital cities could seldom be assaulted, was that the rival empires tended to be closely balanced in their military capabilities (or sometimes in their inabilities). Thus, they engaged for the most part in centuries-long efforts at wearing one another down. Of course, in historical interimperial contests, geography and technology were important factors as well, since it was physically rather difficult to reach very far into expansive rival domains.

In almost every instance of great imperial rivalry, intraimperial affairs attracted far greater core state attention than interimperial affairs. Because of their vastness and internal self-sufficiency, their military invulnerability and the commonly vast physical and cultural distances that separated core state from core state, great empires have tended to mutually isolate themselves. Beyond skirmishing along their borders they have typically had little to do with one another and little interest in one another's societies or internal affairs. "The distance that usually separates empires," Liska observes, "is not only geographical but also psychological. It commonly resides in mutual ignorance, including misassessment of power and objectives. Ignorance and misassessment increase with cultural or ideological differences."[16]

By contrast, core states are typically and constantly involved in securing, consolidating, and deepening their governance within their imperial systems and fixing their hierarchical relations with intraimperial clients. Threats to the efficacy or continuation of core state governance occur frequently, as some parties, somewhere within the empires, are for some reason almost always in revolt. As empires decline, internal disintegration tends to become ever more problematic and eventually becomes the almost total preoccupation of core state governments, thus commanding their attentions and sapping their resources.

Imperial Conflict and American-Soviet Relations

As is typical of great historical interimperial rivalries, conflict between the United States and the Soviet Union was continuous in the post–World War II era, and lasted right up to the time when the Soviet Union collapsed. This conflict, moreover, was often violent. But it was only rarely direct—that is, core state versus core state. In the contest between the Soviet and the American imperial systems, each core state used its own military forces as well as those of client states to do continuing battle with what it saw as incursions or agents of the rival empire. Historically, such indirect conflict is rather typical of the international relations of great empires. Most frequently, such battles have been empire-maintaining exercises conducted principally within the geographic borders of one of the empires and fought between the core state and rebellious elements in a client state. Preoccupations with such intraempire problems are also historically common, as are repeated revolts at imperial peripheries. Otherwise, interimperial contests during the Cold War were fought in portions of the globe not fully incorporated into one of the two systems—that is, in the interimperial marches, where each of the empires aspired either to expand or to check its rival's expansion. As this constant and rather inconclusive skirmishing went on, the interimperial balance of power kept the respective core states reasonably immune from mutual external assault or penetration.

The Beginnings of Interimperial Rivalry

The United States and the Soviet Union had respectively emerged as twentieth-century empires even before the Second World War. But their mutually preoccupying rivalry most realistically dates from the early postwar era. "There probably never was any real possibility," Cold War historian Ernest May writes, "that the post-1945 relationship could be anything but hostility verging on conflict."[17] From Harry Truman to George H. W. Bush and from Josef Stalin to Mikhail Gorbachev, the leaders in each of the two core states managed to see in each other a major threat to their ability to flourish, if not simply to survive. As early as the Potsdam Conference in the summer of 1945, where Truman met Joseph Stalin for the first time, the American president had decided that the Russians had to be confronted with "an iron fist and strong language."[18] He and his inner circle of advisers had determined by the autumn of 1946 that the Soviet Union was an expansionist power bent on conquest. Dwight Eisenhower likewise saw the world imperiled by the "monolithic mass of Communist imperialism."[19] To the authors of NSC-68, the 1950 National Security Council directive that established the Cold War containment policy, the USSR was "the inheritor of Russian imperialism."[20] It needed to be contained.

The view from the Kremlin was no less severe. For Stalin, the enemy during and after the Second World War was not just the Nazis. The enormous losses suffered by the Soviet Union during the war, along with Soviet leaders' historic distrust of the anticommunist European and American powers, generated substantial concern for preserving the security and territorial integrity of the USSR. Notes Robert Messer, "When Stalin insisted upon having only 'friendly' governments on Russia's borders, he declared his refusal even to risk reestablishment of the prewar *cordon sanitaire* of noncommunist, anti-Soviet regimes."[21] "Since World War II," Dimitri Simes underlines, "the relationship with the United States has continually been among the central considerations of Soviet foreign policy. America . . . became for the Soviet Union a source of constant fear, a constraint on further geopolitical advances."[22]

Thus, each of the two empires came to see the other as a distinct threat to its system, and each came to believe that it had to act forcefully to counter efforts by the other to subvert or otherwise detach peripheral states from its imperial system. To fail to do so would be to show weakness, and that, in turn, would likely carry over into unraveling the fabric of imperial control maintained by the respective cores. "As we ourselves demonstrate power, confidence and a sense of moral and political direction," the authors of NSC-68 affirmed, "so those same qualities will be evoked in Western Europe. In such a situation, we may also anticipate a general improvement in the political tone in Latin America, Asia, and Africa. . . . In the absence of affirmative decision on our part, the rest of the free world is almost certain to become demoralized . . . they can become a positive increment to Soviet power."[23]

That Soviet concerns were similar is evidenced in Nikita Khruschev's "For New Victories of the World Communist Movement," where the Russian leader pointed out, "There exists in the world today, not just one country of workers and peasants, but a whole system of socialist countries. It is our duty to safeguard peace and ensure the peaceful development of this grand creation. The struggle against imperialism can succeed only if its [capitalist imperialism's] aggressive actions are firmly resisted. Scolding will not halt the imperialist adventurers. There is only one way in which they will be curbed: steady strengthening of the economic, political and military power of the socialist countries."[24]

Answering exactly why the United States and the Soviet Union emerged as imperial rivals after the Second World War is akin to explaining why Romans and Persians were adversaries in the second century c.e., or why Arabs and Byzantines were rivals, or Austrians and Turks, or perhaps any of the other great antagonists of history. Explanations range from Raymond Aron's notion of *la fatalité des positions,* meaning that proximate great powers are somehow historically determined to be rivals, to George Liska's more persuasive observation that a great-power rivalry tends often to be driven by fear based on mutual cultural ignorance.[25] There is in most cases of interimperial rivalry evidence of extensive "mirror-imaging" where statesmen project their own aggressive intentions onto rivals and thus escalate destructive spirals of mutual suspicion. Nor, of course, is it extraordinary for the political leaders of major powers to actually harbor, and opportunistically act upon, externally expansionistic ambitions. All of these elements, and undoubtedly many others, were ingredients in Soviet-American rivalry as well.

Intraimperial Conflict in the Post–World War II Era

While American and Soviet geostrategic preoccupations defined their global rivalry, their more practical political military preoccupations were with problems occurring within their respective imperial systems. A good proportion of the conflicts that involved the superpowers from the early 1950s onward had to do with what would traditionally be called "putting down rebellions in the outlying provinces of the empire." The patterns in most of the cases are similar, and they recur with remarkable regularity: (1) elements within a client state rise up against local elites that are beholden to the core state; (2) the possible success of the rebels creates some chance that the client state might be separated from the empire; and (3) forces and/or military supplies from the core state are dispatched to suppress the rebellion, thereby maintaining or restoring imperially loyal local elites and preserving the integrity of the empire.

What was rather remarkable in American and Soviet exercises in putting down rebellions in the outlying provinces is that substantial numbers of the respective core state elites repeatedly managed to convince themselves that the rebellions within their respective imperial systems had been caused by the provocations and machinations of their rivals. In fact, there is very little evidence to suggest that most of the intraimperial uprisings were directly fomented by imperial rivals, though there is no denying that many of these rebellions, once initiated, were abetted from the outside. To the extent that the respective imperial elites actually believed that their intraimperial problems were caused by rival provocateurs, they denied themselves the capacity to understand what were often more fundamental causes of the uprisings against them. In any event, combating perceived or proclaimed penetration and subversion from the outside was the standard justification offered by respective core state elites to explain their moves to suppress rebellions.

Client states are not merely passive actors in these processes. For one thing, it is often elites within client states that, acting in their own interest, solicit intervention from the core. The conventional wisdom in Latin America for years was that all the local elites had to do to get whatever assistance they desired from the United States was invoke the threat of communism. The strategy worked well and often. It also frequently embroiled the United States in prolonged and costly affairs, always ostensibly aimed at supporting client elites in their efforts to suppress "leftist rebels." Even in the case of the U.S. invasion of Grenada in October 1983, the client states played an important role. Dominica, with a population of about 75,000, led the way, as its prime minister, Mary Eugenia Charles, petitioned the United States on behalf of the eastern Caribbean states to intervene to save Grenada from "barbarism and communism." Their entreaty served both to provoke the American decision to invade, and to legitimize that decision. Grenada, after all, could not be allowed to slip out of America's imperial domain.

There is no question but that pressures for the suppression of empire-threatening rebellions also flowed in two directions in the Soviet cases. There were certainly those among the local elites in the Soviet client states who stood to lose a great deal from the fragmentation of the Soviet empire, and they were understandably active in encouraging Soviet interventions against their own countrymen, whom they were quick to brand "counter-revolutionaries," "antiparty agitators," and "non-Marxist deviationists," or "hooligans inspired by foreign powers." In Hungary in 1956, for example, at the very first signs of unrest, Erno Gero, the first secretary of the Hungarian Communist Party, called for Soviet and Warsaw Pact intervention to restore order. Likewise, in the Czechoslovakian situation in 1968, the party's hard-liners saw their political futures more closely tied to the communists of the Soviet Union than to their "liberal" colleagues in Prague. They readily made Moscow aware of this by inviting intervention to suppress their countrymen.

Maintaining the United States Empire

Guatemala

Following a successful revolution in October 1944, Guatemala embarked on a ten-year period of reform. The country did away with many of the vestiges of the earlier dictatorship and achieved a democratic opening. Colonel

Jacobo Arbenz Guzmán, who assumed the presidency after Juan José Arevalo in a peaceful transition in 1951, was intent on furthering reform in Guatemala by redistributing uncultivated lands to peasants after duly compensating owners. This land reform effort aroused the opposition of the U.S.-owned United Fruit Company, which owned over 40 percent of the arable land in Guatemala but cultivated only 5 percent. United Fruit then sought the support of the U.S. government for the overthrow of the Arbenz regime. Meanwhile, Arbenz had legalized the Communist Party in Guatemala and invited some of its members into his government. The functioning of the Arbenz government thus began to be perceived in Washington as a challenge to the anticommunist fidelity expected of client elites within the United States imperial system.[26]

Guatemala therefore looked to be in rebellion within the empire, and secretary of state John Foster Dulles was determined to pursue a "clear-cut ... policy ... against the intervention of international communism in the hemisphere," and "to take effective measures, individually and collectively, to combat it."[27] If the articulations of Dulles and other American officials at the time are reliable guides, there is little doubt that Washington (1) saw Arbenz and his policies as unacceptable deviations from appropriate client state elite behavior, and (2) interpreted the Guatemalan situation as instigated and abetted by the Soviet Union.[28] Arbenz, of course, was subsequently overthrown as a result of the U.S. Central Intelligence Agency's now well-known Operation Success; his reforms were rolled back, and Guatemala entered what were to be three decades of repressive and authoritarian rule.[29] But the Guatemalan government remained for those three decades in steadfast support of the anticommunist policies of the United States.

The Dominican Republic

With the assassination of Rafael Trujillo in 1961, thirty years of dictatorship were brought to a close in the Dominican Republic. Despite a period of considerable turmoil, the Dominicans managed to elect a president whose tenure in office was cut short by a military coup in 1963. Then, in April 1965, a rebellion broke out. The rebels sought the overthrow of the military regime and the restoration of the deposed president.

Response from the United States was swift, overt, and military. U.S. president Lyndon Johnson explained on May 2 why he had ordered some 25,000 American troops into the Dominican Republic: "Communist leaders, many of them trained in Cuba, seeing a chance to increase disorder, to gain a foothold, joined the revolution. They took increasing control. [The revolution] was taken over ... and placed into the hands of a band of Communist conspirators."[30]

Challenge to the empire was not acceptable. "Our goal," Johnson said, "is to prevent another Communist state in this hemisphere." As if to forewarn against any future such attempts, he proclaimed what became known as the Johnson Doctrine: "American nations cannot, must not, and will not permit the establishment of another Communist government in the Western Hemisphere."[31]

Central America

Apparently quiescent in the early 1970s, Central America seemed to erupt at the end of the decade. First came the overthrow of Anastasio Somoza in Nicaragua in July 1979, and then, three months later, General Carlos Humberto Romero was ousted in neighboring El Salvador. Meanwhile, violence and insurgency continued to bubble up in Guatemala. In the subsequent decade the United States scrambled to hold the line against what it saw as the threat of communist intrusion and the possible loss of not one but two more Cubas. In Nicaragua, where the incoming Reagan administration found itself confronting a Marxist party in power, the effort was to force the Sandinistas out; and in El Salvador, where the insurgents were a growing force, the strategy was to beef up the local military and defeat the guerrillas on the battlefield.

Despite the efforts of Mexico, Venezuela, Colombia, and Panama—joined later by Argentina, Brazil, Peru, and Uruguay—to persuade the United States that the "battle" being enjoined in Central America was a "north-south" and not an "east-west" one, the U.S. persisted in the view so well articulated by the National Bipartisan Commission on Central America[32]:

> The Soviet-Cuban thrust to make Central America part of their geostrategic challenge is what has turned the struggle in Central America into a security and political problem for the United States and for the hemisphere.
>
> The use of Nicaragua as a base for Soviet and Cuban efforts to penetrate the rest of the Central American isthmus, with El Salvador the target of first opportunity, gives the conflict there a major strategic dimension. The direct involvement of aggressive external forces makes it a challenge quite specifically to the security interests of the United States. This is a challenge to which the United States must respond.[33]

Other Cases

The toppling of Mohammad Mossedeq in Iran in 1953; the "economic destabilization" of Chile from 1970 to the overthrow of Salvador Allende in

1973; the invasion of Grenada in October, 1983; support for the Contras in Nicaragua and other exertions against the Sandinista government, as well as prolific military and economic aid to client elites under siege from leftist insurgents were similarly all empire-maintaining exercises conducted by Washington. As we may glean from the history of empires, someone somewhere within the empire is almost always seen to be in rebellion against the imperial system and its orthodox client elites. The integrity of the empire therefore requires that such rebellions be put down. It is not unusual that the demand for action against such rebellious factions comes from within the client states, at times pushing the core state to a more determined and active position than it might otherwise have taken.

In the first two decades after the Second World War, the United States was reasonably successful in its empire-maintaining efforts. Fidel Castro's successful rebellion, which the Cuban leader himself called an anti-imperial turning point in the Western Hemisphere, was the first successful chipping away at United States dominion. Cuba's move from the U.S. imperial system into the Soviet system and the subsequent Bay of Pigs fiasco combined to produce the only really dramatic early failure of American imperialism. More failures were to come later.

Maintaining the Soviet Empire

Eastern Germany

Although direct Soviet control over Eastern Germany, technically speaking, ended in October 1949, a large Red Army force remained in the German Democratic Republic (GDR), and the Communist Party leaders of the GDR remained strictly beholden to Moscow. Rioting broke out in East Berlin in the summer of 1953, ostensibly over the issue of increased work norms imposed by the East German government on construction workers. This protest escalated into demands to dissolve the East German parliament and calls for free elections. In short order, the uprising that began in East Berlin spread to several other East German cities, and Soviet troops and tanks rolled in to put down the riots with considerable force.

Notably, the origins of the protest stemmed from Germans' dismay with working conditions in the GDR and their frustration with political repression under the communist regime. The episode was fundamentally a rebellion against the communist state and Marxist-Leninist ideological orthodoxy. It was, therefore, an intraimperial revolt. But it was publicly interpreted by the leaders of the Soviet Union, and perhaps even privately understood, as a provocation from the United States. As the Soviet newspaper *Pravda* explained, "the increase in norms was the only pretext for foreign provocateurs from among the number of foreign agents who have settled in East Berlin."[34] Suppressing the East German workers was therefore a move undertaken to protect the Soviet Empire.

Hungary

In the wake of de-Stalinization after 1953, pressures for change built up in some East European countries; these erupted into riots in Hungary in 1956. Shortly after protesters took to the streets in Budapest and elsewhere, Russian tanks rolled in. Opposition escalated into armed conflict, and fighting broke out throughout the country. Response to the rebellion was rapid, and supporters of the Hungarian Revolution were soon crushed. Here, too, the Russians lay blame at the doorstep of the United States and other "reactionary" forces. As was reported in 1953, "It is known that the forces of reaction within the country were acting in close contact with the international reaction, and immediately after the armed putsch was started they were receiving effective aid from the West.... According to official information of the Hungarian Government, ... airplanes arrived from Austria...; they brought a considerable amount of munitions in boxes marked with the Red Cross and persons who acted as the organizers of the counter-revolutionary putsch."[35] Such Western attempts to undermine the Soviet empire were, in Moscow's view, not new. As they claimed the following year in an official publication, *The Truth about Hungary,* "energetic preparations for overthrowing the people's democratic system in Hungary and in other East European countries, have been conducted in the United States of America ... for many years."[36]

Soviet Chairman Nikita Khruschev sought to dispel any doubts concerning the seriousness of Soviet resolve to counter such rebellions in the future when he spoke at Tatabanya, Hungary, in 1958: "If provocateurs or enemies of the workers attempt a 'putsch' or counterrevolution in any Socialist country, then I tell them here and now that all the Socialist countries and the armed forces of the Soviet Union will be ready at all times to give the provocateurs the answer they deserve."[37]

Czechoslovakia

Here once again attempts to weaken a communist regime were viewed as a challenge to Soviet hegemony. Following months of discussions, negotiations, and warnings, the flowering of spring in Prague was brought to an abrupt and violent halt, as Russian and Warsaw Pact troops moved swiftly and massively into Czechoslovakia in 1968. Soviet ambassador Jakob Malik argued at the United Nations that the Czechoslovakian affair had been instigated from outside and that Soviet reaction therefore had been appropriate and necessary: "The Soviet Union has irrefutable data that events in Czechoslovakia can be traced outside that country. There is a dangerous conspiracy of the forces of internal and external reaction to restore the order which had been brought down by the popular revolution."[38]

Malik continued, "Instructions and directives from abroad" went to anticommunist Czechoslovakians who played "the role of imperialist agents in that country." This was all part of an effort by the United States "to undermine and sap the socialist system . . . and create a breach in the Socialist community. The imperialist circles of the United States, by political and ideological means involving secret, clandestine and subversive measures, stubbornly continue trying to tear apart the socialist community, to break its unity and weaken its ability to confront direct aggression."[39]

Afghanistan

Throughout its seventy-year existence, the Soviet Union was vitally concerned with security in its border areas. Afghanistan's geographic proximity put it squarely in the USSR's "backyard," much as Central America and the Caribbean are looked upon by some as the "backyard" of the United States. When it appeared in the late 1970s that the Afghani regime, friendly to the Soviet Union, was likely to be overthrown by indigenous opposition forces, Moscow became greatly concerned. Soviet concerns were amplified by the fact that the Afghan opposition was composed of Islamic fundamentalist groups, whose imminent success could reverberate through Muslim populations inside the Soviet Union. Moscow was also worried that a new Afghan regime might shift the country's alignment away from the USSR and toward the West.

In a preemptive action, the Soviet Union launched a massive invasion of Afghanistan in December 1979, which, despite their technical superiority, got Russian forces bogged down in a decade-long, costly military quagmire. Chairman Leonid Brezhnev explained the Soviet action on the front page of *Pravda*. "Crude interference" from the outside, "tens of thousands of insurgents, armed and trained abroad, whole armed units," he claimed, had been sent to Afghanistan. "In effect," he continued, "imperialism, together with its accomplices, launched an undeclared war against revolutionary Afghanistan." He pointed out that the USSR had warned that it would not abandon the Afghans in their time of need, and that it was "well known, we stand by what we say." He explained, "The unceasing armed intervention, the well advanced plot by external forces of reaction, created a real threat that Afghanistan would lose its independence and be turned into an imperialist military bridgehead on our country's southern border. . . . we could not but respond to the request of the Government of friendly Afghanistan. To have acted otherwise would have meant leaving Afghanistan a prey to imperialism. . . . To have acted otherwise would have meant to watch passively the origination on our southern border of a centre of serious danger to the security of the Soviet state."[40] The Russian invasion of Afghanistan was therefore an empire-maintaining imperative.

Skirmishing in the Interimperial Marches

While the United States and Soviet Union had no common borders save the sea frontier in the remote region of the Bering Strait, their respective imperial systems nonetheless adjoined at the numerous points where respective client states came together. These points and these countries, therefore, were the marches of the empires, and like the borderlands of proximate historic empires, they were contested. However, the contests, while costly in human lives and material resources, never significantly altered the interimperial territorial status quo. The Soviet Union's attempts immediately after World War II to expand its Eastern European domain to include Greece were thwarted by the United States. After three years and more than a half million military and civilian casualties, the Korean War was fought to a stalemate in 1953. The battles for the Taiwan Straits between 1954 and 1957 similarly generated a standoff. The United States, after a costly empire-defending experience, was ejected from Vietnam in 1972, thereby slightly altering the interimperial territorial status quo. On the other hand, the Soviet Union, after a comparably expensive failure at imperial expansion, was forced out of Afghanistan in 1989—again slightly, but again inconsequentially, altering the interimperial status quo. If the civil conflict in Angola was actually a case of interimperial skirmishing in contested borderlands, the conflict there also appeared to have generated impasse. But the main point here is that skirmishing in the marches was constant throughout the Cold War.

Core State–versus–Core State Encounters

Direct confrontations between the United States and the Soviet Union, however, were rare in the post–World War II era, thus lending the appearance of a period of "long peace." As noted earlier, such core state–to–core state confrontations have also been historically rare in interimperial politics, mainly because they were usually perceived as costly, unwinnable because of balanced power, and logistically difficult to manage. In interimperial encounters it has usually been more convenient to fight, rampage, and ravage in client states and in other peoples' countries located in borderlands far away from imperial cores.

Naturally, direct confrontations between imperial powers do from time to time occur. In the American-Soviet relationship, the first true interempire conflict occurred in 1948, when the Soviet Union closed off land and water access through East Germany to the city of West Berlin. Despite some very tense moments, this conflict never escalated past the threshold of large-scale violence. A second and far more serious conflict between the two powers revolved around the placement of Soviet offensive missiles in Cuba in 1962. The United States reacted by declaring a naval quarantine of Cuba. The U.S. Navy, Washington said, would stop and search Soviet ships headed toward the island country. This set the stage for direct confrontation. But the two imperial powers, seeking to avoid direct conflict, and especially to avert escalating to a nuclear exchange, resorted to traditional diplomacy to resolve the crisis.

What Happens When Empires Meet?

How useful is it to model the "long peace" of the Cold War era as a phase of interimperial international relations? Our broad sweep through the history of international relations and our staccato survey of post–World War II Soviet-American relations can only be suggestive. But the suggestions evoked are rather intriguing:

1. The imperial model of United States–Soviet relations would suggest (a) that core states will avoid direct center-to-center clashes, (b) that inter-imperial conflict in borderlands and other contested peripheral areas will be continuous, and (c) that intraempire relations, core state to client state, will consume most of the efforts, if not also most of the attention, of the core states.

2. The emergence of the United States and the Soviet Union as imperial powers, their behavior toward clients within their respective imperial systems, their behavior regarding peripheral and unincorporated states, and their behavior toward each other are all reminiscent of recurrent patterns associated with the great empires and great imperial rivalries of the past. The imperial model is therefore quite informative. The avoidance of direct clashes between imperial core states, or what we describe in Soviet-American relations as the long peace, has strong historical precedents and a sound logic in historical and contemporary balance-of-power thinking. The historical record of Cold War statecraft affirms that imperial statesmen engage in such balance-of-power thinking regarding their direct relations. Yet constant conflict at points of interimperial intersection is also a mode of historical behavior manifestly replayed in Soviet-American relations during the Cold War. For core states, empire-maintaining behavior, "the putting down of revolts in the provinces," or otherwise keeping loyal elites in power in client states has always been a preoccupying aspect of

their international relations. So too was such empire-maintaining behavior the practical preoccupation of both the United States and the Soviet Union.

3. An important aspect of the Soviet-American relationship was an integrated perception, mutually harbored by governing elites in both core states, of an all-encompassing global contest. The contending leadership of the United States and the Soviet Union tended to interpret all aspects of their international relations, intraimperial as well as interimperial, as phases of a single pervasive struggle. The international relations of empires are almost always perceived as great games. During the Cold War, therefore, balancing nuclear power at the strategic level, fighting small wars along the peripheries of the imperial systems, and combating rebellions within client states were all perceived to be connected. In the same way, historically, imperial rivals have consistently been perceived as the instigators and provocateurs of whatever manner of troubles or obstacles core states have confronted in various modes of intra- and interimperial relations. The recurrent "mirror imaging" has been remarkable. It was certainly an aspect of the international relations of the Cold War.

Up to the Present and into the Future

Both the Soviet and the American empires exhibited signs of imperial decline during the last two decades of the Cold War. For one thing, both core states began encountering increasing difficulties in their intraimperial relations, as their authority in peripheral areas appeared to be waning along with their ability to keep subservient elites in power in client states. The Soviet empire actually began to fragment with the pulling away of China after the Sino-Soviet controversies of the middle 1960s. But the next twenty years saw relative stability and even modest expansion in the territorial expanse of the empire. By the late 1980s, however, this empire was clearly disintegrating. The withdrawal of Soviet military forces from Afghanistan in 1989, political upheavals in Eastern Europe, and secessionist activities in the Baltic areas of the Soviet Union, the Caucasus, and elsewhere dramatically signaled the weakening of the imperium. We know, of course, that there was more unraveling to come.

Less momentously—though still indicatively—as early as the middle 1980s United States inability to control events in Nicaragua and El Salvador; Washington's need to occupy Panama militarily in order to depose a defiant, petty dictator; the termination of American influence in Iran; and ebbing respect for U.S. will and authority in Western Europe and Japan all suggested considerable fraying at the edges of the American empire.

Historically speaking, there was nothing extraordinary about what was happening to the American and Soviet empires. Empires decline and the detachment of peripheral client states signals this. Paul Kennedy postulates, probably advisedly, that empires decline because of economic exhaustion impelled by excessive military spending and other empire-maintaining imperatives.[41] The imperial model suggests that "rebellions in the provinces" become more frequent and increasingly successful as processes of imperial fragmentation accelerate. As noted, empires typically do not "fall"; rather, they fragment and "fall apart" as client states become able to claim and enforce increasing autonomy. This was happening to the Soviet and American empires even while the dinosaurs continued to dance.

Historical analogues suggest at least two scenarios for the decline of empires. First, there is the pattern of slow decline and eventual descent into historical, though not necessarily physical, oblivion. Here, one might consider the fates of western Rome, Byzantium, Venice, imperial Spain, or Manchu China. Decline here was halting, fragmentation was piecemeal and intermittent, partial reinvigoration was intermittently in evidence, and traditional rivalries remained alive—though not very vigorously pursued—because they served the internal political or psychological needs of ruling elites. Marshall Shulman is correct: imperial dinosaurs continue to dance because they do not know how to stop. Meanwhile, new centers of power emerge and new interimperial contests eventually become the axes of international relations.

Alternatively, imperial decline can be precipitous, as with Austria-Hungary, the Ottoman Empire, or the Western European colonial empires assembled in the nineteenth century. When this more rapid decline happens, empires dissolve and disappear. Although this is sometimes the case, decline need not spell disaster for former imperial core states, as they frequently become modest, middle powers in postimperial worlds. When empires disappear, the international system expands haphazardly to include numerous new states emerged from the old empires, and constructing a new international order out of small-power pluralism becomes a challenge to diplomacy and a key to stability. If international history is a reliable guide, we can observe that diplomacy frequently falls short of meeting challenges to order in periods of postimperial succession and rather dangerous eras of increased international anarchy ensue.

What, then, can we expect for the future of the Soviet and American empires, given what we have learned from the past? Of course, the future of the then-Soviet empire is the present: it no longer exists. The core state of this empire collapsed in 1993 as a result of a relatively bloodless revolution that transformed the Union of Soviet Socialist Republics into present-day Russia and a ragged collection of successor states. In historically characteristic fashion the weakening of the center set defections in the periphery into motion. The Soviet empire imploded partly because failures of the centrally planned economy could not generate the wealth required to produce the power to keep the Communist Party of the Soviet Union in control. The implosion was also in part the result of liberalizing and liberating forces unwittingly unleashed by Mikhail Gorbachev's efforts to maintain communist control by reforming communist societies. Reform proved both impossible and uncontrollable because the legitimacy of the ruling party was already long lost. *Glasnost* and *perestroika* opened political space inside the core state as well as at the periphery. In both, long-suppressed counterelites leapt at the opportunity not only to fill that space, but to open it even further. Replacing communist elites with anticommunist counterelites had long been the only kind of reforms acceptable in places where Soviet imperialism had been sustained by local leaders selected and supported by Moscow; this is what earlier revolts within the empire had been about. The reaction—throughout Eastern Europe especially—to tossing out the communist parties and communist party leaders signaled the removal of leadership and organizational strata that had been in control for forty years but had been unable to convince the people that they deserved to hold power. As well, in some places where Soviet-installed local leaders were ethnically alien, legitimacy could come only through national self-determination, and this, when finally expressed, tore the "near abroad" from the empire. In several of the peripheral states the physical presence of Soviet troops was canceled by the reluctance of first Mikhail Gorbachev's and then Boris Yeltsin's regimes to use them for empire-maintaining purposes, and in this sense, Soviet imperialism had lost its nerve.

The empire that was the Soviet Union has become the troubled middle power that today calls itself Russia. It is a country seeking identity—postimperial identity, perhaps, not unlike Spain at the end the nineteenth century, Austria and Turkey after 1919, or England and France after losing their world empires. If history is any guide, the most likely future course of Russian development will resemble that of England, France, Austria, Turkey, and Spain. Russia will accept a new identity as a respectable, world-order-supporting middle power, and the Russian people might well find this acceptable. Much will depend on a host of contingencies including economic recovery, democratization, and the wisely conceived and executed foreign policies of important outside interlocutors. Nevertheless, the future will still be one in which whatever remains of the Soviet Empire might attempt to break away in further drives for self-determination, Chechnya being only one case in point. At the same time, and also true to historical form, the symbolism of the former Soviet empire will probably continue to influence the structure and play of Russian politics and foreign policy. Old imperialists never die, and it sometimes takes generations for them to politically fade away. Calls for restoring the glory and prestige of the two-superpower world will continue to be voiced and listened to in Russian politics. Future leadership in Russia could attempt to reassert imperial control, particularly in regions of the "near abroad," even possibly relying on the use of force. Such scenarios, however, are unlikely due to the enormous costs that would be incurred in human and economic resources in conducting military operations in those areas and in addressing predictable tensions that would follow within Russia itself. For similar reasons, reasserting a global imperial vocation is also an unlikely Russian pathway into the future: It is interesting to note that few historic empires, once dissolved, have ever returned to full glory.

The American experience best fits the model of slow decline and piece-meal fragmentation, and a most plausible future for the American empire is one of continuing fragmentation marked by ever-lessening U.S. control over either the internal affairs or foreign policies of peripheral states. This lessening of U.S. control is being prompted, facilitated, and accelerated by increases in the relative power of the peripheral states. Not even the Philippines, South Korea, or Taiwan listen very attentively or behave especially deferentially toward the United States these days, to say nothing of Mexico, Chile, or Brazil. The histories of the post-Alexandrian Seleucid Empire, Byzantium, and Manchu China, which all recorded lessening control from the core because of increasing capabilities combined with drives for autonomy in the peripheries, are interesting analogues against which to gauge the evolution of the American empire in the twenty-first century. Each of these historical core states resisted the fragmentation of their empires at great cost and to little avail.

The good news of the 1990s was that the decline and dissolution of a modern-day empire can occur without having the former core state engage in devastatingly self-destructive behavior, as would likely have been the case if the Soviet Union had attempted to suppress the forces and reverse the course of events that Gorbachev's policies unleashed. The bad news is that the United States appears to be responding to its own relative decline in hegemony by resisting changes in ways that rehearse the experiences of empires that were unable to change gracefully. The United States has not abandoned its imperial vocation. Successive administrations in Washington—Ronald Reagan's, George H. W. Bush's, Bill Clinton's, and George W. Bush's—have endorsed the democratizing, marketizing, liberalizing, and globalizing missions of the United States, all aimed at making the world a safer place for the United States by making it ever more *like* the United States. The imperial mission continues to find considerable support among American political elites; it also resonates in the body politic. The United States has continued to demand allegiance to its ideals on the part of its allies, and it has continued to punish defectors. Ironically, the collapse of the Soviet Union and the dissolution of the Soviet empire have left America's empire the last standing. By every element of George Liska's definition, the United States surely is today the only empire still standing. This turn of events has for the moment removed interimperial relations from the agenda of contemporary world politics. But, it has also, willy-nilly, cast the United States in the role of the "single remaining superpower," and this is being interpreted in Washington as a reaffirmation of America's global hegemonic destiny. There is surprisingly little resistance to the notion of such, not even very much debate about it. In all likelihood then, the United States will continue to pursue its historically and culturally embedded imperial mission. It will face escalating costs, perhaps even to its values, the character of its society, and its way of life. But the last dinosaur will continue to dance—alone—until a new partner steps onto the floor.

CHAPTER 7

International Encounters
of Another Kind

From our perspective at the beginning of the twenty-first century, intercultural encounters should not only command the greater attention of specialists in international relations, but they should do so with a heightened sense of urgency because the dialogue between "the world and West" has already become a debate that is being engaged today in forums as diverse as the human rights organs of the United Nations, the streets of Moscow and Algiers, and the poetry corners of cosmopolitan bookstores. Several analysts, including, most notably, Harvard's Samuel P. Huntington, see the debate turning into a conflict.[1] Today, ideological extremists in both the non-West and the West welcome intercultural conflict and are apparently anxious to provoke it.

Learning from History

That Huntington's *Foreign Affairs* essay on clashing civilizations provoked controversy all over the world is all to the good. His longer study, *The Clashing of Civilizations and the Remaking of World Order*, provoked even greater controversy, and this too is all to the good.[2] Huntington's contentions and predictions are worthy of serious discussion. However, the intellectual level at which the discussion about clashing civilizations is being engaged is both theoretically unsophisticated and historically uninformed. In addition, the discussion of clashing civilizations has to date been remarkably devoid of any conceptual structuring, even in many commentaries to the point of avoiding definitions of important terms like *culture* and *civilization*. The purpose of this essay is not so much to enter into the discussion about whether civilizations will clash in the twenty-first century—although my analysis does lead to conclusions about this—but to help to conceptually frame the discussion itself.

To seek after insights into what happens when civilizations encounter one another, we need to examine history. During the last six thousand years there have been numerous encounters among civilizations and many of them have been elaborately recorded by generations of historians. However, the history of these experiences is so complex, substantively rich, and varied that learning from it requires subjecting it to a conceptual discipline. To usefully conduct a comparative analysis of civilizational encounters we need to inquire about the kinds of things that happen; the kinds of contexts, situations, or settings within which things happen; the kinds of agents or forces that make things happen; and the kinds of entities that things happen to. Doing this, we enter into Max Weber's world of creating "ideal types"— that is, heuristics or thought pictures (*Gedankenbilder*) that may serve as both guides to analysis and building blocks of theory.[3] Fashioning such building blocks is what this chapter is largely about, though it is with some trepidation that I acknowledge, along with Weber, that there is no way of knowing a priori "whether we are dealing simply with a conceptual game or with a scientifically fruitful method of conceptualization and theory-construction."[4] The test of created concepts is ultimately in their analytical usefulness.

Cultures and Civilizations

To be able to say useful things about encounters among civilizations, it is important to begin with some definitions. Since in this analysis cultures are going to be included among the key components of civilizations, it is appropriate first to clarify what *culture* means. Although there exist in the literatures of anthropology, sociology, history, geography, philosophy, and the fine arts scores of definitions of the term, two complementary and fairly commonsensical ones turn out to be the most useful for analyzing civilizations. The first defines culture as essentially everything that is implied by a "way of life." More technically, and in Philip Bagby's words, by this definition, "culture is a particular class of regularities of behavior. It includes both internal and external behavior; it excludes the biologically inherited aspects of behavior. Cultural regularities may or may not recur in the behavior of individuals, but to be called 'culture', they should recur (or fail to occur) in a regular fashion in the behavior of most of the members, and ideally in that of all of the members, of a particular society."[5] Bagby's notion of "internal behavior" includes modes of thinking and feeling, valuing, creating, and other forms of mental behavior, and this brings his definition, and others like it, close to the second widely accepted definition of culture as "shared meaning." People who share a culture find common meanings—utilitarian, social, moral, aesthetic, mythical, or sacred—in the artifacts, institutions, ideas, symbols, myths, and rituals that enter their lives. By this definition, a culture in the collective sense is a community of shared meaning. Clifford Geertz calls it a "web of significance"; Ulf Hannerz sees it defined by "a set of public meaningful forms"; Pitirim Sorokin sees a culture having "its own mentality."[6]

The second concept that needs to be defined is "civilization." Unfortunately, one of the main stumbling blocks to any cumulative understanding of civilizations is that there are no agreed-upon definitions either of *civilizations* or the components of which they are composed. The literature in the field of "comparative civilizations" is rich, though except for the writings of David Wilkinson, which will be considered shortly, and a few of the regular contributors to the *Comparative Civilizations Review,* the main body of this work is rather old. There are classics in the field dating back to Giambattista Vico's *La Scienza Nuova,* published in 1725, and these include in the twentieth century well-known writings by Nikolai Danilevsky, Pitirim Sorokin, Oswald Spengler, and Arnold Toynbee. More recent, though still decades old, are useful contributions by Philip Bagby in his *Culture and History* (1959), and Carroll Quigley in his *The Evolution of Civilizations* (1961). M. F. Ashley Montagu's collection of reviews of Toynbee's work is also valuable.[7] To immerse oneself in this literature is to learn a great deal about macro-history and the relationship between realms of human experience. At the same time, no clear image emerges of what a civilization is or of how many civilizations there are or were. In fact, there appear to be almost as many definitions and rosters of civilizations as there are analysts.

It is impractical here to rehearse the definitional debate concerning "civilization" since others have done it, and much of it is in any event irrelevant to this chapter's purpose. What most analysts agree upon is that civilizations are particular modes of human society centered in urban dwelling, and based upon economic resources and divisions of labor that (1) make urban dwelling feasible and sustainable, and (2) liberate elites from the imperatives of producing daily subsistence and thereby establish contexts for intellectually and artistically creative activities.[8] Civilizations exist in space, inasmuch as they have flourished in identifiable places and typically have geographic centers and roughly traceable cultural frontiers. Civilizations also exist in time, though usually in very extended time.

There is one important definitional disagreement among analysts of civilizations that directly affects this chapter. It concerns the cultural components of civilizations. In the analysis that follows I will look upon civilizations as cultural entities, distinguished from one another by differences in ideas, values, and styles shared among respective elites. However, to look upon civilizations as essentially cultural entities is to register disagreement with David Wilkinson, a current leader in the comparative analysis of civilizations whose very impressive work must be taken seriously.[9] Wilkinson defines a civilization as an "advanced society constituting a self-contained social-transactional network."[10] From his perspective, civilizations are clusters of people(s) who interact with each other more frequently and intensely than with outsiders and thus comprise networks for "fighting, bargaining, trading, traveling, teaching and preaching."[11] Wilkinson likens them to "state systems," although transactions within them range well beyond the political. Such transactional networks, however, are "defined and bounded" by "social bonds or interactions, and not by cultural bonds of similarity."[12] For Wilkinson, then, civilizations are not cultural entities, and we need neither seek nor expect to find cultural coherence within them or cultural differentiation between them.

While such a social-transactional definition of civilization that avoids cultural elements seems to suit Wilkinson's objectives in devising a roster of civilizations, using his method turns up many more "civilizations" than any other analyst has recognized, and it also identifies civilizations that are different from those that appear on most other lists. Wilkinson appears to be identifying social entities of some sort, but calling these civilizations and disqualifying all others identified according to different criteria may be somewhat arbitrary. It also becomes unproductive to compare Wilkinson's findings with those of other analysts, since there is basic disagreement about what constitutes a civilization and therefore nothing to compare. It is true that Wilkinson's social-transactional definition of civilizations immunizes him against having to deal with intangibles like "spirits," "souls," "myths," "ideas," "weltanschauungen," and the like, thus avoiding metaphysical dead ends. The Wilkinson definition also facilitates the search for the evolution of a global civilization because such an entity would logically result from the universal extension of transactional networks. On the other hand, the social-transactional definition also biases this search, since it would be surprising not to find human transactional networks globalizing over time. Wilkinson's definition of civilization therefore gives us somewhat more global homogenization than really exists.

Most important in the context of this chapter's analysis, by excluding cultural coherence from the definition of civilizations, Wilkinson closes off possibilities for examining the cultural impacts of intercivilizational encounters. This sets him apart not only from my main concern here, but also from most other analysts in the field of comparative civilizations who (a) do define civilizations as cultural entities and (b) are interested in the cultural impacts of intercivilizational encounters.[13] Closest to the conception of civilization as a cultural entity used in this chapter is Philip Bagby's notion of "ideas and values" being the defining and distinguishing characteristics of civilizations. According to Bagby, ideas and values are "the most inclusive of cultural phenomena ... they embrace aspects of the largest number of individual character traits and ... it is these same ideas and values which serve to integrate and differentiate our civilizations."[14] When all is said, the question of whether or not the cultural entities identified and analyzed here should be called "civilizations" will remain controversial as long as no agreed definition of the term *civilization* is available. What can be said for the selection included here—that is, the Hellenic, the Greco-Roman, the European (Western), the Russian, the Hindu (Indic), the Persian (Iranic), the Chinese, the Japanese, the Turkic, and the Aztec—is that they satisfy this study's definition of civilization. They have been identified and deeply researched as culture areas, they are intuitively meaningful as such, and they appear on most other analysts' lists of civilizations.

A civilization, then, contains a culture—that is, a community of shared meaning, usually identifiable in the mentality, way of life, and recurring behavior of an elite stratum. And, of course, the characteristic culture of a civilization is normally diffused well beyond elites! Differences in cultural content are the most important differences among civilizations. When civilizations come together, it is the artifacts, institutions, ideas, symbols, myths, and rituals of their respective cultures, along with their meanings, that are bandied. Furthermore, while culture is an attribute of a variety of human collectivities, "high" culture is a hallmark only of civilizations. It is within the social contexts of civilizations that the artifacts of given cultures attain their highest quality, artistic works their most fully developed aesthetic forms, and ideas their most systematic and elaborate expression. Fully developed civilizations have literary languages, scripts, and literatures; styles of art and architecture; systems of philosophy; codes of morality; and higher religions affirmed in sacred texts and elaborated in formal theologies. They also have writers, artists, architects, philosophers, jurists, and theologians. They have cities, academies, universities, and libraries. Civilizations have histories written by their own historians. To all of these tangibles, Toynbee adds that civilizations have "spirits," which A. N. Whitehead calls "profound cosmological outlook(s), implicitly accepted," Christopher Dawson calls "vision," and Oswald Spengler labels "soul" or "form."[15] Worldviews (weltanschauungen), senses of destiny, and illusions of exceptionalism, especially moral superiority, are also hallmarks of civilizations. Civilization-carrying elites are aware of these and of their own status; they are proud of their self-attributed sophistication and not infrequently arrogant about it.[16]

Civilizations also have life cycles. This is commonly acknowledged in the literature of world or universal history. When stripped of determinisms, metaphysics, and organic assumptions, Spengler's work remains the best portrayal of the cyclical rise and decline of civilizations.[17] Civilizations begin as cultures or, by earlier definition, "communities of shared meaning." These communities sufficiently harness their natural environments to produce the economic surpluses that make urban society feasible, sustainable, and contemplative, and aesthetic activities possible. Leisured elites proceed to reproduce their culture in the form of artifacts and ideas of ever-increasing sophistication until the institutional, intellectual, and artistic potentialities of the culture have been fully exploited and expressed. Points of full civilizational development, which are herein referred to as "mature civilizations" (with no organicism implied), are signaled historically by "golden ages" or otherwise-named eras of brilliant and multifaceted accomplishment—for example, Greece in the age of Pericles, Rome in the age of Augustus, Byzantium in the age of Justinian, India at the time of Ashoka, China under the T'ang Dynasty, Turkey in the time of Suleiman, or Europe in the nineteenth century. During its development the civilization will have expanded geographically either because others have been attracted by its culture, or because its elites have chosen to proselytize. At some point beyond its zenith of creativity, the civilization slips into relative or absolute decline as an agent of world cultural history. Some civilizations pass into oblivion.

The literature of cultural history contains any number of variations on the theme of civilizational cycles. Among the more interesting of these are Toynbee's discussion of the *renaissance phenomenon,* which complicates, but also enriches, the parabola-shaped, rise-and-decline model employed by Karl Jaspers, William McNeill, Oswald Spengler, and others.[18] Quigley offers an intuitively appealing seven-phased civilizational cycle.[19] There is also the highly intriguing analysis by Sorokin in *Social and Cultural Dynamics,* where he shows that the cultural content of a civilization may dramatically change over time, while the civilization itself continues. His case in point is Western civilization, which has successively contained several cultures of the "idealistic" or "sensate" variety.[20] It will become clearer in a moment that for the purposes of this essay, it is less important to know the variety of patterns of civilizational development than to understand that there are such patterns and that civilizations do in fact pass through phases in their cultural evolution. By the same token, that we do not yet understand why civilizations pass through cycles is certainly intellectually jolting, and it must remain prominent on our research agenda. However, this essay's inquiry into what happens when civilizations come together depends much more on understanding that there *are* civilizational cycles than upon knowing *why* there are.

Table 7.1. Varieties of Civilizational Encounter

ENCOUNTERS BETWEEN FULLY DEVELOPED CIVILIZATIONS	ENCOUNTERS BETWEEN FULLY AND PARTIALLY DEVELOPED CIVILIZATIONS	ENCOUNTERS BETWEEN CIVILIZATIONS AND OTHER KINDS OF COMMUNITIES
Greeks and Persians, second century B.C.E.	Romans and Greeks, second and first centuries B.C.E.	Northern Chinese and Southern Peoples from Han period, c. 200 onward
Hindus and Chinese, first and second centuries	Arabs and Persians, seventh century	Romans and Germanic tribes, after fifth century
Mongols and Hindus, tenth century	Carolingians and Arabs, ninth century	Byzantines and Bulgars/ Russians, ninth and tenth centuries
Austrians and Ottomans sixteenth–eighteenth centuries	Russians and West Europeans in the era of Peter the Great	Chinese and Mongols, thirteenth and fourteenth centuries
Europeans and Chinese, nineteenth century		Europeans and Africans, nineteenth century

The purpose in dwelling so long on definitions is to open an analytic pathway to comparing civilizational encounters. By establishing what civilizations are and what they are not, it immediately becomes possible to identify at least three kinds of civilizational encounters: (1) those that involve two fully developed or mature civilizations; (2) those that involve one fully developed civilization and another in an earlier stage of development; and (3) those that involve civilizations and other kinds of communities like hordes, tribes, or nations, historically categorized as barbarians. Table 7.1 lists some historical examples of the various kinds of civilizational encounters. All of them are interesting, yet quite different in their outcomes. Therefore, when one is talking about "clashing civilizations" the nature of the interacting entities makes a difference.

Agents of Encounter

Civilizations are not political entities, but they have political organizations within them that serve both to protect their cultures from alien penetration and to project them outward when motivation and opportunity converge. Such political entities are best called "empires" instead of states, because while they are generically states, they tend to be rather extraordinary ones. In his work discussed in chapter 6, George Liska defined an empire as "a state exceeding other states in size, scope, salience and sense of task," and this quite accurately identifies the kinds of states that typically protect and carry the cultures of civilizations.[21] Most civilizations have had one core empire within them—the Persian, Macedonian, Roman, Byzantine, Chinese, Gupta, Holy Roman, Arab, Ottoman, and so on—that assumed the role of protector or extender of the culture. However, both the early Greek and modern European civilizations have had, at times, more than one empire within them, though in these cases, leading imperial roles often passed from one empire to another. The primary ways in which empires have attempted to extend the cultures of their civilizations have been through military conquest, colonization, forced imposition, and the suppression of aliens and their ways. Historically, such coercive measures, with a few notable exceptions like the spread of Islam via jihad, have not been very successful.

Other important carriers of culture from civilization to civilization, and from civilizations to other communities, include peddlers, merchants, and mariners; artists and artisans; monks, priests, and missionaries; teachers and scholars; scribes, translators, and printers; diplomats; slaves; concubines; immigrants; and refugees. In more recent times we would need to add journalists, managers, and media moguls. Though the comprehensive history of such peaceful communicators across civilizations remains to be written, it would not be surprising to discover that the cumulative impact of millions of such cultural agents, like the Buddhist monks who carried their religion to China in the first century, or like the resourceful Fa-hsien at the turn of the fifth century, has enormously affected the course of human cultural evolution.[22]

Looking Over the Historical Record

German Barbarians and Fallen Romans

The Belgian historian Henri Pirenne's *Mohammed and Charlemagne* was written to explain how the Arab conquests of the seventh century and the Mohammedan closing of the Western Mediterranean culturally confined Western Christendom. At the same time these events invited Europeans to develop a self-identity within their cultural confinement and to thereby step finally out of antiquity and into the European Middle Ages.[23] In developing his thesis, however, Pirenne found it useful to begin his narrative just after the fall of the Western Roman Empire, and there to examine encounters between the newly arrived Visigoths, Vandals, Alains, Burgundi, and Ostrogoths (that is, the Germans) and the permanent-resident Romans who naturally constituted the overwhelming majority of the population in the conquered domains. What happened over the course of the sixth century was that the Germans were almost completely "Romanized"—in language; religion; social, political, and juridical institutions; dress; and modes of living—as they assimilated to the resplendent conquered culture. Culturally speaking, Roman antiquity did not end with the fall Rome. "As a matter of fact," Pirenne notes, "a minority can transform a people when it wishes to dominate it effectively. But the Germans wished neither to destroy nor to exploit the Empire. Far from despising it, they admired it. They did not confront it with any superior moral strength. The truth is that in every respect they had much to learn from the Empire. How could they resist its influence?"[24]

Conquering Romans and Conquered Greeks

By the turn of the second century B.C.E. at the end of the Second Macedonian War, Roman armies had extended Roman suzerainty over much of the Aegean Peninsula, and by 147 B.C.E. Roman control over Greece was complete and the political age of the eternally squabbling Greek city-states was over. The Romans at this time retained a tradition-driven martial culture strongly influenced by a public morality of honor, loyalty, patriotism, political participation, and preoccupation with prowess on the field of battle.[25] Rome in this Ciceronian age was a civilization in early evolution: cities dotted the expanding empire, but Roman preferences and pleasures remained in the countryside; the Latin language had literary potential, but Virgil, Horace, and Ovid had not yet appeared; the great feats of architecture and engineering were for the future; sculptural accomplishments awaited Greek stimulus. The first "Roman history" was written by Quintus Fabius Pictor in 198 B.C.E., tellingly, in Greek!

During the first century B.C.E. and for an indeterminate time thereafter, the Greeks won from the Romans in the classroom, studio, and amphitheater what they had lost to them on the battlefield. It is true that culturally the Romans retained their native sense of virtue, their genius for order, their forthrightness and uprightness, and their respect for undiscriminating justice. But in their evolving high culture, the Romans borrowed enormously from the Greeks. Romans imported Greek textbooks, teachers, scientists, physicians, astronomers, astrologers, philosophers by the hundreds, and slaves by the thousands. They learned from all of them to such an extent that Rome by the time of Marcus Aurelius was not only a fully developed, but also an extensively Hellenized Greco-Roman civilization. "Greek influence on Rome," M. L. Clarke observes, "is often thought of as something transmitted through books and expressed in literary imitation. It was more than this. Greek civilization was something living and pervasive, whose influence was impossible to escape. In every branch of learning the Greeks had expert knowledge, teaching experience and systematic textbooks: they taught in their own language and, conscious of the superiority of their culture, saw no reason to modify their teaching for the benefit of the barbarians of Italy who were their latest pupils."[26]

Conversion without Conquest in the Era of the T'ang

In the year 725, the city of Ch'ang-an, called Xi'an today, was the capital of T'ang Dynasty China. With over two million inhabitants, it was the largest city in the world, as well as, perhaps, the most cosmopolitan. Materially and architecturally, Ch'ang-an was one of the most splendid places in the seventh- and eighth-century world, and politically, militarily, intellectually, and aesthetically T'ang China in the seventh and eighth centuries was experiencing the full bloom of Chinese civilization. The T'ang Chinese attained peaks of creativity in poetry, painting, music, porcelain crafting, and temple architecture. Confucian-schooled officials effectively ordered a huge empire; T'ang military strategies, tactics, training, and weapons proved superior time and again. "Never before and never again," Edwin Reischauer and John Fairbank report, "did such a large proportion of mankind look to China as the ... obvious model for government and culture."[27]

While in Wang Gungwu's words the Chinese under the T'ang had an "urge to civilize," what is most remarkable about East Asian international relations in the T'ang era is that almost all of China's neighbors had a complementary urge *to be civilized* by the Chinese. Emergent civilizations in Japan and Korea in particular looked to China for instruction in government, morals, artistic forms, literary forms and themes, and the characters of the written language. Between 630 and 894 the Japanese dispatched nineteen embassies to T'ang China, tasked to thoroughly study and take back to Japan all aspects of Chinese culture. The Japanese capital at Nara was constructed on the pattern of Ch'ang-an; Japanese government and political economy were reformed to approximate Chinese practice; Japanese court life was refined and modeled on the T'ang prototype; Chinese poetry was widely read; the Confucian classics were studied, and Chinese became the literary language of Japan.[28]

What was true for Japan rang equally for Korea and other of T'ang China's neighbors; Zenryu Tsukamoto notes, "The first Tibetan government established in the seventh century, and the state of Nan-chao, founded in Yunnan around 740, were both directly inspired by the T'ang system of rule. The people of Nan-chao were the Thai, who later moved south to found modern Siam. The T'ang political and cultural pattern was even more fully adopted by the peoples to the east. ... [T]he various kingdoms of Korea had for centuries shown strong Chinese influence, and Silla, after uniting the peninsula in 668, became a veritable replica in miniature of the T'ang."[29]

The Hellenistic World after Alexander

Philip II's and then Alexander of Macedon's expeditions through the civilized world between 348 and 323 B.C.E. were in large measure just that—expeditions through the *civilized* world. The Macedonians marched first through Greece, where they temporarily subdued the ever-warring city-states and where they also became converts to and then fervent missionaries of Hellenic culture. They next took on in rapid order the Persians, Egyptians, and Babylonians, all of them mature, though declining, civilizations. Alexander then turned his armies toward regions inhabited by more tribal than civilized peoples in eastern Iran and central Asia, and finally turned south into India, crossed the Indus River, and encountered the Hindu civilization.

Alexander's political project dissipated immediately upon his death, as his empire was divided among his generals, who fought among themselves until approximately 280 B.C.E. Three great monarchies were consolidated: Macedonia under the Antigonids, Asia Minor under the Seleucids, and Egypt under the Ptolemies. Though Alexander's eventual ideal was to breed a world culture by cross-fertilizing all of the cultures he encountered on his expeditions, his initial cultural project was to Hellenize as much of the world as he could expose to the Greek way of life. This was to be accomplished by building "Greek" cities, modeled after the classical poli, by infusing them with the institutions, artifacts, and ideas of Greek civilization, by filling them with Greek colonists, and governing them in Greek manner—by Greeks. At its roots, the strategy was to diffuse culture via colonization, thereby retaining political control.

Libraries of books have been written on the Hellenization of the post-Alexandrian monarchies, and any number of lessons can be extracted concerning this ancient encounter between "the West and the rest" in Western Asia. A significant amount of Hellenization surely occurred. Yet the real significance of the grand Hellenistic cultural project is not in the extent to which it succeeded, but in the extent to which it failed.

Scholarship by Amélie Kuhrt and Susan Sherwin-White and their colleagues, published in *Hellenism in the East,* shows that in Syria at least, post-Alexandrian Hellenism formed only a thinning cultural veneer that affected relatively little of society and less and less of it as time passed.[30] In fact, as time went on, as original colonizing generations passed, and as cultural creativity in Greece itself ebbed, Persian modes, manners, institutions, and visions resurged and either reacted with or replaced Hellenic ones. This is not to say that Hellenic influence was ever fully displaced, and that somehow over a lapse of time the older civilizations reemerged exactly as they were before the Greek colonization; this could never happen. Rather, what emerged were Persian cultures recast, reinvigorated, and probably enriched as a result of their encounter with Hellenism, but newly self-confident enough to reject it. Much the same happened in Ptolemaic Egypt, the experience of which, along with the experience of conquered Persia, is examined in greater depth in chapter 8.

The Spanish and the Aztecs

Michele de Cuneo was a member of Christopher Columbus's second expedition to the West Indies in 1495. He kept a diary, a citation from which sets the somber tone of the encounter between Europeans and Amerindians:

> When our caravels . . . were to leave for Spain, we gathered in our settlement one thousand six hundred male and female persons of these Indians, and of these we embarked in our caravels on February 17, 1495, five hundred fifty souls among the healthiest males and females. For those who remained, we let it be known in the vicinity that anyone who wanted to take some of them could do so, to the amount desired; which was done. And when each man was provided with slaves, there remained about four hundred, to whom permission was given to go where they wished. Among them were many women with children still at suck. Since they were afraid that we might capture them once again, and in order to escape us the better, they left their children anywhere on the ground and began to flee like desperate creatures; and some of them fled so far that . . . they will henceforth be captured only with great difficulty.[31]

When Hernán Cortés reached the central Mexican plateau in 1519, he came upon a community that by most elements of the definition employed in this study would have to be called a civilization. The Aztecs were an urbanized people, with an architecturally magnificent, socially functional capital at Teotihuacán. City-dwelling and leisure-class lifestyles were made possible by an intensive agricultural economy. The society was occupationally specialized, highly stratified, and ordered by a theocratic state apparently legitimized by a polytheistic religion bound up with rituals of animal and human sacrifice. Such cults of human sacrifice kept the Aztecs constantly at war with neighbors, from whom prisoners were taken. The Aztecs were militarily organized and kept a proficient standing army. But their weapons were technologically inferior to those of the Spanish. As the Aztecs had no written language, they had no literature, but they apparently had a rich oral tradition that kept vital a culture-encoding mythology. The quality of their artistic creations, particularly in sculpting with precious metals, is comparable to that of other mature civilizations.

All of this the Spanish haphazardly destroyed over the ensuing three and a half centuries. A handful of priests took interest in Indian culture and learned Indian languages to facilitate conversions to Christianity, which were pursued in Spanish America with crusading zeal. Nevertheless, most Spaniards were in Mexico primarily to extract its wealth by exploiting its inhabitants. This, too, they pursued with crusading zeal. By the end of the eighteenth century, some twenty-four million Indians in Mexico had died

either as a result of massacre, brutal treatment, or enslavement; from dec-
imating European diseases; or from privation and starvation that resulted
from the destruction of their economy. As Tzvetan Todorov notes, "If the
word genocide has ever been applied to a situation with some accuracy, this
is here the case."[32] Monuments, temples, and public buildings were razed
and Indian cities were left to fall into decay while new Spanish settlements
were developed. Simón Bolivar noted in 1819 that even the Indian people as
a race had largely vanished over the course of the Spanish conquest and colonization: "[T]he native population has disappeared. Europeans have mixed
with Indians and the Negroes, and Negroes have mixed with Indians."[33]

Ottomans and Europeans

From somewhat before the accession of Suleiman to the sultanate in 1520 to
some time after the breaking of the second Turkish siege of Vienna in 1683,
two fully developed civilizations—respectively propelled and protected by
two empires, the Ottoman and the Hapsburg—stared at one another ner-
vously. Though the wars of religion had yet to be fought and the modern
state system had yet to emerge, Europe in the early 1500s was passing out of
the darkness of the latter Middle Ages and gaining the cultural heights and
fruits of the Renaissance. Ottoman Turkey during this era was approaching
the outer limits of its geographical extension, and attaining the historical
zenith of its ability to consistently find Sultans of outstanding talent. At this
time Turkey was still relatively, though no longer absolutely, advantaged
militarily on land and sea. Culturally, sixteenth-century Turks fervently adhered to the teachings of their Islamic religion, from which almost all social
relations evolved. They celebrated their religion with marvelous creations
of mosque architecture that "glorified in tangible form the religion of Islam
and the spread of its civilization over a world where the religion of Christ
had beforehand reigned supreme."[34] Turkish design and literary impulses
during the era of Suleiman continued to be strongly influenced by Persian
and other eastern modes. The Ottoman was an oriental civilization.

Not only during the reign of Suleiman but throughout most of the seven-
century encounter between the Ottomans and the Europeans, there was
a peculiar contradiction between intercultural relations within the Turkish
civilization and intercultural relations between it and neighboring European
civilization. Constantinople remained throughout the Ottoman centuries
one of the most cosmopolitan cities in the world, and the empire itself was
an ethnic and religious congeries, within which, save for occasional fits of
sultanic pique, diversity was respected and protected. On the other hand,
with regard to the outside world, and particularly the *Christian* outside
world, the foreign policy of the empire up to the late seventeenth century
was military confrontation, and thereafter political-military immunization
through the manipulation of the European balance of power. Culturally, the

Turkish attitude toward Europe was one of disdain and disinterest. Christian antagonists were dubbed "infidels" and "devils." European art treasures (and artisans) were carried away as booty after military campaigns in the Balkan marches. But little interest or effort was apparently expended in attempting to understand Western culture. When compelled after their military decline in the seventeenth century to begin to deal regularly with Europe via diplomacy, the Turks "traditionally aloof in their attitude to the foreigner, ... were now obliged to organize a foreign service" but "few Turks at this time ... had any knowledge of European languages or indeed any appreciable experience of the outside world."[35]

The aloofness was mutual, for the crusading impulse remained entrenched in Christian mentality and the era of learning from the Mohammedans that had contributed to Europe's twelfth-century renaissance was over. There was no longer very much interest in learning from the East, nor, save in Venice perhaps, was there much linguistic or other expert ability to do so. In addition, there was in sixteenth-century Hapsburg Europe a grave anxiety about the "Turkish menace," a readily recallable history of calamitous defeats at Turkish hands, as at Mohacs in Hungary in 1526, and the (accurate) understanding that Suleiman aimed to surpass Alexander at world-empire building. Even at the folk level, anti-Turkish sentiments were reflected in the Hungarian expression, "[N]o matter what disaster strikes, more was lost on Mohacs field," or the sixteenth-century German doggerel depicting Suleiman:

> From Hungary he's soon away
> In Austria by break of day,
> Bavaria is just at hand,
> From there he'll reach another land
> Soon to the Rhine perhaps he'll come.[36]

The Bactrian Roundabout

Located in the basin formed by the flow of the Oxus and Jaxartes Rivers in what is today northern Afghanistan, Bactria, circa 350 B.C.E., was a frontier province of the Persian empire. As a result of Alexander's conquest, Bactria was made a Greek colony, and, after breaking away from the post-Alexandrian Seleucid monarchy around 250 B.C.E., it became an autonomous Hellenic state that survived until 55 C.E. During its history, Bactria expanded southward from its capital at Aï Khanum and gained control over a large portion of what is today northern India.[37] One theme in Bactria's evolution pertinent to this analysis is that this Greek eastern outpost, though it remained Greek longer than some others, also eventually lost its Hellenistic veneer. Its first ruler, Diodotus, was culturally Greek in every respect; its last ruler, Menander, was a convert to Buddhism, much more Eastern than Western in culture.

But what is more significant at this point in the analysis is that Bactria constituted what Toynbee identifies as a *cultural roundabout*. Such roundabouts are geographic locations "where traffic coming in from any point of the compass can be switched to any other point in a great number of alternative combinations and permutations."[38] What can happen within such regions is a mixing of cultures to produce hybrids of great originality, even entirely new embryonic civilizations. Otherwise, the roundabout regions can serve as conduits linking civilizations by transferring artifacts, ideas, and institutions. Toynbee saw Bactria serving as a cauldron of cross-fertilizing cultures, from which emerged the Mahayana Buddhism that was later transported cross Central Asia to China and eventually to Japan. Bozeman also saw Bactria functioning as a cultural transfer station, "the crossroads of the Indian, Chinese, and Hellenic culture realms," through which elements of each of these cultures reached each of the others.[39]

From occidental perspectives of the time, Bactria in 200 B.C.E. was at the outer fringe of the civilized world. But in more a universal perspective and looking back from our time, Bactria can be seen as being at the very center of human civilization, almost exactly midway among India, China, and the Mediterranean. Its population was culturally diverse, and its leaders, to maintain their legitimacy, therefore had to become increasingly cosmopolitan. As Adda Bozeman notes,

> This Greco-Bactrian "land of the thousand cities" was not only a proving ground for the compatibility of Greek and Asian institutions. Until the very end of its political existence it was also a junction of the land routes from China and India to the West and a meeting place of numerous and dynamic nations and cultures. As such, it was a filter through which artistic styles, religious forms, and political ideas radiated in all directions. In the first century B.C. Greek, Iranian, and Chinese products and art-motifs met in distant Mongolia. We know also that Hellenism exercised a certain artistic influence on the art of Siberia, and that the Greek calendar, as used in Bactria, swept Asia west of India. On the vaster stage of international relations the Greco-Bactrian state was a bridge, both geographically and culturally, between the Mediterranean and Far Eastern realms, notably China and India.[40]

What Happens When Civilizations Meet?

Naturally, the episodes of intercultural and intercivilizational encounter described here were much more complex than these abstracted accounts reveal. However, the particular encounters described were selected because they are representative instances of more generally recurring phenomena, and what was abstracted from them were elements of historical experience about which it may be possible to generalize. Each of the episodes discussed involved encounters between *civilizations at various levels of development or maturity,* including at least one variety of encounter between a civilization and a noncivilization. Each episode also involved a *flow of cultural influence,* usually a directional flow, but in at least one case a nonflow. The cases all produced *outcomes:* in fact, the seven cases produced seven different outcomes. All of the cases also have identifiable analogues, thus suggesting that they may be representative instances of more generally recurring phenomena. Table 7.2 is constructed to summarize the discussion to this point, and to frame further analysis.

The Significance of the Cases

The episode of the Germans and the Romans is a rather interesting case of the phenomenon of *absorption.* Throughout ancient and medieval history "barbarians" of various ilks, either driven by pressures jeopardizing their own survival or whipped on by fanatical, charismatic chieftains, assaulted advanced civilizations when the protecting empires of such civilizations weakened.[41] The political result of such encounters between civilizations and hordes frequently was the destruction of the protecting empire, the plundering of the material wealth of the civilization, the massacre of a portion of the population, and the subjugation of the remainder under a militarily superimposed, culturally alien elite. However, the cultural result of such encounters, particularly when the aliens stayed for a long time, was frequently the absorption of the aliens into the culture of the vanquished civilization, and the ultimate abandonment by them of whatever cultures they carried with them at the time of their initial occupation.

Of course, analogies are never perfect, and particular instances have to be carefully examined to ascertain whether given analogies hold at all. But bearing this in mind, the case of the Germans and the Romans seems analogous to the case of the Macedonians and Greeks after Philip II's descent into Greece and conquest in the middle of the fourth century B.C.E.; it is also analogous to the encounter between the Chinese and their Mongol conquerors in the thirteenth century, and to the encounter between the Chinese and the Manchus during the seventeenth to nineteenth centuries.

In the episode of the Romans and Greeks after the Roman conquests of the second century B.C.E., an emergent civilization encountered a mature civilization, resulting in a hybridization that created what we call today Greco-Roman civilization. Much that the Romans encountered in Greek culture

Table 7.2. Encounters, Results, and Analogues

ENCOUNTER	LEVELS OF CIVILIZATION INVOLVED	MAIN DIRECTION OF CULTURAL INFLUENCE	MAIN RESULT OF ENCOUNTER	ANALOGOUS ENCOUNTERS
Germans and Romans, c. 600 C.E.	Noncivilization versus civilization	Romans→ Germans	Absorption	Macedonians and Greeks, c. 300 B.C.E. Mongols and Chinese, c. 1200 Manchus and Chinese, 1700–1900
Romans and Greeks, c. 200 C.E.	Emergent civilization versus mature civilization	Greeks→ Romans	Hybridization	Carolingians and Moslems, c. 800
T'ang Chinese and Japanese/Koreans, c. 700	Mature civilization versus emergent civilization	Chinese→ Japanese/ Koreans	Hegemony	Europe and Russia, c. 1700 Europe and Japan, 1876+
Hellenes and Persians/ Egyptians, c. 300 B.C.E.	Mature civilization versus mature civilizations	Initially: Hellenes→ others Later: others→ Hellenes	Rejection/ resurgence	Europeans and Indians, 1700–1994
Spanish and Aztecs, 1500+	Mature civilization versus mature civilization	Spanish→ Aztecs	Genocide/cultural obliteration	Moslems and Hindus, c. 1100–1600
Ottomans and Europeans, 1300–c. 1870	Mature civilization versus mature civilization	Little appreciable flow of cultural influence	Isolation, insulation, suspicion, hostility	Japanese and Europeans, c. 1600–1850 Russians and Westerners, 1900–1990
Bactria, c. 100 B.C.E. 200 C.E.	Mature civilization versus myriad cultural influences	Mixing and merging of flows from many directions	Creative cross-fertilization	Syria, 200 B.C.E.–600 C.E. Southeast Asia New York City, Hong Kong, London, Paris, c. 2000

excited and attracted them, and they adopted it. But by the time that this encounter occurred, the Romans had already put in place many of the building blocks of a civilization of their own—that is, a written literary language, a religion suited to an urban-based existence, and a mythology buttressing political legitimacy. What they took from the Greeks, then, were elements missing from their culture—such as a moral philosophy, sophisticated aesthetic modes, and science—that when adopted and adapted significantly enriched Roman civilization.

Encounters analogous to the Greek-Rome episode include the interactions between Arab Muslims and European Christians in the Carolingian and succeeding Frankish eras, after Muslim expansion was halted at Tours in 732 and up through the time of the Crusades. During this period Arab civilization was more advanced than European, though in Europe some elements of what Spengler was to depict as "Faustian" civilization were already in place. Nevertheless, up to about 1300, the direction of cultural flow was decidedly from the Arabs to the Europeans, as for example with the influence of Greek philosophy via Arabic translation on Christian thinking—from Aristotle through Averroës to Thomas Aquinas—and numerous other Arab intellectual influences on Europe's twelfth-century renaissance. Even more directly analogous to the Roman-Greek encounter was the experience of the Arab conquest of North Africa, Iberia, Persia, and the Levant in the seventh century, where a nomadic culture invigorated by a powerful, messianic religion combined with aggressive military prowess transformed itself, in the course of two centuries, into a remarkable civilization by absorbing the best of what the ancient civilizations it overran had to offer.[42]

The episode of the T'ang Chinese encounter with the emergent Japanese civilization in the seventh century may not have any close analogues. Neither of these peoples overran the other, yet the emergent civilization, Japan, borrowed from the culture of the more mature civilization, China, deliberately, appreciatively, systematically, and very extensively, with the result that China attained a cultural hegemony over Japan, vestiges of which (for example, in the written language), persist even to the present. China's encounter with Korea was somewhat more conventional inasmuch as there was conquest and imposition, but still, the most ambitious and systematic cultural borrowing, and the most intense period of cultural hegemony, occurred during the T'ang era, when Korea was united as Silla and politically autonomous. Episodes structurally similar to these T'ang Dynasty cases include Russia's seeking Western culture during the time of Peter the Great, and Japan's turning to the West after the Meiji Restoration. However, in both of these later episodes, cultural borrowing was more constrained because powerful indigenous reactionary forces prevented deep penetration from the outside.

The experiences of the Hellenes, Egyptians, and Persians in the post-Alexandrian era are cases of mature civilizations encountering mature civilizations. The conquest and colonization of one mature civilization by another can be accounted for by the relative military capabilities of the respectively associated empires. At the time of the Alexandrian conquests, Macedonia was more powerful militarily than Persia, Egypt, or Babylon. But while conquest and colonization were accomplishable, Hellenization was not. The ultimate result was the *rejection* of alien hellenic culture and the *resurgence*, though with modification, of ancient indigenous ways.

We need not search long or hard for analogues to these episodes of failed colonization. Western civilization encountered the mature Islamic, Hindu, and Chinese civilizations of the non-West from the sixteenth through the twentieth centuries, conquered them in consequence of the superior power of the empires associated with Western civilization, and colonized them. Not a few observers fully expect a twenty-first-century rendition of "rejected Hellenism" in the form of "rejected Westernism." While the most recently outspoken of these observers is Samuel Huntington, one of the most eloquent is Will Durant, who wrote in 1935, "At this historic moment—when the ascendancy of Europe is so rapidly coming to an end, when Asia is swelling with resurrected life, and the theme of the twentieth century seems destined to be an all-embracing conflict between the East and the West—the provincialism of our traditional histories, which began with Greece and summed up Asia in a line, has become no merely academic error, but a possibly fatal failure of perspective and intelligence. The future faces into the Pacific, and understanding must follow it there."[43]

While the coming together of mature civilizations containing empires of unequal power has several times set in motion the colonization-rejection scenario, it has more rarely, but also more tragically, led to genocide and *cultural obliteration*. The episode of the Spanish and the Aztecs is one of these cases. The Islamic suppression of Hindu culture in northern India under the Moguls in the ninth and tenth centuries is another, described by Durant as "the bloodiest story in history."[44] If biblical accounts are at all reliable, there were probably additional episodes of this sort in ancient Mesopotamia. What appears to distinguish these experiences from less tragic encounters of mature civilizations are the attitudes of the conquerors toward the conquered. In instances of genocide and cultural obliteration, the alien conquerors tend to be driven by essentialistic ideologies, religious or secular, that render toleration unacceptable and intercultural learning impossible, combined with insatiable lusts for material acquisition, which together enable them to rationalize the dehumanization of their victims. The great cost to mankind from such episodes has been the removal from the course of human evolution of experiences and ideas that may foreclose cultural options for centuries, or forever.

Yet another variant among encounters between mature civilizations is the case of the Ottomans and the Europeans. Here relative military parity between respective empires proscribed conquest or colonization (or genocide). At the same time, essentialistic ideologies, mutual illusions of cultural superiority, self-satisfactions with civilizational attainment, and mutual fear all mitigated against appreciable cultural borrowing. What resulted was intercivilizational *isolation, insulation, suspicion,* and *hostility.* Such cultural "cold wars," where borrowing and cross-fertilization are eschewed, can also set back the human race morally, religiously, artistically, socially, and technologically. Easily identifiable analogues to the Ottoman-European experience are to be observed in the cases of Japan and the West during the closing of Japan from the seventeenth to the mid-nineteenth centuries, and, more recently in the encounter between Western civilization and the Russian in the twentieth century, which by midcentury was as much a cultural cold war as a political-military one.

The experience of the Bactrian roundabout seems to be one way in which the human race has managed willy-nilly to short-circuit historical obstacles of pride, prejudice, and fear that have hampered intercultural learning between and among mature civilizations. Roundabout settings and patterns of communication have made it possible for mature civilizations to encounter one another *indirectly* in cosmopolitan, tolerant, pluralistic, and non-hegemonic environments where ideas can be bandied about, institutions experimented with, forms and styles interspersed and interwoven, and hybrids and innovations concocted. The historical result of intercivilizational intermingling within and via cultural roundabouts has been *creative cross-fertilization.* Toynbee suggests that greater Syria, comprising the Levant, Palestine, Mesopotamia, and Northern Arabia in the centuries before the birth of Christ, was also a historical roundabout that facilitated the cross-fertilization of Judaic, Hellenic, and Persian cultures to produce the Christian religion in the first and second centuries and later the Islamic religion as well.[45] Others have identified Southeast Asia as the historical roundabout that integrated Indian, Chinese, Javanese, Polynesian, and Western influences to yield rather distinct cultures of present-day Vietnam, Cambodia, Thailand, the Philippines, and Indonesia.[46]

The cultural roundabouts of the twenty-first century are more likely to be places where wires meet, rather than places where caravan routes converge. World civilizations are meeting today in the cosmopolitan marketing hubs of the advanced capitalist world—New York City, Toronto, Tokyo, Hong Kong, Frankfurt, London, and Paris—and to a lesser extent in the world diplomatic hubs of New York, Geneva, Washington, Rome, Vienna, and Nairobi.

Culturally speaking, to be in one of these cosmopoli is to a pronounced extent to be in all of them, and to be in any of them culturally is to be within a culture very different from any of the respective hinterlands. World-class cities today have a culture of their own. These may be the brewing kettles for a global civilization in the twenty-first century.

Looking across the Encounters

While remaining sensitive to Max Weber's cautioning that social scientists who seek profound generalities often end up with meaningless trivialities, there are some interesting consistencies to be noted among the different kinds of intercivilizational encounters.[47]

Civilizations Do Not Often Clash

It would appear that the most frequent outcome of intercivilizational encounters is intercultural borrowing that results in either the cultural enrichment of the borrower's civilization, or hybridization. The reason for this is that the most frequent kinds of intercivilizational encounters tend to be between civilizations at different levels of maturity. In such instances, the less mature civilization borrows from the culture of the more mature civilization. Uncivilized cultures are frequently transformed by encounters with civilizations: when barbarians overrun civilizations, the barbarian cultures are often abandoned and the barbarian peoples are absorbed into the cultures of the overrun civilizations. Cases of civilizations subduing barbarians did not come under the purview of this study, though a first impression is that when civilizations subdue barbarians, they either civilize them, enslave them, or eliminate them.

Cultural Borrowing Is Primarily Unidirectional

As noted, barbarians borrow from civilizations, and emergent civilizations borrow from mature civilizations. This is not say that there are no reverse flows of influence from lower levels of civilization to higher ones; there are. But the prevailing flow in cultural influence is unidirectional. This is because civilizations tend toward completeness, which implies solving economic problems having to do with achieving and sustaining urban modes of existence; arriving at moral doctrines that define justice and secure stable human relations; arriving at social and political philosophies that lend rectitude to patterns of governance; arriving at theologies or cosmologies that speak to issues of origin, being, death, and relations with divinities consistent with advanced or advancing levels of intellectual sophistication; arriving at sciences that address technological needs; and arriving at aesthetic tools and practices that yield beauty and insight also consonant with advanced or advancing levels of intellectual sophistication. Emergent civilizations borrow from mature civilizations those elements of completeness still lacking in their own cultures. They also borrow the blueprints for building powerful empires. Generally speaking, what makes the mature civilization attractive to the emergent one is that the former has answered questions that the latter is still asking.

Mature Civilizations Do Clash

In one sense, at least, Spengler was correct: at advanced stages of their development, civilizations tend to become hermetically sealed. In their arrogance, illusory superiority, and spiritual and material self-satisfaction, the elite carriers of advanced civilizations resist learning from each other. This is even true in instances when one advanced civilization superimposes itself upon another via the military prowess of its associated empire(s). Depending upon the relative military capabilities of their associated empires and the religious or secular myths of their cultures, direct encounters between mature civilizations tend to yield either colonization, which is often culturally unsuccessful; mutual insulation; or genocide. By contrast, indirect encounters between mature civilizations mediated through cultural roundabouts have proven historically to be integrative and by and large rewarding to humankind overall.

Advanced Civilizations Are Culturally Resilient

This is perhaps just another way of saying that the superimposition of one advanced civilization upon another seldom succeeds. It is also a way of saying again that when two mature civilizations engage, colonization with the aim of cultural assimilation does not work. Civilizations, once completed, are difficult to extinguish save by genocide, and even this is never complete. When suppressed, civilizations tend to rest latent, but their cultures remain alive in languages, myths, social relations, historical narratives, books, monuments, and religions. With suppression removed, civilizations reconstitute themselves by reinstalling their culture-carrying elites. Reconstitution, however, is always with some modification because human culture is evolving and so too must the cultural contents of civilizations evolve if they are to remain purveyors of meaning.

The Empires Associated with Civilizations Drive Intercivilizational Relations

Historically, the most consequential intercivilizational encounters have resulted from imperial behavior. Therefore, whether or not civilizations have had associated empires has influenced patterns of encounter, as has the balance of capabilities among empires associated with different civilizations.

The relative maturity of civilizations has historically had little to do with whether they were able to protect or extend themselves. But the power of associated empires, on the other hand, has had a great deal to do with the fates of civilizations. Making this point is not merely another way to "bring the state back" into intercivilizational relations. What it suggests is that only certain states, and rather few of them, have had impacts on human cultural history. Their historical significance, moreover, is not that they won or lost wars; made rational choices or irrational ones; or behaved realistically, neorealistically, or unrealistically; but that they protected or extended the civilizations with which they were associated, or they failed at this.

Twenty-First Century Encounters?

Nothing is impossible regarding intercivilizational encounters in the future. If Robert Kaplan's 1994 contribution to the *Atlantic Monthly* titled "The Coming Anarchy" is accurate, it is even possible to contemplate a new barbarism in the future, with twenty-first-century hordes again assaulting civilizations' gates.[48] What is more certain is the progressive reemergence of the non-Western civilizations suppressed under Western colonialism, which ultimately will have proven no more culturally successful than was Hellenic colonization in post-Alexandrian Western Asia. We might expect that these civilizations—the Arab, Persian, Hindu, and Chinese—will culturally reemerge with traditions, first principles, and worldviews intact, with an experientially acquired, robust anti-Westernism folded in, and with other elements modified to accommodate technological and intellectual modernity. Also foreseeable is the reemergence of Russian culture and the revitalization of Russian civilization, along with the ready rejection of Western civilization's halfhearted attempt to superimpose itself upon the Slavic east. The Japanese civilization is at full maturity, and will remain there for much of the foreseeable future. Of course, Western civilization, too, remains vital and as messianic as ever, though the differentiating cultural contents of American and European civilizations may soon no longer justify talking about a Western civilization per se.

If history can shed light on the future, then the twenty-first century world is likely to abound in mature civilizations, and, historically speaking, this could be a very dangerous situation. As we observed, encounters among mature civilizations have not been very productive in terms of pushing humanity toward heightened moral sophistication or cultural integration. Some of the encounters between mature civilizations have been tragic. Whether we shall see cultural imperialism, colonization and superimposition, or mutual insulation or genocide, come from encounters of mature civilizations in the future will depend upon the relative power and sense of cultural mission of the empire(s) associated with the respective civilizations. Beijing, New Delhi, Teheran, Tokyo, Moscow, Brussels, and Washington should be monitored closely. Kaplan instructs us to watch Ankara as well.

Still, we would be well advised to also watch future goings-on in the world-class cities, because humankind's cultural future may lie in a global civilization that is today being fashioned within these roundabouts. A twenty-first-century world civilization—with universal morality, philosophy, social relations, governance, science, art, and—who can say? even religion—may already be congealing in those places where the wires, air routes, sea lanes, markets, marketeers, priests, and poets converge.

CHAPTER **8**

Colonization and Culture in the Ancient World

The point of departure for this essay is the observation that today a forceful reassertion of non-Western cultures is occurring in many parts of the former European colonial world. Following from this, my inquiry asks three questions:

1. How is such a reassertion of non-Western cultures possible even after several hundred years of Western colonial imposition?
2. What exactly happens interculturally during colonial experiences?
3. What may eventuate from the postcolonial reassertion of non-Western cultures today?

Asked differently, and more broadly, What happens when civilizations encounter one another in colonial situations? And what follows culturally as imperialism invariably looses its political vigor?

One way to begin to answer such questions is to turn to history, because over the breadth of human experience, what is here described as *cultures encountering one another in colonial situations* has recurred numerous times. Let it be noted, however, that when I turn to history in this study I do not do so as a historian. As a scholar of international relations, and an inquirer into the intercultural aspects of relations among states and peoples, I am much more a beneficiary of historians' writings than a contributor to their field. Therefore, the events that I recall and describe are already well known to students of history, and I seek no improved or revised understanding. I propose instead to use history—here, ancient history—as a laboratory in which to closely examine episodes in human relations and perhaps to draw lessons from them.

An episode comparable to the European imperial projection outward in modern times is the first European projection outward in ancient times— that is, the Greco-Macedonian thrust into western Asia during the Hellenistic era.[1] Examining the processes and outcomes of intercultural relations during this period and interrogating them for contemporary relevance are the main concerns of this essay. Politically, the Hellenistic era extended roughly from 331 B.C.E., when Alexander the Great defeated Darius III at Gaugamela and extinguished the Persian empire, to 30 B.C.E., when Cleopatra VII committed suicide as the Roman Octavian entered Alexandria and the Ptolemaic empire collapsed. Culturally, the Hellenistic era lasted considerably longer, as Greek cities established in Western Asia struggled to maintain their distinctiveness and as rulers in Parthia, Bactria, and other entities in the East continued to identify as "philhellenes." Greek remained the language of government, literature, and religion in Byzantium until its fall in 1453, though the Hellenic way of life had disappeared from Constantinople long before this, as well as from almost everywhere else that the Greeks had once been in western Asia.

Setting the Historical Stage

Between 359 B.C.E., when he ascended the throne of Macedonia, a kingdom located to the north of the Aegean peninsula, and 336 B.C.E., when he was as- sassinated, Philip II conquered, consolidated, and subjugated the Greek city states to his south, thus establishing a Macedonian Empire. Culturally, the empire remained Greek, and the polis and its associated way of life remained emblematic. Philip II was succeeded by his son Alexander, who acted upon his father's ambition to defeat the proximate and powerful Persian empire. In this Alexander probably sought retribution for previous Persian invasions of Greece and for the Persian subjugation of Greek cities in Asia Minor. Less generous accounts of his motives, however, attribute Alexander's empire building more simply to a primal lust for conquest.[2] By 326 B.C.E., Alexander the Great had not only overrun the vast Persian realm, which extended from Egypt in the west to Bactria and Sogdiana in central Asia, but he had in addition penetrated India to the Indus River. After Alexander's death in 323 B.C.E., when the main concerns of this study historically commence, a forty- year struggle for succession carved three Greco-Macedonian entities out of Alexander's empire—the Ptolemaic empire, centered in Egypt, the Seleucid empire, which extended at its fullest from the Phoenician Coast in the west to the Jaxartes River deep in central Asia in the east and from Asia Minor in the north to the Persian Gulf in the south; and the Macedonian empire (variously named), centered on the Aegean Peninsula. For later reference it is important to note that the Seleucid Empire was a unit only to the extent that the reigning monarchs claimed jurisdiction over its total expanse. Otherwise, it consisted mainly of *Syria*, which extended from the Phoenician coast (Coele-Syria) across ancient Mesopotamia to the Euphrates River, and *Iran*, the heart of the former Persian (or Achaemenid) Empire, which extended east from the Euphrates outward toward central Asia, north to the Caspian Sea, and south to the Persian Gulf.

This study focuses mainly on intercultural encounters in two regions of this Hellenistic world, Ptolemaic Egypt and Seleucid Iran. It also gives cameo treatment to Palestine and the Jewish temple state of Judah therein, where the anti-Hellenistic revolt of the Maccabees in the middle of the second century B.C.E. was much too spectacular to be left out of a discussion of interacting cultures in this ancient world. Egypt and Iran were selected for analysis because much of the historical writing about these regions colonized by the Greco-Macedonians suggests that Hellenism, that is, the colonizers' way of life, neither took hold among the indigenous peoples, nor even remained unadulterated among the Greek settlers. Hellenism apparently had somewhat more appeal elsewhere in the conquered lands, particularly in the Syrian areas of the Seleucid empire, although this is somewhat controversial.[3]

Ptolemaic Egypt and the realms of the Seleucids were areas of extensive Greco-Macedonian colonization, which in substance consisted of (1) the founding of Greek cities, modeled on the polis, that reproduced and sustained the Greek, urban way of life on foreign soil; (2) immigration and settlement, which deposited large numbers of the veterans of the conquering armies on granted lands and encouraged similarly large numbers of fortune-seekers and others to move from Greece to the new eastern domains; (3) garrisoning, which stationed loyal troops at locations strategically selected to protect Greeks in the conquered regions from both external predators and indigenous troublemakers; and (4) exploitation, which to greater or lesser extents, depending upon local circumstances, took the form of allocating the bulk of the wealth and political power in the conquered lands to the Greco-Macedonian conquerors at the expense of most of the indigenous population.

While there is something short of full consensus among scholars concerning the identity of the colonizers of post-Alexandrian conquered domains, it is reasonably clear that the actual conquerors were Macedonians, not Greeks, and that there were definite cultural differences between these peoples. Alexander's army, for example, was largely composed of Macedonian units and its commanders were almost entirely Macedonian.[4] Similarly, the Ptolemaic and Seleucid monarchs were Macedonian and the colonial ruling classes were likewise mostly Macedonian. But, as Peter Green has reported in his *Alexander to Actium*, these were "hellenized Macedonians" inasmuch as they spoke Greek and cultivated Greek lifestyles. Moreover, the preponderance of immigrant settlers who populated the newly founded cities of the Hellenistic world were Greeks who carried their culture with them and sought to preserve it within the overseas empires. The imperial culture was Greek. "When we come to assess the ubiquitous Greek temples, Greek theaters, Greek gymnasia, Greek mosaics, Greek language inscriptions scattered throughout the oikoumene," Green notes, "we should never forget that it was the Hellenized Macedonian ruling minority and its Greek supporters, professional or commercial, that such home-from-home luxuries—not to mention the *polis* that housed them—were, in the first instance, provided."[5]

Contributors to the literature of the Hellenistic era underline that "Hellenization"—in the sense of assimilating indigenous populations to the Greek way of life—was not an aim of the Greco-Macedonian regimes, or promoting such acculturation was, at least (and with only a very few exceptions), not a high-priority consideration. Alexander the Great reportedly entertained the notion of fusing Eastern and Western cultures to form a unity of mankind. His marriage to the Iranian princess Roxanne, and his command that his officers also take oriental brides, were assumedly meant to symbolize this universalistic ideal. More practically, Alexander also arranged to have some thirty-thousand Persians instructed in the Greek language.[6] Yet, from all we know, such transcultural idealism, if not entirely mythical, barely outlived Alexander. Nearer to fact, according to Pierre Jouguet, what "Hellenization" actually meant was exploiting the native population for the benefit of the Greek colonists; confiscating land; replacing natives with Greeks in all positions of high, secular authority; encouraging immigration, particularly from Greece and Macedonia; and establishing Greek institutions wherein Greek culture could flourish—among Greeks.[7]

There was in the lands conquered by the Greco-Macedonians the constant juxtaposition of Western and Eastern cultures, which amounted in places like Egypt and Iran to the interplay of venerable, established civilizations.[8] For their part, at the outset of the colonization experience the Greeks were confident in the superiority of their culture. Initially they were just as self-assured about the inferiority of oriental cultures, and they were fully open to the idea that their colonial subjects should want to become culturally Greek. Again, there were some exceptions to this attitude, like the ban on intercultural intermarriage within the Greek cities in Egypt, and there were also some contradictions, which will be taken up later. But, in general, colonial subjects, while hardly encouraged, were nonetheless not discouraged from acculturating, if they so chose. What was required was learning the Greek language, frequenting the gymnasium and engaging there in physical exercise in the Greek manner, learning about the literary classics underpinning

Greek civilization, educating children in Greek schools, and accepting Greek gods—particularly local cults (while not necessarily abandoning gods formerly worshipped). It was to be expected, at least among the Greeks, that other more subtle traits of Greekness, like faith in the power of reason, commitment to human freedom, and moderation in temper and behavior, would follow from exposure to the socializing influences of Greek institutions.[9] Still, "the dissemination of Hellenism, when it came, was incidental rather than conscious or deliberate," and this is an important point.[10]

Processes and Outcomes in Intercultural Relations

While there is some disagreement among scholars about how deeply Hellenism actually penetrated the souls of converts, there is rather widespread acknowledgment that cultural Hellenization—deep, superficial, or otherwise—was probably the least frequent outcome of the very complex intercultural interplay that occurred in Egypt and Iran during the Hellenistic Age. Again, this was partly because the Greeks were indifferent to the assimilation of the native populations, and, as will become clearer in a moment, it was also because the colonized peoples so resented the Greeks that assimilation would likely have been rare even if it were encouraged. Relatively speaking, very few oriental peoples became culturally Greek, and Hellenization in this cultural sense diminished almost everywhere in the conquered lands over time. However, Hellenization was not the only identity-transforming or reinforcing process that was occurring in the colonized lands. What makes the intercultural relations of the Hellenistic era fascinating is that several kinds of integration and alienation appear to have been happening almost simultaneously, sometimes among different populations in the conquered lands at the same time, sometimes within the same population at different times and sometimes within the same population at the same time. At the risk of considerable oversimplification, the observable intercultural processes can be cataloged as follows.

Hellenization

Although this was not the primary outcome of intercultural relations between the Greeks and their colonial subjects, some Hellenization—that is, natives adopting Greek ways of life—did in fact take place. Most authorities agree with Michael Avi-Yonah that the Hellenized elements of the subject populations constituted only a "thin Greek veneer" on their societies, and perhaps also that Greekness constituted only a thin veneer over the thinking and behavior of the Hellenized individuals themselves.[11] Still, some natives did seek to become culturally Greek. But such Hellenization as did occur was almost entirely a class phenomenon. Those from the indigenous populations who chose to assimilate came almost universally from privileged (or formerly privileged) strata of the native populations—Egyptian official-dom, and the priestly and military-aristocratic classes to a limited extent, and the Iranian military-aristocratic strata also, to a limited extent—and they came largely from the cities. Their motives for changing their lives were no doubt complex, and we have only limited evidence to substanti-ate our speculations about them. There are indications that many of these people advanced materially, professionally, and socially after their accultur-ation, which suggests that opportunism may have been involved.[12] As Green notes, "There were intelligent and ambitious collaborators who set out to make a career in the administrative system of the occupying power . . . (and) by so doing they committed themselves to the foreign regime they served in a social no less than a professional sense."[13] Some others may have been taken with admiration for the prowess of their conquerors. Others, too, may have been enchanted by the robust, sophisticated, and liberating nature of Greek culture, for to be Greek in the Mediterranean world of the second and first century B.C.E. was to be "modern."[14] In fact, some of the modern ingredients of Hellenism, such as rationalistic thinking, Greek science, mili-tary science, and modes in art and architecture, were accepted even by those who otherwise rejected most of the rest of the Greek way of life.[15]

What is interesting, though perhaps not surprising, is that the accul-turation of some elements of the indigenous elites in the colonized lands spurred the alienation of others. Such Hellenization also widened the chasm between elites and masses, although rigid social stratification was already a signal characteristic of ancient Mediterranean society. In contemporary terms we would say that what Hellenization produced in the conquered lands was a *comprador native elite*. In the eyes of their neighbors, these Hellenized natives were seen as having sold out to the foreign oppressors, and, perhaps even more seriously in the thinking of the time, to have broken sacred laws and blasphemed against traditional gods. Because these people usually ben-efited under the colonial regime while their fellow countrymen suffered, they were often confronted with "angry contempt mixed with jealousy" and subjected to even greater local disdain than were the Greek overlords.[16] When native uprisings occurred, as in upper Egypt during the last half of the third century B.C.E. or in Palestine from 173–164 B.C.E. with the revolt of the Maccabees, indigenous zealots were quick to massacre their Hellenized neighbors.

Hellenization was fraught with trepidation for both the Greeks and the natives. To allot the natives any reasonable degree of respect when it re-mained profitable to continue to exploit them, when it was inconvenient and perhaps somewhat dangerous to share power with them, and when it was in any event difficult to think of them as anything but barbarians had to render Hellenization ambiguous for the Greeks. As Green points out, it is problematic to think about sharing a way of life with others "when you are busy conquering their territory, exploiting their natural resources and manpower, taxing their citizens, imposing your government on them and unloading their accumulated gold reserves onto the international market in the form of military loot."[17] For their part, the indigenous peoples were as likely as not to look upon Hellenization with skepticism, since there was no guarantee that prejudices against them would cease after they assumed the cultural trappings of Greekness. Or, if they saw acculturation as an opportunity to move from the class of the exploited into the class of the exploiters, they may have looked askance at the idea of joining the foreigners who were suppressing their countrymen.

Rejection and Resistance

If some few and ambitious colonial subjects admired Hellenism for its "modernity" it was more frequently the case that the arrogant, exploitative behavior of Greco-Macedonian overlords was repugnant in native eyes. Therefore, more prevalent during the period of Greek colonization, and much more culturally consequential over the long run, was a more-or-less resolute rejection of aspects of Greek culture that threatened traditional, indigenous values and institutions. Because "Greekness" was rejected, meaning was sapped from the symbols of legitimacy and the institutions of authority that accompanied colonial rule. This rejection of Greek culture was combined with a tenacious clinging to native ways. We might call this denial and resistance "anti-Hellenism" to emphasize its rejectionist aspects and to underline that it surely embodied hostility toward the Greeks and their culture. H. Idris Bell describes this as "sullen hostility"; Samuel Eddy and others see it as "hatred of the invader."[18] Anyone familiar with the intercultural dynamics of more recent European imperialism, or indeed with the "sullen peoples" of Rudyard Kipling's poetry, might find some resemblance between then and now.[19] More about this later.

Otherwise, we might think of the rejection of and resistance to Hellenistic influences as native "nationalism" to emphasize that it aspired toward the reestablishment of social and political contexts wherein indigenous cultures could flourish unrivaled and undisparaged. Here, however, it should be born in mind that nationalism, patriotism, and kindred ideologies and sentiments had distinctive meanings in ancient settings that were closely linked to godly legitimization and religious orthodoxy.[20] "Nationalism" meant supporting and enthroning kings selected by appropriate gods, or descended from them, while opposing any who lacked divine sanction. Therefore, "nationalists" in Egypt, Iran, and elsewhere during the Hellenistic period were much more likely to be religious zealots than political reformers, and their opposition to the Greek colonizers rested in a questioning of their sacred legitimacy.

The centers of resistance against Hellenism were where they might have been expected. Geographically, resistance was much more prevalent in the countryside than in the cities, or at least it was much more manifest there. It flourished more extensively and openly in regions like upper Egypt, eastern Iran, and Judea, where native inhabitants greatly outnumbered Greek settlers, and it persisted and grew in regions like upper Egypt (again) and Persis, which lacked goodly numbers of Greek-founded cities. Socially, resistance against Hellenism simmered in traditional temples, among the priestly classes like the Magi of Persia, among the aristocratic and military classes of the conquered lands who had been discredited and then impoverished by the Greeks, and among the displaced officials and scribes of the former regimes—that is, "from those people who had been a part of or close to the dynasty,"[21] and to some extent from peasants yoked by the economic policies of exploitative Greco-Macedonian kings.[22] Needless to say, none of these groups anywhere in the conquered lands could be identified as *wholly* anti-Hellenistic, since the penetration of Greek culture tended to fracture indigenous classes by splitting off collaborators from rejectionists. On balance, however, there appears to have been much more resistance to Hellenism than there was conversion to it, so we may conclude—with Ehsan Yarshater—that, regarding indigenous elites at least, anti-Hellenism, active or passive, was a sentiment shared by "a silent but hopeful majority."[23]

Indigenous cultural resistance against Hellenism was by and large passive, taking the form of the "sullen resentment" reported above. Yet there is rather copious evidence that the resistance also assumed more active forms. Occasionally it exploded into open revolt, as was the case in Egypt in 246 B.C.E. during the reign of Ptolemy III, and again in Egypt in 216 B.C.E. during the reign of Ptolemy IV. This latter rebellion, lasting from 216 B.C.E. to approximately 186 B.C.E., resulted in the temporary secession of portions of upper Egypt, and the virtual independence of these areas. When the revolt was finally put down with great brutality, the city of Thebes, stronghold of the rebels, was reduced to rubble and never permitted to be rebuilt. Pierre Jouguet's early analysis of the Egyptian revolts led him to conclude that they were of a nationalist nature and that "what roused them [the indigenous population] was the impetuosity of the conquest, the regret over lost national independence and the hate of a foreign dynasty that governed them rudely."[24] Later historians of the period, and more recently discovered source materials, show that the native revolts in Egypt were more complex because they involved intradynastic feuding and class warfare as well as rallies around indigenous symbols and challenges to alien rule.[25] Yet it is reasonably clear that the revolts were led by Egyptian priests and old-regime aristocrats and that anti-Hellenistic propaganda, like the *Demotic Chronicle* and the *Oracle of the Potter,* discussed below, fired the passions of rebel forces.[26] It is also clear that the revolt of 216 B.C.E. was linked to the success of Egyptian soldiers in the Battle of Raphia (217 B.C.E.), and that veterans of Raphia joined the revolt on the "nationalist" side. At Raphia, at the climax of the Fourth Syrian War (217–216 B.C.E.), Ptolemy IV was compelled by his weakness to use native Egyptian soldiers as frontline troops for the first time. Their fine showing in battle against the Macedonian forces of the Seleucid king Antiochus III not only gained the victory for Ptolemy, but also raised Egyptian self-confidence and inspired the Egyptian nationalism that exploded in the native revolts of 216–186 B.C.E.[27]

Then there was the Revolt of the Maccabees; this episode, which inspired two apocrypha, Maccabees I and Maccabees II as well as *The Book of Daniel,* is far too complex to be fully examined here. *The Cambridge Ancient History* introduces the circumstances surrounding the Maccabean revolt as "the classic case of a hellenizing movement, which did not penetrate the more dense strata of the population and, although it made headway among some of the aristocracy, [it] ran up against national and religious resistance with strong popular support."[28] In barest outline, the temple state of Judah, center of the Judaic religion and home of the Jews in Palestine, was taken from the Ptolemies of Egypt by the Seleucid king Antiochus III in 200 B.C.E. and granted the right to exist under Mosaic law and the rule of the high priest of the temple of Jerusalem.[29] Subsequently, however, conflict within the Jewish community in Jerusalem pitted Hellenizers, who sought to modify Judaic culture and law to make these compatible with Greek culture, against traditionalists who sought to preserve the Mosaic law and the way of life that it mandated.[30] Stated overly simply, but not altogether inaccurately, one faction of Jews welcomed Hellenism while the other rejected it. In 169 B.C.E., the Seleucid king Antiochus IV intervened in Jerusalem on the side of the Hellenizers, which earned for him the scorn of the traditionalists and demonized him ever after in Jewish history. Thereafter followed the withdrawal of Antiochus III's grant of autonomy, the abolition of the Jewish temple state, the desecration of the Temple of Jerusalem, the persecution of devout Jews, the establishment of a Greek polis on the Acra or citadel in Jerusalem, and the stationing of a Macedonian garrison on the Acra. These events incited a Jewish revolt, with active fighting commencing in 167 B.C.E. under the leadership of Matthias, a priest of a Jewish family from Modin. Upon the death of Matthias, the leadership of the rebelling Jews was assumed by his son Judas Maccabaeus. The Revolt of the Maccabees was fought with great ferocity and atrocity owing to the religious zeal driving it. The revolt went on nearly continuously until 134 B.C.E. when the Hellenistic community in Jerusalem was finally eliminated.

The Revolt of the Maccabees, like other indigenous risings in the conquered lands, was driven by anti-Hellenistic propaganda. *The Book of Daniel*, for example, was most likely written between 167 and 164 B.C.E. by a Jewish author (or authors) who, according to one interpreter, "felt revulsion for the ways of Hellenism and the tyranny by which it was imposed upon the Jews."[31] The text was intended to inspire those in rebellion against the Seleucid regime to fight on. It prophesied the end of the "Syrian" empire, the death of the "evil king," and "the Temple . . . restored."[32] Prophetic writings similar to *The Book of Daniel* were widely circulated in the conquered lands during the Hellenistic period, and they had great appeal among religiously devout peoples who acknowledged the powers of prophets and believed in oracles and legends. The writings were essentially items of anti-Hellenistic political propaganda, sometimes bluntly referring to the Greeks as "bringers of Chaos and Unright," as "Demons with Disheveled Hair," or as "dreadful monsters."[33] However, the writings were usually immersed in religious symbolism because theology and political theory were thoroughly intertwined. Their common themes concerned the illegitimacy of the Macedonian kings, the need to regain native rule to guarantee social order, and the need to regain native rule to protect indigenous religions. The writings were intended either to fire revolt, as in Egypt or Judea, or, as in Iran, to counsel patience and passive resistance.

Circulating around the time of the native revolts in Egypt were prophecies contained in the *Demotic Chronicles* and the *Oracle of the Potter*, which, with only slight veiling in metaphor, professed contempt for the alien rulers and their ways, hatred especially for their city of Alexandria, and the eventual overthrow of their regime.[34] During the same period Egyptians repeated for one another a heritage of legends such as the "Sesostris Legend," the "Ramses Legend" and the "Osiris Legend," which according to Samuel Eddy, had in common "an Egyptian hero, greater than Alexander, [who] was true king because he ruled for the benefit of his subjects, and thereby fulfilled the Egyptian ideal of kingship emphasized from the Middle Kingdom onwards."[35] In the Seleucid empire at the same time, there also existed an apocalyptic literature—*The Sibylline Oracles,* the *Oracle of Hystaspes,* and the *Bahman Yasht,* for example—that was also essentially anti-Hellenistic propaganda. A standard prophecy foresaw Iran regaining world empire after expelling the Greeks. As Yarshater notes, "Literature of protest and apocalyptic prophecies of the same kind were produced in other parts of the Middle East under Greek domination, and folk-histories of local and national heroes were elaborated and enhanced as a reaction to the alien rule."[36]

The majority of people in the conquered lands also rejected the religion of the Greeks. The significance in this should not be underestimated because in the context of the time, all legitimacy, order, and justice were believed to follow from godly injunction. To reject the authenticity of a deity was to reject the way of life connected with its worship. Indigenous religions continued to thrive throughout the Hellenistic era, and except among the Hellenized natives, who accepted Greek gods and were scorned by their neighbors for this, Egyptians, Iranians, Jews, and others clung to their traditional religions. "The Iranians did not succumb to the charm of the Greek gods," the *Cambridge History of Iran* reports. "Syncretism was no more than verbal."[37] Instead, the Zoroastrian supreme deity Ahura Mazdā and his fire temples continued to focus Iranian religious life, and Alexander was portrayed in the Zoroastrian Pahlavi literature as "as the destroyer of fire-temples, the burner of the holy scriptures, the murderer of the magi."[38] Meanwhile, in Egypt, a need for legitimacy, and the apparent lack of appeal of Greek gods among the Egyptians prompted Ptolemy I to establish the cult of Sarapis, a composite deity with both Greek and Egyptian attributes who, however, assumed a form, persona, and ritual that were distinctly more Greek than Egyptian. Brady tells us that "the cult of Sarapis turned out to be eminently successful as far as the Greek population was concerned." But "Sarapis was unknown to the priests and the Egyptian population."[39] What the Jews thought of the Greek gods has already been reported.

Resistance to Hellenization in the conquered lands was also registered in countless more subtle ways throughout the period of colonization. Iranians, for example, clung to the Zoroastrian calendar, which dated *their* national history, and they refused to abandon the Aramaic script, even though transcribing the Iranian language using the Greek alphabet would have been much simpler. In Egypt, the demotic tongue continued to be the language of the temple, in part, perhaps, because it was inaccessible to the Greeks. Manifested in countless ways, cultural resistance, then, was one very pronounced response to Greco-Macedonian colonization during the third century B.C.E. The preponderance of evidence suggests that it was a very successful response, inasmuch as most of the indigenous population of the conquered lands did not choose to Hellenize and native cultures flourished in the face of, or even perhaps because of, the Greek conquerors' derision and distaste. "However great the difference in technical ability between victor and vanquished," Avi-Yonah has observed, "the latter in the course of time will always find the means to bridge the technological gap." "Unless the conquered are liquidated physically," he continues, "the defeated will at some moment overcome the shock of the lost war and try to resist on the cultural plane."[40] The ancient Egyptians and Iranians certainly tried.

Indigenization and Orientalization

Rejection and resistance were, however, only initial cultural responses to the Hellenistic imposition. As it turned out, rejection and resistance in the short term contributed to the later reascension of indigenous cultures and the decline of Greek forms.[41] In many of the conquered lands indigenous religions, traditional ways of life, traditional art forms, native languages, native literary genres, native social and political institutions, and native rulers and dynasties eventually reemerged and prevailed again. Naturally, but interesting in the context of comparing ancient and contemporary experiences in decolonization, the native cultures did not reemerge in pure, precolonial forms after the encounters with Hellenism. The interplay of cultures during colonialism made impacts and bestowed legacies; Greek as an official language remained in usage in some principalities up to the fifteenth century; Greek learning, for example, was incorporated into many national traditions with its Hellenistic origins often obscured; other cultural borrowings were adopted and adapted in areas where Greek ways were recognized and accepted as superior. But Hellenism as a way of life—via the polis, the gymnasium, classical education, the Olympian gods, Homeric values, cold rationalism and freedom of the human spirit—was overwhelmed in the reflourishing of indigenous cultures, which was already under way in the conquered lands in the second century B.C.E.

It is important to distinguish between *indigenization* and *orientalization*. Indicative of the former in the conquered lands was an engulfing of Hellenistic society by native society, which typically had the effect of turning Greek settlements and cities into isolated enclaves of Hellenistic culture surrounded and besieged within indigenous cultural areas. Except within their walled cities, the Greeks were vastly outnumbered by the natives, and this situation worsened for the settlers as time went on. The stream of immigration from Greece and Macedonia diminished to a trickle during the second century B.C.E. and ultimately dried up. In their enclaves, the Greeks tended to resist the ways of their indigenous neighbors, sometimes with considerable tenacity, as was apparently the case in Egypt after the native revolts during the second century B.C.E. and even more in Iran near the end of the Seleucid reign and into the Parthian period.[42] Here, initially at least, the Greek settlers were not orientalized in the sense of being assimilated to the native culture; they were rather isolated and marginalized and left to culturally wither in alien environments, as usually happened over the space of time. Yarshater, for example, has found that in many parts of the Seleucid Empire, "the Greek settlements and cities were only islands in the Iranian Sea," to which Avi-Yonah adds that "the colonists were too few and too distant from the main body of Hellenistic culture, to be able to spread Hellenism among the natives... they had quite enough trouble to keep up their own Hellenism, and in the end... were submerged by the Oriental flood."[43] After 141 B.C.E., with the imposition of Parthian rule from the Euphrates River eastward, Greek cities and settlements in what had been the eastern Seleucid empire no longer enjoyed even the succor of a Greco-Macedonian royal house, and indigenization consequently proceeded more rapidly. Indigenization, then, had much more to do with natives reclaiming their own cultural space than with natives converting Greeks.

Orientalization, on the other hand, had much more to do with transforming the cultural identities of the Greeks. The slowing of immigration from the Greek and Macedonian homelands not only affected the demographic ratio of settlers to natives, but also cut off the flow of cultural innovation, vitalization, and inspiration, and this left settler communities susceptible to orientalization. In many areas in the conquered lands, and particularly in places where Greeks and natives intermixed outside of the Greek-founded cities, the Greeks assimilated to native ways. Such orientalization was spurred by intermarriage—again, particularly outside the walled cities, where physically and environmentally over time it became more and more difficult to "stay Greek." For example, with regard to Egypt, Michael Rostovzeff has observed that, "the Greeks as the dominant nation tried to organize their new life in the new places *a la grècque*. . . . But the up-country Greeks were living outside the atmosphere of the *polis*. . . . The greater part of the people around them were Egyptians. . . . Of course in the first generation the children talked Greek and received a Greek upbringing; without that they would not have felt themselves at home in the privileged class. But they, and still more their children, very likely by a half-Egyptian mother, were already only half Greek and the Egyptian cast of mind was nearer to them than that of their fathers."[44] To this Green adds that orientalization was also in some instances and aspects a class phenomenon more prevalent among the Greek lower classes, who mixed more frequently and intensely with the native populations: "Such assimilation as took place tended in the first instance to be among the illiterate or culturally indifferent lower classes; and here it was the alien Greeks, who, by intermarriage and religious syncretisim, slowly Egyptianized, a pattern that repeats itself elsewhere in the *oikoumene* from the second century onwards."[45]

But orientalization was not a lower-class phenomenon only. An important index of the orientalization of the Greek communities was the increasing appeal of oriental gods, first among settlers in the countryside and later even among the ostensibly Hellenistic royal households. Where, for example, the Greek-invented deity Sarapis failed to attract much following, "Isis and Harpokrates, the more Egyptian members of the triad, were infinitely more popular with the mass of worshippers, and Sarapis himself gradually tended to revert to the character of Osiris, the original Egyptian consort of Isis."[46] "The Hellene," Pierre Jouguet has observed, "came to be seduced by the pomp and the rituals of Egyptian religion, of which the myths, from well before the Macedonian conquest, appeared to him to secret within them a

profound wisdom."[47] Respect among Greeks for Egyptian gods also grew
after the strong Egyptian showing at the Battle of Raphia, because, during
this epoch, winning on the battlefield signaled the superior power of the
victor's gods. In an intensely religious age, evidence of conversion must be
taken as a strong indicator of assimilation. More subtly, but still very significantly, there was the dilution of Greek rationalism by oriental mysticism
exhibited in the increasing attraction of magic and astrology, and by a progressive leaning toward royal rituals that signified the orientalization of the
Macedonian kingships.

Greco-Macedonian colonialism also involved political and institutional
contradictions that probably made orientalization more likely over the long
run. For one thing, imperial kingship was not a Hellenistic institution (although it was not alien to Macedonian political culture, which confronted
even the Aegean regions of the post-Alexandrine world with political-
theoretical contradictions and fomented resistance). The absolute monarchies installed in the conquered lands were *oriental* forms of government.
As such, they were anathema to Greek political theorists and diametrically
opposed in structure and functioning to the Greek-idealized, self-governing
polis. They were, of course, congenial to Macedonians, and they were also
made imperative by the nature of conquest and imperialism and by the
necessities of internal order and external defense in the Alexandrine successor states. Nor even were the poli established in the conquered lands true
Greek city-states, for while they displayed the trappings of self-government,
they too were subject to royal dictates, which could override any and all
decisions taken by city councils. The monarchies of the Ptolemies and the
Seleucids were oriental despotisms—that is, centrally controlled, rigorously
hierarchical, bureaucratic states. As time went on, the Ptolemaic regimes in
Egypt became ever more pharaonic and the Seleucid regimes became ever
more Persian even in matters of ceremony and ritual. To maintain Greco-
Macedonian rule in Egypt, Jouguet notes of Ptolemy II (Philadelphos, 283–
246 B.C.E.) that he "had to revive in his person the despotic and divine power
of the ancient Pharaohs," but in doing so he had to "incarnate a personality
the most contrary to the Greek ideal, the most guilty of that 'immoderation,'
of that hubris, which, since Homer, is that great sin against the Hellenistic
gods."[48] Even more to the point is Bell's observation that within the absolute
despotisms of the Greek colonial system, "the spirit of Hellenism, the mental freedom, that fullness of humanity, that exquisite balance, that fearless,
cloudless facing of concrete reality, which are the glory of Hellas, could not
but wither."[49]

In other ways orientalization (and for that matter indigenization, also)
in the conquered lands may be attributed in some measure to failings of

the Greek culture itself. Again, religion was central, because during the Hellenistic age the influence of the gods was the accepted explanation for all facets of temporal existence. Significantly, among the Greeks, and particularly among the Greeks of the western Asian diaspora, the Hellenistic age was a time of growing religious skepticism. *The Greek colonizers doubted the efficacy of their own gods.* The social and political turmoil of the times, which must have appeared to many as a profound randomness, raised questions about the will and wisdom of the Olympians, about the meaning of events, and about the foundations of virtue, and about heavenly mandates and the legitimacy of kings. Pervasive skepticism was reinforced by the philosophers of the time, who reasoned away the need for gods. Contemporary Greek poets mocked the deities.[50] "Already in the third century B.C.E. there were symptoms of that profound spiritual malaise which marked the last centuries of paganism," Bell comments, to which Avi-Yonah adds that "the possibility of a religious acculturation of the Orient with all its tremendous consequences was prevented from the beginning by the decline of religious belief in Greece."[51] The "tremendous consequences" of which Avi-Yonah speaks involved persuading the conquered peoples that the Greco-Macedonian despots were legitimate kings. This could not be done when even the Greeks themselves questioned the sacred mandates that these kings embraced. To the extent that the Greeks doubted their own gods, they undermined their assumed right to rule. They raised doubts (including self-doubts) about their legitimacy as rulers and they lost their nerve as imperialists.

Orientalization was a good deal more pronounced in Ptolemaic Egypt than in Seleucid Iran, where indigenization was the more pervasive. Yet it certainly affected Greek settlers in the Seleucid empire as well. "This was engendered," Ghirshman points out, "by the frequency of mixed marriages and by the appeal of oriental cults and religious ceremonies. . . . Some Greeks, while not renouncing their language and institutions, nevertheless passively accepted the Iranian way of life and religion with a consequent weakening of their former intellectual interests."[52] The combined impacts of indigenization and orientalization over the course of time were, if not to obliterate, then at least to denature, much of the culture of Hellenism in Egypt and Iran (as well as elsewhere in the conquered lands). Speaking with specific reference to Iran, but in easily extrapolated terms, the *Cambridge History of Iran* reports that Hellenism in the East was largely transient in the long run, "and the spirit and outlook of Greek culture, which nourished Western civilization many centuries later, proved in the end alien to and incompatible with the Iranian way of life. So complete was this reversion," the author goes on to say, "that one can easily lose sight of the fact that Iran went through a period of Greek and Macedonian ascendancy."[53]

Greco-Macedonian Colonization As a Cultural Failure

The Greco-Macedonian colonization of Egypt and Iran could perhaps be considered a political success at least as regards the duration of the empires. Regimes descended from the Alexandrine conquests reigned in Egypt for nearly three hundred years until the Romans militarily overwhelmed them during the first century B.C.E. Such post-Alexandrine imperial governments lasted even longer in Iran until they were ultimately replaced by reestablished indigenous dynasties. Politically, then, the Greco-Macedonian imperium was relatively long lasting; this was an accomplishment.

Yet, *Greco-Macedonian colonization in Egypt and Iran clearly failed culturally.* The index of this failure was not so much the infrequency of native-to-Greek assimilation, which was neither the colonizers' objective nor the predilection of most of the natives, but rather the Greeks' inability to establish legitimacy for their rule, even by the prenationalistic standards for political legitimacy prevailing at the time. Despite living in the colonized lands for several centuries, the Greek settlers were still looked upon as aliens by their indigenous neighbors, and the colonial rulers were still considered "unrightful" kings. This was not an age when political legitimacy depended upon ethnic identities between rulers and ruled. But still—until quite late in the colonial era, when orientalization became significant—the juxtaposition of Greek and indigenous cultures tended more frequently than not to fortify cultural identities within both communities and to foment frictions. Among the indigenous peoples this cultural vitalization tended to mobilize political dissent and hence to continuously undermine the colonial regimes' claims to legitimacy and their abilities to govern in secure social environments.

Crucially important for explaining the cultural incompatibilities and the resulting frictions was the fact that, in Egypt and Iran, the colonizers' Hellenistic civilization encountered indigenous civilizations that were venerable, mature, sophisticated, and fully developed. These cultures considered "barbarian" by the Greeks were in many ways every bit as rich as the Hellenistic culture, and they were therefore not to be readily or easily disparaged, suppressed or transcended. The Egyptian and Iranian civilizations, and certainly the Jewish culture in Palestine as well, had strong religious foundations, sacred texts, highly developed cosmologies, moral and legal philosophies, political theories and political institutions, literary languages, sacred and secular literatures, and appealing and meaningful mythologies. They had had all of these attributes of mature civilization for centuries. It is true that the Egyptians and Iranians borrowed from the Greeks in some areas, but it is also true that during the last three centuries before Christ these peoples, and their elites in particular, felt that there was relatively little that they needed to borrow.

That the Egyptians, Iranians, most Jews, and many others did not accept the superiority of Greek culture was because they fervently believed in the superiority of their own. "The Persians," Samuel Eddy found, "undoubtedly felt culturally superior to the Europeans. . . . They believed in their own excellence because they had seen that their high god had given them rule of the Near East for over two centuries of time [and this] was considered to be part of the order of things."[54] For their part, not only did the Egyptians reject the Greek culture, but they too continued to believe that their own was superior. *They looked upon the Greeks as barbarians!* Egyptian civilization had an intricately manufactured cosmology that made Egypt the font of all creation and the repository of wisdom, which explained to Egyptians why their religion was true and their social and political institutions were incomparable.[55]

Cultural sanctuaries also flourished in the conquered lands during the centuries of Greco-Macedonian colonization. That is, there were places, people, and practices that preserved indigenous cultures and protected them against Hellenistic penetration or dilution. Indigenous religious institutions, for example—texts, temples, rituals, and priestly classes—persevered in fending off Hellenism while keeping indigenous religions alive and well. Not only did these institutions protect religions, but they also preserved languages and scripts, as well as legends and myths, both sacred and secular. Languages themselves, Egyptian recorded in the demotic script, Aramaic in Iran and Judea, and literatures written in these languages, plus art and architectural forms, all harked back in Egypt to Pharaonic epochs and in Iran to the Achaemenian centuries. Families—particularly old, aristocratic families—preserved customs, revered ancestors, passed inheritances, communicated in vernaculars and socialized and educated children. Women, especially, were repositories and transmitters of traditional cultures.[56] In the end, the most significant cultural sanctuaries were probably the countrysides, and there the cycles of agricultural life, which the colonizers did not greatly affect because they did not wish to, but could not greatly affect in any event since here they had nothing to offer. Commenting on the Egyptian countryside, for example, Claire Preaux has observed that "nothing essential was shattered, nor profoundly transformed by the arrival of the Greeks."[57]

Yet it was also the case that the arousal of native cultural resistance to Greco-Macedonian colonization probably had as much to do with Greek attitudes toward the natives as with native attitudes regarding the Greeks. To exploit the conquered peoples efficiently it was necessary to maintain a system of social and economic segregation, and to preserve the mentality of the subjugator among the Greeks and that of the subject among the natives. Again, the preponderance of evidence suggests that both of these conditions carried through the entire colonial era, although some amelioration may have occurred near the end of both the Seleucid and the Ptolemaic empires. That the Greeks held fast to their prejudices concerning the inferiority of the "barbarians" is well documented. Polybios "thought those [Egyptians] in Alexandria quite keen to be civilized," meaning that the Greeks considered them to be uncivilized. Strabo rejected the natives entirely, considering them to be hot-tempered and apolitical and determined in their hostility to foreigners. He thought Egyptian architecture ugly, a vain and megalomaniac display. Apollodoros repeated stories that the Egyptians sacrificed foreigners to their outlandish gods. An unknown writer, a fragment of whose work is in Athenaios, was not so harsh. He thought the Egyptians were merely drunkards.[58] None of this manifest ethnic prejudice could have enamored the Greek colonizers in the eyes of the colonized peoples. Instead, the Greeks' ethnic prejudices undoubtedly raised native cultural consciousness.

Ancient Experience: Contemporary Relevance

Cognizant of all the admonitions about the pitfalls in postulating recurrence in history, we must nonetheless acknowledge that there are rather intriguing similarities between what happened in Western Asia after the Alexandrine conquests and what has happened throughout much of the non-Western world between the sixteenth and the twentieth centuries during and after the more recent European colonization. The common theme, ancient and modern, in the most general sense, is that *cultural resistance incites political resistance.* But many other apparent similarities in intercultural dynamics between then and now may also be noted, suggesting, therefore, that conclusions about the Greek experience with imperialism during the last three centuries B.C.E. might provide interesting food for contemporary thought.

For one thing, it would appear that *the political dynamics of colonization and eventual decolonization after Alexander were neither unique nor even extraordinary.* Conquerors came and they exploited the indigenous peoples. Their reigns, while comparatively long, were nevertheless temporary. In Egypt, the Greeks were eventually displaced by more powerful conquerors. Here, one colonial regime was superseded by another—a familiar political-historical pattern. In Iran the Greeks were exhausted and overwhelmed by indigenous resistance. Here, colonization eventuated in decolonization, again a historically recurrent outcome. What is of interest is that the Greco-Macedonian colonial regimes in Egypt and Iran were never *culturally* accepted, and this contributed notably to their insecurity and in Iran at least to their eventual, and almost total, disappearance. In the eyes of all but a few colonial subjects the Greeks were never looked upon as anything more than alien overlords, and they were resented, indeed disdained, not only because their rule was harsh, but because their culture was objectionable.[59] The Greek colonial rulers could not aspire to political legitimacy because the fonts of legitimacy recognized in the Greek culture—namely, the favor of Greek gods—were not recognized in the indigenous cultures. And by contrast, the politically legitimizing forces and sources acceptable to the indigenous peoples could not succor and sustain aliens. Under conditions of cultural alienation, transcultural political legitimacy tends to be elusive, and, more than this, indigenous cultural symbols and institutions become focal points for the mobilization of political dissent and the launching pads for native rebellions.

Although mutual cultural alienation was the main theme, it was not the whole story in the conquered lands, because in much more complex fashion *the encounter of Hellenistic and indigenous cultures actually initiated a variety of different integrative and alienating processes and experiences.* Hellenization, indigenization, and orientalization occurred simultaneously in some places, sequentially in others. Indigenous rejection and resistance, although paramount, were nevertheless paralleled within some strata by conversion and acculturation. Some natives acculturated to Hellenistic culture, while some Greeks assimilated to native cultures, depending upon a host of conditioning factors. Even ruling dynasts alternatively Hellenized or orientalized their regimes in floundering quests for legitimacy. The Hellenization that did occur appeared associated with personal considerations of status and aspirations for social and economic mobility, plus perhaps the attractiveness of "modernity" associated with "Greekness." Orientalization, on the other hand—that is, "going native"—was linked both to the allure of the exotic in the Eastern cultures and to the conquerors' self-doubts about "Greekness." There were also pragmatic realizations among the colonizers that native practices and institutions better suited physical survival in the eastern environments. To some extent, then, assimilation during colonization was a bidirectional phenomenon.

As a result of the fact that some within the indigenous societies Hellenized while most did not, *the short-term cultural result of Greek colonization in Egypt and Iran was to culturally fragment the native societies, and in so doing to politically fragment them as well.* The Hellenization that did take place among the indigenous populations, although limited, was nonetheless disproportionately consequential, because in colliding with the Greeks and their culture the native societies were shattered and then reconstituted into differently reacting and adapting groups. Indigenous cultural reactions to the Greek imposition ranged from rejection to admiration, from native patriotism to treachery against native elites and institutions, from ambiguity about identity to determined clinging to native identity, and, in the crucial domain of religion, from piety to syncretism to agnosticism to atheism.

Each kind of reaction politically defined a faction, stratum, or association of the like-minded, and these groups contended within the native societies. Most significantly, the Hellenistic cultural imposition sharply divided indigenous elites into Hellenized and non-Hellenized segments, and this fostered considerable and lasting hostility between them. Greco-Macedonian colonialism more broadly divided the societies of the conquered lands into compradors and resisters, Hellenistic and Hellenized bourgeoisies on the one hand and indigenous proletariats responsive to traditional elites on the other. The major fulcrum of the culture-based politics in the colonized lands was an alliance of the moderns or modernizers resisted by an alliance of tradition bearers or otherwise motivated anti-Hellenes. These lines of political cleavage were obvious during the Revolt of the Maccabees and during most of the Greco-Macedonian colonial era in Iran. Although they were complicated and blurred by Ptolemaic court intrigues, pro- and anti-Hellenistic culture-based politics also clove colonial Egypt. Interestingly, such culture-based alliances and political cleavages also appeared in British India, in western and eastern Africa, and in the British Caribbean during the modern era of European colonialism, and they continue to influence postcolonial politics in these places today.

Over the course of time indigenous cultures in the conquered lands reasserted themselves. Indigenous cultures were never submerged or effectively repressed. They flourished in juxtaposition to the overlaid Hellenistic culture of the colonizers, and, if anything, were vitalized by the encounter with Hellenism. The eventual outcome of this encounter of Hellenistic and indigenous civilizations in Egypt and Iran was a decline of the Hellenistic culture, which ensued even while colonial regimes remained in power. Most manifestations of Greek culture eventually disappeared, particularly in Iran, after Greek political authority weakened, or, as Yarshater has observed, when the colonizers' power ebbed, Hellenism, "which had been superimposed on latent national tendencies, was cast off in a moment."[60] The "casting off" of which the historian speaks involved complex processes of indigenization and orientalization that occurred in an environment of growing indigenous self-confidence set against increasing Greek cultural malaise and isolation from cultural wellsprings. As time moved on, the Greeks in the conquered lands became less Greek as Egyptians became more Egyptian and Iranians more Persian.

There may not be a contemporary analogue to orientalization, although something of this sort may be occurring among former European settler populations that were left culturally stranded in parts of the decolonized non-Western world. But present-day indigenization is certainly happening, particularly in southern and eastern asia, in Africa, and across the Islamic world. William Pfaff calls this "moral recovery"; Benjamin Barber dubs it "jihad"; for Rhoda Howard it is "occidentalism"; Lee Kwan Yew describes it as the assertion of "Asian values"; Arnold Toynbee called it "cultural renaissance"; and Samuel Huntington sees it as "clashing civilizations."[61] The cultural aftershocks of European colonialism are being felt today wherever indigenous populations encountered colonizing Westerners in the non-Western world. Indigenous expressions of present-day postcolonial cultural reassertion abound. One conclusion, strongly endorsed and sharply voiced by many non-Westerners, is that during the era of colonization the culture of the colonizers insinuated ignoble, alien values while belittling more admirable indigenous ones. "This land of Syria gave the West a Prophet / Of purity and pity and innocence," wrote the Muslim poet Muhammad Iqbal, "And Syria from the West as recompense / Gets dice and drink and troops of prostitutes."[62] Similarly, African playwright Ngugi wa Thiong'o likens the pressing of European modes, values, and ideas onto colonial peoples to the destructiveness of a "culture bomb," the effect of which is to "annihilate a people's belief in their names, in their languages, in their environment, in their heritage of struggle, in their unity, in their capacities and ultimately in themselves."[63] Many more such postcolonial expressions are being voiced—very forcefully, for example, in the works of Edward Said, Ali Mazrui, Claude Ake, and Kishore Mahbubani.[64] Interestingly, the centers of the present-day, postcolonial tossing off of Westernism are in the lands and among the peoples where venerable, rich, established, matured cultures prevail—Persia, China, India, Pakistan, and Egypt.

If what happened in Western Asia roughly 2300 years ago can offer food for contemporary thought, we might note that the reassertion of "Egyptianness" and "Persianness" after the eclipse of Greco-Macedonian colonization so long ago was less an atavistic return to an unretrievable past than it was an expression of a new modernism. It had been both influenced by the cultural encounter with European colonialism and driven by it. If some analogue of what happened then is indeed happening now, then the homogenization of cultures widely associated with globalization, Westernization, and liberalization may not be the cultural order of our day;[65] nor may cultural confrontations be as irrelevant to twenty-first-century world politics as the globalizers are choosing to believe.

CHAPTER 9

Myth, History, and Morality

The publication in 1986 of William McNeill's *Mythistory and Other Essays* rekindled interest in the notion of public myths and their social impacts. Myths, according to McNeill, are publicly held beliefs that unite peoples, comfort them by alleviating uncertainties, and mobilize them to act. They are "general statements about the world and its parts... that are believed to be true and then acted on whenever circumstances suggest or require common response." Myths, McNeill notes, are "mankind's substitute for instinct." Without them, "coherent public action becomes very difficult to improvise or sustain."[1]

The social and socializing importance of myths is also at the heart of Robert MacIver's explanation of the coherence of political communities. In his classic study, *The Web of Government,* MacIver observes that shared myths define political communities and contribute to rendering them governable. By myths, MacIver says, "we mean the value-impregnated beliefs and notions that men hold, that they live by or live for. Every society is held together by a myth-system, a complex of dominating thought-forms that determines and sustains all its activities. All social relations, the very texture of human society, are myth-born and myth-sustained.... Wherever he goes, whatever he encounters, man spins about him his web of myth, as the caterpillar spins its cocoon."[2] Enduring myths are embedded in cultures. They cement communities, even possibly global ones.

Even though the truth of myths is always uncertain, or in any event beyond determination, the epistemological claims that support them are important because plausibility recruits and retains believers. The longing of individuals to believe, to locate themselves within cosmic, cultural, and social contexts, is deep-seated in the human psyche, but *believability* requires *plausibility*.[3] Therefore, surrounding all enduring public myths, we can expect to find relentless efforts to prove or otherwise explain their validity. Yet, as Ernst Cassirer makes clear, myths are almost never grounded in epistemologies congenial to modern science, at least to empirical science. They are more often grounded in forms of revelation that associate mythology and religion. He notes, "In mythical imagination there is always implied an act of *belief*. Without the belief in the reality of its object, myth would lose its ground.... In this respect it seems to be possible and even indispensable to compare mythical with scientific thought. Of course they do not follow the same ways. But they seem to be in quest of the same thing: reality."[4]

The Myth of the Moral Unity of Humankind

This chapter inquires into the presence in different cultures of a particular belief, which affirms that humankind constitutes a moral community. Hereafter I will call this belief the *myth of the moral unity of humankind*. Those who hold this belief would accept that in fundamental moral and ethical matters common humanity transcends cultural differentiation among peoples. They would also accept that the moral obligation to treat others sympathetically, respectfully, charitably, and humanely extends across cultures—indeed, across civilizations—and that outsiders ought to be considered the moral equals of insiders. Morally there are no insiders and outsiders. Ethical obligations, believers in the myth of the moral unity of humankind would say, are universal, and the myth highlights the oneness of all humanity. Whether or not such a belief exists, and whether or not it is held across civilizations, may be more important even than whether it is true in any ontological sense. Who can say whether humankind actually constitutes a moral community? It does if one believes it does. Idealism, moreover, postulates that the future has to be imagined before it can be constructed; reality begins with ideas. What can be imagined today may be built tomorrow. By reverse reasoning, what is unimaginable is probably also unrealizable.

Esoteric interests aside, there are also today some very practical reasons for looking into moral universalism. It is on the agenda of world politics. The promotion of human rights as these are presently defined requires shared assumptions concerning moral universalism. Otherwise, "human rights" become culturally relative, the tenets of the Universal Declaration of Human Rights become options instead of imperatives, distinctions between cultural insiders and cultural outsiders become central instead of irrelevant, and attempts to assign the protection of human rights to global institutions like the United Nations become immediately controversial and ultimately futile.

Moral universalism is rejected today by a growing number of governments. To be sure, some of these regimes are standing against moral universality because they are themselves abusers of the human rights defined in the Universal Declaration. Others value national sovereignty more than moral universality and eschew interference in their domestic affairs even in the name of humanity. Nevertheless, some governments, representing some cultural communities, are taking genuine philosophical exception to notions of moral universality, so that there is an intensifying debate going on today at the interface of world politics and moral philosophy. This was very much in evidence, for example, at the United Nations Vienna Conference on Human Rights in 1993, which turned out to be a political donnybrook instead of a celebration of progress toward human security. The outcome of the debate over moral universalism may determine the future fate of "human rights" as an international institutional mission. This makes it all the more important to know whether there is a myth of the moral unity of humankind that transcends cultures.

This chapter examines the ethical foundations of three civilizations, the Western, the Confucian, and the Hindu, as manifested in the works of representative moral philosophers or schools of ethical thought within each tradition; as such, it can offer no definitive answers concerning moral universalism, because whatever generalizations emerge pertain specifically to these three cases. Several other cultural communities—the Islamic, the Persian, the Russian, and the African, for example—have yet to be examined. Yet, preliminary findings reported here do suggest that it would be well worthwhile to extend the inquiry to these other cultural communities.

Moral Universalism and the Western Tradition

Like its counterparts in other cultural contexts, the Western moral-philosophical tradition is so extensive and complex that its treatment here is necessarily selective. Analysis in this essay is also historically selective, partly because of the vastness of the subject, but also because occurrences of cosmopolitan thinking in Western intellectual history have been episodic.

For the most part, emphasis in this essay will be on secular thought in the West, though it must be underlined that there is also a Christian moral tradition that is in some ways intertwined with secular thinking and in other ways quite distinct. Christian thinking has always been rather ambiguous regarding salvation, as it is not entirely clear—and also disputed among churches—who is eligible for ultimate passage into heavenly bliss and how eligibility is established.[5] On the other hand, the Christian tradition is quite unambiguous regarding moral universalism. The injunction to "love one's neighbor" is at the heart of Christian ethics, with the meaning of "love" coming to embody the proscriptions against harming others contained in the last seven commandments of the Decalogue (Exodus 20:2–17), in the imperatives of benevolence contained in Christ's Sermon on the Mount (Matthew 5–7), and in the moral guidance contained in St. Paul's letter to the Romans (Romans 13). The Christian notion of "neighbor," moreover, is inclusive: one's neighbors include all of humanity; moral tenets are therefore universal. The inclusiveness of the human moral community was given classic expression in St. Paul's letter to the Galatians, where he told his readers, "There is neither Jew nor Greek, there is neither slave nor free, there is neither male nor female, for you are all one in Christ Jesus" (Galatians 3:28). Inclusiveness was emphasized by Jesus in the Sermon on the Mount, dramatized in St. Luke's Gospel in the *Parable of the Good Samaritan* (Luke 10:29–37), and later echoed by St. Augustine and succeeding generations of Christian interpreters. Christian convictions regarding both goodness and human inclusiveness are grounded first in divine revelations, beginning with the Hebrew prophets and extending through the teachings of Christ. But Christianity, particularly in the Thomist tradition, also acknowledges that human reason can access the will of God and discern divinely promulgated natural laws.[6] It is here in the consideration of natural law that the Christian tradition epistemologically intersects the Western secular tradition in moral thinking.[7]

In Western secular thought, three periods in history are of particular interest with regard to affirmations about the moral unity of humankind—the Greco-Roman era, and especially the Augustan Age in ancient Rome, roughly from the time of Cicero (106–143 B.C.E.) to the reign of Marcus Aurelius (121–180); the era of the eighteenth-century Enlightenment, and particularly French and British thinking during this time; and the present day.

Greco-Roman Stoicism and Roman Cosmopolitanism

History records that the Roman Empire was administered by what would today be called a "transnational elite."[8] Public officials were recruited from all the regions of Roman reign, and, as far as is known, in their official doings at least, most of these people thought and acted as internationals rather than nationals. Their demeanor, and, as far as we can know, their convictions, too, were as citizens of the (Roman) world. These people believed in the universal applicability of Roman law, universal entitlement (among citizens and free men, at least) to equal treatment under this law, justice as a result of such treatment and order in a just society. They also believed in service to the Roman state and in a direct link between performing such service and attaining personal virtue.

It is also recorded that many among this Roman transnational elite were influenced by the ideas of Greek philosophers of the Stoic school, Epictetus perhaps most important among them, and that Romans like Cicero and Marcus Aurelius also contributed their own thinking and writing to the corpus of Stoic philosophy. Stoicism, they believed, justified the cosmopolitanism they accepted because it cast humanity as a single moral community. The Stoic philosophy offered to these Roman "citizens of the world" a justification for their self-chosen status and it rationalized a linkage among individual virtue, cosmopolitan values, and universal moral law. Stoicism rested on a belief in a rational universe, usually referred to as nature, an identity between reason and goodness and a conviction that humankind constituted a unity wherein all people were equal in both their capacities to reason and to do good. As Cicero put it so eloquently, "No single thing is so like another, so exactly its counterpart, as all of us are to one another. . . . However we define man, the same definition applies to all; this is sufficient proof that there is no difference in kind between man and man. . . . Reason is common to all. . . . There is no human being of any race who cannot find a guide to attain to virtue. Thus man is made for a mutual relationship of justice."[9]

For the individual, conformity with nature required a life of virtue because the universe mandated harmony, and harmony among people followed from an ethics that connected personal virtue with upholding public order. The Stoic accepted that the dictates of reason, and therefore the determination of nature, counseled forbearance, tolerance, humanitarianism, and justice. When convictions about the unity of humankind were combined with strivings after personal virtue, forbearance, tolerance, humanitarianism, and justice had to be universally rendered. Indeed, they would be universally rendered by all good people. Cosmopolitanism therefore was the only acceptable standpoint, or, at least Marcus Aurelius so believed when he wrote, "If the power of thought is universal among mankind, so likewise is the possession of reason, making us rational creatures. It follows, therefore, that this reason speaks no less universally to us all with its 'thou shalt' or 'thou shalt not.' So then there is a world-law; which in turn means that we are all fellow-citizens and share a common citizenship, and that the world is a single city. Is there any other common citizenship that can be claimed by all of humanity? And it is from this world-polity that mind, reason, and law themselves derive."[10] Several aspects of Greco-Roman Stoicism are of interest for comparative purposes. First, Stoic thinking obviously embraced what is here called the myth of the moral unity of humankind—that is, convictions about humanity's moral oneness. The commonality among people was in their capacity to reason, a quality believed to distinguish humans from beasts and a quality that rendered humans unique among mortal beings. Humankind's moral unity was based upon imperatives created by the laws of an ordered universe. To live a life in accord with the natural order, or in compliance with natural law, an individual was obliged to treat all others in ways that reinforced, or at least did not disrupt, the natural harmony. But nature was more than simply an "order" somehow set in place and left ever running thereafter. Nature was instead a force, a spirit, a "will," perhaps, that had a benign purpose. Stoic ethics were metaphysically founded: the unseen force, nature, legislated righteousness, and set its moral laws before mankind. Nature's will could be accessed by man; human reason was the channel of communication. One learned of the will of nature, or about the dictates of natural law, by reasoning—by following courses that reason charted. Reason pointed all thinking human beings in the same moral directions. The good was reasonable, the bad was unreasonable, the good was virtuous and the bad was not, and every reasoning being, no matter where within the human race this person was located, could discern the difference and act accordingly.

Western Cosmopolitanism during the Enlightenment

In a period extending from the late seventeenth to the early nineteenth century, and largely within a British, Continental European, and North American epistemic community, ideas about the unity of mankind blossomed again in Western thinking. The perpetrators of these ideas, at least in the first generation, identified themselves as *philosophes*. Somewhat like their ancient counterparts in Rome, the philosophes of the eighteenth-century Enlightenment were an intellectual elite. They were not for the most part professional philosophers as much as they were thinking individuals representing a variety of professions and disciplines. They formed a transnational society interlinked through friendship, kinship, correspondence, and travel. They read each other's writings and exchanged criticisms. Unlike their ancient Roman counterparts, the eighteenth-century philosophers were not public administrators, although many, like Benjamin Franklin and Voltaire, had served governments, and some notables among them, like Prussia's Frederick II, reigned during the eighteenth century as so-called enlightened despots.

Generally speaking, the thrust of the philosophes' political discourse was critical of the governments of the monarchical ancien regime and their "princely" international relations. On the surface the professions of world citizenship voiced by the philosophes were reactions against the perceived irrationalities of the international relations of their time. Though peoples had no quarrels with each other, Denis Diderot noted, princes did, petty though they were, and peoples were the inevitable victims of the princes' bickerings.[11] For J. W. von Goethe it was the hatreds aroused by nationalism that were irrational. He wrote in 1830 that, "National hatreds are peculiar things. You will always find them strongest and most vigorous among the lowest stages of culture. But there is a stage when they entirely vanish, and where one stands in a certain measure above all nations, and feels the happiness or the woe of a neighboring people as though it were his own. This stage of culture suited my nature, and I was firmly rooted in it before I had reached my sixtieth year."[12] For many among the eighteenth-century philosophers, intermediate loyalties between the individual and humanity were artificial, usually contrived to gain advantage over somebody else, and frequently destructive. No reasoning person could therefore harbor such loyalties.

As a result, the cosmopolitan agenda of the eighteenth century's citizens of the world called for universal toleration. To be other than tolerant in a politically and religiously pluralistic world was to foolishly court conflict. But, the philosophes' agenda also called for the promotion of "the rights of man," and about abuses of these they were intolerant. The rights were accepted as universal and inalienable because people everywhere were seen to have similar interests, aspirations, and entitlements. Humanitarianism was also a universal imperative in Enlightenment thinking, best captured in the French idea of *bienfaisance*. Human dignity was seen as an absolute entitlement and men everywhere were responsible for confronting its abuse anywhere.[13]

In a way that was remarkably analogous to the morality-based world citizenship of the Romans, the cosmopolitanism of the eighteenth-century thinkers was also founded on a moral philosophy. Revealingly, the two moral philosophies—the Stoicism of the ancients, and what has been called the neo-Stoicism of the philosophes—were directly linked via the philosophes' immersion in the ancient literatures. "Voltaire," Thomas Schlereth comments, "repeatedly turned to Cicero, Epictetus, and Marcus Aurelius as a 'pagan' trinity of ancients who adhered to a cosmopolitan theism parallel to his own. By a revealing coincidence, David Hume's list of ancient counselors is precisely the same."[14] Like the ancients, but greatly fortified by the flowering of science all around them, the philosophes accepted that the universe had been created by rational forces or at the inspiration of a benevolent deity, who was more like a dispassionate master architect or engineer than the paternal, though sometimes vindictive, almighty king of Christian theology. In this eighteenth-century universe, morality was no less determined by natural law than was physical nature, and the laws of morality were as accessible to human reason as the laws of physics.

To confirm their beliefs, Enlightenment thinkers, like their Stoic intellectual ancestors, looked to nature as the validator, and nature in the eighteenth century, and for some time thereafter, was Sir Isaac Newton's nature—a complex machine that nonetheless operated according to a parsimonious set of unalterable, knowable natural laws. Just as natural laws determined the structure and functioning of Newton's cosmos, so too did natural laws determine the good and the moral in relations among human beings. These laws, both physical and moral, were self-evident, which meant, in eighteenth-century discourse, that they became apparent to all educated, *reasoning* human beings. Natural laws defined the true and the good; the laws were immutable, and, most important, human reason revealed these laws. Behaving in accord with them was ethical because the good corresponded to naturally ordained orderliness and acting in accord with it yielded temporal orderliness in a harmony that was beneficial to all people. Ethical standards were affirmed to be universal. "Since human nature is always and everywhere the same," Randall notes, "rules useful in France will be equally useful in Persia, China, the forests of America or the South Sea Islands."[15] Many among the eighteenth-century thinkers, who accepted that the intricately ordered universe was a divine creation, pursued their commitment to law-founded morality with religious intensity.

Adding an empirical dimension to their otherwise purely rationalistic epistemology, some of the eighteenth-century writers felt that to help discover nature's laws for human conduct it was helpful to compare the great moral systems of mankind, but only after these had been stripped of the myths, mysteries, metaphysics, rituals, and conventions derisively called the "ossified orthodoxy" of organized religions.[16] The principles of universal morality, Benjamin Franklin believed, were to be found in the "essentials of every religion," while others, like Voltaire and Oliver Goldsmith, found inspiration in Confucianism because it focused on earthly ethics instead of supernatural mysteries.[17]

The result of the Enlightenment's quest for universal moral principles was unspectacular: tolerance, benevolence, justice, and the Golden Rule's injunction to do unto others as you would have them do unto you were the prime ethical tenets. Not surprisingly, applying human reason to moral problems led to reasonable conclusions about ethical behavior. Still, these reasoned principles appropriately justified world citizenship by linking personal virtue to ethical universalism. The world was a universe of morally equivalent individuals who had to be treated according to naturally ordained and universal ethical standards. To be virtuous required a person to adhere to natural laws regarding morality, and as the laws were universal, moral universalism was the only reasonable standpoint. Humankind was a moral community.

Contemporary Neo-Aristotelianism and Moral Universalism

Collapsing an immense amount of Western thinking into this very limited space requires another leap over centuries, during which (1) cosmopolitanism and attendant moral universalism remained as strains of thought, although nineteenth-century Romanticism, later nationalism, and then cultural relativism challenged and all but overwhelmed them; (2) metaphysical justifications for ethical behavior largely disappeared; (3) rationalism was shaken was by Freudianism and by modernism and psychologism more generally; (4) quantum physics raised important questions about order in the universe; (5) moral philosophy itself fell into decline, and (6) empiricism gained epistemological ascendancy, leaving little intellectual space for alternative, purely rationalistic pursuits after truth. Needless to say, the horrendous bloodshed, inhumanity, chaos, and anarchy of the first half of the twentieth century did little to encourage new cosmopolitan thinking (at least in the West). The United Nations was founded in 1945 upon the cosmopolitan principles of the eighteenth-century Enlightenment. They were noble indeed, but most of them had already lost their philosophical grounding at the time they were written into the UN's charter.[18]

Very recently, however, a renaissance has begun in Western moral philosophy, and one strain especially—called neo-Aristotelianism, or essentialism—has taken up the cosmopolitan banner. Among the most forceful contemporary arguments in support of moral universalism are those being articulated by the American philosopher Martha Nussbaum, who labels her thought "neoessentialist," which means that she builds her argument not from metaphysical assumptions about God or physical ones about an ordered nature, but rather from considerations concerning the essence of human beings. Because we are human beings, Nussbaum argues, we are entitled to be allowed to flourish in our human way of life. The basis of our morality is in our obligation as human beings, as individuals and in our societies, to allow and help one another to flourish as human beings. And since the human essence is universal, requirements for human flourishing are universal, obligations to promote such flourishing are universal, and therefore so is human morality.

Central to Nussbaum's philosophy is her inventory of human entitlements. To what are we entitled by virtue of our humanity? What, if denied to us, will constrain our flourishing? What, therefore, are we as human beings obligated to promote and protect in our dealings with one another? Nussbaum lists ten "basic human functional capabilities," and states that "a life that lacks any one of these, no matter what else it has, will be lacking in humanness."[19] These are:

- Being able to live to the end of complete human life, as far as is possible; not dying prematurely, or before one's life is reduced as to be not worth living.
- Being able to have good health; to be adequately nourished; to have adequate shelter; having opportunities for sexual satisfaction; being able to move from place to place.

- Being able to avoid unnecessary and nonbeneficial pain and to have pleasurable experiences.
- Being able to use the five senses; being able to imagine, to think, and to reason.
- Being able to have attachments to things and persons outside ourselves; to love those who love and care for us, to grieve at their absence, in general, to love, grieve, to feel longing and gratitude.
- Being able to form a conception of the good and to engage in critical reflection about the planning of one's own life.
- Being able to live for and with others, to recognize and show concern for other human beings, to engage in various forms of familial and social interaction.
- Being able to live with concern for and in relation to animals, plants, and the world of nature.
- Being able to laugh, to play, to enjoy recreational activities.
- Being able to live one's own life and nobody else's; being able to live one's own life in one's very own surroundings and context.[20]

Not surprisingly perhaps, Nussbaum's list of requirements for human flourishing, and hence our entitlements as human beings, closely approximate the contents of the Universal Declaration of Human Rights, not only with respect to civil and political rights but also with respect to economic, social, and cultural rights. This is, in a way, a restatement of the Enlightenment creed, leavened with ideas from nineteenth- and twentieth-century democratic socialism. In all of this Nussbaum is very much within the Western tradition. So, too, in the Western tradition are the ethical rules that would guarantee the itemized moral entitlements—toleration, compassion, humanitarianism, charity, justice, and respect.

What is innovative in Nussbaum's contribution is the justification for the entitlements and the grounding for the ethics. Both the justifications and groundings take the form of empirical inferences: if particular conditions must prevail for human beings to flourish, and the object of morality is to facilitate human flourishing, then morality demands that appropriate conditions for human flourishing must be sought, and ethics demand morally appropriate behavior. No metaphysics or mysticisms are involved; human needs arise from the human condition, and acknowledging this condition defines the good as meeting the needs. But ultimately the system comes to rest upon its epistemology, which is empiricism, largely of the kind practiced in twentieth-century social science. How are we to know what the requirements are for human flourishing? Obviously, we must study human beings.

I have spent perhaps too long a time with Western thinkers, and it is appropriate now to move to other civilizations. As analysis shifts focus, however, several points need to be stored for later comparisons. First and most obvious, the myth of the moral unity of humankind is well represented in Western moral thinking. All human beings are moral equals and are therefore entitled to equal ethical treatment. The myth is deeply embedded in Western culture, both sacred and secular. It has appeared more prominently is some periods of Western intellectual history than in others, but it has never disappeared. Second, rationalism consistently underpins the Western justification for believing that mankind constitutes a moral unity. There has been scant allowance for mysticism in Western moral thinking, or at least in secular renditions, and over time there has been increasing impatience with the metaphysical in particular and the nonempirical in general. Finally, the ethical imperatives of Western cosmopolitanism have tended to remain remarkably consistent: various ways of reasoning from a variety of premises have resulted in the same conclusions concerning what constitutes virtuous behavior and how widely it applies.

Moral Universalism and the Confucian Tradition

But what of the non-West? Is there a philosophical foundation for cosmopolitanism in non-Western cultures? Do we find in non-Western thinking notions akin to moral universalism, beliefs about the similarity of human beings everywhere, and justifications for believing that humanity constitutes a single moral community? An examination of Confucian thought as it evolved in China and neighboring countries over nearly two millennia begins to answer some of these questions.

What is obvious to the Confucian scholar, but not so clear to the Western novice, is that the Confucian tradition has been assembled from a history of ponderings, pronouncements, perceptions, and prescriptions that pre-dated Confucius himself (551–479 B.C.E.). The tradition, of course, contains and reveres the works of Confucius the master, though there are continuing debates about their authenticity. There are also contributions by later Confucian scholars, such as Mencius (371–289? B.C.E.) and Chu Hsi (1130–1200) that almost rival those of the master. Then there is a vast, continuing literature contained in hundreds of volumes of commentary, and thousands of essays of interpretation and reinterpretation that have appeared since the time of Confucius and continue to be produced even today. As it turns out, much of Confucianism is only remotely related to the actual pronouncements of Confucius, so that the Confucian tradition might more generically be thought of as "the teachings of the . . . Chinese Classics about cosmology, the social order, government, morals and ethics."[21] Distributed along the two-millennium-long way, and of particular relevance for insights into moral universalism are *The Book of Change* (*I Ching*), *The Book of Rites*

(*Li chi*) and *The Doctrine of the Mean* (*Chung Yung*), dating from Confucius's era, but drawing upon the insights from much earlier times. Later there are *The Book of Mencius* (*Mêng Tsu*) written in the third century B.C.E.; the neo-Confucianist commentaries of Lu Hsiang-shan, Chang Tsai, and Chu Hsi produced in the eleventh and twelfth centuries; the work of Wang Yang-ming, written in the fifteenth century; and the early-twentieth-century writings of K'ang Yu-wei, particularly *The Great Unity* (*Ta Tung Shu*), and of his disciple T'an Ssu-T'ung. What is fascinating is that the Confucian tradition is at the same time both very ancient and very contemporary; contributors speak to one another meaningfully and continuously across some twenty centuries. One intellectually profitable way to study the Confucian tradition is to spread the contributions out along their two-thousand-year intellectual continuum, look at them holistically, and consider all of them alive and contemporary.

Like most Chinese philosophy, Confucianism "is predominantly a system of ethical realism."[22] It situates people in a universe that is ordered and benign, posits the reality of both humankind and universe, but then makes understanding humankind its central problem. Confucianism shares with most Chinese thinking an ethical philosophy based on the notion that "running through life and the universe is one all-pervading principle" that is rational and ethical in nature.[23] It is humankind's duty to follow this principle, which brings it into harmony with society and in tune with the universe. Deviation from the way of principle is the origin of evil. Every individual can attain moral perfection, and striving toward this should be everyone's goal. It is the obligation of those who have moved farthest toward human perfection—i.e., the sages—to guide others. To say that Confucianism shares its ethics with Chinese philosophy in general understates the centrality of Confucian ethics in Chinese thought. In fact, Confucian ethics are at the core of Chinese ethical thinking, and "the Confucian way of life remains the key to a study of values in Chinese philosophy."[24]

Confucian Ethics and Moral Universalism

Understanding the Confucian concept of *jen* is the key to identifying the moral universalism in Confucian doctrine. In broadest terms, *jen* is a moral capacity peculiar to human beings and common among them. Jen is an imperative to do right and to pursue the good in human relations that has been variously translated as "compassion," "magnanimity," "reciprocity," "humanity," "propriety," "commiseration," "true manhood," "man-to-manness" or in various other ways that capture the sense of thinking, feeling, and acting appropriately and benignly toward others. In Y. P. Mei's rendering, jen is "the common denominator of humanity . . . and the mark which distinguishes man from animal, . . . the innermost and highest ideal of true manhood, the beginning and the end of the way of life. . . . the super-virtue of virtues."[25] Some have summarized jen as spontaneous behavior in accord with the Chinese Golden Mean, which prescribes not doing unto others that which one would not want done unto oneself. Others have defined it as the "one principle" that underlies all moral contemplation and action. When Confucius was pressed by a disciple to explain the meaning of jen, he replied, "Love men."[26]

Whether Confucius believed that this capacity was innate or whether he thought it was acquired by reflecting upon nature and human experience is not entirely clear. In *The Doctrine of the Mean*, for example, Confucius is quoted as saying that "the moral sense is a characteristic attribute of man," thus suggesting innateness. But he is also quoted as saying that "the life of the moral man is an exemplification of the universal moral order," which could be interpreted as behavior by imitation rather than from innate nature.[27] However, most Confucianists since Mencius have accepted that human goodness is inborn. Mencius said, "If you let people follow their feelings . . . they will be able to do good. This is what is meant by saying that human nature is good. If man does evil, it is not the fault of his natural endowment. The feeling of commiseration is found in all men; the feeling of shame and dislike is found in all men; the feeling of right and wrong is found in all men. . . . Humanity, righteousness, propriety and wisdom are not drilled into us from the outside. We originally have them with us."[28]

At another point, Mencius elaborated on the meaning of common humanity, by dwelling on human beings' innate and universal responses to suffering. He observed that "[a]ll men have the mind which cannot bear to see the suffering of others," and went on to say,

> When I say that all men have the mind which cannot bear to see the suffering of others, my meaning may be illustrated thus: Now, when men suddenly see a child about to fall into a well, they all have a feeling of alarm or distress, not to gain friendship with the child's parents, nor to seek the praise of their neighbors and friends, nor because they dislike the reputation of lack of humanity if they did not rescue the child. From such a case we see that a man without the feeling of commiseration is not a man; a man without the feeling of shame and dislike is not a man; a man without the feeling of deference and compliance is not a man; and a man without the feeling of right and wrong is not a man. The feeling of commiseration is the beginning of humanity; the feeling of shame and dislike is the beginning of righteousness; the feeling of deference and compliance is the beginning of propriety; and the feeling of right and wrong is the beginning of wisdom. Men have these four beginnings just as they have their four limbs.[29]

The parable of the "child about to fall into the well" remains the Confucian symbol of innate humanity, confirming the inherence of jen, and the *Doctrine of the Four Beginnings* remains a most elegant rendition of human beings' inborn moral endowment. It is also an explicit instruction in the Confucian meaning of moral behavior. To treat fellow human beings as human beings, one must show compassion, practice righteousness (or justice), exhibit appropriate deference or propriety, and call upon the wisdom that discriminates between right and wrong. Various Confucian thinkers over the centuries have added nuances to Mencius's pronouncements, as for example K'ang Yu-wei, who found inborn in humans a kind of magnetic attraction—an electricity—that binds them to one another and to the universe.[30] But the basic beliefs have come down from ancient times largely unaltered: men are moral by nature, and the moral inclination is universal.

The theme of moral universality was explicitly voiced by Mencius when he acknowledged that all men can become sages, meaning that the moral sense is everywhere inborn and can be cultivated by anyone willing to develop it. Moral universality was referenced by Mencius in more homely fashion when he recited the parable of the shoemaker: "Therefore all things of the same kind are similar to one another. Why should there be any doubt about men? The sage and I are the same in kind. . . . If a man makes shoes without knowing the size of people's feet, I know at least he will not make them to be like baskets. Shoes are alike because people's feet are alike."[31]

Echoing the same theme in his essay *The Western Inscription*, the eleventh-century writer Chang Tsai acknowledged that "all men are my brothers, all things are my relatives," and again in the work of the twentieth-century Confucian interpreter K'ang Yu-wei one finds that "mankind in the ten thousand countries are all my brothers . . . (and) being that I have knowledge of them, then I have love for them."[32]

To understand why Confucianism considers jen to be innate and universal requires that we step from Confucian ethics into Confucian metaphysics, which is a small step intellectually because in Confucian thinking "the feeling of kinship between man the universe is so strong that it is difficult to know where ethics ends and where metaphysics begins."[33] The universe, referred to interchangeably as nature, heaven, or God in a non-anthromorphic sense, is in the Confucian conceptualization an ordered cosmos, indeterminate and unchanging. This universe is methodical, harmonious, law-driven, and benign. It is also all-embracing: human beings are elements of it and therefore share in its character. "I have a body," K'ang Yu-wei wrote, "then I share with coexisting bodies that which permeates the air of Heaven, permeates the matter of the Earth, permeates the breath of man."[34] Heaven, earth, and humanity are one, a triune; they *are* the universe, and the same cosmic drivers—identified as "spiritual forces" according to Confucius; "moral laws" according to *The Doctrine of the Mean;* the "universal mind" according to Lu Hsiang-shan; the "Way" of the Taoists; the "Principal of Heaven," according to Chu Hsi; or the "all-embracing Primal Ch'i," according to K'ang Yu-wei—affect heaven, earth, and humanity uniformly. Material things are transitory, including, of course, human beings, but during their existence they are simply determinate differentiations of the indeterminate universe that produced them. Heaven, earth, and humanity are one.

Jen, or humankind's moral nature, then, is a revelation of the design of the universe, or, perhaps more than this, an aspect of the reality that is the universe. Only a moral humanity could be an aspect of an ordered and harmonious universe. Confucian writers have expressed this notion in different ways:

Confucius
The power of spiritual forces in the Universe—how active it is everywhere! Invisible to the eyes, and impalpable to the senses, it is inherent in all things, and nothing can escape its operation.[35]

The Doctrine of the Mean
These moral laws form one system with the laws by which Heaven and Earth support and contain, overshadow and canopy all things. These moral laws form the same system with the laws by which the seasons succeed each other and the sun and moon appear with the alterations of day and night. It is this same system of laws by which all created things are produced and develop themselves each in its order and system without injuring one another, and by which the operations of Nature take their course without conflict or confusion; . . . It is this one system running through all that makes the Universe so impressively great.[36]

Chu Hsi
The mind of Heaven and Earth is to produce things. In the production of man and things, they receive the mind of Heaven and Earth as their mind. . . . For *jen* as constituting the Way (Tao) consists of the fact that the mind of Heaven and Earth to produce things is present in everything.[37]

K'ang Yu-wei
The all-embracing Primal Ch'i created Heaven and Earth. "Heaven" is composed of a single soul-substance; "Man" is likewise composed of a single soul-substance. Although individual forms may differ in size, still, they are all but parts of the all-embracing ch'i of the ultimate beginnings of the universe.[38]

As with most moral philosophies, occidental as well as oriental, Confucian ethics and the metaphysics that create the ethical imperatives must give rise to epistemological questions. How do Confucianists know that human beings are inherently and universally moral, and how do they justify their claims about an ordered, benign, and all-embracing universe? Confucius appears to have espoused what we might call *intuitive empiricism*. He advised the study of things to understand their nature and to gain insights about the cosmos of which they were manifestations. He studied history and therein observed the experiences of the ancients; he studied music to sense harmonies; he studied nature and derived analogies. But his methods were not analytical as much as they were appreciative or aesthetic. One acquires wisdom by allowing immediate experience to simultaneously impact upon the senses and the intellect—that is, by *appreciating* what the universe has to offer. Following the method of Confucius, truth is not so much discovered as felt: "It is the one-ness provided by this immediately apprehended aesthetic continuum common to all men, which gives the Confucian . . . his compassionate fellow-feeling for all men," and which assures him of the truth of his experience.[39]

Most propagators of Confucian doctrine through the centuries continued to rely more or less upon intuitive empiricism to justify their claims to moral knowledge, though several, like Lu Hsiang-shan and later Wang Yang-ming leaned rather excessively toward introspection. Lu, for example, posited that the ways of the universe were invested in the minds of men, so that little was to be learned by observing external objects. Mencius relied largely upon intuitive empiricism, which generated instructive analogies. But he also favored a variety of rationalism, which permitted him to induce generalities from particulars and to move logically from the homely to the profound. Others like Chu Hsi were also convinced that because the universe was a rational order, human reason could fathom its laws and its meaning. Because the universe was as it was, everything else, including the moral nature of human beings, followed rationally from it, and the application of human reason could decipher it. Of course, as the corpus of Confucian works expanded over the centuries, succeeding authors were increasingly able to justify their truth claims by citing the authority of renown predecessors.

Confucianism and the Myth of Moral Universalism

By the tenets of science and the epistemological foundations that support it, the case for the truth, or even for the plausibility, of Confucian ethical doctrines is fairly weak. In this sense those who have classified Confucianism as a religion are not far off the mark. One ultimately accepts Confucian claims concerning the universality of humankind's inherently moral nature on faith; or, one rejects Confucian doctrine out of skepticism or disbelief. However, none of these epistemological considerations impinge in the least upon Confucianism's rather profound mythological qualities and the enduring power of the public myths it has propagated. Confucianism's initial impacts and its enduring appeal have resided not in any unimpeachable truths in its doctrine, but in its unquestioning acceptance by scores of generations of Chinese and neighboring Asian peoples. Its mythological appeal is in its description of a way of life, founded upon the pursuit of virtue, to which all could aspire in the hope of attaining fulfillment in human perfection. That few, if any, ever achieve human perfection only strengthens Confucianism's mythological appeal, likening it perhaps to the ancient Greek Myth of Sisyphus or medieval Christendom's Myth of the Holy Grail. Confucianism also embodies a myth of moral universalism, constructed about the notion of jen. The proposition that all human beings are similar in their moral endowments, and as such are obligated to treat one another compassionately, justly, respectfully, and benignly is firmly embedded in Confucian lore, and therefore also in Chinese and Asian culture.

Moral Universalism and the Hindu Tradition

If the Confucian tradition can claim two millennia of continuous impact on East Asian thought, the Vedic tradition at the core of Hindu culture can claim at least a four-millennium-long influence over South Asian thought. In fact the indeterminate, but very ancient, origin of the Vedic scriptures is in itself an element of the Hindu tradition because it allows for the claim that the Vedas had no earthly origin. The sacred texts have always existed; they are therefore eternal and unimpeachable. Whatever mystery shrouds the Vedas' beginnings, they remain, in the form of the Vedic hymns or mantras, particularly the Reg Veda, the ritualistic prescriptions of the Brahmanas and the metaphysical-psychological explorations of the Aranyakas and the Upanishads the fundamental, and still living, sources of Hindu philosophy, theology, and ethics. They were the inspiration for the *Bhagavad-Gita*, or *Divine Song*, which is perhaps the single most important ethical text in the Hindu culture, and the Vedas were also the sources of the so-called orthodox schools of Indian philosophy, which evolved during approximately two millennia prior to the Mohammedan invasions of the subcontinent. The drive to find new, contemporary meaning in the Vedic literature was a main force behind the renaissance of Hindu philosophy, which began in the last half of the nineteenth century. It was reflected in the works of Mahatma Gandhi, Nikhilananda, Sarvepalli Radhakrishnan, Ramakrishna, Rabindranath Tagore, Vivekananda, and many others, and it continues today.[40]

In seeking insight into Hindu thinking concerning moral universalism it makes most sense historically to begin in the contemporary period and then to work back to Vedic scripts, where, as noted, almost all Indian philosophy finds its foundations. It should, however, be underlined at the outset that whether or not mankind constitutes a moral community has never been problematized in Indian philosophy: instead, the moral unity of humanity is taken as a given; Indian moral thinkers conceive of a man as man, never as *Hindu* man, or any other kind of segregated community, and this has been consistently the case through the millennia. But whereas in the historically remote writings moral universalism was more frequently implicit rather than explicit, in the recent literature of the philosophical renaissance expressions of universalism are explicit and abundant.

Mahatma Gandhi, for example, proclaimed the moral unity of mankind time and time again. "We will work for the unity of mankind," Gandhi told his followers; "All my actions have their rise in my inalienable love for mankind. I have known no distinction between relatives and strangers, countrymen and foreigners, white and coloured, Hindus and Indians of other faiths whether Mussulmans, Parsees, Christians or Jews...All men are brothers and no human being should be a stranger to another. The welfare of all ... should be our aim."[41]

On another occasion Gandhi summarized his cosmopolitanism most succinctly by noting that "there is no limit to extending our services to our neighbors across State-made frontiers. God never made those frontiers."[42]

Sarvepalli Radhakrishnan, a contemporary of Gandhi, and one of India's most perceptive modern-day moral philosophers, also developed his vision of a better world from convictions concerning humankind's moral unity. "If we leave aside the fanatics," Radhakrishnan noted in his *Future of Civilization*, "the leaders of every historical civilization to-day are convinced that mankind in all its extent and history is a single organism." Immediately following this, the Indian philosopher acknowledges his agreement with Dante that "there is not one goal for this civilization and one for that, but for the civilization of all mankind there is a single goal."[43] Before Radhakrishnan there was India's greatest modern poet-philosopher, Rabindranath Tagore, whose cosmopolitanism was summarized in the oft-repeated aphorism: "When a man does not realise his kinship with the world, he lives in a prison house, whose walls are alien to him."[44] Reaching back in time, we find that moral universalism is an integral and integrating theme of the *Bhagavad-Gita*, "the song divine, which advocates toleration, universal brotherhood and coexistence of all people and all religions."[45] And out of ancient mists there were Upanishadic musings on the transcendent unity of the human soul and Vedic injunctions concerning humankind's common obligations under the laws that ordered the universe, and about which more will be said shortly.

The Metaphysical Foundations of Hindu Universalism

Since the Indian philosophical commitment to moral universalism is so obvious, analytical interest comes to center on exactly why this commitment is so emphatic and so consistent through time. Pursuing answers carries one immediately into metaphysics, perhaps into mysticism, where distinctions between Indian philosophy and Hindu religion disappear. This is an area where Westerners must tread with greatest caution because ignorance could easily lead to misinterpretation.[46] But it is also the area where the Hindu locates ultimate knowledge.

In Hindu philosophy, empirical reality, which includes beings as well as objects, represents the transitory and partial manifestation of an all-embracing spiritual force, most often referred to as Brahman, although it is designated in many ways in various texts. Brahman is sometimes person-alized as God, but the Hindu god is best understood as a force rather than an anthromorphized agent. Brahman is the ultimate reality: it is formless, changeless, timeless, inaccessible to the senses, inexplicable via reason and indescribable. Brahman is pure being. Everything that exists, animate and inanimate, is a manifestation of it, but again only a partial manifestation, for the complete reality, the Absolute that is Brahman, is empirically imper-ceptible. In the *Bhagavad-Gita*, for example, the seer, Krishna, attempts to convey to the novice, Arjuna, that,

- Brahman is the indestructible, the supreme. (8:3)
- It is outside and within all beings. It is unmoving and moving. It is too subtle to be known. It is far away and it is also near. (13:15)
- It is undivided and yet seems to be divided in all beings. It is to be known as supporting all beings and as absorbing and creating them. (13:16)
- It is also, it is said, the light of lights beyond darkness; it is knowledge, the object of knowledge, and the goal of knowledge; it is seated in the hearts of all. (13:17)
- He who sees the supreme Lord abiding equally in all beings, not perishing when they perish, he [truly] sees. (13:27)[47]

Because Brahman is omnipresent, every human being is a manifestation of this abiding spirit. But since the human body is transitory and destructible, the essence of the self which partakes of ultimate reality is the soul, and this life force, or Atman, in each individual is but a differentiated manifestation of the single life force of the universe, which is Brahman. Oneness—that is, monism—then, is the most widely accepted basis of Hindu metaphysics.

This is emphatically expressed by Samakara, founder of the Aviata Vendanta school, but it certainly extends back to Upanishadic pantheism and to the Vedic notion of Prjapati, or Lord of Creation.[48] What this means is that the unity of humankind is in essence a spiritual unity: all beings are one with each other because they are one with the universe, and one with God because ultimate reality is an undifferentiated, absolute, and eternal oneness.

This is what Gandhi means when he says that "there is an indefinable mysterious Power that pervades everything."[49] For Gandhi the implication is that "I believe in the absolute oneness of God and, therefore, of humanity. What though we have many bodies? We have but one soul."[50] That Radhakrishnan was also much imbued with the Upanishadic tradition, and that his cosmopolitanism flowed from it becomes clear in his observation that "in spite of appearances to the contrary... there is a secret spirit in which we are all one, and of which humanity is the highest vehicle on earth...."[51] Elsewhere, Radhakrishan observes that "the universality of the great facts of religious experience, their close resemblance under conditions of race and time, attest to the persistent unity of the main spirit"; he then adds that "adherents of this creed are citizens of the world."[52] Likewise, for Tagore, "man and nature are both expressions of the universal spirit.... One can obtain endless joy the moment one adjusts one's individual self to the universal spirit, [which] is made practical by the inclination of love for all human beings."[53] And most succinctly, Swami Nikhilananda instructed his followers to "love your neighbor because your neighbor is yourself."[54] The implication in all of this is that humankind cannot be other than a unity because all being is absolute unity.

Knowing through Feeling

Where the Hindu tradition diverges sharply from the Western, and to an extent also from the Confucian, is in the realm of epistemology. How does one know that ultimate reality is an undifferentiated spiritual continuum, and how does one gain knowledge about this level of pure being, which by its very concept is indefinable, imperceptible, and indescribable? What is important in terms of this essay's thesis is that Indian thinkers are impelled toward cosmopolitan standpoints because they believe that ultimate reality is a universal oneness and that this unity necessarily embraces all of humanity. Therefore, it is useful to determine how they have come to believe what they believe.

Gandhi offers some insight in the continuation of a passage quoted earlier. About the "indefinable mysterious Power that pervades everything," Gandhi goes on to say, "I feel it, though I do not see it... [it] makes itself felt, yet defies all proof... it transcends the senses."[55] Hindu epistemology distinguishes between two kinds of knowledge; that which is attainable through the senses, termed *Vijana* or scientific learning, and that which is gained through meditation and introspection, termed *Jnana*, or intuitive knowledge. Vijana results in learning concerning the empirical world, which is differentiated, changeable, destructible, and transitory. On the other hand, knowledge of the absolute, of Brahman, comes only in the form of Jnana, and it comes only by transcending the intellect, by moving beyond the fallibilities of the senses, the limitations of reason, and the contrivances of categorization and conceptualization, and from merging one's total being with the oneness that is Brahman. According to Radhakrishnan, "So long as we are bound by intellect and are lost in the world of many, we shall seek in vain to get back to the simplicity of the one."[56] The process and procedures by which and through which Brahman is intuited are intense, exhaustive, and extensive. They require extraordinary discipline, both mental and physical.[57]

Describing the intuitive experience in pursuing knowledge of the absolute is probably impossible, though in a brilliant passage from his *Eastern Religions and Western Thought* Radhakrishnan comes very close:

> While outer knowledge can be easily acquired, inner truth demands an absolute concentration of the mind on its object. So in the third stage of *samadhi* or identification, the conscious division and separation of the self from the divine being, the object from the subject, which is the normal condition of unregenerate humanity, is broken down. The individual surrenders to the object and is absorbed by it. He becomes what he beholds. The distinction between subject and object disappears. Tasting nothing, comprehending nothing in particular, holding itself in emptiness, the soul finds itself as having all. A lightning flash, a sudden flame of incandescence, throws a momentary eternal gleam on life in time. A strange quietness enters the soul; a great peace invades its being. The vision, the spark, the supreme moment of unification or conscious realization, sets the whole being ablaze with perfect purpose. The supreme awareness, the intimately felt presence, brings with it a rapture beyond joy, a knowledge beyond reason, a sensation more intense than that of life itself, infinite in peace and harmony. When it occurs our rigidity breaks, we flow again, and are aware, as at no other time, of a continuity in ourselves and know more than a little section of it that is our life in this world.[58]

For any given individual, seeking knowledge of the absolute may extend well beyond the mortal limits of a single lifetime. To elaborate this point, however, would move discussion deeply, and not very relevantly, into Hindu religion and mysticism. Therefore, let it suffice to note that seeking the ultimate truth about reality, or rather seeking the truth that is reality, is every Hindu's obligation, and coming upon this truth at the end of the exhaustive quest through successive reincarnations is the Hindu's reward, called *Moksa*, which is tantamount to beatification and final liberation from mortal suffering. Moksa is the supreme goal and pursuing and attaining it is the paramount meaning of life. The pursuit after Moksa is also the linkage between Indian metaphysics and Indian ethics and it is at this juncture that it becomes directly relevant to this essay's argument.

The Imperatives of Goodness

The main thrust of Hindu ethics is contained in the notion of *Dharma*, which concerns appropriate behavior. Here again the problem is not about what constitutes good behavior, or how human beings individually and collectively ought to act toward one another. Ethical goodness and rectitude are quite clearly defined in the Indian philosophic tradition, although the Hindu code of ethics is greatly complicated by distinctions between *varnasramadharma* and *sadharnadharma*. The former concerns appropriate behavior within different social castes and at different stages of life and the latter has to do with behavior that is obligatory for all people toward all people. *Sadharnadharma* is of most interest here; not surprisingly, as far as appropriate social behavior is concerned, the general tenets of Hindu ethics said to be obligatory for all people are in essence remarkably similar to those contained in Western and Confucian moral philosophy. People are generally obliged to treat one another with dignity, and lovingly, compassionately, honestly, charitably, chastely, modestly, and humbly. So that they can fulfill their moral obligations, individuals and groups are admonished to develop their characters and nurture and display virtues. The *Bhagavad-Gita*, for example, "mentions the virtues of non-violence, truth, freedom from anger, renunciation, tranquility, aversion to fault-finding, compassion for living beings, freedom from greed, gentleness, modesty, steadfastness, forgiveness, purity, freedom from malice, and excessive pride, anger, harshness, and ignorance."[59] Vaiseska's inventory of virtues includes many of those already noted, plus "kindness to all living creatures," "physical purity," and "devotion to the deity," and Gandhi's register of virtues of course gave the most prominent place to *Ahimsa*, or "nonviolence," which for him would be better translated as "universal love and brotherhood."[60]

Discerning exactly why humankind is expected to behave ethically moves one back into metaphysics and at the same time closes the circle of consideration that opened by inquiring into the foundations of moral universalism in Indian philosophy. Several answers are available. The most basic and for many still the most compelling is that righteous behavior is in compliance with moral laws that accord with imperatives for harmony in the universe. This interpretation stems from the origins of the notion of Dharma in the Vedic texts and associates moral acts with maintaining order and staving off chaos. Vedic sources add the further notion that the gods, or God, constantly monitor human behavior.[61] Later interpretations link Dharma, or righteous behavior, much more directly to attaining Moksa, which is to say that they bridge empirical and eternal existence. The *Bhagavad-Gita*, for example, instructs that clearheadedness and balanced thinking are necessary preparations for commencing the quest for Brahman. The clear-thinking person sorts her temporal tasks, performs her duties, and recognizes that the spiritual ascent toward the Absolute is long and gradual. Similarly, the *Bhagavad-Gita* as well as the works of later thinkers affirm that self-purification must precede self-realization, that a morally defective person cannot merge with God, who is perfect, and that therefore the pathway toward Moksa cannot even be entered upon until moral righteousness is achieved. As the God of the Gita makes known, "these cruel and hateful men, these wicked ones, I constantly throw back into the cycle of existence, into demoniac wombs" (16:19).

Most mystical, but nevertheless most consistent with Hindu metaphysics, is the recognition that within the oneness of the timeless, spaceless, undifferentiated realm of Brahman there is no distinction between humankind and God. All is unity in eternal oneness. To enter this realm, to attain Moksa, therefore means to become one with God, to achieve divinity, and by implication to achieve perfection. Acknowledging this, Radhakrishnan comments that "man is not divine, but has to become divine [i.e., to attain Moksa]. His divine status is to be built up by good thoughts, good words and good deeds."[62] Even more revealingly, E. Washburn Hopkins concludes that "the identity of man as spirit with the Supreme God, which is now pure spirit, has a strong ethical effect. In God is no evil and man must strive for his own perfection and for the world's perfection, for man is one with God."[63] Striving for goodness in the temporal realm may not be sufficient to become one with Brahman, but it is absolutely necessary.

The Mythical Foundations for a World Culture

The obvious conclusion that emerges from comparing the results of analyzing the moral bases of three civilizations is that the myth of the moral unity of humankind is central to all three cases. Among Western thinkers in the secular tradition this myth first found its substantiation in natural law, as displayed in the pantheism of the Stoics and in the theism of the *philosophes*. Some force or mind had ordered the universe. Goodness among people resided in recognizing the principles of this order, reasoning to the ethical implications of it, and acting accordingly. Such reasoning yielded an ethics of toleration, compassion, humanitarianism, justice, and respect, and any who could reason would reason to the same conclusions. Since all human beings could reason, the ethics of toleration, compassion, humanitarianism, justice, and respect were universal, and humankind therefore constituted a moral unity. The Christian tradition in the West recognizes the same panoply of human virtues and endorses the same moral universalism, but grounds their truth in the will of an Almighty God made known through both revelation and reason. Interestingly, Confucian and Indian metaphysics produced very similar ethical results. Belief in the existence of transcendental moral laws also grounds both of the Asian moralities: the dictates of heaven, for the Confucians, and the will of the Vedic Lord of Creation for the Hindus (or, for them, more mystically, the ultimate reality of Brahman). The transcendental powers are impartial; they invest and embrace everyone and hand down the same ethical imperatives to everyone. So here too humankind cannot be other than a moral unity.

Eastern thinking never abandoned its metaphysics: the transcendental groundings remain intellectually intact today, and this lends Eastern moral thought a spiritual dimension that is presently missing from Western secular philosophies. But the West has not abandoned moral universalism. Cosmopolitanism has reentered Western moral philosophy in the form of neo-Aristotelianism, and this school's adherents claim that moral universalism is more compelling than ever precisely because is it shorn of metaphysics. No faith is necessary to affirm moral universalism; empirical observation and cold logic show well that humankind constitutes a moral community because every human being's ethical claims on every other human being are identical.

It is also apparent from comparing the moral foundations of the three civilizations that the pathways that lead to moral knowledge are different for each. Eastern epistemologies are intuitive and require meditation; Western epistemologies are mainly empirical and rational, and require observation and inference. Between Confucianism and Hinduism, the former achieves knowledge by deriving insight from immediate experience, and the latter achieves knowledge by transcending immediate experience. These epistemological differences are profound, but their variety is also liberating to the extent that it becomes clear that there must be more than one pathway to ultimate wisdom and that the human capacity to understand reality is surely more powerful than many would care to admit. Even so renowned a thinker as Immanuel Kant concluded that the human intellect was probably so constrained as never to be able to discern ultimate reality or "things in themselves," but Hindu philosophers since ancient times have insisted that ultimate reality—"things in themselves"—can be known, though not solely via the intellect. What is most striking, however, is that with regard to the fundamental tenets of morality and the imperatives of ethics, the profoundly different Eastern and Western epistemologies lead to the same moral insights. They also generate very similar ethical imperatives. Across cultures we find a similar recognition of mankind's universal moral nature, which everywhere compels compassion, respect, justice, and magnanimity. This is the central finding of this study.

But let us be clear concerning where these conclusions lead. This chapter's odyssey through the moral thinking of East and West has revealed that there are no fatal incompatibilities among the different civilizational traditions regarding moral universality and human goodness. At least this is the case with regard to the three civilizations investigated. This finding is important because it contradicts notions fashionable today about cultural relativism and "clashing civilizations."[64] It suggests that those who claim that there are fundamental moral and ethical differences among contemporary civilizations may be deficient in understanding not only other cultures, but their own as well. Or, more significantly, those who excuse the maltreatment of human beings with the claim that cultural standards allow it might be asked about the cultural standards to which they are referring.

However, what all of this amounts to is that there are reasons, deeply embedded in the mythological lores of different civilizations, for believing that humankind constitutes a moral and ethical community. Rather strong philosophical justifications have been mustered to support such beliefs. There is a myth of the moral unity of humankind, and it is transculturally shared. But the problem today is that the myth of the moral unity of humankind is only one of the public myths that inspire people to act socially and politically, and it is surely not the most powerful among these. To reach universalism one must pass through dense and contradictory layers of provincialism, tribalism, nationalism, regionalism, sectarianism, racism, exclusivism, exceptionalism, ethnocentrisms, orientalism, occidentalism, proletarianism, and any number of other myths that persuade human beings that they are different from one another and that motivate them to act accordingly. Such particularistic myths continue to feed conflicts and justify mutual indifference. If conflict and indifference are undesirable in human affairs, the challenge to statesmanship in the decades ahead is to bolster the salience of the myth of the moral unity of humankind. The challenge to scholarship is to study carefully the historical conditions under which such a myth flourishes.

CHAPTER 10

Liberal Theory and Linear History

International liberalism is both a theory of international relations and a political ideology. But since proponents of the theory are most often also believers in the ideology, it is sometimes difficult to separate articles of fact from professions of faith. As a result, liberal theory in international relations usually combines scientific findings and fond hopes, and liberal theorists, suspended between objectivity and subjectivity, alternate between reporting and exhorting. Liberals are predispositionally optimistic. They have "an ameliorative view of progress in human affairs," and they believe that a freer, more ordered, and less violent world is not only desirable but also possible.[1]

As an ideology, international liberalism looks askance at alternative worldviews, most notably political realism, where liberals cannot accept realist visions of indelible conflict in human affairs.[2] Like political liberalism more generally, international liberalism affirms a cluster of values, including individualism, freedom, political equality, popular sovereignty, constitutional government, private property, unrestricted commerce, and peace. Some of these values come from the Judeo-Christian tradition, while others were born of Europe's eighteenth-century Enlightenment. Culturally, they are all Western, though most liberals believe them to be universal. The liberal ideology also embodies assumptions about human nature, Lockean assumptions for the most part, and about sociocultural evolution as outlined by Immanuel Kant and more generally contained in Enlightenment thinking.[3] As a program of action, "liberalism is committed to the steady, if uneven, expansion of human freedom through various political and economic strategies, such as democratization and free and open commerce, ascertained through reason and, in many cases enhanced by technology."[4] Internationally, Michael Doyle says, liberals "protect human rights, support international cooperation, profess international law, and support international norms."[5] They favor international organizations because these offer frameworks for constructive diplomacy and mechanisms for enforcing international rules. Liberals also encourage global capitalism, because they believe that such economic intercourse and institutions promote peace.

In contrast to their ideologically committed cohorts, liberal theorists of international relations seek to determine whether their science can support their worldview. As a theory of international relations, international liberalism aspires to explain relations among states in terms of a set of conceptualized processes that includes integration, institutionalization, modernization, liberalization, and democratization. The causes and apparent effects of these processes are objects of continuing scientific inquiry. Significant among these effects are cooperation and ordered, lawful behavior among countries that together contribute causally to world peace. Other effects of liberalizing processes include liberty, democracy, and enhanced human security within countries. The causes of some of the processes that liberal theorists see transforming international relations have proven elusive. Still, the benign international outcomes that liberal theorists problematize and analyze are certainly important enough to command intense intellectual attention.

Liberal Internationalism and the Problem of Directional Change

Liberal ideology offers an interpretation of history that, depending upon the articulator, ranges from mild to wild optimism. Liberals, Yale Ferguson and Richard Mansbach observe, believe that "history is going somewhere."[6] For international liberals, Mark Zacker and Richard Matthew add, "world politics is about evolution," and the evolution is in the direction of a better world.[7] Although few liberal internationalists writing today can agree with Francis Fukuyama that a fully liberal world is imminent, many accept that this world is already partially in place and they expect the "liberal revolution" to continue.[8] "Liberalism is an extraordinary beacon of hope in the long run," Doyle says.[9] Or, as Robert Keohane more modestly points out, liberalism "constitutes an antidote to fatalism and a source of hope for the human race."[10]

Many liberal writers, perhaps most of them, believe that international history is directional, that it is progressive, and that it is evolving toward the ascendance of liberal values worldwide. A good many international relations scholars are liberals, Zacker and Matthew observe, because "they think...that the underlying forces of change are creating opportunities for increased cooperation and a greater realization of peace, welfare and justice."[11] As prophets, international liberals believe in such "underlying forces of change," and as scholars international liberal theorists have been seeking to establish their existence and explain their workings. *But are there actually underlying forces driving world politics in what international liberals would define as progressive directions?* Are world politics really about evolution, as Zacker and Matthew find liberals believing?[12] Are relations among states and peoples ineluctably moving toward a greater realization of peace, welfare, and justice?

Liberal theorists have been phrasing and rephrasing these questions in various ways. For example, Kant, whose writings have become a font of inspiration for liberal theorists of international relations, wanted to know whether relations among states were evolving toward perpetual peace. He wondered more specifically whether the emergence and expansion of liberal societies would result in peaceful relations among them. G. W. F. Hegel wanted to know whether human cultural evolution was moving in the direction of freedom. That is, would the whole world eventually be a liberal one? Karl Marx, very much in the liberal tradition, pondered the relationship between capitalism, a liberal institution, and peace, drawing gloomy conclusions at least in the short run, while Joseph Schumpeter later considered the same relationship with more promising results.

Among contemporary liberal theorists there has been a good deal of attention to the future of international relations. Doyle, for example, has been concerned with whether the cluster of liberal democracies that presently includes more than half of the countries of the world will continue to expand, or, more precisely, "[C]an the liberal zone of peace be effectively preserved and expanded?"[13] Fukuyama asks Hegel's question again: "[I]s there some longer-term pattern of development at work that will eventually lead all countries in the direction of liberal democracy?"[14] In other words, are we to have a liberal world and an accompanying liberal world politics? In separate analyses, both Robert Keohane and James Lee Ray turn Kant's question around and ask whether an increasingly liberal world will generate increasingly liberal societies.[15]

The deeper, broader, and to me more interesting questions underlying the liberals' evolutionary concerns have to do with linear history. *Is there a direction to international history, and even more tantalizingly, is there an end?* These questions are hardly new ones. Robert Nisbet, for example, traces teleological inquiry in the West back to writings of the Greek philosopher Heraclitus, who articulated a notion of organic growth, which, through numerous permutations eventually blossomed into the idea of "development" that is so deeply embedded in the Western worldview.[16] In another attempt at the intellectual history of teleological inquiry, Frank E. Manuel goes back to the Hebrew biblical tradition and the prophecies of the *Book of Daniel* and then moves forward through the Christian tradition beginning with St. Augustine's vision of humanity's progression from Creation to Final Judgment.[17] Many of the social thinkers of the eighteenth-century Enlightenment asked about directionality in history and then affirmed that the human race was pointed in the direction a perfectibility that would result in a world of increasing social harmony, material abundance, and peace. The Marquis de Condorcet, for one, believed this, and wrote about it even as he was seeking refuge from the guillotine.[18] Voltaire also believed in human progress, as did Anne Robert Jacques Turgot, Bernard Le Bovier de Fontenelle, the Count de Saint-Simon, among the French philosophes; and in Germany, of course, there were the well-known writings of Immanuel Kant, who believed that if a universal history of humankind were written it would show a progression from savagery in relations among peoples toward a future "union of nations wherein each, even the smallest state, could expect to derive its security."[19]

Though challenged, especially in Germany by thinkers in the Machiavellian tradition, the idea that history was directional and progressive and that international history was a story of growing harmony among states persisted through the nineteenth century. Such thinking fell into disrepute in the twentieth century, because amid the crises and carnage in this century's first half, any progressive interpretation of history had to appear ludicrous. Nevertheless, liberal international theorists, carrying forward the international "idealist" tradition of the 1920s and '30s, have not stopped wondering where the world is headed and they have not stopped trying to find out.

Liberal Theory, International History, Democratization, and Peace

Some of the most definite liberal prophecies have to do with democratization. Classically, these are to be found in the writings of Kant and many other writers of his era, where "a regular procession of improvements in constitutional government" is assumed, leading to what we would identify as the universalization of liberal democracy.[20] Some present-day liberal writers also foresee a universally democratized world and look for its realization in the near to midterm future. Fukuyama, for example, is most confident that history is "a single, coherent, evolutionary process" and that "it dictates a common evolutionary pattern for *all* human societies—in short, something like a Universal History of mankind in the direction of liberal democracy."[21] Then, in a most remarkable passage, in his essay titled "A Liberal View: Preserving and Expanding the Liberal Pacific Union," Doyle offers approximate dates for the democratization of the world. "We can project when all regimes will have become liberal," Doyle writes. This should happen between 2050 and 2100, depending upon conditions of war and peace during the twenty-first century.[22] Elsewhere Doyle is more cautious about the future of liberal democracy, acknowledging that extrapolating for the past is methodologically questionable and that a number of factors "could upset Kantian expectations."[23] But Doyle, like many other liberal internationalists, nevertheless expects the spread of democracy.

Democracy and international relations come together in the analysis of the causes of peace. *Peace*, not democratization, is what liberal international theory is seeking to explain. What liberal theorists postulate, however, is that democratization explains peace. That d*emocracies do not go to war with one another* has proven to be much more than an article of liberal ideological faith. Extensive, careful, and methodologically sound empirical testing recently conducted by several scholars has established a definite positive correlation between democratic regimes and nonviolent diplomacy during the last two centuries. This is virtually the entire time during which there have actually been democratic regimes, so that, empirically speaking, democratic international relations are peaceful. Summarizing a good deal of work preceding their own, John Oneal and Bruce Russett note that "most political scientists now agree that contemporary peacefulness can be traced in part to the so-called democratic peace, wherein established democratic states have fought no international wars with one another and the use or threat of force among them, even at low levels, has been rare."[24] Ray, in an intensive analysis of democratic peace, agrees that the empirically established relationship between democracy and peace "supports the conclusion that the proposition is worthy of continued serious consideration."[25]

Exactly why democracies refrain from warring among themselves is a matter of debate among analysts. Some postulate that democratic public opinion is peace oriented and that Kant was correct when he observed that "nothing is more natural than that those who would have to decide to undergo all the deprivations of war will very much hesitate to start such an evil game."[26] Leaders in democratic countries are therefore more constrained to act accommodatingly in foreign affairs than their authoritarian counterparts. Other analysts explain that the peoples of democratic societies share values, and recognizing this, they also share identities that catalyze the peaceful resolution of disputes among them. Still others note that the ethos of democratic politics itself instills norms of bargaining and compromise, as well as an eschewal of political implacability, that also favor nonviolent conflict resolution. It could be the case as well that democratic governments and peoples in liberal societies harbor mutual expectations about how others in similar societies are likely to behave in conflict situations. Nonviolent conflict resolution thus becomes a self-fulfilling prophecy stemming from such expectations. Or, it may well be that democratic societies generally share other attributes, like open market economies and rule of law traditions, that better explain their pacific behavior than does the attribute of democracy itself. To this point, we do not really know *why* democracies tend toward nonviolent conflict resolution in their mutual relations, although it is pretty well established that they do.[27]

It is important to underline that the correlation between democracy and peace pertains only to relationships among democratic regimes. Democracies *do* fight wars with nondemocracies, indeed many such wars, so that historically overall democracies fight about as much as other kinds of states. Therefore, *the promise of a peaceful world follows not from the fact that democracies do not fight one another, but rather from the spread of democracy*. A uniformly and universally democratic world would presumably be a peaceful one. Notes Ray, "If relationships among democratic states are fundamentally different from those among combinations of democratic and undemocratic states, as well as among uniformly undemocratic states, then a significant trend toward democracy, even if restricted to most powerful states in the international system, could transform international politics."[28]

Yet, is there such a historical trend toward democracy, and, if so, how is it to be explained? These are key questions confronting liberal international theory today. To resolve them affirmatively would not only require demonstrating democracy's diffusion, but also identifying the force(s) driving it. Such findings would endow liberal international theory with a rather impressive degree of predictability. If the trend were established and the driving mechanism(s) were known, and if it could be further established that these mechanism(s) are relentlessly chugging along, then a liberal, democratically peaceful future could be anticipated rather than simply hoped for. Identifying such drivers, moreover, would also amount to affirming directional history, perhaps even to endorsing teleology in human affairs. On the other hand, to conclude that there are no explicable forces necessarily driving the spread of democracy would be to deprive liberal international theory of predictability, thus weakening the theory intellectually. Some would say that denying predictability to liberal international theory also renders it inferior in this regard to political realism, which can at least reliably anticipate cycles of rising and falling power.[29]

Research has shown that there is a three-century-long *empirical trend* toward an increasing number of democratic regimes in the world. Numbers of democratic regimes and patterns of progression and diffusion vary somewhat from study to study, mainly because different researchers define democracy in different ways. Most, however, include in their definitions constitutional government, the popular election of top political leaders, representative legislative institutions, the rule of law, and guaranteed civil and political rights. In one counting of "liberal communities" that begins in the eighteenth century and moves forward to the late twentieth, Doyle observes that the world's "liberal zone" has expanded over time from three democracies to sixty-eight.[30] Fukuyama's list of democracies grows from three in 1790 to sixty-one in 1990, leading him to conclude that "while there have been cycles in the worldwide fortunes of democracy, there has also been a pronounced secular trend in a democratic direction."[31] Ray reviews the work of several scholars who have examined the spread of democracy, most of whom agree that there has been a "global democratizing trend" operating worldwide for quite some time.[32] For his part, Samuel Huntington observes that there have been three periods since the beginning of the nineteenth century—1828 to1926, 1943 to 1962, and 1974 to circa 1991— during which the number of democratic regimes in the world increased.[33] Each of the first two periods was followed by a "reverse wave" during which the number of democracies decreased, and Huntington supposes that this might also be the case regarding the most recent wave. He concludes, however, that over time a ratcheting effect has been in evidence so that reverse waves never completely cancel democracy's general expansion. Huntington acknowledges that "history is messy and political changes do not sort themselves into neat historical boxes." Nevertheless, "democratization waves and the reverse waves suggest a two-step-forward, one-step-backward pattern," and "to date each reverse wave has eliminated some but not all the transitions to democracy of the previous democratization wave."[34] Thus, empirically speaking, democracy is spreading.

But exactly why has democracy been spreading? "Without theory," Patrick McGowan and Howard Shapiro remind us, "we can only make predictions of the crudest sorts upon projections from empirical trends."[35] Therefore, if the future of democratic peace is to be rendered predictable, then the future of democracy also must be rendered predictable. The apparent empirical trends toward diffusing democracy therefore need to be *explained*.

Immanuel Kant had no problem identifying the historical driver that was moving democratization forward. This was nature itself. A liberal world was foreordained: institutionalizing freedom was the plan of providence; the plan would be realized no matter whether humans cooperated or not. "Nature's mechanical course evidently reveals a teleology: to produce harmony from the very disharmony of men even against their will."[36] In Enlightenment thinking more generally, progressive history was either predetermined by a metaphysical eminence and manifested in "natural law," or syllogistically provable via the application of right reason.[37] But since the foundations of Enlightenment thinking have been rather mercilessly trampled by the twentieth-century marches of philosophy, psychology, physics, art, and literature, neither confidence in nature nor in logical necessity is much in evidence today. To search, therefore, for the mechanisms producing progressive history, or more precisely progressive democratization, requires looking elsewhere.

From Modernization to Democratization to Peace?

A number of liberal theorists have looked to economic modernization to explain progressive democratization. *Economic modernization leads to political democratization,* they say, and therefore a modernizing world will be a democratizing world and ultimately a peaceful world. It all begins with science and technology, and it dates from the very dawn of history. From their very early emergence, the cumulatively increasing power, remarkable and cumulative achievement, and worldwide diffusion of science and technology have been the most readily identifiable directional trends in history. Some say, in fact, that the relentless march of science and technology is the *only* identifiable linear trend in history. Since the appearance of *Homo sapiens* on our planet, there has been a trend in human affairs toward an ever-increasing control over physical nature, and if accomplishments in the life sciences, again both very ancient and very modern, are added, the trend has also been one of increasing control over biological nature. The progression of science and technology is not teleological, inasmuch as there is no foreseeable end point or definable purpose. But the trend is unilinear: humanity overall has never opted for primitive technologies when more advanced ones were known, affordable, available, and applicable, and technological advances occur continuously.[38]

Theories of modernization begin by assuming this evolution of science and technology and proceed by linking technological progress to the satisfaction of human material needs.[39] Advancing technology applied to satisfying human needs first makes possible and then makes imperative changing modes of production, and changing modes of production make possible and then imperative changing social, political, and cultural institutions. Marxists, probably wrongly, saw in this developmental sequence concurrent social, political, and institutional changes that would eventuate in a classless society, a socialist economy, and a stateless polity. Liberal theorists, on the other hand, postulate a linkage between economic modernization and political democracy; Fukuyama makes this argument rather well.[40] The historical advance of science and technology leads eventually to industrialism, that is, to a revolutionary change in the dominant mode of production occasioned in the first instance by technical applications of previous scientific discoveries. Inevitable social and cultural innovations accompany the new mode of production and ensure that it results not only in greater output, but also in greater wealth for those who control the new technologies. These sociocultural innovations invariably include the institutionalization of market capitalism, and this economic institution creates and nurtures a new *industrial middle class*. Then, to protect its interests—and its wealth—this class applies its economic power to the pursuit of enhanced political power and ultimately forces the liberalization of authoritarian regimes.

But the onset of industrialism has additional social effects, among these the creation of industrial working classes, which also come to demand and acquire political influence. More important, perhaps, advancing industrialism requires an increasingly highly skilled labor force, and meeting this requirement in turn requires education. "The effect of education on political attitudes is complicated," Fukuyama explains, "but there are reasons for thinking it at least creates the conditions for democratic society."[41] Among other things, better-educated people are prone to question the legitimacy of traditional political authorities, to better recognize their self-interests and to "acquire a certain sense of dignity, which they want respected by their fellow citizens and the state."[42] They therefore come to demand social and political institutions that meet their social expectations.

The sequence *technology–industrialism–capitalism–middle-class society–democracy* reappears with considerable frequency in the literatures of economic development and political modernization. However, there are some interesting variations on the main themes. For example, in his important early study on *The Dynamics of Modernization,* Cyril Black first describes the economic progression toward industrialism occasioned by the advance of science and technology. He then associates these transformations of the economy with transformations of society, which initially involve a broadening of elites. "There is a considerable broadening of the ruling group," Black explains, "as the sources of recruitment change from land ownership to business, commerce, and areas requiring university-trained specialists." In the course of this social transformation from agrarian to industrial society, Black observes, "executive, managerial, and service strata may come to embrace as much as one-half the population of a society."[43] There then follows the emergence of mass society, because "mass production cannot be maintained without mass consumption."[44] Nor can mass production occur without mass education, which, among other things, equips much greater numbers of people with skills for political participation. Comparing the modernization experiences of a number of different societies, Black writes that "at the start, the individuals directly concerned with political power constitute no more than a fraction of the population, and the great majority are peasants or rural and urban workers who have no political role."[45] But all of this changes as traditional agrarian society becomes middle-class industrial society. While Black does not link these social transformations directly to democratization, he does connect them to the degeneration of traditional authoritarian regimes. Basing government on a miniscule, narrowly competent ruling class recruited largely by ascription becomes increasingly unworkable (to say nothing of questionably legitimate) as industrial society matures. Political transformation in the direction of dismantling authoritarianism therefore usually follows upon social transformation, which followed upon economic development.

Samuel Huntington also examines the interrelationships among economic, social, and political changes during modernization. His emphasis, however, is on attitudinal changes in society that accommodate democratic institutions and politics. In other words, social-psychological changes occasioned by economic development establish a political-cultural environment hospitable to democracy. The logic of Huntington's argument begins with the increased and significantly broader distribution of wealth that almost invariably occurs during industrialization. Historically, the heightened well-being of a much-expanded middle class occurs first, followed later by the heightened well-being of the working class. As the level of societal affluence rises, Huntington observes, "the values and attitudes of ... citizens" change. In particular, "interpersonal trust, life satisfaction and competence" all increase, and these feelings "correlate strongly with the existence of democratic institutions."[46] Concurrently, as others have observed, economic development requires better-educated people, and along with new practical skills, Huntington says, "more highly educated people tend to develop the characteristics of trust, satisfaction, and competence that go with democracy."[47] To his explanation of linkages between economic modernization and democratization, Huntington adds that generalized increases in wealth and well-being in society also facilitate accommodation and compromise, which are themselves elements of democratic political culture. Overall, Huntington's variations on the theme of economic change leading to social change leading to political change inserts "civic culture attitudes" into the causal nexus. Although, like Cyril Black, Huntington stops short of democratization itself by explaining that his model leads only to "support for democratization."[48]

Among the numerous attempts to identify a historical progression toward democracy, Talcott Parsons's essay "Evolutionary Universals in Society" remains one of the most intriguing.[49] Here he proposes that a process of cultural evolution has long underscored the course of human development. Employing a Darwinian logic, Parsons argues that human development in all of its manifestations has occurred when societies have discovered and adopted certain "universals" in the form of structures and processes that have been necessary for societal success in progressively changing historical environments. Universals are in fact universal because all societies must adopt each of them at appropriate times if their evolution toward modernity is to progress. Technological, physical, and social environments surrounding human communities have been changing over the long course of history, very generally in the direction of increasing populations, increasing size of societal units, increasing sophistication of technology, increasing capacities for production, increasing functional specialization, and increasing complexity in all dimensions of human affairs. All human communities, Parsons postulates, have faced similar environmental challenges at comparable stages of their evolution toward modernity. To adapt to these environmental changes, Parsons proposes, societies have been impelled to progressively innovate social institutions. Moving at their own historical pace, but in similar directions, societies tend to "hit upon" cultural innovations through various kinds of experiences, not infrequently painful ones. Appropriate innovations guarantee societal survival and competitive success, while inappropriate ones, or reluctance to innovate, relegate failed societies either to history's margins (where a number of societies languish today) or to its dustbin.

Very early on, imperative innovations included communication through language, social organization through kinship, and technology. Later universals included social stratification and political legitimation beyond kinship roles. Even later came money and the market system, bureaucratic organization, and generalized, universalistic legal systems. Then, finally, Parsons explains, the environment of advanced modernity impelled "democratic association." The transition to democracy is a necessary stage in political-institutional evolution, because only democracy can "mediate consensus" in the large and complex societies characteristic of the modern world. "At high levels of structural differentiation in the society itself and in its governmental system . . . providing structured participation in the selection of leaders and formation of basic policy, as well as opportunities to be heard and exert influence and to have a real choice among alternatives, is the crucial function of the associational system."[50] And, Parsons insists, "no institutional form basically different from the democratic association" can meet these political requirements. Parsons acknowledges that political democracy is probably not a final form in human cultural evolution. But, those societies that do not democratize will not move on the next stage.

Francis Fukuyama was right to point out that "modernization theory looks much more persuasive in 1990 than it did fifteen or twenty years ago when it came under heavy attack in academic circles."[51] Today it does appear that societies experiencing modernization are coming to look more and more like one another. Critics of modernization theory built their attack around the accusation that such a theory was ethnocentric. Modernization theorists, they said, strongly suggested that being "modern" was tantamount to being "Western" and that the only trail to modernity was the one historically blazed in the West.[52] With regard to some works, this criticism was justified because authors were unabashedly ethnocentric.[53] In other instances the "theory" of modernization became a social scientifically stylized rendition of British history.[54] However, closer examination of this literature thirty years later reveals that the more sophisticated among the modernization theorists, such as Cyril Black and Barrington Moore, for example, were quite sensitive to a variety of permutations in different societies' modernization experiences.

What is most important for purposes of this essay is that not one of these more historically and culturally sensitive scholars was prepared to posit that modernization necessarily leads to democratization. For Black, dictatorships of both the Left and the Right turn out to be compatible with economic modernization, and how a society evolves politically depends at least as much on ideologies favored by elites and on state-society relationships as on the social effects of industrialism.[55] Moore's well-known study *Social Origins of Dictatorship and Democracy* tells a similar story about economic and political changes in the context of modernization. According to Moore, there is no necessary relationship between modernization and democracy. By itself, economic modernization does not explain democratization. Transformations from authoritarianism to democracy are possible, but they occur under particular conditions of interclass relationships. Otherwise, industrialization is also fully compatible with both fascism and communism, as both theory and history amply demonstrate.[56]

Despite his observation that economic development can create attitudinal conditions that support democracy, Huntington ultimately concludes as well that modernization does not explain transitions from authoritarianism to democracy. Again there is no necessary linkage. Beyond this, Huntington argues that there is no single explanation for transitions to democracy— that is, no model processes; no ineluctable pathways, no directional history. "The causes of democratization differ substantially from one place to another and from one time to another," so that "the combination of causes producing democracy varies from country to country" and "the combination of causes generally responsible for one wave of democratization differs from that responsible for other waves."[57] According to Huntington, transitions to democracy only occur when they are historically overdetermined, meaning that many causes must be present to ensure that a transition to democracy will take place. If any further evidence is required on this point, Ellen Comisso's review of the respective collapses of communist regimes in Eastern Europe in the late 1980s provides it.[58] While on the surface all of these transitions toward democracy appeared to be cut from the same historical cloth, in actuality they were all quite different in their causes, political dynamics, and institutional results. At the end of the day, even Fukuyama comes to the conclusion that modernization does not always lead to democracy, as "none of these theories is . . . adequate to establish a necessary causal connection." And, "if we look more deeply into the process, we find that democracy is almost never chosen for economic reasons."[59]

The implications of these findings for liberal internationalism both as a scientific theory and a political ideology have to be disappointing. Modernization is not the historical driver that is going to expand the liberal international community and thereby lead to a future democratic peace; or, at least, modernization is not a very reliable historical driver because it does not always drive toward democracy. Economic development could underpin political transitions to democracy for all of the reasons that the modernization theorists enumerate, and it could very well be that attaining a certain level of economic well-being might be a necessary condition for democratic transition. However, it does not appear to be a sufficient condition. Then too, economic development may not even be necessary for democracy, as the experience of India suggests. There democracy preceded economic development. For all we know as well, Parsons might have been right in postulating a long-term progression in human cultural evolution that makes democratization a required condition for societal success under conditions of modernity. But there is not very much corroborating evidence for Parsons's thesis, and, again, there are several contemporary contradictions.[60] Parsons's theory, for example, predicts the democratization of China, or, failing such political reform, China's marginalization or collapse. However, none of these outcomes is foreseeable in the near future, and since we have no reliable theories to project into the longer term, whether China will democratize or not can only be a matter of hope, dread, or speculation. Modernization theory, in sum, does not endow liberal internationalism with predictability. From it we can say only that the world may move toward more democracy and therefore toward democratic peace. On the other hand, it may not.

Modernization theories, however, are not the only bodies of thought that attempt to explain the diffusion of democracy. Some theorists suggest, for example, that democracy spreads by emulation. One successful democratic revolution encourages the next; one constitution proven successful at furthering particular values inspires replication; one institutionalization of an appealing political philosophy captures imaginations and aspirations elsewhere. Ray offers a very interesting discussion of political-institutional diffusion via emulation, although the implication of his argument is that democracy is not the only object of others' emulation.[61] Different kinds of regimes have proven attractive at different times, depending upon whether they are seen as able to deal effectively with problems confronting societies in particular historical contexts. Therefore, the diffusion of any particular kind of regime at any given time—say, the diffusion of democracy after the Cold War—cannot be interpreted as a linear historical process driven by emulation.

From a very different perspective, but still in pursuit of an explanation for progressive democratization, Robert Keohane suggests that as much as liberal states may contribute to creating a liberal world, a liberal world in turn may create liberal states.[62] The process is therefore canonical, with each phase—international liberalization and national democratization—pushing the other forward. The underlying force driving the overall liberalization process is international commerce. That is, for international commerce to expand, markets must be opened and barriers removed. But to take best advantage of international economic liberalization, national markets have to be liberalized to heighten competitiveness. Such economic liberalization unleashes the forces and impacts of market capitalism on societies, and presumably it structurally transforms such societies and their political institutions in ways described by modernization theorists. Progressive democratization then may be an indirect consequence of a globalizing market economy. Still, we have to ask whether international commerce is in fact a historical driver, whether it relentlessly expands, whether it has the domestically liberalizing and democratizing effects that Keohane postulates, and whether only democratically governed societies can take best advantage of liberalized international markets. This last question is particularly salient in light of a number of Asian countries' seeming success in the late twentieth century at melding market capitalism and political authoritarianism. Reflecting upon economic globalization, Thomas Friedman suggests that what competitive success increasingly demands in a globalized economy are not necessarily democratic states, but strong ones.[63]

Coming nearly full circle in the search for historical forces that may be driving progressive democratization brings one back to Francis Fukuyama and this time to his ventures into psychology. At the deepest level, Fukuyama argues, the forces driving history are idealistic, not material. Technology is a tool, not a primal force. The force is discovered only when we ask why humankind has been using this tool since time immemorial. Fukuyama finds the answer in human psychology, in a drive he calls "desire," which, according to him, is universally embedded in our species. *Desire* is the will to enhance well-being, and it ultimately explains the aeon-long progression of what we may refer to economic development. But, as Fukuyama acknowledges, "desire" does not lead to democracy. *Thymos* does.[64] Also primordially and universally embedded in our species is a need for what Fukuyama calls "recognition," which might be interpreted to mean "respect," "dignity," "autonomy," "individuality," or "freedom," or perhaps all of these or some otherwise-named quality that includes them all. *Thymos* is the human drive to secure this quality. By Fukuyama's reckoning, what has been progressively moving political history through the ages has been this innately human quest for recognition—for freedom. Understandably, this progression leads finally to democracy.

Although Fukuyama's work has been raked over by critics, it is surprising that almost no one has taken him to task for his amateurish psychology.[65] Since his authority on human nature is Hegel, he invariably produces a metaphorically told story about the freeing of the human spirit. But of course notions of "human spirit," "human nature," and even "innate human drives" have been largely abandoned by modern psychology and replaced by empirically tested theories about human personalities. There are many different kinds of personalities, and any given one may change in the course of a human lifetime. Hence, there is likely no such thing as "human nature" in the encompassing sense that Fukuyama postulates. According to contemporary understanding, humans are both psychologically complex and psychologically diverse. Anthropologically speaking, humans are also culturally diverse, so that attributing universal strivings is likely to be incorrect. This probably has always been the case, so that basing a universal, linear history on questionable conceptions of human nature and universality, as Fukuyama has, must be somewhat suspect. Fukuyama's argument, therefore, is surely not persuasive enough to be the answer to liberal theory's quest for predictability.

Still, the idea that political development in the direction of democracy is being historically driven by causes other than material ones remains intriguing. Shortly before his death in 1994, historian Donald Treadgold published a rather remarkable volume that one reviewer described as "an encyclopedic history of freedom."[66] Here, Treadgold takes as his hypothesis Raymond Aron's assertion that "freedom is the strongest and most enduring desire of all mankind," and accordingly compiles a survey of political institutions that spans all of recorded history and encompasses the entire world.[67] By *freedom* Treadgold means individual autonomy—that is, "the natural wish of the human being not to be interfered with." He observes that this kind of autonomy can be nurtured and protected only under conditions of political pluralism, incorporated above all in democratic forms of government.[68] Scouring history, Treadgold locates countless attempts to institutionalize human freedom. They have occurred and recurred rather haphazardly through time and across space, suggesting thereby an historical pattern of "try, try again" as regards humans' quest for freedom. From his research, Treadgold draws two conclusions: first, "past history should inculcate a healthy skepticism concerning whether democracy is about to be attained everywhere in the world," but second, "the whole story, with its fits and starts and triumphs and tragedies, deserves ... thoughtful reflection ... for along with failure and misery it holds much that is noble and uplifting, tells of much gain for humanity through patient suffering and self-sacrifice, and catches a vision of liberty for all in the present and possible future that was inconceivable at the dawn of history."[69] There is no ineluctable trend toward democracy. But, the struggle to attain and institutionalize freedom appears to be a historical constant.

From Interdependence, to Institutions, to Peace?

Is it possible that a world of diverse political regimes—that is, democracies, nondemocracies, and variations in between—might also be a peaceful one? Or, even among democracies, might there be more to explaining their peaceful relations than their similarly liberal societies and comparable forms of government? Keohane reminds us that "for Kant republicanism only produces caution; it does not guarantee peace" so that "to prevent war, action at the international level as well as the national level is necessary."[70] Peace is a passive state of international relations—that is, the absence of war. In this sense, it is the effect of causes contained in more active modes of international relations that are also of great interest to liberal theorists. These more active modes include processes and projects in international cooperation, and among these in particular the establishment of international institutions.

While it has become rather fashionable of late for liberal international theorists to turn to the work of Kant for inspiration and direction, it is not really necessary to go that far back into intellectual history to talk theoretically about relationships between international institutions and world peace. Kant does indeed postulate that peace can be buttressed by "federations" of states as well as by international law. But so do modern-day functionalists make such claims, and their formulations are much more elaborately spelled out, and much less in need of contemporary interpretation, than are Kant's. From early on, functionalists have suggested that key causal relationships in international relations tie international institutionalization to peace.[71] In this regard, the transformation of intra-European international relations during the last half of the twentieth century offers rather impressive prima facie evidence.

There also exists a good deal of more systematic evidence concerning the interrelationship between international institutionalization and peace. For example, in 1998, Bruce Russett, John Oneal, and David Davis published the results of a carefully executed quantitative analysis of interrelationships among (1) mutual memberships in international organizations, (2) kinds of national political regimes, (3) economic interdependence, and (4) involvement in wars.[72] Mutual membership in international organizations is a fairly direct measure of international institutionalization. The study revealed first that democratic regimes, economic interdependence, and mutual memberships in international organizations "substantially correlated with one another," which led the authors to underline that "good things do go together."[73] Second, each of the three conditions was separately related to peaceful relations between countries, and according to the authors "the independent benefits of democracy, interdependence, and shared IGO [intergovernmental organization] memberships are . . . substantial."[74] Data analyzed in this study spanned the years 1950 to 1985 only, but in a follow-up project, Oneal and Russett extended their data historically back to 1885 and reached similar conclusions about relationships among democracy, economic interdependence, membership in international organizations, and peace.[75] These findings rather strongly suggest that there are other important correlates of peace besides democracy, and therefore, there may be other processes besides democratization that are driving toward the more benign kind of international relations that liberal theorists envision. In particular, *progressive international institutionalization* may be one of these processes.

But is international institutionalization progressive? Do the proliferation of international organizations and the expansion of international law (which also must be looked upon as an international institution) represent linear historical trends in the direction of diminishing anarchy in relations among states? Or, more positively, is there a linear historical trend in the direction of increasing international governance, and can we therefore be assured that tomorrow there will be greater regulation of states' behavior in the common interest, greater numbers of institutions that regulate such behavior, and more international order and less international disorder than today?

Most analysts would agree that there is an historic trend toward the increasing regulation of international behavior. International law, for example, has been expanding both with regard to its subjects and to its subject matter for a very long time.[76] The beginnings of positive international law—that is, rules and regulations contracted by states (and today by other parties as well)—have been traced by archaeologists to early human civilizations in Mesopotamia and China.[77] Treaties between ancient states regulated war, peace, and commerce. Regulations affecting the conduct of war were observed among the ancient Greeks and became increasingly important in the West during the Middle Ages. The regulation of international maritime affairs dates at least from the Rhodian Codes that were aimed at pacifying the Mediterranean and recorded between 500 and 800 C.E.[78] Rules regarding permanent diplomatic representation and diplomatic immunities probably first entered into widespread practice during the Renaissance in Italy. Later, the emergence of the Westphalian state system in Europe gave birth to modern international law focused on the privileges, immunities, and responsibilities of sovereign states. The early twentieth century saw major extensions of the laws of war and peace and first attempts at international tribunals. During the nineteenth and twentieth centuries, the system of international law that originated in Western Europe universalized.[79] More recently, the subjects of international law have come to include not only states but also international and transnational organizations, and even individuals, with respect to the protection of their human rights. In our time, too, there has been a major expansion in the range of international regulation into new matters of commerce, communication, and transportation; and matters regarding the oceans; outer space and Antarctica; health; migration and environmental protection; whales; ivory; diamond smuggling; trafficking in drugs, women, and children; and much, much more.

The expansion of international law has been cumulative over the longest stretch of time: save perhaps the collapse of the *jus gentium* after the fall of the Roman empire, there has never been *less* international law at historically later dates than at earlier ones.[80] But the expansion of international law has also been sporadic inasmuch as there have been periods of great innovation interspersed with periods of minimal activity. In recent decades the corpus of international law has expanded very rapidly, suggesting that the second half of the twentieth century may have been another period of international legal innovation. Such innovation seems to be continuing at present, but might conceivably soon run its course. Alternatively, we may be currently witnessing a change in the shape of international law's progressive growth curve, which from 1945 onward appears to have become almost exponential. Louis Henkin acknowledges this and explains that what we have been seeing in our time is the expansion of a new kind of international law that he calls the "law of cooperation." This kind of international law establishes ground rules and fashions instruments for collective international problem solving. Henkin says that it should be distinguished from the more traditional kind of international "law of 'abstention' that prescribes limits on the freedom of action of governments" in the interest of creating conditions for orderly intercourse.[81]

Allowing that Henkin is correct, we might further assume that different processes probably have been driving the international "law of abstention" and the international "law of cooperation." In the formation of traditional international law—that is, the "law of abstention," Edward Morse explains, "there was the premise that state survival required the maintenance of a minimal system of order among state actors."[82] Henkin agrees: "Nations have a common interest in keeping the society running and keeping international relations orderly."[83] Attaching value to order has not only served the interest of survival but also of commerce, day-to-day diplomacy, and other necessary and ongoing transactions among states. In fact, despite obvious and frequent lapses into disorder, pursuing order through law has been a *constant* in the history of international relations, and as a constant it explains a prevailing condition—normal orderliness—and not a historical trend. Conducting transactions among societies requires minimal order. This has always been so, and the requirement for order continues to found international law and regulate international relations today. Ordering via the international "law of abstention" will likely continue at least as long into the future as states remain principal international actors. But it is important to note that while yielding minimal order, this kind of traditional international law has not produced the peaceful world that liberal theorists envision. In this regard, projecting it into the future is not especially promising. States have always had other interests besides order, and these too are likely to continue into the future.

Trends in the "international law of cooperation," however, are more interesting because they match trends in the founding of international organizations. In the twentieth century the expansion of the international law of cooperation and the proliferation of international organizations had similar trajectories: they both increased very rapidly, particularly after the middle of the century. There was 1 intergovernmental international organization in 1860, but there were 11 by 1900, 31 by 1930, 81 by 1950, 242 by 1970 and 293 by 1990.[84] In his important study *Modernization and the Transformation of International Relations*, Morse explains that these trends in the international law of cooperation and the founding of international organizations constitute a single pattern of historical development in the direction of greater international institutionalization.

What is most important, according to Morse, is that this pattern can be explained. It is a product of economic modernization.[85] Thus, here again *modernization* becomes the driver of historical change in the direction of a liberal, peaceful world. However, in Morse's formulation, what is being driven by modernization is not democratization but international institutionalization. The causal sequence again begins with accumulating technology. By familiar reasoning, the increasing sophistication of technology leads ultimately to industrialism, and this leads both to greatly enhanced capacities for international interaction, and to greatly expanded opportunities as well as needs for conducting economic activities beyond national borders. All kinds of international transactions increase.

Under modern conditions, one frequent result of conducting economic activities beyond national borders is the forging of bonds of interdependence between and among interacting societies. Societies come to depend upon one another as customers, suppliers, and financiers, and they respectively come to depend upon their mutual relationships to contribute to national employment, or provide necessary flows of investment, or buttress price stability or all of these amounting to furthering national economic well-being in general. Under conditions of interdependence, therefore, the economic well-being of one society comes to depend upon prevailing conditions—and decisions made—in another society, and vice versa. Moreover, in most countries in our modern era, the political tenure of the government (or sometimes political stability overall) is linked to the economic well-being of the society because governments are increasingly put upon to make citizens' lives materially better and are politically penalized when they fail to do so. Consequently, international economic interdependence can crucially affect the political fates and fortunes of national ruling elites. Partner governments, however, can often assist one another both economically and politically by exploiting the bonds of interdependence to accommodate mutual needs.

However, international interdependence need not be benign. Under conditions of interdependence economic adversity as well as prosperity can be exported, and so can political pressures and problems. Furthermore, insensitivity on the part of one linked partner, indifference to the external effects of domestic policies, or actions deliberately undertaken in the name of narrowly defined national interests can gravely penalize dependent others, and conflicts—even wars—can follow. *Herein lies the linkage between interdependence and international institutionalization.* "Modernization," Morse observes, "is accompanied by increased levels and types of interdependences among societies, which require . . . a high level of international cooperation."[86] To produce mutually benign results and hedge against penalties, relations between interdependent societies must be conducted according to rules that encourage accommodating behavior and discourage disruptive behavior. Moreover, as international interdependence broadens and deepens, the need for international rule-making increases. When responded to appropriately, this need generates rules, laws, and organizations aimed toward managing interdependence, and the proliferation of such management mechanisms amounts to the progressive institutionalization of international relations. Hence the causal sequence: from technology to economic modernization, to international interdependence, to international institutionalization, and by observed correlation, to a higher probability of peace.

In his *Beyond Sovereignty,* Marvin Soroos looks at international interdependence from another perspective that usefully complements and extends the earlier work of Edward Morse.[87] For Soroos, the states and peoples of the modern world are circumstantially interdependent because they are all more or less adversely affected by a number of global problems that none of them can unilaterally solve. They will all be further affected by whether, how, and when these problems are dealt with, and to this extent, observes Soroos, their "destinies are intertwined."[88] Such global problems include, for example, nuclear proliferation, the deterioration of our planet's ecosystems, the pollution of the oceans, diminishing natural resources like fresh water, overpopulation, increasing poverty in many parts of the world, and the spread of deadly new diseases. These are, for the most part, problems of modernity. While Soroos does not spell out the causal sequences that created our global problems, many, if not most, have at their core the adverse effects of the relentless march of technology. Like Morse, Soroos perceives a growing propensity to respond to this interdependence of "entwined destinies" through international institutionalization: "A highly interdependent world must be managed to avoid disruptions and chaos that can be detrimental to the interests of all nations."[89] There is, therefore, in Soroos's estimation "a substantial undercurrent of world politics directed toward cooperative efforts at international problem solving."[90] Here the causal sequence runs from the adverse effects of modern technology, to international interdependence, to international institutionalization.

Robert Keohane and Joseph Nye's *Power and Interdependence* also implicitly incorporates a modernization model to explain the emergence of "complex interdependence" as a present-day mode of international relations.[91] "Multiple channels of contact among societies," themselves consequences of modernization, are signal characteristics of this complex interdependence. Observing this leads the authors "to predict a significant role for international organizations in world politics."[92] Later in *Power and Interdependence*, and then more definitively in Keohane's *After Hegemony*, "international regimes" are identified as increasingly important international institutions. International regimes are informal international institutions, consisting of agreed-upon principles, norms, and rules that by mutual understanding and adherence regulate states' behavior regarding particular issues or sectors.[93] In the late twentieth century and certainly continuing today, international regimes have been perhaps the most rapidly proliferating kinds of international institutions. Conditions requiring collective action, Keohane says, create a "demand for regimes," and such demand under contemporary conditions of complex interdependence has been high. In a new chapter on globalization in the 2001 edition of *Power and Interdependence*, Keohane and Nye see increasing global interdependence as the most probable trajectory for international society. Today, "more dimensions than ever ... are beginning to approximate our ideal type of complex interdependence."[94] To the extent that modernization is driving international history and to the extent that its correlates reliably follow, intensifying interdependence predicts increasing international institutionalization, and this for some liberal theorists predict a more peaceful world.

And yet, do the correlates reliably follow? First there is some question about the reliability of the observed trends themselves. Increasing and increasingly complex interdependence, the expansion of the international law of cooperation, the proliferation of international institutions (including regimes)—all are mainly late-twentieth-century phenomena. Theoretically, they all have their roots in the Industrial Revolution, which was itself a result of evolving science and technology in the West, which can be traced through numerous casual linkages all the way back to the emergence of Greek rationalism in the sixth and fifth centuries B.C.E. But why does all of this begin to transform international relations only in the twentieth century? Why is it not equally reasonable to assume that these manifestations of international cooperation in our time index a phase in a historical cycle instead of a linear historical trend? Most things that increase increase for a while, but most increase *only* for a while. It may therefore be too soon to tell whether the observed trends are actually trends. Or, one might at least have more confidence in the directionality of the trends if they had been ongoing for a longer time.

Still, the real rub here again is that no necessary pathway to a benign future can be projected from the modernization mechanism assumedly underlying the institutional trends. Modernization produces international interdependence, *but interdependence invites a variety of responses* and only some of these result in greater international institutionalization. Governments, for example, may reject international cooperation, and they especially shy away from institutionalization because it unreasonably restricts their autonomy. They may therefore opt instead to decrease their dependence on others, even if this is painful and unpromising. Nationalists, fascists, and communists all chose this option in the twentieth century, and until quite recently, international authorities—to say nothing of schools of academics—were advising the governments of poorer countries to choose similarly. Major powers also tend to shirk collective undertakings when unilateralism appears feasible. Or again, as Morse observes, "as the advanced industrialized countries have become significantly interdependent with one another, the objectives of the various societies have become more and more incompatible."[95] In this sense, imperatives of domestic politics, particularly in democratic countries, could lead governments to eschew or abandon international cooperation even when such cooperation might be in their best interest or in the world's best interest. Here the stillbirth of several international environmental regimes comes readily to mind. Otherwise, the annoyances of unmanaged interdependence can spark crises and conflicts before institutions for management can be put in place. Such episodes often set back rather than encourage international cooperation and institutionalization. This was surely the case regarding international monetary affairs during the period between the two world wars, and manifestations of it were also apparent during the Asian financial crisis of the mid-1990s. What frequently ensues in such instances instead of cooperation and institutionalization is a flurry of self-protective "free-for-all" behavior.

Considering the indefiniteness of responses to international interdependence and acknowledging its numerous correlates other than international institutionalization leads Edward Morse to conclude that "interdependences among societies...require but do not always obtain a high level of international cooperation."[96] In the same vein, Soroos concludes that "whatever peace and prosperity is enjoyed in an interdependent world can be a very fragile condition."[97] "National governments," he explains, "frequently display a reluctance to work together to manage interdependence. They persist in pursuing self-help strategies, failing to consider that the welfare of their societies in an interdependent world may be better served by sacrificing some of the prerogatives of state sovereignty."[98] For Keohane and Nye, "history always has surprises," and for Ferguson and Mansbach, "interdependence is thus what actors of many sorts make of it, but the concept remains essentially nonpredictive."[99] Industrialism does not necessarily lead to interdependence and interdependence does not necessarily lead to international institutionalization. Therefore, liberal theory's quest for predictability comes up short again.

International Liberalism and the Transformation of World Politics

To the extent that the findings of my study are valid, liberal theorists of international relations must be disappointed. A liberal future cannot be ascertained. Yet, nothing that was discussed here should cloud the fact that liberal international theory contains a highly sophisticated—and by and large, accurate—description *of the state of contemporary international relations.* In the world in which we live today, and perhaps have been living in for quite some time, cooperation is an evident mode of international relations; international governance via international law, organizations, and regimes is present, reasonably effective, and apparently expanding; a zone of peace characterizes relations among democratic countries; democracy appears to be spreading; and complex interdependence binds most countries today caught up in globalization. All of these happenings, liberal international theory, and *only* liberal international theory, alerts us to look for and challenges us to understand. The ongoing debates between liberal international theorists and political realists, though esoteric, have largely been about the ontology of contemporary international relations—that is, about what is really going on out there. Here, greater perceptiveness is surely on the side of the liberals. Their world is much richer, much more complex, and in many aspects much more real than that of the political realists.

Nevertheless, at this stage of its intellectual development, liberal international theory is unable to say very much either about the future paths or the eventual outcomes of the historical trends that it has purportedly identified. Liberal theorists do not really know whether democracy will continue to spread; neither do they really know whether international relations will become more highly institutionalized. Consequently, they do not really know whether we are moving toward a more peaceful world. What all of this really means is that liberal international theory is not yet a theory. To make it scientifically respectable, and to endow it with predictability, liberal theory needs to investigate and validate a host of contingent relationships. To begin with, liberal international theorists need to tell us under what conditions democracy spreads and under what conditions international interdependence leads to international institutionalization. They then need to tell us about the causes of these causal conditions, and once this is accomplished, they need to inform us about the likelihood that these causes and hence these conditions will materialize in the future. Liberal assumptions about the causes of international political change are presently too simplistic. To be sure, modernization explains something about historical change, but it does not explain enough about progressive change to make even a probabilistic future plausible. The contributions to progressive history of other proffered mechanisms like innate human drives, aspirations for freedom, human propensities to make rational choices, or human abilities to learn remain to be demonstrated. And if it is to be a theory of international relations, liberal internationalism cannot be only about the twentieth century and beyond. In this sense, liberal international theory will likely mature as the analysis of world political change bows more deeply to the complexities of international history.

Those who are ideologically committed to international liberalism may be a bit confounded by my findings. The better world they seek can still be imagined and hoped for, but it cannot necessarily be anticipated because it is unclear where international history is going. They also have to confront the possibility that there is "fallacy in believing that history is going somewhere."[100] Liberals can, of course, continue to urge statesmen to act in reasonable ways and in this manner move toward trying to make their ideological beliefs into self-fulfilling prophecies. Michael Doyle does this, for example, when he prescribes reinforcing "the steadying institutions of multilateral security, whether UN or regional organizations."[101] Robert Keohane does it when he concludes that "liberalism holds out the prospect that we can affect, if not control, our fate, and thus encourages both better theory and improved practice."[102] Or again, Keohane and Nye do it when they specifically advise the U.S. government to "support international institutions that facilitate decentralized enforcement of rules," and to "reflect, in advance of crises, on how international institutions can help achieve cooperation."[103] Of course, there is no necessary reason why statesmen will improve their practice, or why we should expect that they would. Immanuel Kant was wrong when he assumed that providence would create a better world whether humans cooperated or not.

Most disappointed of all with this study's findings must be those who believe that international history is linear, perhaps teleological, and that there are mechanisms driving human affairs in identifiable directions. Very little turned up in this study to suggest that "underlying forces of change" are driving international history in preset directions. Stephen Korbin, therefore, was well advised to remind us to avoid "the very modern assumption that time's arrow is unidirectional and that progress is linear."[104] Yet, all that this study really determined is that there are apparently no immutable forces driving international history in *progressive* directions. Therefore, we must at some point consider that there could be forces driving international history in *degenerative* directions.

Decades ago, in his classic *International Politics in the Atomic Age,* John Herz peered into what was for him the abyss of international history and observed that technology was indeed a directional driving force—military technology.[105] Herz took perennial competition among states, power balancing, frequent failures of deterrence, and consequent wars to be constants in international history, and when he set these in the dynamic context of advancing military technology the degenerative pattern of international history became apparent. Crossing the nuclear threshold had set humankind onto a historical slippery slope to disaster. At this moment, international history became directional (or, with regard to the exponentially increasing destructiveness of military technology over time, perhaps it always has been directional). In response, Herz urged a shift in consciousness toward a new human universalism and counseled statesmen to change their traditional ways because war was no longer rational. The author nevertheless had to lament that "logical preclusion, of course, offers no guarantee against actual resort to all-out war in disregard of rationality."[106] Herz was not alone in fearing that human kind had set itself on a collision course with nuclear disaster, as other writers like Kenneth Boulding and Raymond Aron reached similar conclusions about the same time.[107] Liberals by and large do not accept this degenerative model of international history. But, if for no other reason than that a great deal of historical evidence can be mustered to lend them credence, the notions that advancing military technology is a principle driver of international history and that the end of history is human disaster should not be set aside.

CHAPTER 11

Beyond the Divided Discipline

In 1903, when the editorship of the journal *Archiv für Sozialwissenschaft und Sozialpolitik* passed into the hands of Max Weber, Werner Sombart, and Edgar Jaffé, Weber used the occasion to inquire into the state of German social science at the turn of twentieth century. "When a social science journal . . . appears for the first time," Weber wrote, "it is customary to ask about its 'line'"—that is, in the case at hand, what standards of social scientific scholarship were the editors of *Archiv* going to establish?[1] Weber's inquiry of course became the classic essay "'Objectivity' in Social Science and Social Policy." This needed to be written, Weber reasoned, because there was at the time some urgency in asking about the scope and especially the methods of social science. German scholarship at the turn of the twentieth century was still caught up in a *Methodenstreit,* or quarrel among methods, that, in Weber's words, led to "bitter conflict about the apparently most elementary problems of our discipline."[2]

Max Weber's efforts, not only in his methodological essays but in much of his later work, were attempts to bridge the epistemological chasm that separated the positivists from the idealists, or "objectivists" and "historicists" as they were sometimes called, among European scholars. The former held that human affairs could and should be studied by social scientists using methods similar to those employed by natural scientists. They also expected that similar results in the form of causal laws would follow. The latter, for their part, denied "the possibilities of scientific work in the field of human culture."[3] They stood by their interpretative approaches and doubted whether useful generalizations could ever be gleaned from the countless contingencies of historical experience. Weber managed to transcend the positivist/idealist divide in his own work, integrating as he did systematic observation leading to theoretical generalization and interpretative historiography in works like *The Protestant Ethic and the Spirit of Capitalism.*[4] Not surprisingly, Weber's work drew criticisms from both the positivists and the idealists, which encouraged his colleagues and successors to continue their intellectual feuding.

Déjà Vu?

As we in the field of international relations are well aware, the *Methodenstreit* continues even today. It even raises some of the same issues that divided European scholars in the nineteenth century. We in international relations call it the "third great debate." There is, among many of us who are professionally involved in trying to better understand the world of relations among states and peoples, a rather urgently felt need to more clearly define— or redefine—our field of study. Needed too, perhaps, is a methodological/epistemological truce, and assuredly some increased communication, greater tolerance, and more civility among scholars. This essay, I believe, speaks to all of these needs, although it is hardly the last word regarding any of them. What I offer is one vision of the field of international relations. It combines reflections on the literature(s) of the field and the controversies swirling around them, with conclusions that I reached while researching and writing the several essays that comprise this book.

To the extent that the discipline of international relations is in disarray, the major differences and disagreements among scholars are not for the most part about the contours, concerns, or even the causes of the post–Cold War world. There is, I believe, substantial agreement that studying international relations today requires examining interactions between states and peoples, with at least as much attention paid to peoples as to states. Intercultural interactions are likely to be as consequential in shaping the world of the twenty-first century as intergovernmental interactions. Encounters among cultures via their agents need to be studied more intensely and much more creatively than has heretofore been the case. It is also accepted that contemporary international relations, or perhaps more accurately *trans*national relations, increasingly involve consequential interactions among organizations other than states. This we have been aware of at least since Robert Keohane and Joseph Nye's *Power and Interdependence,*[5] but now such transnational phenomena are best conceptualized as elements of *globalization,* and this poses a number of fascinating questions about borders, markets, networks of interaction, diffusing values, civil society, and global governance—all of which warrant the increasing analytical attention that they are today receiving.[6] The Westphalian state system has not been eliminated, since states, their sovereignty, their interests, their power, and their governments' geopolitical calculations and machinations all continue to be agents and ingredients of international politics.[7] But it appears that in the post–Cold War world international politics are most likely to take the form of states reacting to domestically generated events abroad amplified and echoed via networks of interdependence, and states reacting to social, economic, demographic, and physical movements and forces impacting everywhere. States moving about geopolitical chessboards, contending for power, wealth, glory, and domain, seem no longer to be what international relations are centrally about. There *were* international relations before Westphalia; they were *not* Westphalian. If these were more systematically examined and better understood, what appears today to be the lessening relevance of sovereignty, the reduced importance of territoriality and the marginalization of inter*state* politics per se might be seen as less than extraordinary.[8] Whatever the agents, old or new, international relations—particularly in political modes—are still about values: identity, equity, justice, autonomy, security, and more, usually embedded in ideologies and acted upon by protectors and projectors. It is as likely as not that twenty-first-century international relations will be about liberalism and its challengers, just as twentieth-century international relations were.[9] Enduring challenges to the Enlightenment project are hibernating in Russia, and new ones are coming from Asia and the Islamic world.[10] These need to be attentively assessed and set appropriately into the contexts of a world where race, ethnicity, religion, and culture are internationally politicized as perhaps never before.

When problematized, all of these aspects of the changing world around us add to a promising research agenda for our field. The real problem, and the thrust of this essay, is how to proceed through the agenda. As most of us are well aware, considerable controversy surrounds how research in international relations should be conducted, and there are even questions about who is qualified to conduct it. Here, our discipline is surely again immersed in a "great debate." One might dismiss the great debates in the study of international relations as intellectual diversions, describe them as "games that professors play," deconstruct them as Foucaultian genealogies or dignify them as Kuhnian paradigm shifts. But the questions debated are intellectually important because they are about the identity of an institution—that is, our field, international relations. Moreover, the debates themselves have been anything but trivial in their consequences. Scholarly careers have been (and are today being) established, challenged, and in some cases ruined depending upon academic partisanship. Journals have been turned into ramparts, book reviews into cannonades, academic meetings into gatherings of cults, academic departments into cathedrals, tenure and promotion processes into inquisitions, graduate students into foot soldiers or pawns, and idealists into cynics. Concurrently, contributions to understanding have slipped between subcultural cracks, or been garbled in mutually incomprehensible discourses or politicized into issues about intellectual turf. Would that academic debates were only diversions, but they almost never are.

Questions about the focus, nature, integrity, procedures, and objectives of scholarship in the field of international relations are certainly not new. During the last half century, many of us working in this field have seen such issues debated at least three times, once by "realists" versus "idealists," then by "traditionalists" versus "scientists," and at present by what I suppose we could call "mainstreamers" versus "dissidents." The issues were framed and focused somewhat differently at different times: the first debate centered on questions of ontology and concerned the true or real nature of relations among states. E. H. Carr, as we all know, debated the first debate with himself and displayed his thinking for the rest of us in his classic *The Twenty Years' Crisis.*[11] This exercise, initiated in the late 1930s, prompted three succeeding scholarly generations to take sides, which indeed they did. The second debate centered on questions of methodology—that is, on what are the most reliable ways to study international relations. Raymond Aron, Hedley Bull, and Stanley Hoffmann, among others, rallied the traditionalists around interpretative historiography and historical sociology, while Morton Kaplan, Charles McClelland, J. David Singer, and others affirmed a science of international relations with nomological aims.[12] The methodological confrontation was highlighted in Klaus Knorr and James Rosenau's *Contending Approaches to International Politics.*[13] Its intensity was dramatized in Oran Young's memorable "naked emperor" review of Bruce Russett's *International Regions and the International System* in the April 1969 issue of *World Politics.*[14] This second debate prompted two succeeding generations to take sides, and again they did.

Neither the first nor the second of the great debates were really debates at all, inasmuch as contenders spoke past one another and closure was never reached; the debates never really ended. Acknowledging this, Yosef Lapid signaled in 1989 that the first and second debates about the study of international relations had evolved into a third, which is racking our field today.[15] The issues that centered both of the earlier debates are still in contention among us, and some insist that ontology and/or methodology remain the principal concerns. However, this third debate is really much broader because it raises questions about the identity of the academic field of international relations. It is also much deeper because it brings to the surface epistemological issues concerning what we can know.

In contrast to what happened during the second debate, what is currently dividing scholars in our field is much more than a quarrel about research methods. For one thing, methodological issues per se are less contentious than they once were since the usefulness of quantification has been largely taken off of the debating table. Nowadays most would agree that statistical analyses have their uses, and also, of course, their limitations. The issues today are much more epistemological than methodological. Concerns about the philosophy of knowledge were largely circumvented in earlier renditions of the great debates about the study of international relations. Notably, even Max Weber wanted to avoid questions such as these, and sidestepped them in his methodological essay as "questions far deeper than those raised here."[16] But, as I will explain in moment, epistemological issues can no longer be avoided in the study of international relations (or in social science more generally) because gauntlets have been tossed by both postmodernism and constructivism. Complicating the epistemological debate is the question of whether the study of international relations ought to be an exclusively social-scientific undertaking. Some opt for this exclusiveness, while others point out that the works of humanists, not only historians, but also novelists, poets, dramatists, sculptors, and painters, constitute legitimate and oftentimes important contributions to understanding the realm of human experience we call international relations. Whether our field can accommodate the artists' insights, and handle the methodological/epistemological and pedagogical questions that such intellectual catholicity would raise, is an interesting question.

Of course, all of these concerns about foundations, methods, and scope beg the question of what exactly our field is. What is it that the student of international relations studies? What is central? What is marginal? What belongs intellectually elsewhere? Is the student of international relations a contributor to a discrete academic discipline, or a putterer within a curious subfield of one or another of the broader disciplines? In whatever way this question is answered, or even if the issue of disciplinary autonomy is dismissed as not being very important,[17] with us still is the question of *why* we are studying international relations. Should we be seeking pronouncements of recognizable relevance to the world of practical affairs, or will esoteric communications among ourselves meet our professional obligations?[18] Questioning the policy relevance of our work interestingly brings us back to Max Weber. But it also raises some gnawing normative issues, not least of which is the matter of where our "ideologies"—realism? liberalism?—end and where our "theories" begin.

A Third Debate?

The battle lines in the third debate are not as readily discernable as in the earlier ones, although it is not too far off the mark to say that one main group of contenders deems the study of international relations to be a project for social science and in so doing accepts rather uncritically the epistemological assumptions that support a correspondence theory of truth.[19] This was the position of the majority of contributors to *Visions of International Relations*, a recent symposium that assessed the field of International Relations.[20] Here, a number of contributors made the case for science rather forcefully. To wit, there is an objective reality "out there" that is not only knowable, but also sufficiently regular in its causes and effects to be understood nomologically. The careful invocation of inductive and deductive logics applied to the analysis of systematic observations, as required by the scientific method, will render the real world incrementally intelligible. Charles Kegley, for one, insists that "science can best provide a set of principles for the reunification of scholarship in international relations."[21] The scientific approach to the study of human behavior is systematic, efficient, elegant, and compelling, as long as the assumptions about the world and about knowledge that philosophically ground it are accepted.

Among the scientists we also find the "dueling theorists" who are at the moment esoterically debating, largely among themselves, whether liberalism, realism, or one or another of the "neo-isms" best describes international relations. This ancillary debate makes good theater: it fills anthologies, decorates journals, and suggests questions for doctoral examinations. But it contributes rather little to furthering our understanding of contemporary international relations. To be sure, the work of some of the giants in international relations theory is insightful, at times brilliant; it must be read and pondered. But the derivative writings of disciples, apostles, and novices too often amount to little more than intellectual clutter. The arcane vocabularies in which the debaters choose to cast their discourses also obscure more than they clarify. As already discussed in this volume, to the extent that liberalism depicts a pluralistic, norm-regulated, complexly interdependent international arena, the picture thus displayed is largely accurate but hardly new. It may have to be repeatedly reaffirmed for the edification of realists, but not for the rest of us. To the extent that liberalism projects a culturally undifferentiated, ideologically homogenizing, democratizing world, it is probably wrong.[22] As for realism, structural, classical, neo- or otherwise, its project in parsimony, assumptions about anarchy, and fixation upon geopolitical gamesmanship among major powers tend to reproduce trivial truisms, such as the "discovery" that we live today in a unipolar world. Moreover, by attributing motives derived from the logic of games to abstract agents, rather than directing analytical attention toward the actual motives of statesmen, realism may perhaps capture some of the form of interstate relations, but it misses the substance. It creates a logically elegant world in which nobody lives. Realism does have a respectable intellectual track record when it comes to charting the course of international history, although importing vocabularies from the field of economics and elsewhere is hardly necessary to show this.

Many among the scientists would keep the study of international relations for themselves. Some political scientists in particular insist upon relegating the study of international relations to the status of a subfield within their discipline, designating it "international politics."[23] Conceptual, methodological, and terminological borrowing from other social sciences is approved and encouraged, and works from the humanities are sometimes looked upon as sources of data. History, for example, is to be mined for facts to be packed into databases. But the products of the humanities are seldom accepted as sources of explanation, causal or otherwise, or as legitimate contributions to the corpus of knowledge about international relations, because, in the case of history, researchers' methods are deemed unsystematic, subjective, atheoretical, and nonreplicable, and therefore unreliable. One can, after all, find in history almost anything that one seeks, and one can invariably also find there its antitheses. Artistic works, including histories, are more generally suspect because their epistemological groundings are questionable. Revelation, intuition, introspection, and interpretation are not easily accepted by international relations scientists as pathways to truths about objective reality.

Because science as applied to the study of international relations is considered by many to be the disciplinary mainstream today, we need to call the other contenders in the third debate "dissenters." They question not only the results of four decades of scientific efforts, but also the assumptions underpinning such efforts. "Rigorous empiricism has not achieved for our field what it promised when J. David Singer proclaimed victory over 'traditionalists' three decades ago," writes Richard Mansbach.[24] He is certainly not alone in his skepticism: great fanfare, methodological virtuosity, and prodigious efforts have thus far yielded rather few notable findings and even fewer "laws" of international behavior. Granted that normal science is slow moving, as the scientists of international relations are quick to emphasize, but it has been forty years since the scientific study of international relations was launched with great anticipation, and we might perhaps expect somewhat more from the project.

Still, the most important issues are epistemological, not methodological. Since I have already offered my critique of scientific epistemologies in chapters 2 and 3, there is no need here to make my case anew. What needs to be noted, however, is that I am not the only one making the case. There has been considerable philosophic pondering in recent decades about the origins of knowledge—scientific, humanistic, or otherwise. Much of this points to the recognition that there are no unimpeachable groundings for anything we might like to define as "truth," particularly when truth is conceived of as observational or propositional correspondence with something we define as "reality."[25] Critics therefore contend that science, and particularly social science, as an approach to knowledge is not sufficiently distinct from other approaches to warrant any privileged epistemological position.[26] Some in the field of international relations welcome this as refreshing news.

The harshest critics of science as applied to the study of international relations are the apostles of postmodernism.[27] Postmodernists deny that there is a an "objective reality" that can be known, or that, in any event, there is no objective language in which knowledge can be coded and inter-subjectively transmitted. Therefore, what are purported to be scientific truths based on correspondence to reality can be nothing more than justifications for beliefs.[28] Statements about reality invariably privilege the values of subjects—that is, those making the statements—and these utterances therefore can and should be deconstructed down to their normative cores. The postmodern project reduces knowledge about international relations (or anything else) to subjective prejudice, and while it can evoke skepticism about science, as it surely has, it nevertheless offers no alternative. In postmodernism there is no research agenda for international relations save deconstruction, because there can be no attainable knowledge. This is harsh criticism, indeed. However, those of us who remain committed to trying to better understand international relations are entitled to wonder where it gets us.

More moderate dissenters against the mainstream recognize that science is but one of the several meaningful discourses available for describing and explaining the human experience.[29] Yet, unlike the postmodernists, these scholars accept that such experiences can be explained in intersubjectively meaningful ways. Constructivists, for example, posit that the only "reality" we can know is that which we construct using the signs and symbols of our language.[30] This, of course, also makes "objective reality" an oxymoron and similarly challenges the epistemological foundation of science. However, the constructivists say that we are able to "socially construct" our worlds through communication and conversation, which permits us to reach intersubjective agreements about their contours and dynamics. We may even verify these worlds by intersubjectively agreeing upon what constitutes evidence for their existence, which is probably what many of us as scholars have been doing anyway, although we have seen ourselves as doing science. We then live in the worlds we have socially constructed until believing in them contradicts our experience to such a degree as to require reconstruction.

International relations research in the constructivist mode consists in describing the worlds that the agents of international relations socially construct. This is accomplished by studying and interpreting the vocabularies of their discourses. Since these worlds are built of symbols, we gain access to them by interpreting these symbols. The methods here are essentially hermeneutic, which amounts, interestingly, to the diametric opposite of scientific procedures. Instead of distancing oneself from the object under investigation to *observe* it, the researcher empathetically approaches the object, or "lives into it," as Wilhelm Dilthey long ago instructed, in order to understand it.[31] Explaining and predicting behaviors accordingly follow from understanding the constructed realities.

Is it not also possible that we may sometimes intuit the truth? And, is it not also possible that revelations can be intersubjectively transmitted, and inspirations intersubjectively shared? Demoting science from an epistemologically privileged position to the status of one promising discourse among many opens the way to tapping the wisdom of the humanities.[32] History, for example, need not only be mined for facts to be converted into social scientists' data. Historians' work can be studied for insights into causes, effects, and meanings in human affairs. Literature and literary criticism, painting, sculpture, and architecture embody visions of the human condition that artists and their interpreters identify as "truths." Are these not worth pondering? Perhaps even accepting? Artists' renderings also send signals about emotions and passions that perhaps ought to be taken into greater account by those of us who study international relations. How do international relations feel? An interesting question.

My own brief in criticism of social science's hegemony over the study of international relations, which I suppose allies me with the dissenters in the third debate, is that the humanities have been systematically, and rather arrogantly, excluded from so-called mainstream international relations. Do history, religion, comparative literature, language, philosophy, art, and music really have nothing to contribute to our better understanding international relations? I have written elsewhere,

> As if not only Thucydides (who has apparently been admitted as a proto-IR theorist) but also Herodotus, Xenophanes, Seneca, Ceasar, Cicero, Livy, St. Augustine, St. Jerome, Vico, Voltaire, Croce, Burkhardt, Pirenne, Gibbon, Ranke, Macaulay, Acton, Adams, Taylor, Toynbee, McNeill and Kennedy have no insights to offer concerning relations among states and peoples! As if the *Old Testament* is not a textbook in International Relations, or that the *Koran* or the *Bhagavad Gita* instruct us not all about statesmanship and moral choice. As if Homer, Euripides, Shakespeare, Marlowe, Milton, Kipling, Conrad, Tolstoy, Remarque, Vonnegut, Hemingway, Giraudoux, Camus, Malraux, Tennyson, Elliot, Brittan and Auden do not deepen our grasp of the meaning of relations among states and peoples! As if Goya's "Execution of the Defenders of Madrid,"

his "Horrors of War" and Picasso's "Guernica" are not about international relations, or that Dvorak's "New World," Shostakovich's "Leningrad" or his "Eighth Symphony," Tchaikovsky's "1812," Bob Dylan's "Blowin' in the Wind" or Bob Marley's "Sheriff" for that matter, are not about war and peace or the coming together of cultures![33]

Some of the most penetrating questions we are wont to ask about the world may not be questions about fact or cause, but rather questions about *meaning* that concern such matters as historical significance, moral rectitude, mythological import or aesthetic quality. Such questions of interpretation are typically handled poorly by social scientists, but they can be elegantly dealt with by humanists and brilliantly broached by artists. Ought we not as students of international relations to have in our methodological quivers the interpretative tools required to extract truths from artists' visions?

The Discipline of International Relations

If we in international relations become too engrossed in third debating, chances are good that we will overlook our common interests, or perhaps even forget about our intellectual identity. International relations is an academic *discipline*: full-fledged, full-blown, autonomous, intellectually legitimate, and accomplished. A number of colleges and universities in the United States have departments for the study of international relations; several of these grant degrees in international relations, including the doctorate. We might call international relations a *field* if we are so predisposed, as long as we understand that what we mean by *field* is the intellectual canvas that displays the phenomena in which we are interested. This would be similar to Hayden White's use of the term *field* when, discussing historiography, he described the historian's field as a phenomenal range, extending through time and across space that displays the chaos of human motivations, perceptions, actions, relationships, and results that intellectuals seek to render intelligible.[34] Our field too is to be identified in terms of the world in which we are interested, and the purpose of our discipline is to render this world intelligible. Let us, then, avoid thinking of our discipline as a subfield of something else; it's not. Our discipline has subfields of its own.

Despite all of the differences and debates among us, the discreetness of our discipline is in the objects of our attention, and our unity is in our research agenda. Scholars in the discipline of international relations seek to identify and explain phenomena that result from encounters among states and peoples, and in particular to contemplate the uniqueness of such phenomena. We seek to identify and understand what happens when states encounter one another, when other organizations operating across political or cultural boundaries encounter one another, when peoples as cultural communities encounter one another, and when entities of all of these varieties encounter all others. Such encounters involve agents that need to be identified, processes that needed to be tracked, and outcomes that need to be inventoried and explained. As a result of the efforts of generations of scholars, our discipline has made considerable progress toward building a sophisticated understanding of encounters among states. We now have a rather comprehensive inventory of outcomes and reasonable understandings of when, how, and why such outcomes occur. With regard to other kinds of interorganizational encounters, our discipline has some way yet to go, and with regard to intercultural encounters, which we have neglected for far too long, we have not yet reached the point of even identifying exactly what happens, or may happen, when cultural communities meet in either space or time. There is, therefore, a great deal of work still to be done.

To be sure, phenomena analogous to those in which our discipline is interested may occur in other fields of human affairs and the student of international relations can gain insight by examining these. It is also the case that scholars working in cognate disciplines may wish to carve out subfields within their disciplines concerned with international or transnational manifestations of problems that interest them. They are welcome to do this, and we can learn from them. But the distinctiveness of international relations as a discipline is that we focus our attentions on a cluster of interorganizational and intercultural phenomena that *we have theoretically identified and conceptually constructed,* and that are preeminently of interest to us because they occur in a realm of human affairs that we are both motivated and trained to study. Our investigations into these outcomes have contributed to a distinctive corpus of knowledge that may or may not inform the "international" subfields of other disciplines. Other disciplines should perhaps be learning more from international relations than they apparently are, but this is something about which we can do little. Our concerns must be with the phenomena that we are trying to explain and not with what cognate disciplines are trying to explain.

As for our intradisciplinary debates, they will likely continue. The third debate, however, may turn out to be salutary by establishing that there are multiple pathways to knowledge about international relations, and this at least should open the way to the incorporation of the insights of the humanities into our discipline. As discussed in chapter 3, acknowledging that there are multiple pathways to knowledge might also lead us to accept what William James frequently referred to as *pragmatic truth,* or knowledge that is useful enough to guide human behavior reasonably successfully toward human objectives.[35] If epistemological exclusiveness could be waived, and today it is largely up to international relations scientists to waive it, the way would also be opened to transforming the study of international relations from a battleground of contending factions into a continuing, and indeed exciting, dialogue among intellectuals interested in better understanding relations among states and peoples. What those of us who study international relations might agree on is that we are seeking *edification*. This is different from objective truth, which is at least elusive and possibly mythical. Edification, Richard Rorty wrote in his *Philosophy and the Mirror of Nature*, means human intellectual and spiritual growth arrived at by considering and contrasting constantly new or alternative ways of describing reality.[36] Each project—that of mythology, religion, history, art, or science—has its own discourses, and each of these yields interpretations of human beings and human affairs by its own methods and its own justifications. Edification comes from a continuing conversation among discourses. Would it not be refreshing if such continuing conversation, and not periodic great debates, became the intellectual mode of international relations?

Notes

Chapter 1

1. Review by Harold D. Lasswell, *Saturday Review* 44:2 (1961), 31.
2. Review by C. A. McClelland, *American Political Review* 55:1 (1961), 209.
3. Carl G. Hempel, *Philosophy and Natural Science* (Englewood Cliffs, N.J.: Prentice-Hall, 1966).
4. Hedley Bull and Adam Watson, eds., *The Expansion of International Society* (Oxford: Oxford University Press, 1984), 9.
5. Alexander E. Wendt, "The Agent-Structure Problem in International Relations Theory," *International Organization* 41:3 (1987), 368.
6. Yale H. Ferguson and Richard W. Mansbach, *Polities: Authority, Identities and Change* (Columbia: University of South Carolina Press, 1996), 21–30.
7. John Gerard Ruggie, "Continuity and Transformation in the World Polity: Toward a Neutralist Synthesis," *World Politics* 35:2 (1983), 261–85; and Ruggie, "Territoriality and Beyond: Problematizing Modernity in International Relations, *International Organization* 47:1 (1993), 139–74.
8. Stanley Hoffman, "Suggestions for the Study of International Relations," in *Contemporary Theory in International Relations,* ed. Stanley Hoffmann (Englewood Cliffs, N.J.: Prentice-Hall, 1960), 174–79; See also Bert F. Hoselitz, "On Comparative History," *World Politics* 9:2 (1957), 267–79.
9. Hoffmann, "Suggestions," 178–79.
10. See, for example, Michael Mann, *The Sources of Social Power II: The Rise of Classes and Nation-States, 1760–1940* (Cambridge: Cambridge University Press, 1993); Charles Tilly, *The Formation of Nation-States in Western Europe* (Princeton, N.J.: Princeton University Press, 1975).
11. Raymond Aron, "Conflict and War from the Viewpoint of Historical Sociology," in Hoffmann, ed., *Contemporary Theory in International Relations,* 191–208.
12. Hoffmann, "Suggestions," 174.
13. Hedley Bull, "International Theory: The Case for a Classical Approach," in *Contending Approaches to International Politics,* ed. Klaus Knorr and James N. Rosenau (Princeton, N.J.: Princeton University Press, 1969), 20.
14. Darryl S. L. Jarvis, *International Relations and the Challenge of Postmoderism* (Columbia: University of South Carolina Press, 2000).
15. Samuel P. Huntington, "The Clash of Civilizations?" *Foreign Affairs* 72:3 (1993), 22–49; and Huntington, *The Clash of Civilizations and the Remaking of World Order* (New York: Simon and Schuster, 1996).

Chapter 2

1. "Untitled Poem Attributed to Betrand Russell by Harold Morick," in *Challenges to Empiricism,* ed. Harold Morick (Indianapolis: Hackett, 1980), vii.
2. See Albert Somit and Joseph Tanenhaus, *American Political Science: A Profile of a Discipline* (New York: Atherton Press, 1964), 28–41.
3. Fred Warner Neal and Bruce D. Hamlett, "The Never-Never Land of International Relations," *International Studies Quarterly* 13:3 (1969), 283.
4. Kenneth Waltz, *Man, the State and War* (New York: Columbia University Press 1959); Hedley Bull, *The Anarchical Society: A Study of Order in World Politics* (Oxford: Oxford University Press, 1984); Louis Henkin, *How Nations Behave: Law and Foreign Policy* (New York: Praeger, 1968); Raymond Aron, *Peace and War: A Theory of International Relations,* trans. Richard Howard and Annette Baker Fox (Garden City, N.Y.: Doubleday, 1966).

5. Yale H. Ferguson and Richard W. Mansbach, *The Elusive Quest: Theory and International Politics* (Columbia: University of South Carolina Press, 1988), 32–48; see also the revised edition, *The Elusive Quest Continues* (Upper Saddle River, N.J.: Prentice-Hall, 2002).

6. Michael Haas, "International Relations Theory," in *Approaches to the Study of Political Science*, ed. Michael Haas and Henry S. Kariel (Scranton, Penn.: Chandler, 1970), 446–48; Carl Hempel's *Philosophy and Natural Science* (Englewood Cliffs: N.J., 1966) and Karl Popper's *The Poverty of Historicism* (New York: Harper and Row, 1961) were required reading for graduate students.

7. Oran R. Young, "Aron and the Whale: A Jonah in Theory," in *Contending Approaches to International Politics*, ed. Klaus Knorr and James N. Rosenau (Princeton, N.J.: Princeton University Press, 1969), 131.

8. J. David Singer, "Data-Making in International Relations," *Behavioral Science* 10 (1965), 68–80.

9. J. David Singer, ed., *Quantitative International Politics* (New York: Free Press, 1968).

10. Ferguson and Mansbach, *The Elusive Quest*, 220–21.

11. F. Parkinson, *The Philosophy of International Relations: A Study in the History of Thought* (Beverly Hills, Calif.: Sage, 1977), 186.

12. Neal and Hamlett, "Never-Never Land," 295–306.

13. Hedley Bull, "New Directions in International Relations Theory," *International Studies* 14:2 (1975), 279.

14. Oran R. Young, "Professor Russett: Industrious Tailor to a Naked Emperor," *World Politics* 21:3 (1969), 486–511; Bruce M. Russett, *International Regimes and the International System* (Chicago: Raud McNally, 1967).

15. Neal and Hamlett, "Never-Never Land," 294.

16. Paul K. Feyerabend, "Science without Experience," in Morick, ed., *Challenges to Empiricism*, 163.

17. Susanne K. Langer, *Philosophy in a New Key* (Cambridge, Mass.: Harvard University Press, 1960), 14–16.

18. Ibid., 20–25 and passim; Ernst Cassirer, *The Philosophy of Symbolic Forms* (New Haven, Conn.: Yale University Press, 1957), 105–204 and passim; others mentioned have representative writings in Morick, ed., *Challenges to Empiricism*.

19. Morick, introduction to *Challenges to Empiricism*, 1.

20. Langer, *Philosophy*, 21–22.

21. Feyerabend, "Science," 163.

22. Langer, *Philosophy*, 16.

23. Ernst Cassirer, *An Essay on Man* (New Haven, Conn.: Yale University Press, 1962), 22.

24. Louis Arnaud Reid, *Knowledge and Truth* (London: Macmillan, 1923), 219.

25. Robert O. Keohane, "Theory and World Politics: Structural Realism and Beyond," in *International Relations Theory*, ed. Paul R. Viotti and Mark V. Kauppi (New York: Macmillan, 1987), 129.

26. Kenneth Boulding, *The Image: Knowledge in Life and Society* (Ann Arbor: University of Michigan Press, 1956), 64–81; C. A. W. Manning also deals with the notion of theory as the pursuit of an understanding of social wholes in his discussion of "social cosmology"; see Manning, *The Nature of International Society* (London: John Wiley and Sons, 1962) 64–77, 200–216. Manning also explicitly links his work to Boulding's and offers Kenneth Waltz's *Man, the State and War* as an interesting example of eiconics employed in theorizing about international relations (75). Waltz in fact uses a vocabulary of "images." See Waltz, *Man, the State and War*.

27. Morton Kaplan, "The New Great Debate," in Knorr and Rosenau, eds., *Contending Approaches to International Politics*, 42.

28. Langer, *Philosophy*, 26–102.

29. Reid, *Knowledge and Truth*, 222–38. See also Richard Kostelanetz, "Contemporary American Esthetics," in *Esthetics Contemporary*, ed. Richard Kostelanetz (Buffalo: Prometheus, 1978), 20–24.

30. This art gallery metaphor should not be taken too literally, though it is in the realms of symbolization, abstraction, and metaphysics that philosophy, science, and art commingle. In deference to the aesthetically inclined, let me note that the kind of experience one receives

in an art gallery is of a different quality from what one receives in reading international relations theory.

31. Paul K. Feyerabend, "How to be a Good Empiricist—A Plea for Tolerance in Epistemological Matters," in Morick, ed., *Challenges to Empiricism,* 166.

32. Paul Johnson, *Modern Times: The World from the Twenties to the Eighties* (New York: Harper and Row, 1983), 49–104, 261–309.

33. Kenneth Waltz, *Theory of International Politics* (Reading, Mass.: Addison-Wesley, 1979); Hans J. Morgenthau, *Politics among Nations: The Struggle for Power and Peace,* 4th ed. (New York: Alfred A. Knopf, 1967), 161–218.

34. Raymond Aron, *Peace and War: A Theory of International Relations* (Garden City, N.Y.: Doubleday, 1966), 71–124.

35. Morton Kaplan, *System and Process in International Politics* (New York: Columbia University Press, 1957).

36. Hedley Bull, *The Anarchical Society: A Study of Order in World Politics* (London: Macmillan, 1977).

37. Robert O. Keohane and Joseph S. Nye, Jr., *Power and Interdependence: World Politics in Transition* (Boston: Little, Brown, 1977), 3–62. See also the revised edition of *Power and Interdependence* published by Longman in New York in 2001.

38. Samuel P. Huntington, *The Clash of Civilizations and the Remaking of World Order* (New York: Simon and Schuster, 1996).

39. Harold D. Lasswell, *World Politics and Personal Insecurity* (1935; reprint New York: The Free Press, 1965), 3–72.

40. Aron, *Peace and War,* 150–76.

41. Robert Gilpin, *War and Change in World Politics* (New York: Cambridge University Press, 1981).

42. Paul Kennedy, *The Rise and Fall of the Great Powers* (New York: Vintage Books, 1989). From the same analytical components, Paul Kennedy also paints an interesting picture of the international relations of the twenty-first century; see Kennedy, *Preparing for the Twenty-First Century* (New York: Vintage Books, 1994).

43. Andrew B. Schmookler, *The Parable of the Tribes: The Problem of Power in Social Evolution* (Boston: Houghton Mifflin, 1984), 3–13.

44. Karl W. Deutsch, et al., *Political Community and the North Atlantic Area* (Princeton, N.J.: Princeton University Press, 1957).

45. David Mitrany, *A Working Peace System* (Chicago: Quadrangle, 1966), 29–33; Amitai Etzioni, "The Epigensis of Political Communities at the International Level," *American Journal of Sociology* 68 (1963), 407–42; Oran R. Young, *Global Governance in World Affairs* (Ithaca; N.Y.: Cornell University Press, 1999); Marvin S. Soroos, *Beyond Sovereignty: The Challenge of Global Policy* (Columbia: University of South Carolina Press, 1986).

46. Schmookler, *The Parable,* 5.

47. R. S. Woolhouse, *The Empiricists* (New York: Oxford University Press 1988), 2.

48. Philip Green, *Deadly Logic: The Theory of Nuclear Deterrence* (Columbus: Ohio State University Press, 1966), 93–102, 293–94.

49. Anatol Rapoport, *Strategy and Conscience* (New York: Schocken Books, 1969), 83.

50. Green, *Deadly Logic,* 98.

51. Stanley Hoffmann, ed., *Contemporary Theory in International Relations* (Englewood Cliffs, N.J.: Prentice Hall, 1960), 177–84.

52. Joseph Strayer, "Introduction," in *The Interpretation of History,* ed. Jacques Barzun et al., (New York: Peter Smith, 1950).

53. James Hutchinson Stirling, *Text-Book to Kant: The Critique of Pure Reason* (Edinburgh: Oliver and Boyd, 1881), 169, 171.

54. Langer, *Philosophy,* 41.

55. Hedley Bull, "International Theory: The Case for the Classical Approach," in Knorr and Rosenau, eds., *Contending Approaches,* 20.

56. Richard W. Mansbach, "Deterritorializing Global Politics," in *Visions of International Relations,* ed. Donald J. Puchala, (Columbia: University of South Carolina Press, 2002), 101–18; See also Robert D. Kaplan, *The Ends of the Earth: A Journey to the Frontiers of Anarchy* (New York: Vintage Books, 1997), 336–37.

57. Johnson, *Modern Times,* 2–3.
58. Not all historians, however, are quite this modest about the theoretical implications of their work and the aspirations of their discipline. See, for example, Strayer, "Introduction," 1–26.
59. W. B. Gallie, *Philosophy and the Historical Understanding* (New York: Schocken Books, 1964), 90.

Chapter 3

1. Adda B. Bozeman, *Politics and Culture in International History* (New Brunswick, N.J: Transaction Press, 1994).
2. Hedley Bull and Adam Watson, eds., *The Expansion of International Society* (Oxford: Clarendon Press, 1984); Adam Watson, *The Evolution of International Society: A Comparative Historical Analysis* (New York: Routledge, 1992); Edward W. Said, *Culture and Imperialism* (New York: Alfred A. Knopf, 1993); Francis Fukuyama, *The End of History and the Last Man* (New York: The Free Press, 1992); and Michael W. Doyle, *Empires* (Ithaca, N.Y.: Cornell University Press, 1986).
3. William H. McNeill, *The Rise of the West* (Chicago: University of Chicago Press, 1963); McNeill, *Mythistory and Other Essays* (Chicago: University of Chicago Press, 1986).
4. Fernand Braudel, *The Perspective of the World: Civilization and Capitalism, Fifteenth–Eighteenth Centuries* (New York: Harper and Row, 1984); Paul Kennedy, *The Rise and Fall of the Great Powers: Economic Change and Military Conflict from 1500 to 2000* (New York: Random House, 1987); Paul Kennedy, *Preparing for the Twenty-First Century* (New York: Random House, 1993).
5. See, for example, Arnold Toynbee (with Jane Caplan), *A Study of History* (New York: Portland House, rev. and abr. ed., 1988), passim; and Toynbee, *The World and the West* (London: Oxford University Press, 1953), passim.
6. Yale Ferguson and Richard Mansbach, *Polities: Authority, Identities and Ideology* (Columbia: University of South Carolina Press, 1996).
7. F. S. C. Northrop, *The Meeting of East and West* (Woodbridge, Conn.: Ox Bow Press, 1979). See also Bozeman, *Politics and Culture.*
8. Immanuel Wallerstein, *The Capitalist World-Economy* (New York: Cambridge University Press, 1979).
9. Hayden White, *Tropics of Discourse: Essays in Cultural Criticism* (Baltimore: Johns Hopkins University Press, 1978), 41. William McNeill issues a similar appeal to use history to instruct about the present in his *Mythistory,* 18–19, and Ernst Cassirer concludes that history, in the sense of learning from experience, has always been a prime source of practical knowledge; see Cassirer, *An Essay on Man* (New Haven, Conn.: Yale University Press, 1944), 171–206.
10. Yale Ferguson and Richard W. Mansbach, *The Elusive Quest: Theory and International Politics* (Columbia: University of South Carolina Press, 1988), 220–22; see also Immanuel Wallerstein, "Should We Unthink Nineteenth-Century Social Science?" *International Social Science Journal* 18 (1988), 525–31.
11. Madan Sarup, *An Introductory Guide to Post-Structuralism and Postmodernism,* 2d ed. (Athens, Ga.: University of Georgia Press, 1993), 97–98, 150–52.
12. For a comprehensive review of the evolution of hermeneutics as applied to the interpretation of human experience see Hans-Georg Gadamer, *Truth and Method* (New York: Seabury Press, 1975), 153–334.
13. See Peter Novick, *That Noble Dream: The "Objectivity Question" and the American Historical Profession* (New York: Cambridge University Press, 1988), 1–21, 415–629. The nineteenth-century *Methodenstreit* in German sociology was also basically about historical method. In this regard see Theodor W. Adorno et al., *The Positivist Dispute in German Sociology* (Aldershot, England: Avebury, Ashgate, 1994), xv–xxvii; and H. Stuart Hughes, *Consciousness and Society* (New York: Alfred A. Knopf, 1958), 278–335.
14. The pursuit after determinative essences, spirits, and teleological programmings has fallen out of fashion, though it could be creeping back in as long-cycle theorists are compelled to ask "why" questions. See Joshua S. Goldstein, *Long Cycles: Prosperity and War in the Modern Age* (New Haven, Conn.: Yale University Press, 1988), 174ff.; William R. Thompson, *On Global War: Historical-Structural Approaches to World Politics* (Columbia: University of

South Carolina Press, 1988), 3–84; and George Modelski and William Thompson, *Leading Sectors and World Politics: The Co-Evolution of Global Economics and Politics* (Columbia: University of South Carolina Press, 1996). See also Fernand Braudel, *On History* (Chicago: University of Chicago Press, 1980), 25–54.

15. It should be noted that this is not exactly the "historicism" that Karl Popper so classically criticized in *The Poverty of Historicism* (New York: Harper and Row, 1961). Popper's attack was leveled mainly against the "philosophy of history," in the writings of authors like G. W. F. Hegel, Karl Marx, Oswald Spengler, and Arnold Toynbee, where claims were made about essences that were driving history, where appearance could not disclose essence, though theory, derived intuitively, could. Popper's position was not that these works were bad history, but rather that they were unacceptable science.

16. White, *Tropics*, 101.

17. Hughes, *Consciousness*, 183–248. See also Richard Swedberg, "The New 'Battle of Methods,'" *Challenge* 33:1 (1990), 33–38.

18. The nineteenth-century foundations for what came to be called positivism were constructed in the writings of Auguste Comte. See David Frisby, "Introduction to the English Translation," in Adorno et al., *Positivist Dispute*, x–xiii. See also Jürgen Habermas's discussion of Comte's work in *Knowledge and Human Interests* (London: Heinemann, 1972), 74–77.

19. Hyppotyte Taine, cited in Ernst Cassirer, *The Logic of the Humanities* (New Haven, Conn.: Yale University Press, 1960), 14.

20. Wesley C. Salmon, *The Foundations of Scientific Inference* (Pittsburgh: University of Pittsburgh Press, 1979), 4.

21. Ibid., 10.

22. Richard Rorty, *Philosophy and the Mirror of Nature* (Princeton, N.J.: Princeton University Press, 1979), 347. Rorty goes on to quote from Karl-Otto Apel's *Analytic Philosophy of Language and the Geisteswissenschaften* (Dordrecht, 1967), 30, as follows: "the protagonists of 'understanding' (i.e., of the *Geisteswissenschaften*) always attack the supporters of the theory of explanation (i.e., of the objective social or behavioral sciences) from behind—and vice versa. The 'objective scientists' point out that the results of 'understanding' are only of pre-scientific, subjectively heuristic validity, and that they at least must be tested and supplemented by objective analytic methods. The protagonists of understanding, on the other hand, insist that the obtaining of any data in the social sciences—and therefore any objective testing of hypotheses—presupposes 'actual understanding' . . . of meaning."

23. Max Weber, *The Methodology of the Social Sciences*, trans. and ed. Edward A. Shils and Henry A. Finch (New York: The Free Press, 1949), 78–79.

24. Ibid., 80.

25. Ibid., 72.

26. Adorno et al., *Positivist Dispute*, 138.

27. Ibid., 11.

28. Ibid., 78.

29. Ibid., 135.

30. Hans Albert, "The Myth of Total Reason: Dialectical Claims in the Light of Undialectical Criticism," in Adorno et al., *Positivist Dispute*, 166–67.

31. See chapter 2, of this volume.

32. Rorty, *Philosophy*, 357–94.

33. George E. Marcus and Michael M. J. Fischer, *Anthropology As Cultural Critique* (Chicago: University of Chicago Press, 1986), 7–16.

34. White, *Tropics*, 29.

35. See, for example, Hughes's account of the classic nineteenth-century debate between Wilhelm Windelband and Heinrich Rickert in Hughes, *Consciousness*, 186–95.

36. According to Adorno (on a point I accept), "The procedure of operational or instrumental definition . . . sanctions the primacy of method over the object, and ultimately sanctions the arbitrariness of the scientific enterprise itself. The pretence is made to examine an object by means of an instrument of research, which through its own formulation decides what the object is; in other words, we are faced with a simple circle." Adorno et al., *Positivist Dispute*, 73.

37. H. S. Thayer, *Meaning and Action: A Critical History of Pragmatism* (Indianapolis: Hackett, 1968), 10–16.

38. Weber, *Methodology*, 49–60.
39. David Hume, *The Treatise on Human Nature*, quoted in Robert Livingston Schuyler, "Indeterminism in Physics and History," *Social Studies* 27:8 (1936), 510.
40. This is Michel Foucault's point. History is entirely contingent; things just happen. Intellectuals impose interpretations upon these happenings, but they are artificial. See Foucault, *The Archaeology of Knowledge* (New York: Pantheon Books, 1972), 9–14; and Sarup, *Introductory Guide*, 58–59.
41. Marcus and Fischer, *Anthropology*, 8.
42. Seyla Benhabib, "Epistemologies of Postmodernism: A Rejoinder to Jean-François Lyotard," *New German Critique* 33 (1984), 107–8.
43. Hayden White, "Foucault Decoded: Notes from Underground," in *Tropics of Discourse*, 230–260. White's essay upon which I am drawing is essentially a review of Foucault's two books most pertinent to the critique of the social sciences, *The Order of Things: An Archaeology of the Human Sciences* (New York: Random House, 1970) and the *Archaeology of Knowledge.*
44. White, 233.
45. Ibid., 232.
46. Ibid., 259. White, paraphrasing Foucault, writes that all systems of thought in the human sciences can be seen as little more than terminological formalizations of poetic closures with the world of words, rather than with the "things" they purport to represent and explain.
47. Thomas Kuhn, *The Structure of Scientific Revolutions*, 2nd ed. (Chicago: University of Chicago Press, 1974).
48. Rorty, *Philosophy*, 275–76.
49. William James, *Pragmatism* (Buffalo: Prometheus Books, 1991), 98.
50. Rorty, *Philosophy*, 285.
51. White, "Foucault," 240.
52. Ibid., 241.
53. Rorty, *Philosophy*, 173.
54. Ibid., 187. See also David Braybrooke, "Through Epistemology to the Depths of Political Illusion," in *Through the Looking Glass: Epistemology and the Conduct of Inquiry*, ed. Maria J. Falco (Washington, D.C.: University Press of America, 1979), 75–76.
55. Rorty, *Philosophy*, 181.
56. Ibid., 170. See also Wilfrid Sellars, *Science, Perception and Reality* (London: Routledge and Kegan Paul, 1963), 167ff.
57. William James, *The Meaning of Truth* (Cambridge, Mass.: Harvard University Press, 1975), xxxiii.
58. Suzanne Langer, *Mind: An Essay on Human Feeling*, vol. 2 (Baltimore: Johns Hopkins University Press, 1972), 141–356.
59. William James, *The Meaning of Truth*, xxvii–xxxi.
60. Ibid., xxxvi.
61. James, *Pragmatism*, 83. James's idea of useful and useless truths is captured in his frequently cited commentary on formal philosophies: "Locke, Hume, Berkeley, Hegel, have all been utterly sterile, so far as shedding any light on the detail of nature goes, and I can think of no invention or discovery that can be directly traced to anything in their peculiar thought. . . . The satisfactions they yield to their disciples are intellectual, not practical; and even then we have to confess that there is a large minus-side to the account."
62. James, *The Meaning of Truth*, xxxiv.
63. Weber, *Methodology*, 104. Weber in fact presents his ideal types as pragmatic devices whose value is in assisting our understanding and therefore coping with our circumstances. In remarking on the "transiency of *all* ideal types" and "the inevitability of *new* ones," Weber suggests that when a conceptualization ceases to be useful, as all conceptualizations about human affairs eventually do, it should rightly be discarded.

Chapter 4

1. Pitirim Sorokin, *Social Philosophies of an Age of Crisis* (Boston: Beacon Press, 1950), 3–4.
2. Paul Johnson, *Modern Times: The World from the Twenties to the Eighties* (New York: Harper and Row, 1983), chaps. 8–16.

3. Francis Fukuyama, *The End of History and the Last Man* (New York: The Free Press, 1992), 3–71.

4. John A. Garraty and Peter Gay, eds., *The Columbia History of the World* (New York: Harper and Row, 1972), 49–67, 154–63; Frederick L. Schuman, *International Relations, The Western State System and the World Community* (New York: McGraw-Hill, 1958), 31–38.

5. Some non-Marxist students of imperialism have looked rather insightfully into pre-Westphalian interstate relations. See, for example, Michael W. Doyle, *Empires* (Ithaca, N.Y.: Cornell University Press, 1986), 51–103; George Liska, *Imperial America* (Baltimore: Johns Hopkins University Press, 1967), 9–35; Joseph Schumpeter, *Imperialism and Social Classes* (Cleveland: World, 1955), passim. On the whole, contemporary theorizing about international relations has either ignored the pre-Westphalian eras or forced the interpretation of such eras into "comparative state system" molds where the Westphalian system, or the concepts of political realism, constitute implicit or explicit interpretative norms.

6. Arnold Toynbee, *A Study of History* (New York: Portland House, 1988), 379–477; see also Kenneth W. Thompson, "Toynbee and the Theory of International Politics," *Political Science Quarterly* 71:3 (1956), 365–386; Adda B. Bozeman, *Politics and Culture in International History* (Princeton, N.J.: Princeton University Press, 1960), 57–133 and passim, F. S. C. Northrop, *The Meeting of East and West* (Woodbridge, Conn.: Ox Bow Press, 1979), 1–15, 436–79.

7. Thompson, "Toynbee," 369.

8. Yale H. Ferguson and Richard W. Mansbach, *The Elusive Quest: Theory and International Politics* (Columbia: University of South Carolina Press, 1988), 32–48.

9. Max Weber, *The Methodology of the Social Sciences,* ed. and trans. Edward Shils and Henry Finch (New York: The Free Press, 1949), 90.

10. E. H. Carr, *The Twenty Years Crisis, 1919–1939: An Introduction to the Study of International Relations* (New York: Harper Torchbooks, 1964), 11–63; Karl Polanyi, *The Great Transformation: The Political and Economic Origins of Our Time* (Boston: Beacon Press, 1957), 130–222.

11. Hedley Bull and Adam Watson, eds., *The Expansion of International Society* (Oxford: Clarendon Press, 1984), 1–13; 117–127, 289–308; and James Piscatori, "Islam in the International Order"; Elie Kedourie, "A New International Disorder," and Adda Bozeman, "The International Order in a Multicultural World," in Bull and Watson, 309–322, 357–370, 387–406. See also Adda Bozeman, *Strategic Intelligence and Statecraft* (McLean: Brassey's, 1992), passim; William Pfaff, *Barbarian Sentiments: How the American Century Ends* (New York: Hill and Wang, 1989), 3–21 and passim.

12. Hans Kohn, *The Twentieth Century: A Mid-Way Account of the Western World* (New York: Macmillan, 1949), 185–97 and passim; John Herman Randall Jr., *The Making of the Modern Mind: A Survey of the Intellectual Background to the Present Age* (Cambridge, Mass: Houghton Mifflin, 1940), 334–88.

13. Fukuyama, *The End of History,* xi–xxiii; Daniel Patrick Moynihan, *On the Law of Nations* (Cambridge, Mass.: Harvard University Press, 1990), 33–54; Alfred, Lord Tennyson, *Locksley Hall,* quoted in Randall, *Modern Mind,* 444.

14. For an excellent review of apocalyptic thinking in the Western tradition, see Frank E. Manuel, *Shapes of Philosophical History* (Stanford, Calif.: Stanford University Press, 1965), 1–70.

15. Andrew B. Schmookler, *The Parable of the Tribes: The Problem of Power in Social Evolution* (Boston: Houghton Mifflin, 1984), 1–121.

16. Or, as Schmookler himself would have it, the ominous handwriting on civilization's wall compels a change in human nature and culture that extinguishes the predatory drives.

17. Ludwig Dehio, *The Precarious Balance: Four Centuries of the European Power Struggle* (New York: Vintage Books, 1965), passim; Leopold von Ranke, "The Great Powers," in *The Theory and Practice of History,* ed. Georg Iggers and Konrad von Moltke (New York: Bobbs-Merrill, 1973), 65–101; A. J. P. Taylor, *The Struggle for Mastery in Europe, 1848–1918* (London: Oxford University Press, 1954), xix–xxxvi; Raymond Aron, *Peace and War: A Theory of International Relations,* trans. Richard Howard and Annette Baker Fox (Garden City, N.Y.: Doubleday, 1966), 150–77. Edward V. Gulick, *Europe's Classical Balance of Power* (New York: W. W. Norton, 1967), 3–94; A. F. K. Organski, "The Power Transition," in *International Politics and Foreign Policy,* ed. James N. Rosenau (New York: The Free Press of Glencoe, 1961), 367–75.

18. Robert Gilpin, *War and Change in World Politics* (Cambridge: Cambridge University Press, 1981), 1–38; Paul Kennedy, *The Rise and Fall of the Great Powers: Economic Change and Military Conflict from 1500 to 2000* (New York: Random House, 1987), xv–xxv and passim.

19. Fernand Braudel, *The Perspective of the World: Civilization and Capitalism, Fifteenth–Eighteenth Centuries* (New York: Harper and Row, 1984), vol. 3, 21–88; Immanuel Wallerstein, *The Capitalist World-Economy* (New York: Cambridge University Press, 1979), 1–36, and passim.

20. For particularly interesting examples, see Robert A. Kann, *A History of the Habsburg Empire, 1526–1918* (Berkeley and Los Angeles: University of California Press, 1974); George Ostrogorsky, *History of the Byzantine State* (New Brunswick, N.J.: Rutgers University Press, 1969); Lord Kinross, *The Ottoman Centuries: The Rise and Fall of the Turkish Empire* (New York: Morrow Quill, 1977).

21. Conceptualizing here amounts to an abbreviated exposition of Liska's insightful chapter "Empire and Imperial Politics," in his *Imperial America*, 9–22.

22. Harold D. Lasswell, *World Politics and Personal Insecurity* (1935; reprint New York: The Free Press, 1965), 3–39.

23. Ibid., 3.

24. This definition rather closely approximates Arnold Toynbee's; see Toynbee, *A Study of History*, 43.

25. The literature on the emergence and expansion of great cultures is vast. Sorokin, *Social Philosophies,* summarizes some of the most outstanding works. Sorokin's *Social and Cultural Dynamics,* one vol. abr. (New Brunswick, N.J.: Transaction, 1991), is itself a major contribution. See also Oswald Spengler, *The Decline of the West,* abr. ed. (New York: Oxford University Press, 1991); Christopher Dawson, *The Movement of World Revolution* (New York: Sheed and Ward, 1959), 69–98; K. M. Panikkar, *Asia and Western Dominance: A Survey of the Vasco Da Gama Epoch of Asian History, 1498–1945* (London: George Allen and Unwin, 1959); and Bozeman, *Politics and Culture,* 3–237 and passim.

26. See Kennedy, *Great Powers,* 228–29.

27. Joseph S. Nye Jr., *Bound to Lead: The Changing Nature of American Power* (New York: Basic Books, 1990), 31–32.

28. Zbigniew Brzezinski should be credited with anticipating the collapse of communism in Eastern Europe and the Soviet Union and writing with some prescience about the causes before the effects were readily discernible; see Brzezinski, *The Grand Failure: The Birth and Death of Communism in the Twentieth Century* (New York: Collier Books, 1989), passim.

29. America's penchant for intervention was demonstrated, for example, in the unseating of Mohammed Mussadeq in 1953, the overthrow of Jacobo Arbenz Guzmán in Guatemala in 1954, the Bay of Pigs fiasco in 1961, the invasion of the Dominican Republic in 1965, the undermining of Salvador Allende in the 1970s, the financing of the Nicaraguan Contras throughout the 1980s, the bombing of Libya in 1987, and the invasion of Panama in 1989. Washington's flouting of world opinion was displayed in episodes such as its long opposition to the seating of Mainland China in the United Nations, its reluctance to sanction the apartheid regime in South Africa, its persistent refusal to deal with the Palestine Liberation Organization, its extreme negativism during the debates concerning a new international economic order, its refusal to pay assessed dues for United Nations membership, its refusal to recognize World Court jurisdiction, its refusal to sign the Law of the Sea Treaty, and its rejectionist stances at the 1992 United Nations Conference on Environment and Development, and recently, its rejection of the International Criminal Court.

30. Susan J. Pharr, "Japan and the World: The Debate in Japan," *International Review,* April/May 1980, 35ff; Sadako Ogata, "The Changing Role of Japan in the United Nations," *Journal of International Affairs* 37:1 (1983), 30ff; Japan Economic Institute, *Japan's Role in Multilateral Aid Organizations* (Washington, D.C.: Japan Economic Institute, 1988); John Hughes, "Emerging Japan," *Christian Science Monitor,* September 2, 1988, 14; and Susan Chira, "Japan and the World: Applying Assertiveness Training to Foreign Policy" *New York Times,* September 6, 1988, A8.

31. David P. Calleo, *Rethinking Europe's Future* (Princeton, N.J.: Princeton University Press, 2001); and Elizabeth Pond, *The Rebirth of Europe,* 2d ed. (Washington, D.C.: Brookings Institution, 2002).

32. Paul Kennedy, 458, 447–58; Jonathan Pollack, "China and the Global Strategic Balance," in *China's Foreign Relations in the 1980s*, ed. H. Harding (New Haven, Conn.: Yale University Press, 1984), 146–76; and A. D. Barnett, "Ten Years after Mao," *Foreign Affairs* 65:1 (1986), 130–31.

33. Zbigniew Brzezinski, *The Grand Chessboard: American Primacy and Its Geostrategic Imperatives* (New York: Basic Books, 1997), 87–122, 194–216.

34. G. Vernadsky, *The Mongols and Russia* (London: Oxford University Press, 1953), 390.

35. George Washington, quoted in Richard W. Van Alstyne, *The Rising American Empire* (New York: W. W. Norton, 1974), 69.

36. Robert W. Tucker and David C. Hendrickson, *The Imperial Temptation: The New World Order and America's Purpose* (New York: Council on Foreign Relations, 1992), 192–97 and passim.

37. Bozeman, *Strategic Intelligence*, passim.

38. The argument developed here closely follows Hans Kohn's interpretation of the intellectual history of the nineteenth and twentieth centuries; see Kohn, *The Twentieth Century*, 3–75 and passim.

39. Kohn, *The Twentieth Century*, 59–60.

40. Ibid., 59.

41. Lasswell, *World Politics*, 5.

42. Westerners might note with particular interest the ideological ferment currently underway in the People's Republic of China under the rubrics "new authoritarianism" or "neoconservatism." The movement is led by younger members of the ruling elite who are apparently seeking to formulate a post-Marxist ideological justification for continuing authoritarian rule.

43. The notion of "mobilized and alienated populations" follows from Karl Deutsch's analysis of social-psychological conditions conducive to the spread of new political ideas; see Karl W. Deutsch, *Nationalism and Social Communication* (Cambridge, Mass.: MIT Press, 1953), 97–138.

44. Compare also Karl A. Wittfogel, *Oriental Despotism: A Comparative Study of Total Power* (New Haven, Conn.: Yale University Press, 1957), 49–100, and passim.

45. In somewhat broader perspective the Cold War becomes an episode in interimperial relations, not entirely unlike the relations between the Roman and Parthian empires, the Byzantine and Turkish empires or the Austrian and Ottoman empires. See Dehio, *Precarious Balance*, 19–71; Walter L. Dorn, *Competition for Empire, 1740–1763* (New York: Harper and Brothers, 1940), passim; Arthur J. Marder, *From Dreadnought to Scapa Flow: The Royal Navy in the Fisher Era, 1904–1919* (London: Oxford University Press, 1961), vol. I, passim; Raymond J. Sontag, *Germany and England, Background of Conflict, 1848–1918* (New York: Appleton-Century, 1938), passim; John A. Garraty and Peter Gay, eds., *Columbia History of the World*, 257; George Ostrogorsky, *Byzantine State*, 87–147, 466–572; Lord Kinross, *Ottoman Centuries* 182–336.

46. One need not accept Spengler's organic metaphors to appreciate his analysis of the blossoming of Faustian (Western) civilization, which, he argues, reached apogee in the eighteenth century; see Spengler, *Decline*, 97–159. For insightful analyses of the outward diffusion of Western culture and its impacts, see Christopher Dawson, *The Movement of World Revolution* (New York: Sheed and Ward, 1959), 5–98; Panikkar, *Asia and Western Dominance*, 21–176; and Nirad C. Chaudhuri, *The Autobiography of an Unknown Indian* (New York: Macmillan, 1951), passim.

47. Panikkar, *Asia and Western Dominance*, 13.

48. The consensus about Western decline among cultural historians is remarkably broad. Sorokin reviews this in *Social Philosophies of an Age of Crisis*, where he examines and constructively criticizes the work of Nikolai Berdyaev, Nikolai Danilevsky, Alfred Kroeber, F. S. C. Northrop, Walter Schubart, Albert Schweitzer, Oswald Spengler, and Arnold Toynbee; see Sorokin, *Social Philosophies*, 49–186. Sorokin concurs regarding "the twilight of our sensate culture" in his own monumental *Social and Cultural Dynamics*, 699–704.

49. Panikkar, *Asia and Western Dominance*, 197–278; Dawson, *Movement*, 139–158; Edmund Stillman and William Pfaff, *The Politics of Hysteria: The Sources of Twentieth Century Conflict* (New York: Harper and Row, 1964); William Pfaff, *Barbarian Sentiments*, 131–59 and passim; and David C. Gordon, *Images of the West: Third World Perspectives* (Savage, Md.: Rowman and Littlefield, 1989), 61–109.

50. F. S. C. Northrop, *Meeting*, 1–14, 405–36.

51. Dawson, *Movement*, 143.
52. Ibid., 143, 157.
53. David Diop, "The Vultures," in *The Penguin Book of Modern African Poetry,* ed. Gerald Moore and Ulli Beier (London: Penguin, 1963), 246.

Chapter 5

The idea for this essay dates back to 1997, when Arthur Vanden Houten and I prepared a paper titled "The Tragedy of International Relations" for a workshop on morality and international relations sponsored by the Walker Institute at the University of South Carolina.

1. See, for example, Eberhard Fisch, *Guernica by Picasso: A Study of the Picture and Its Context* (Lewisburg, Penn.: Bucknell University Press, 1988).
2. Adda B. Bozeman, *Politics and Culture in International History* (Princeton, N.J.: Princeton University Press, 1960).
3. Jacob Burckhardt, *The Civilization of the Renaissance in Italy* (New York: Modern Library, 1954). For a discussion of phenomenology as applied to the study of international history, see Donald J. Puchala, "Harold Laswell's Legacy and Twenty-first Century International Relations," in *Visions of International Relations: Assessing an Academic Discipline,* ed. Donald J. Puchala (Columbia: University of South Carolina Press, 2002), 145–46.
4. Thucydides, *The History of the Peloponnesian War,* ed. and trans. Sir Richard Livingston (New York: Oxford University Press, 1960); Raymond Aron, *Peace and War: A Theory of International Relations,* trans. Richard Howard and Annette Baker Fox (Garden City, N.Y.: Doubleday, 1966); Robert Gilpin, *War and Change in World Politics* (Cambridge: Cambridge University Press, 1981). Stanley Hoffmann, ed. *The State of War: Essays on the Theory and Practice of International Politics* (New York: Praeger, 1965); Lewis Fry Richardson, *Arms and Insecurity: A Mathematical Study of the Causes and Origins of War* (Pittsburgh: Boxwood Press, 1960); J. David Singer, *The Correlates of War* (New York: Free Press, 1979); Pitirim Sorokin, *Social and Cultural Dynamics: A Study of Change in Major Systems of Art, Truth, Ethics, Law, and Social Relationships* (New Brunswick, N.J.: Transaction, 1991), 534–605; Kenneth Waltz, *Man, the State and War* (New York: Columbia University Press, 1959); Quincy Wright, *A Study of War,* 2 vols. (Chicago: University of Chicago Press, 1942).
5. C. V. Wedgewood, *The Thirty Years' War* (London: Jonathan Cape, 1938), 526.
6. Polybius, *On Roman Imperialism: The Histories of Polybius Translated from the Text of F. Hultsch,* trans. Evelyn S. Shuckbaugh (South Bend, Ind.: Regnery/Gateway, 1980), 510.
7. Hans-Georg Gadamer, *Truth and Method* (New York: Seabury Press, 1975), 153–334; see also Richard Rorty, *Philosophy and the Mirror of Nature* (Princeton, N.J.: Princeton University Press, 1979, 357–62, and Joseph J. Kockelman, ed., *Hermeneutic Phenomenology: Lectures and Essays* (Washington, D.C.: Center for Advanced Research in Phenomenology and University Press of America, 1988).
8. Gadamer, *Truth and Method,* 259.
9. Wilhelm Dilthey, *Selected Writings,* ed. and trans. H. P. Rickman (Cambridge: Cambridge University Press, 1976), 155–264; see also Rudolph A. Makkreel, *Dilthey: Philosopher of the Human Studies* (Princeton: Princeton University Press, 1975), 205–344.
10. Hayden White, *Metahistory: The Historical Imagination in Nineteenth-Century Europe* (Baltimore: Johns Hopkins University Press, 1978), 5–7.
11. Max Weber viewed this intellectual activity as the connection between history and the social sciences; see Weber, "'Objectivity' in Social Science and Social Policy," in *The Methodology of the Social Sciences,* ed. and trans. Edward A. Shils and Henry A. Finch (New York: Free Press, 1949), 72–79.
12. White, *Metahistory,* 7.
13. Hayden White, "Interpretation in History," in *Tropics of Discourse: Essays in Cultural Criticism* (Baltimore: Johns Hopkins University Press, 1978), 51–80; See also Northrop Frye, *The Anatomy of Criticism: Four Essays* (Princeton, N.J.: Princeton University Press, 1957.
14. White, "Interpretation," 58.
15. Ibid.
16. R. G. Collingwood, *The Idea of History,* ed. Jan Van Der Dussen, rev. ed. (New York: Oxford

Universtiy Press, 1994), 245, 240–49. See also William H. McNeill, *Mythistory and Other Essays* (Chicago: University of Chicago Press, 1986), 18–19 and passim.

17. White, "Interpretation," 58.
18. White, *Metahistory*, 7–11.
19. Ibid., 8–9.
20. White, *Tropics*, 6–12, 70–75.
21. Ibid., 60.
22. McNeill, *Mythistory*, 7–19.
23. Francesco Gabrieli, *Arab Historians of the Crusades* (New York: Dorset Press, 1957), 135.
24. John Weltman, *World Politics and the Evolution of War* (Baltimore: Johns Hopkins University Press, 1995), 24.
25. Geoffrey Parker, *The Thirty Years' War* (New York: Military Heritage Press, 1987), 164.
26. Ibid., 125.
27. Alan Lloyd, *Destroy Carthage!* (London: Souvenir Press, 1977), 179–80.
28. Robin Neillands, *The Hundred Years War* (New York: Routledge, 1990), 227.
29. Geoffrey Parker, *Thirty Years' War*, 164–65.
30. John Keegan, *War and Our World* (New York: Vintage Books, 2001), 4.
31. Harold D. Lasswell, *World Politics and Personal Insecurity* (New York: McGraw-Hill, 1935).
32. Iris Chang, *The Rape of Nanking: The Forgotten Holocaust of World War II* (New York: Basic Books, 1997).
33. F. Tillman, "All Captives Slain," *New York Times,* December 18, 1937, 1, 10.
34. Keegan, *War*, 2.
35. Michael Ignatieff, *The Warrior's Honor: Ethnic War and the Modern Conscience* (New York: Metropolitan Books, 1998); see also International Commission on the Balkans, *Unfinished Peace: Report of the International Commission on the Balkans* (Washington, D.C.: Carnegie Endowment for International Peace, 1996), passim.
36. Richard H. Palmer, *Tragedy and Tragic Theory* (Westport, Conn.: Greenwood Press, 1992). Palmer usefully surveys a number of literary interpretations of tragedy and analyzes the differences among them. See also John Kekes, *Facing Evil* (Princeton, N.J.: Princeton University Press, 1990), 34.
37. The *Iliad,* cited in Simone Weil, "The Iliad, or Poem of Force," trans. Mary McCarthy, *Politics* 2:11 (1945), 324.
38. Richard B. Sewall, "The Vision of Tragedy," *Review of Metaphysics* 10:2 (1956), 197.
39. Ekbert Faas, cited in Palmer, 33; see also Ekbert Faas, *Tragedy and After: Euripides, Shakespeare, and Goethe* (Kingston, Ont.: McGill-Queens University Press, 1984), 5, 141.
40. Richard B. Sewall, "The Tragic Form," *Essays in Criticism* 4:4 (1954), 350.
41. Arthur Schopenhauer, *The World As Will and Idea,* trans. R. B. Haldane and J. Kemp (London: Kegan Paul, Trench, Trubner, 1907), 62.
42. John Kekes, *Facing Evil*, 35.
43. Ibid., 26.
44. Ibid., 23.
45. Sigmund Freud, *Civilization and Its Discontents* (New York: W. W. Norton, 1962); and Joseph Conrad, *Heart of Darkness* (New York: W. W. Norton, 1971).
46. Kekes, *Facing Evil,* 25.
47. Eugene O'Neill, *Mourning Becomes Electra,* in *Three Plays of Eugene O'Neill* (New York: Vintage Books, 1959), 376.
48. Euripides, *Medea,* in *Ten Plays by Euripides,* translated by Moses Hadas and John McLean (New York: Bantam, 1960), 62–63.
49. Euripides, *The Trojan Women,* in *Ten Plays by Euripides,* 183.
50. Fisch, *Guernica by Picasso,* 43.
51. Ibid., 45.
52. Ernst Cassirer, *Essay on Man* (New Haven, Conn.: Yale University Press, 1962), 146.
53. Keegan, *War and Our World,* xi.
54. Weil, "The Iliad," 326.
55. William Shakespeare, *Macbeth;* act 5, scene 5, 26–28.
56. Euripides, *The Trojan Women,* 183.
57. The Athenian attempt to capture Syracuse was to cost 20,000 Athenian lives, widow countless Athenian women, and leave countless children fatherless.

58. Moses Hadas, commentary in *Ten Plays by Euripides*, 173.
59. Jan Kott, *Shakespeare Our Contemporary*, trans. Boleslaw Taborski (Garden City, N.Y.: Doubleday, 1964), 4–5.
60. Ibid., 34.
61. Shakespeare, *Richard III*, act 4, scene 4, 85–86.
62. Jan Kott, *Shakespeare*, xix. Quoted from "Preface" by Peter Brook.
63. Cyril E. Robinson, *A History of Greece* (London: Methuen Educational, 1983), 247–331.
64. C. V. Wedgwood, *The Thirty Years' War*, 525, 526.
65. Wedgwood, *The Thirty Years' War*, 526.

Chapter 6

1. Marshall D. Shulman, "The Superpowers: Dance of the Dinosaurs," *Foreign Affairs* 66:3 (1987–88), 494.
2. John Lewis Gaddis, *The Long Peace: Inquiries in the History of the Cold War* (New York: Oxford University Press, 1987).
3. It is also rather commonplace to use the conflict between Rome and Carthage in the period of the Punic Wars (264–146 B.C.E.) as an analogue for the American-Soviet rivalry during the Cold War—i.e., as another bipolarity of sorts. Or, sometimes the rivalry between ancient Athens and Sparta that generated the Peloponnesian War (431–404 B.C.E.) is recalled. Unfortunately, both of these historical episodes are frequently used to teach inaccurate lessons. For one thing, most historic imperial rivalries have not ended as did the rivalry between Rome and Carthage, with the total physical annihilation of the vanquished by the victor. Many have in fact ended in the manner of Athens and Sparta, with the utter exhaustion of both contenders. However, the conventional image of the outcome of the Peloponnesian War is that Sparta won the conflict and the "totalitarian" power thus vanquished the "democratic" one. It would be more accurate, however, if we simply recalled that both powers lost.
4. Richard Koebner, *Empire* (New York: Grosset and Dunlap, 1965), 61.
5. Walter Lippmann, *Men of Destiny* (Seattle and London: University of Washington Press, 1927), 215–216.
6. John Spanier, *American Foreign Policy Since World War II*, 11th ed. (Washington, D.C.: Congressional Quarterly Press, 1988), 158–67.
7. George Liska, *Imperial America: The International Politics of Primacy* (Baltimore: Johns Hopkins University Press, 1967), 9–10.
8. Frederick M. Watkins, *The State As a Concept in Political Science* (New York: Harper and Bros., 1934), 48–49.
9. Christer Jönsson, "The Ideology of Foreign Policy," in *Foreign Policy:USA/USSR*, ed. Charles W. Kegley Jr. and Patrick McGowan (Beverly Hills, Calif.: Sage, 1982), 103–4.
10. Richard W. Van Alstyne, *The Rising American Empire* (New York: W. W. Norton, 1974), 69.
11. Ibid., 87.
12. For a discussion of "soft power," see Joseph S. Nye Jr., *Bound to Lead: The Changing Nature of American Power* (New York: Basic Books, 1990), pp. 31–34.
13. Susan Strange, "Cave! Hic Dragones: A Critique of Regime Analysis," in *International Regimes*, ed. Steven D. Krasner (Ithaca, N.Y.: Cornell University Press, 1984), 340.
14. G. Vernadsky, *The Mongols and Russia* (London: Oxford University Press, 1953), 390.
15. Lionel Kochan and Richard Abraham, *The Making of Modern Russia*, 2d ed. (Hammondsworth, England: 1983), 24.
16. Liska, *Imperial America*, 12. This point was borne out in Robert S. Nichols's study of U.S. and USSR perceptions of their military balance. He found that "nations base their policies on their perceptions of balance rather than on the *objective* data." See Nichols, "Factors Influencing Perception of the US/USSR Military Balance" (Carlisle Barracks, Penn.: Strategic Studies Institute, U.S. Army War College, 1978), 11.
17. Ernest May, "The Cold War," in *The Making of America's Soviet Policy*, ed. Joseph S. Nye, Jr. (New Haven, Conn.: Yale University Press, 1984), 209.
18. Robert L. Messer, "World War II and the Coming of the Cold War," in *Modern American Diplomacy*, ed. John M. Carroll and George C. Herring (Wilmington, Del.: Scholarly Resources, 1986), 123.

19. Richard H. Immerman, *The CIA in Guatemala: The Foreign Policy of Intervention* (Austin.: University of Texas Press, 1982), 15.
20. Jerry W. Sanders, *Peddlers of Crisis: The Committee on the Present Danger and the Politics of Containment* (Boston: South End Press, 1983), 33.
21. Messer, "World War II," 109.
22. Dimitri K. Simes, "Soviet Policy Toward the United States." in Nye, ed., *America's Soviet Policy,* 291.
23. Sanders, *Peddlers of Crisis,* 25.
24. H. Bradford Westerfield, *The Arms Race and Current Soviet Doctrine* (New Haven, Conn.: Yale University Press, 1959), 86–87.
25. See Raymond Aron, *Peace and War: A Theory of International Relations* (London: Weidenfeld and Nicholson; 1967); Liska, *Imperial America,* 14.
26. Immerman, *The CIA in Guatemala,* 128–129.
27. Robert Trudeau and Lars Schoultz, "Guatemala," in *Confronting Revolution: Security through Diplomacy in Central America,* ed. Morris J. Blachman, William M. LeoGrande, and Kenneth Sharpe (New York: Pantheon, 1986), 50.
28. Guatemala was the first major post–World War II "challenge" to U.S. hegemony in the hemisphere. Not only did the United States intervene with a CIA operation, but it worked to use the regional Organization of American States to endorse its general anticommunist position. This was accomplished with relative ease as the Tenth Inter-American Conference in Caracas adopted the Declaration of Solidarity for the Preservation of the Political Integrity of the American States against International Communist Intervention. See Thomas M. Franck and Edward Weisband, *Word Politics: Verbal Strategy among the Superpowers* (New York: Oxford University Press, 1971), 51–52.
29. Immerman, *The CIA in Guatemala,* 177; Trudeau and Schoultz, "Guatemala," 25–33; and Franck and Weisband, *Word Politics,* 53–54.
30. Franck and Weisband, *Word Politics,* 79.
31. Ibid., 79.
32. Terry Karl, "Mexico, Venezuela and the Contadora Initiative," in *Confronting Revolution,* Blachman, LeoGrande, and Sharpe eds., 272–292.
33. Henry Kissinger, *Report of the National Bipartisan Commission on Central America, Submitted to the President of the United States January 10, 1984,* 12, 126–27.
34. *Pravda,* cited in "Moscow Lays Riots to 'Alien Hirelincs' " *New York Times,* June 18, 1953, A8.
35. *Izvestia,* cited in Franck and Weisband, *Word Politics,* 59.
36. Ibid.
37. *Keesing's Contemporary Archives,* June 14–21, 1958, 16237.
38. Franck and Weisband, *Word Politics,* 107.
39. Ibid., 107–8.
40. *Keesing's Contemporary Archives,* May 9, 1980, 30236.
41. Paul Kennedy, *The Rise and Fall of the Great Powers: Economic Change and Military Conflict from 1500 to 2000* (New York: Random House, 1987), 488–535.

Chapter 7

1. The phrase "the world and the West" alludes to Arnold Toynbee's book of that title (London: Oxford University Press, 1953), in which he, too, anticipates intercivilizational conflict; see also Samuel P. Huntington, "The Clash of Civilizations?" *Foreign Affairs* 72:3 (1993), 22–49.
2. Samuel P. Huntington, *The Clash of Civilizations and the Remaking of World Order* (New York: Simon and Schuster, 1996).
3. There is admittedly some tension between the vocations of the historian and the social scientist. In the estimation of the renowned Dutch historian Johan Huizinga, "the term 'case' does not belong in history at all," to which intellectual historian W. Warren Wagar adds that once the scholar "begins looking on people or institutions or civilizations primarily as 'examples' of a generalization, he is no longer a historian." Still, some of the most interesting scholarship in both history and social science tends to be done either by historians willing to generalize, by social scientists able to reflect on history, or, in any event, by scholars working at the convergence of the disciplines. It is at this convergence that this essay is intellectually

located. See W. Warren Wagar, *World Views: A Study in Comparative History* (Hinsdale, Ill.: Dryden Press, 1977), 9.

4. Max Weber, *The Methodology of the Social Sciences,* trans. Edward A. Shils and Henry A. Finch, (New York: Free Press, 1949), 92.

5. Philip Bagby, *Culture and History: Prolegomena to the Comparative Study of Civilizations* (Berkeley and Los Angeles: University of California Press, 1959), 88.

6. Clifford Geertz, *The Interpretation of Cultures* (New York: Basic Books, 1973), 5; Ulf Hannerz, *Cultural Complexity: Studies in the Social Organization of Meaning* (New York: Columbia University Press, 1992), 3; and Pitirim Sorokin, *Social and Cultural Dynamics: A Study of Change in Major Systems of Art, Truth, Ethics, Law and Social Relationships,* rev. and abr. ed. (New Brunswick, N.J.: Transaction Publishers, 1991), 24.

7. M. F. Ashley Montagu, *Toynbee and History: Critical Essays and Reviews* (Boston: Porter Sargent, 1956).

8. This definition follows closely from Toynbee's formulation. See Arnold Toynbee (with Jane Caplan), *A Study of History,* rev. and abr. ed. (New York: Portland House, 1988), 44. A very similar definition is derived more systematically in Carroll Quigley, *The Evolution of Civilization: An Introduction to Historical Analysis* (New York: Macmillan, 1961), 25–37.

9. See David Wilkinson, "Sixteen Papers in Gray Covers," unpublished manuscript distributed at the University of California, Los Angeles, 1996; particularly, "A Definition, Roster, and Classification of Civilizations," paper presented at the eleventh annual meeting of the International Society for Comparative Civilizations, Pittsburgh, May 27–30, 1982; "Civilizations, States Systems, and Universal Empires," paper presented at the twelfth annual meeting of the International Society for the Comparative Study of Civilizations, Buffalo, May 26–28, 1983; "Encounters between Civilizations: Coexistence, Fusion, Fission, Collision," paper presented at the annual meeting of the International Society for the Comparative Study of Civilizations, Boone, North Carolina, June 14–16, 1984; and "Sorokin versus Toynbee: Congeries and Civilizations." See also Wilkinson, "Twelve Articles in Blue Covers," unpublished manuscript distributed at the University of California, Los Angeles, 1995.

10. David Wilkinson, "A Definition, Roster and Classification," 3.

11. Ibid., 5.

12. David Wilkinson, "Sorokin versus Toynbee," 380.

13. Pitirim Sorokin, *Social Philosophies of an Age of Crisis* (Boston: Beacon Press, 1950), 275.

14. Bagby, *Culture and History,* 191.

15. Toynbee, *A study,* 44; A. N. Whitehead, *Adventures of Ideas* (London: Cambridge University Press, 1933), 14; Christopher Dawson, *The Dynamics of World History* (London: Sheed and Ward, 1957), 41; Oswald Spengler, *The Decline of the West,* abr. ed. (New York: Oxford University Press, 1991), 7–28.

16. These themes have been central to Edward W. Said's writings about Western civilization; see *Orientalism: Western Conceptions of the Orient* (London: Penguin, 1991), passim; and *Culture and Imperialism* (New York: Alfred A. Knopf, 1993), 3–14.

17. Spengler, *Decline,* 3–40, 70–86. Of particular interest with regard to civilizational cycles are the tabular chronologies included in the original two-volume translation of *The Decline of the West.*

18. Toynbee, *A Study,* 445–73; Karl Jaspers, *The Origins and Goal of History* (New Haven, Conn.: Yale University Press, 1953); and William H. McNeill, *The Rise of the West* (Chicago: University of Chicago Press, 1963).

19. Quigley, *Evolution,* 66–94.

20. Sorokin, *Social Philosophies,* 288–90.

21. George Liska, *Imperial America: The International Politics of Primacy* (Baltimore: Johns Hopkins University Press, 1967), 9. Liska's definition is actually more elaborate, since by "scope" he refers to broad-ranging interests; "salience" means importance or centrality in the eyes of all other relevant statesmen, and "sense of task" connotes moral or political vision and messianic drive.

22. H. G. Quaritch Wales,*The Indianization of China and of South-East Asia* (London: Bernard Quaritch, 1967), 2–15. Fa-hsien was a Chinese convert to Buddhism who sought to bring the full text of the *Vinaya,* translated from the Sanskrit, to China. He departed overland through central Asia in 399, descended into India across the Pamirs, read and translated the sacred texts and returned with them, and with deep insight into Hindu culture, by sea to

China some twelve years later; see H. A. Giles, *The Travels of Fa-hsien* (London: Cambridge University Press, 1923).

23. Henri Pirenne, *Mohammed and Charlemagne* (New York: Barnes and Noble, 1992), passim.
24. Ibid., 37–38.
25. M. L. Clarke, *The Roman Mind: Studies in Roman Thought from Cicero to Marcus Aurelius* (New York: W. W. Norton, 1968), 3–5.
26. Ibid., 1–2.
27. Edwin O. Reischauer and John K. Fairbank, *East Asia* (Boston: Houghton Mifflin, 1960), 177.
28. Zenryu Tsukamoto, "Chinese Culture Overseas," in *Half of the World: The History and Culture of China and Japan,* ed. Arnold Toynbee (London: Thames and Hudson, 1973), 189.
29. Reischauer and Fairbank, *East Asia,* 177.
30. Amélie Kuhrt and Susan Sherwin-White, eds., *Hellenism in the East: The Interaction of Greek and Non-Greek Civilizations from Syria to Central Asia* (Berkeley and Los Angeles: University of California Press, 1987), passim.
31. Michele de Cuneo, cited in Tzvetan Todorov, *The Conquest of America* (New York: Harper Perennial, 1992), 47–48.
32. Todorov, *Conquest,* 133.
33. John A. Garraty and Peter Gay, eds., *The Columbia History of the World* (New York: Harper and Row, 1972), 658.
34. Lord Kinross, *The Ottoman Centuries: The Rise and Fall of the Turkish Empire* (New York: Morrow Quill, 1977), 214.
35. Ibid., 619.
36. Ibid., 189.
37. Peter Green, *Alexander to Actium: The Historical Evolution of the Hellenistic Age* (Berkeley and Los Angeles: University of California Press, 1990), 330–35. The main English-language reference work on Bactria is W. W. Tarn, *The Greeks in Bactria and India* (London: Cambridge University Press, 1951).
38. Toynbee, *A Study,* 395.
39. Adda B. Bozeman, *Politics and Culture in International History* (Princeton, N.J.: Princeton University Press, 1960), 113.
40. Ibid., 117.
41. Tim Newark, *The Barbarians: Warriors and Wars of the Dark Ages* (Dorset: Blandford Press, 1985); René Grousset, *The Empire of the Steps: A History of Central Asia* (New Brunswick, N.J.: Rutgers University Press, 1970); and Bertold Spuler, *History of the Mongols* (New York: Dorset Press, 1988).
42. Albert Hourani, *A History of the Arab Peoples* (New York: Warner Books, 1992), 7–12.
43. Will Durant, *Our Oriental Heritage* (New York: MJF Books, 1935), viii–ix.
44. Ibid., 459–72. Durant elaborates the story of Sultan Firoz Shah, who "invaded Bengal (and) "offered a reward for every Hindu head (and) paid for 180,000 of them," or Sultan Ahmad Shah, who "feasted for three days whenever the number of defenseless Hindus slain in his territories in one day reached twenty thousand."
45. Toynbee, *A Study,* 394.
46. C. P. FitzGerald, *The Southern Expansion of the Chinese People* (London: Barrie and Jenkins, 1972), 127ff; Tsukamoto, "Chinese Culture," 191; Michael Haas, "Asian Culture and International Relations," in *Culture and International Relations,* ed. Jongsuk Chay (New York: Praeger, 1990), 172–90.
47. Weber, *Methodology,* 72–80, esp. 80.
48. Robert D. Kaplan, "The Coming Anarchy," *Atlantic Monthly,* February, 1994, 44–76. Since publishing this first provocative piece, Kaplan has elaborated his thinking in *The Ends of the Earth: A Journey to the Frontiers of Anarchy* (New York: Vintage, 1997) and *Warrior Politics: Why Leadership Demands a Pagan Ethos* (New York: Random House, 2002).

Chapter 8

1. The era of Greek influence in western Asia after the conquests of Alexander the Great is identified by most historians as the "Hellenistic" era, although some call it the "Hellenic"

era. In this essay "Hellenistic" is used to identify the era, while "Hellenic" is used to refer to values and ideals associated with classical Greece.

2. Pierre Jouguet, *Alexander the Great and the Hellenistic World,*   online at <http://www.macedon.org/anmacs/jouguet.html>, 3; David G. Hogarth, *Philip and Alexander of Macedon,* as cited at <http://www.macedon.org/anmacs/hogarth.html>, 4.

3. Susan Sherwin-White, "Seleucid Babylonia: A Case-Study for the Installation and Development of Greek Rule," in *Hellenism in the East: The Interactions of Greek and Non-Greek Civilizations from Syria to Central Asia After Alexander,* ed. Amélie Kuhrt and Susan Sherwin-White (Berkeley and Los Angeles: University of California Press, 1987), 1–31. But, see also Fergus Millar, "The Problem of Hellenistic Syria," in Kuhrt and Sherwin-White, eds., *Hellenism,* 110–33.

4. A. B. Bosworth reports that there were some Greek cavalry units and about seven thousand infantry soldiers from various Greek cities attached to Alexander's preponderantly Macedonian army of some forty thousand. Greek units apparently played only minor parts in major battles, as Alexander assigned them mostly to garrison duties in conquered cities. See Bosworth, "A. B. Bosworth on the Macedonian Language," online at <http://www.macedon.org/anmacs/bosworth.htm>, 2–3.

5. Peter Green, *Alexander to Actium: The Historical Evolution of the Hellenistic Age* (Berkeley and Los Angeles: University of California Press, 1993), 319.

6. Roman Ghirshman, *Iran: From the Earliest Times to the Islamic Conquest* (Hammondsworth, England: Penguin, 1954), 217.

7. Pierre Jouguet, "L'Égypt Ptolémaïque," in *Histoire de la Nation Égyptienne,* ed. Gabriel Hanotaux, vol. 3 (Paris: Librarie Plon, 1931), 35ff.

8. In this chapter I choose not to reopen the conceptual discussion of the nature of civilizations and about definitional and analytical distinctions than can be drawn among civilizations and cultures. For my thinking on these matters, see chapter 7.

9. Elias J. Bickerman, "The Seleucid Period," in *The Cambridge History of Iran: The Seleucid, Parthian and Sassanian Periods,* vol. 3, pt. 1. Ehsan Yarshater, ed. (London: Cambridge University Press, 1983), 17.

10. Green, *Alexander to Actium,* 313.

11. Michael Avi-Yonah, *Hellenism and the East: Contacts and Interrelations from Alexander to the Roman Conquest* (Jerusalem: Institute of Languages, Literature, and the Arts, The Hebrew University, 1978), 163, 178ff.

12. Pierre Jouguet, "Les Lagides et les Indigènes Égyptiens," *Révue belge de philosophie et d'histoire* 2 (1923), 442.

13. Green, *Alexander to Actium,* 316.

14. R. Ghirshman, *Iran,* 230; Sammuel K. Eddy, *The King Is Dead: Studies in the Near Eastern Resistance to Hellenism* (Lincoln: University of Nebraska Press, 1961), 39; and J. Grafton Milne, "Egyptian Nationalism under Greek and Roman Rule," *Journal of Egyptian Archeology* 14 (1928), 227.

15. Eddy, *The King,* 333; Green, *Alexander to Actium,* 316.

16. Ghirshman, *Iran,* 231; Samuel K. Eddy, *The King,* 38.

17. Green, *Alexander to Actium,* 325.

18. H. Idris Bell, *Egypt: From Alexander the Great to the Arab Conquest* (London: Oxford University Press, 1948), 37; Eddy, *The King,* 257.

19. Rudyard Kipling, "The White Man's Burden," in *Great English Poets: Rudyard Kipling,* ed. Geoffrey Moore (New York: Clarkson N. Potter, 1992), 16–18.

20. Eddy, *The King,* 56, 296.

21. Eddy, *The King,* 37.

22. From what little is known of peasant attitudes and involvements during the Hellenistic period, it appears that resistance from these strata was much more likely to be economically than ideologically motivated. In the Seleucid realm in particular there did not appear to be sufficient interaction between the masses and the Greco-Macedonian conquers to foment intercultural frictions. See Claire Preaux, "Esquisse D'Une Histoire Des Révolutions Égyptiennes Sous Les Lagides,"*Chronique d'Égypte* 22 (1936), 522–52.

23. Ehsan Yarshater, "Introduction," in *The Cambridge History of Iran: The Seleucid, Parthian and Sassanian Periods,* vol. 3, pt. 1 (London: Cambridge University Press, 1983), xxix.

24. Jouguet, "Les Lagides," 422.
25. Claire Preaux, "Esquisse D'Une Histoire Des Révolutions Égyptiennes Sous Les Lagide": "≪Chasser le Grec≫ est peut-être un des ces cris de guerre; ce n'est ni le but premier, ni las cause profonde de l'inlassable révolte égyptienne" (522). ["'Drive out the Greek' is perhaps one of the war cries; it is neither the primary goal, nor the fundamental cause of the untiring egyptian revolt."]
26. Green, *Alexander to Actium,* 323.
27. Jouguet, "L'Égypte Ptolemaïque," 118–20.
28. Domenico Musti, "Syria and the East," in *The Cambridge Ancient History,* vol 7, pt. 1: *The Hellenistic World,* 2d ed., F. W. Walbank, A. E. Austin, M. W. Frederiksen, and R. M. Ogilvie, eds. (Cambridge: Cambridge University Press, 1984), 217.
29. Still one of the best sources on the subject of the Revolt of the Maccabees is Elias Bickerman, *The God of the Maccabees: Studies on the Meaning and Origin of the Maacabean Revolt,* trans. Horst R. Moehring (Leiden: E. J. Brill, 1979); compare also 1 Maccabees, *Good News Bible: With Deuterocanonicals/Apocrypha* (New York: American Bible Society, 1978), 148–87; 2 Maccabees, ibid., 188–217; John R. Bartlett, *The First and Second Books of the Maccabees* (Cambridge: Cambridge University Press, 1973).
30. This is an admittedly oversimplified rendition. Also involved in these events was a power struggle between rival families and political factions in Jerusalem, where the stake was the office of high priest, supreme ruler of the temple state and agent of the Seleucid monarch. Events were further complicated by the fact that Antiochus IV was fighting a war with Ptolemaic Egypt in 169–168 B.C.E. and factions in Jerusalem, expecting a Ptolemaic victory, sided with the Ptolemies against the Seleucids, thus further dividing the Jews among themselves. See Bickerman, *The God of the Maccabees,* 32–61.
31. H. Dean Garrett, "Daniel: Ancient Prophet for the Latter Days," in *The Old Testament and the Latter-Day Saints: Proceedings of the Fourteenth Annual Sidney B. Sperry Symposium* [February 8, 1986, Brigham Young University] (Sandy, Utah: Randall, 1987), 261.
32. *The Book of Daniel,* in *Good News Bible,* 976, 971–72.
33. Eddy, *The King,* 293.
34. Eddy, *The King,* 272–93.
35. Ibid., 283.
36. Yarshater, "Introduction," xxix.
37. Bickerman, "Seleucid Period," 14.
38. Yarshater, "Introduction," xxiii.
39. Thomas Allan Brady, "The Reception of the Egyptian Cults by the Greeks (330–30 B.C.)," *University of Missouri Studies* (1935), 17. H. Idris Bell was not even willing to give Sarapis much of a following among the Greeks. "Outside Memphis and Alexandria, the chief centers of the cult, Sarapis seems to have had little appeal for the native Egyptians and not a very great deal more for the majority of Greek settlers." Bell, *Egypt,* 35.
40. Avi-Yonah, *Hellenism,* 48.
41. Some authors describe this phenomenon as "de-Hellenization," but such a designation is somewhat misleading because, regarding the native populations, very little Hellenization had occurred.
42. Michael Rostovtzeff, "Ptolemaic Egypt," in *The Cambridge Ancient History Vol. 7, The Hellenistic Monarchies and the Rise of Rome,* S. A. Cook, F. E. Adcock, and M. P. Charlesworth, eds. (New York: Macmillan, 1928), 152; Bell, *Egypt,* 60–61; Bickerman, "Seleucid Period," 12.
43. Bickerman, "Seleucid Period," 12; Avi-Yonah, *Hellenism,* 176.
44. Rostovtzeff, "Ptolemaic Egypt," 148–149.
45. Green, *Alexander to Actium,* 315.
46. Milne, "Egyptian Nationalism," 229.
47. Jouguet, "L'Égypte Ptolémaïque," 173.
48. Pierre Jouguet, "Les Lagides," 113.
49. H. Idris Bell, "Hellenic Culture in Egypt," *The Journal of Egyptian Archeology* 8 (1922), 146.
50. Avi-Yonah, *Hellenism,* 30.
51. Bell, *Egypt,* 40; Michael Avi-Yonah, *Hellenism,* 29.
52. Ghirshman, *Iran,* 230.
53. Yarshater, "Introduction," xxviii.

54. Eddy, *The King,* 59.
55. Ibid., 260–72.
56. Sarah B. Pomeroy, *Goddesses, Whores, Wives, and Slaves: Women in Classical Antiquity* (New York: Schocken Books, 1975), 120–49.
57. Preaux, *Chronique D'Égypt,* 149.
58. Eddy, *The King,* 260.
59. Notes Green, "The parallel to British India springs to mind, where the acceptance of English as a *lingua franca,* and the appetite of numerous educated Indians for such plums of power as they could grab . . . in no way mitigated the deep-abiding resentment of British rule, much less made any inroads against India's own long-standing cultural and religious traditions"; *Alexander to Actium,* 320.
60. Yarshater, "Introduction," xxvii.
61. William Pfaff, *Barbarian Sentiments: How the American Century Ends* (New York: Hill and Wang, 1989); Benjamin Barber, *Jihad vs. McWorld* (New York: Random House, 1994); Rhoda Howard, "Occidentalism, Human Rights, and the Obligations of Western Scholars," *Canadian Journal of African Studies* 29:1 (1995), 110–26; Fareed Zakaria, "Culture is Destiny: A Conversation with Lee Kwan Yew, *Foreign Affairs* 73:2 (1994), pp. 109–26; Arnold Toynbee (with Jane Caplan), *A Study of History,* abr. ed. (New York: Portland House, 1988), 445–76; and Samuel P. Huntington, *The Clash of Civilizations and the Remaking of World Order* (New York: Simon and Schuster, 1996).
62. Muhammad Iqbal, "Europe and Syria," *Poems From Iqbal* (London: Murray, 1955), 75.
63. Ngugi wa Thiong'o, *Decolonizing the Mind: The Politics of Language in African Literature* (London: James Currey, 1986), 3.
64. Edward W. Said, *Culture and Imperialism* (New York: Alfred A. Knopf, 1993); Ali Mazrui, *Cultural Forces in World Politics* (London: James Currey, 1990); Claude Ake, "The New World Order: A View from Africa," in *Whose World Order?,* ed. Hans-Henrik Holm and Georg Sorensen (Boulder, Colo: Westview Press, 1995), 19–42; Kishore Mahbubani, *Can Asians Think?* (Singapore: Times Editions, 1999). For a review of contemporary non-Western thinking see Donald J. Puchala, "Third World Thinking and Contemporary International Relations," in *International Relations and the Third World,* ed. Stephanie G. Neuman (New York: St. Martin's Press, 1998), 133–58.
65. Ali Mazrui, "Islamic and Western Values," *Foreign Affairs* 76:5 (1997), 118–32.

Chapter 9

1. William H. McNeill, *Mythistory and Other Essays* (Chicago: University of Chicago Press, 1986), 23.
2. R. M. MacIver, *The Web of Government* (New York: Macmillan, 1947), 4–5.
3. Joseph Campbell, *Creative Mythology: The Masks of God* (New York: Viking Penguin, 1968), 4–6.
4. Ernst Cassirer, *An Essay on Man: An Introduction to a Philosophy of Human Culture* (New Haven, Conn.: Yale University Press, 1944), 75; see also Cassirer, *The Myth of the State* (New Haven, Conn.: Yale University Press, 1946), 37.
5. Ronald Preston, "Christian Ethics," in *A Companion to Ethics,* ed. Peter Singer (Oxford: Blackwell, 1991), 91–105.
6. John Finnis, *Aquinas: Moral, Political, and Legal Theory* (Oxford, Eng.: Oxford University Press, 1998), 56–102.
7. Thomas Jefferson, *The Jefferson Bible: The Life and Morals of Jesus of Nazareth* (Boston: Beacon Press, 1989).
8. Crane Brinton, *From Many One: The Process of Political Integration: The Problem of World Government* (Cambridge, Mass.: Harvard University Press, 1948), 30ff.
9. M. L. Clarke, *The Roman Mind: Studies in the History of Thought from Cicero to Marcus Aurelius* (New York: W. W. Norton, 1968), 50.
10. Marcus Aurelius, *Meditations* (Hammondsworth, England: Penguin, 1964), 65.
11. Thomas J. Schlereth, *The Cosmopolitan Ideal in Enlightenment Thought: Its Form and Function in the Ideas of Franklin, Hume, and Voltaire, 1694–1790* (Notre Dame, Ind.: University of Notre Dame Press, 1977), 113.

12. J. W. von Goethe, quoted in, John Herman Randall Jr., *The Making of the Modern Mind: A Survey of the Intellectual Background of the Present Age* (Cambridge, Mass.: Houghton Mifflin, 1940), 379.
13. Schlereth, *Cosmopolitan Ideal*, 79.
14. Ibid., 83.
15. Randall, *Modern Mind*, 367.
16. Schlereth, *Cosmopolitan Ideal*, 73.
17. In this interpretation they misread Confucianism, as will become apparent later in this study.
18. Donald J. Puchala, "The Ethics of Globalism," John F. Holmes Memorial Lecture, Academic Council on the United Nations System, New York, June, 1995.
19. Martha C. Nussbaum, "Human Functioning and Social Justice: In Defense of Aristotelian Essentialism," *Political Theory* 20:2 (1992), 222.
20. Ibid.
21. Leonard Shihlien Hsü, *The Political Philosophy of Confucianism* (New York: E. P. Dutton, 1932), xvi.
22. Y. P. Mei, "The Basis of Social, Ethical, and Spiritual Values in Chinese Philosophy," in *The Chinese Mind*, ed. Charles A. Moore (Honolulu: East-West Center Press, 1967), 150.
23. Ibid.
24. Ibid., 152.
25. Mei, "Chinese Philosophy," 152–53.
26. Ibid., 152.
27. Lin Yutang, *The Wisdom of Confucius* (New York: Modern Library, 1938), 105, 116.
28. Mencius, quoted in Wing-Tsit Chan, *A Source Book in Chinese Philosophy* (Princeton, N.J.: Princeton University Press, 1963), 54.
29. Ibid., 65–66.
30. K'ang Yu-wei, *Ta T'ung Shu: The One-World Philosophy of K'ang Yu-Wei*, trans. Laurence G. Thompson (London: George Allen and Unwin, 1958), 64–65.
31. Wing-Tsit Chan, *Source Book*, 55.
32. Ibid., 162; K'ang Yu-wei, *One-World Philosophy*, 65.
33. Mei, "Chinese Philosophy," 150.
34. K'ang Yu-wei, *One-World Philosophy*, 64.
35. F. S. C. Northrup, *The Meeting of East and West: An Inquiry concerning World Understanding* (Woodbridge, Conn.: Ox Bow Press, 1946), 332.
36. Lin Yutang, *Confucius*, 129–30.
37. Wing-Tsit Chan, *Source Book*, 594.
38. K'ang Yu-wei, *One-World Philosophy*, 65.
39. Northrup, *East and West*, 399.
40. Donald H. Bishop, ed., *Thinkers of the Indian Renaissance* (New Delhi: Wiley Eastern Limited, 1982), passim.
41. UNESCO, *All Men Are Brothers: Life and Thoughts of Mahatma Gandhi as Told in His Own Words* (Paris: UNESCO, 1958), xiv.
42. Ibid., 121.
43. Paul Arthur Schilpp, ed., *The Philosophy of Radhakrishnan* (New York: Tudor, 1952), 732.
44. Durlab Singh, *The Sentinel of the East: A Biographical Study of Rabindra Nath Tagore* (New York: Haskell House, 1974), 132.
45. I. C. Sharma, *Ethical Philosophies of India* (Lincoln, Nebraska: Johnsen, 1965), 265.
46. Northrup, *East and West*, 319, 326.
47. *The Bhagavad Gita*, trans. Eliot Deutsch (New York: Holt, Rinehart and Winston, 1968), passim.
48. E. Washburn Hopkins, *Ethics of India* (Port Washington, N.Y.: Kennikat Press, 1968), 45–86.
49. UNESCO, *Brothers*, 56.
50. Ibid., 110.
51. S. Radhakrishnan, *Eastern Religions and Western Thought* (Oxford: Clarendon Press, 1949), 33.
52. Ibid., 296.
53. Sharma, *Philosophies*, 309.
54. Austin B. Creel, *Dharma in Hindu Ethics* (Columbia, Mo.: South Asia Books, 1977), 83.
55. UNESCO, *Brothers*, 57.

56. A. N. Marlow, ed., *Radhakrishnan: An Anthology* (London: George Allen and Unwin, 1952), 25.
57. S. Radhakrishnan, *An Idealist View of Life* (London: George Allen and Unwin, 1964), 100–137.
58. Radhakrishnan, *Eastern Religion and Western Thought,* 50.
59. Sharma, *Philosophies,* 60.
60. Ibid., 182, 208.
61. Hopkins, *Ethics,* 40–41.
62. Marlow, ed., *Radharkrishnan,* 39.
63. Hopkins, *Ethics,* 59.
64. Samuel P. Huntington, "The Clash of Civilizations?" *Foreign Affairs* 72:4 (1993), 22–49; and Huntington, *The Clash of Civilizations and the Remaking of World Order* (New York: Simon and Schuster, 1996).

Chapter 10

1. Robert O. Keohane, "International Liberalism Reconsidered," in *The Economic Limits to Modern Politics,* ed. John Dunn (New York: Cambridge University Press, 1990), 174.
2. Yale H. Ferguson and Richard W. Mansbach, *The Elusive Quest Continues* (Upper Saddle River, N.J.: Prentice Hall 2002), 29–30.
3. Michael W. Doyle, *Ways of War and Peace: Realism, Liberalism, and Socialism* (New York: W. W. Norton, 1997), 216–19; see also Carl Becker, *The Heavenly City of the Eighteenth Century Philosophers* (New Haven, Conn.: Yale University Press, 1932).
4. Mark W. Zacker and Richard A. Matthew, "Liberal International Theory: Common Threads, Divergent Strands," in *Controversies in International Relations Theory: Realism and the Neoliberal Challenge,* ed. Charles W. Kegley Jr. (New York: St. Martin's Press, 1995), 111.
5. Michael W. Doyle, "A Liberal View: Preserving and Expanding the Liberal Pacific Union," in *International Order and the Future of World Politics,* ed. T. V. Paul and John A. Hall (New York: Cambridge University Press, 1999), 213.
6. Ferguson and Mansbach, *The Elusive Quest Continues,* 213.
7. Zacker and Matthew, "Theory," 140.
8. Ibid., 117–20; see also Francis Fukuyama, *The End of History and the Last Man* (New York: The Free Press, 1992), 45ff.
9. Doyle, "A Liberal View," 261.
10. Keohane, "Liberalism," 194.
11. Zacker and Matthew, "Theory," 140.
12. Zacker and Matthew, "Theory," 149.
13. Doyle, "A Liberal View," 241.
14. Fukuyama, *The End,* 47.
15. Keohane, "Liberalism," 177; James Lee Ray, *Democracy and International Conflict: An Evaluation of the Democratic Peace Proposition* (Columbia: University of South Carolina Press, 1995), 47–73.
16. Robert A. Nisbet, *Social Change and History: Aspects of the Western Theory of Development* (New York: Oxford University Press, 1969), 22–24 and passim; see also Frederick J. Teggart, *Theory and Process of History* (Berkeley and Los Angeles: University of California Press, 1977). The first edition of Teggart's work appeared in 1925.
17. Frank E. Manuel, *Shapes of Philosophical History* (Stanford, Calif.: Stanford University Press, 1965), 25–32.
18. See Jean Antoine Nicolas Condorcet, *Sketch of a Historical Survey of the Progression of the Human Mind* (New York: Noonday Press, 1955).
19. Immanuel Kant, "Idea for a Universal History with Cosmopolitan Intent," in *The Philosophy of Kant: Immanuel Kant's Moral and Political Writings,* ed. Carl J. Friedrich (New York: The Modern Library, 1949), 124.
20. Ibid., 130.
21. Fukuyama, *The End,* xii, 48.
22. Doyle, "A Liberal View," 261–62.
23. Doyle, *Ways of War and Peace,* 480, 481.
24. John R. Oneal and Bruce Russett, "The Pacific Benefits of Democracy, Interdependence,

and International Organizations, 1885–1992," *World Politics* 52:1 (1999), 1–2; for a comprehensive review of the democratic peace literature, see Ray, *Democracy*, 1–46.

25. Ray, *Democracy*, 41.
26. Immanuel Kant, "Eternal Peace," in Friedrich, ed., *Philosophy of Kant*, 438.
27. Ray, *Democracy*, 30–41.
28. Ibid., 201.
29. See chapter 4 of this volume.
30. Doyle, *Ways of War and Peace*, 261–64.
31. Fukuyama, *The End*, 48–50.
32. James Lee Ray, *Democracy*, 47–49.
33. Samuel P. Huntington, *The Third Wave: Democratization in the Late Twentieth Century* (Norman: University of Oklahoma Press, 1991), 13–17.
34. Ibid., 15, 25.
35. Patrick J. McGowan and Howard B. Shapiro, *The Comparative Study of Foreign Policy: A Survey of Scientific Findings*, vol. 4 (Beverly Hills: Sage, 1973), 2, 4.
36. Kant, "Eternal Peace," 448.
37. For both a sympathetic rehearsal and a brilliant critique of such Enlightenment thinking, see Nisbet, *Social Change*, 105–36.
38. This is despite the fact that some agents in all ages have railed against advanced technologies and urged reversions to more primitive ones. Here, our age is no different from others past. See Jared Diamond, *Guns, Germs, and Steel: The Fates of Human Societies* (New York: W. W. Norton, 1999), passim.
39. This is not to belittle or sidestep the fact that advancing technology has also been continuously applied to enhancing the destructiveness of warfare. This progression, however, is better accommodated within the framework of realist rather than liberal theory.
40. Fukuyama, *The End*, 71–97.
41. Ibid., 116.
42. Ibid.
43. Cyril E. Black, *The Dynamics of Modernization: A Study in Comparative History* (New York: Harper and Row, 1966), 79.
44. Ibid., 83.
45. Ibid., 79.
46. Huntington, *The Third Wave*, 65.
47. Ibid., 67–68.
48. Ibid., 69.
49. Talcott Parsons, "Evolutionary Universals in Society," *American Sociological Review* 29:3 (1964), 339–57.
50. Ibid., 355–56.
51. Fukuyama, *The End*, 133.
52. For an informative review of the controversy surrounding modernization theory, see Leonard Binder, "The Natural History of Development Theory," *Comparative Studies in Society and History* 28 (1986), 3–33, esp. 12–18.
53. See, for example, Daniel Lerner, *The Passing of Traditional Society: Modernizing the Middle East* (New York: The Free Press, 1958), where the author contends in his preface, "What the West is, the Middle East seeks to become" (ix).
54. See W. W. Rostow, *The Stages of Economic Growth: A Non-Communist Manifesto* (Cambridge: Cambridge University Press, 1960).
55. Black, *Dynamics*, 136ff.
56. Barrington Moore Jr., *Social Origins of Dictatorship and Democracy: Lord and Peasant in the Making of the Modern World* (Boston: Beacon Press, 1966), xv–xvi; see also Theda Skocpol, "A Critical Review of Barrington Moore's Social Origins of Dictatorship and Democracy," in *Social Revolutions in the Modern World*, ed. Theda Skocpol (New York: Cambridge University Press, 1994), 25–54.
57. Huntington, *The Third Wave*, 38.
58. Ellen Comisso, "Crisis in Socialism or Crisis of Socialism?" *World Politics* 42:4 (1990), 563–606.
59. Fukuyama, *The End*, 117, 134.
60. Ibid., 240–44.

61. Ray, *Democracy*, 52–55.

62. Keohane, "Liberalism," 166–67.

63. Thomas Friedman, *The Lexus and the Olive Tree: Understanding Globalization* (New York: Farrar, Straus and Giroux, 1999).

64. Francis Fukuyama, *The End*, 181–91.

65. Critics have mostly latched onto Fukuyama's claim that political-ideological history essentially ended with the collapse of communism in the late twentieth century and have made a critics' cottage industry out of offering reasons why history has not ended. Reviewers have not gone much deeper into Fukuyama's work, with perhaps the notable exceptions of John Gray, "The End of History and the Last Man," *National Review* 44:9 (1992), 46ff, and H. Stuart Hughes, "On 'The End of History and the Last Man,'" *Los Angeles Times Book Review*, November 8, 1992, 3, 13.

66. Donald Treadgold, *Freedom: A History* (New York: New York University Press, 1990); reviewed in the *American Historical Review* 97:2 (1992), 512, by Karl F. Morrison.

67. Treadgold, *Freedom*, 416; see also Raymond Aron, *Democracy and Totalitarianism* (New York: Praeger, 1969), 229.

68. Ibid., 10.

69. Ibid.

70. Keohane, "Liberalism," 176.

71. David Mitrany, *A Working Peace System: An Argument for the Functional Development of International Organization* (London: National Peace Council, 1946).

72. Bruce Russett, John Oneal, and David R. Davis, "The Third Leg of the Kantian Tripod: International Organization and Militarized Disputes, 1950–1985," *International Organization* 52:3 (1998), 441–68.

73. Ibid., 455.

74. Ibid., 456.

75. Oneal and Russett, "Benefits," 34.

76. Commentators on international law refer to its "vertical" and "horizontal" expansion over time. See, for example, Edward L. Morse, *Modernization and the Transformation of International Relations* (New York: The Free Press, 1976), 166–71.

77. Adam Watson, *The Evolution of International Society: A Comparative Historical Analysis* (New York: Routledge, 1992), chap. 12.

78. Adda B. Bozeman, *Politics and Culture in International History* (Princeton, N.J.: Princeton University Press, 1960), 110–12.

79. Adam Watson, *Evolution*, chap. 19; and Gerrit Gong, *The Standard of Civilization in International Society* (Oxford: Oxford University Press, 1984), passim.

80. The Roman *jus gentium* may or may not be considered international law, since its purpose was to regulate commerce and private dealings between "nations" *within* the empire.

81. Louis Henkin, *How Nations Behave: Law and Foreign Policy* (New York: Praeger, 1968), 21.

82. Morse, *Modernization*, 156.

83. Louis Henkin, *How Nations Behave*, 48.

84. Edward Morse, *Modernization*, 163; Russett, Oneal, and Davis, "Third Leg," 443.

85. Morse, *Modernization*, 114–51.

86. Ibid., 80.

87. Marvin S. Soroos, *Beyond Sovereignty: The Challenge of Global Policy* (Columbia: University of South Carolina Press, 1986).

88. Ibid., 25.

89. Ibid., 25.

90. Ibid., 7.

91. Robert O. Keohane and Joseph S. Nye Jr., *Power and Interdependence*, 3d ed. (New York: Longman, 2001).

92. Ibid., 30.

93. Ibid., 17–19; see also Robert O. Keohane, *After Hegemony: Cooperation and Disorder in World Political Economy* (Princeton, N.J.: Princeton University Press, 1984), 49–64; and Stephen D. Krasner, ed., *International Regimes* (Ithaca, N.Y.: Cornell University Press, 1983).

94. Keohane and Nye, *Power*, 262.

95. Morse, *Modernization*, 20.

96. Ibid., 80.
97. Soroos, *Beyond Sovereignty,* 15.
98. Ibid., 25.
99. Keohane and Nye, *Power,* 262; and Ferguson and Mansbach, *The Elusive Quest Continues,* 184.
100. Ferguson and Mansbach, *The Elusive Quest Continues,* 213.
101. Michael Doyle, "A Liberal View," 262.
102. Keohane, "Liberalism," 194.
103. Keohane and Nye, *Power,* 300.
104. Stephen Korbin, "Back to the Future: Neomedievalism and the Postmodern Digital World Economy," *Journal of International Affairs* 51:2 (1998), 364.
105. John H. Herz, *International Politics in the Atomic Age* (New York: Columbia University Press, 1959).
106. Ibid., 243.
107. Kenneth E. Boulding, *Conflict and Defense: A General Theory* (New York: Harper Torchbooks, 1962); Raymond Aron, *Peace and War: A Theory of International Relations,* trans. Richard Howard and Annette Baker Fox (Garden City, N.Y.: Doubleday, 1966).

Chapter 11

1. Max Weber, " 'Objectivity' in Social Science and Social Policy," in *The Methodology of the Social Sciences,* trans. and ed. Edward Shils and Henry A. Finch (New York: The Free Press, 1949), 50.
2. Ibid., 51.
3. H. Stuart Hughes, *Consciousness and Society* (New York: Alfred A. Knopf, 1958), 302.
4. Max Weber, *The Protestant Ethic and Spirit of Capitalism* (New York: Scribner's, 1958).
5. Robert O. Keohane and Joseph S. Nye Jr., *Power and Interdependence* (Boston: Little, Brown, 1977); see also Joseph S. Nye Jr. and Robert O. Keohane, "Transnational Relations and World Politics: An Introduction," *International Organization* 25:3 (1971), 326–50.
6. See, for example, William Greider, *One World, Ready or Not: The Manic Logic of Global Capitalism* (New York: Simon and Schuster, 1998); David Held et al., *Global Transformation: Politics, Economics and Culture* (Stanford, Calif.: Stanford University Press, 1999); Michael Mann, "Has Globalization Ended the Rise and Rise of the Nation-State," in *International Order and the Future of World Politics,* ed. T. V. Paul and John A. Hall (Cambridge: Cambridge University Press, 1999), 237–61; and James H. Mittelman, *The Globalization Syndrome: Transformation and Resistance* (Princeton, N.J.: Princeton University Press, 2000).
7. Zbigniew Brzezinski, *The Grand Chessboard: American Primacy and Its Geostrategic Alternatives* (New York: Basic Books, 1997).
8. John Gerard Ruggie, "Territoriality and Beyond: Problematizing Modernity in International Relations," *International Organization* 47:1 (1993), 139–74; Yale H. Ferguson and Richard W. Mansbach, *Polities: Authority, Identities and Ideology* (Columbia: University of South Carolina Press, 1995).
9. Hans Kohn, *The Twentieth Century: A Mid-Way Account of the Western World* (New York: Macmillan, 1949).
10. Aileen Kelly, *Toward Another Shore: Russian Thinkers between Necessity and Chance* (New Haven, Conn.: Yale University Press, 1998); Aileen Kelly, *Views from Another Shore: Essays on Herzen, Chekhov and Bakhtin* (New Haven, Conn.: Yale University Press, 1999); Ali Amin Mazrui, *Cultural Forces in World Politics* (London: James Currey, 1990); Edward Said, *Culture and Imperialism* (New York: Alfred A. Knopf, 1993); and Kishore Mahbubani, *Can Asians Think?* (Singapore: Times Books International, 1998).
11. Edward Harlett Carr, *The Twenty Years' Crisis* (London: Macmillan, 1939).
12. Raymond Aron, *Peace and War* (London: Weidenfield and Nicolson, 1966); Hedley Bull, "International Theory: The Case for the Classical Approach," *World Politics* 18:3 (1966), 361–77; Stanley Hoffmann, ed., *Contemporary Theory in International Relations* (Englewood Cliffs, N.J.: Prentice-Hall, 1960); Morton Kaplan, "Problems of Theory Building and Theory Confirmation in International Politics," in *The International System: Theoretical Essays,* ed. Klaus Knorr and Sidney Verba (Princeton, N.J.: Princeton University Press, 1961), 6–24; Charles A. McClelland, *Theory and the International System* (New York: Macmillan, 1966);

and J. David Singer, "The Incompleat Theorist: Insight without Evidence," in *Contending Approaches to International Politics*, ed. Klaus Knorr and James N. Rosenau (Princeton, N.J.: Princeton University Press, 1969), 62–86.

13. Knorr and Rosenau, eds., *Contending Approaches*.

14. Oran Young, "Professor Russett: Industrious Tailor to a Naked Emperor," *World Politics* 21:3 (1969), 486–511; Bruce M. Russett, *International Regions and the International System: A Study in Political Ecology* (Chicago: Rand McNally, 1967).

15. Yosef Lapid, "The Third Debate," *International Studies Quarterly* 33:3 (1989), 235–54.

16. Weber, "Objectivity," 49.

17. Harvey Starr, "Visions of Global Politics as an Intellectual Exercise: Three Questions without Answers," in *Visions of International Relations: Assessing an Academic Field*, ed. Donald J. Puchala (Columbia: University of South Carolina Press, 2002), 43–44.

18. James Kurth, "Inside the Cave: The Banality of IR Studies," *National Interest* 53 (1998), 29–41.

19. Richard Rorty, *Philosophy and the Mirror of Nature* (Princeton, N.J.: Princeton University Press, 1979), 131–64.

20. See Puchala, ed., *Visions*.

21. Charles W. Kegley Jr., "Bridge Building in the Study of International Relations: How 'Kuhn' We Do Better?" in Puchala, ed., *Visions*, 71.

22. John Gray, *Enlightenment's Wake: Politics and Culture at the Close of the Modern Age* (New York: Routledge, 1995).

23. Brian Schmidt, *The Political Discourse of Anarchy: A Disciplinary History of International Relations* (Albany, N.Y.: State University of New York Press, 1998).

24. Richard W. Mansbach, "Deterritorializing Global Politics," in Puchala, ed., *Visions*, 110–11.

25. George E. Marcus and Michael M. J. Fischer, *Anthropology As Cultural Critique* (Chicago: University of Chicago Press, 1986); see also chapters 2 and 3 of this volume.

26. Hayden White, *Tropics of Discourse: Essays in Cultural Criticism* (Baltimore: Johns Hopkins University Press, 1978), 29.

27. See, for example, Steve Smith, "The Self-Images of a Discipline: A Genealogy of International Relations Theory," in *International Relations Theory Today*, ed. Ken Booth and Steve Smith (Cambridge: Cambridge University Press, 1995), 1–37; contributions to *International Theory: Positivism and Beyond*, ed. Steve Smith, Ken Booth, and Marysia Zalewski (Cambridge: Cambridge University Press, 1996); James Der Derian, ed., *International Theory: Critical Investigations* (New York: New York University Press, 1995); and James Der Darian and Michael Shapiro, *International/Intertextual Relations: Post-Modern Readings of World Politics* (New York: Lexington Books, 1989).

28. Rorty, *Philosophy*, 170.

29. For philosophic context, see Ernst Cassirer, *An Essay on Man: An Introduction to a Philosophy of Human Culture* (New Haven, Conn.: Yale University Press, 1944).

30. Nicholas Onuf, *World of Our Making: Rules and Rule in Social Theory and International Relations* (Columbia: University of South Carolina Press, 1989); Alexander Wendt, "Anarchy Is What States Make of It: The Social Construction of State Politics," *International Organization* 46:2 (1992), 391–425.

31. Hans-George Gadamer, *Truth and Method*, trans. and rev. Joel Weinsheimer and Donald J. Marshall, 2d ed. (New York: Continuum, 1994); and Hajo Holborn, "Wilhelm Dilthey and the Critique of Historical Reason," in *European Intellectual History Since Darwin and Marx*, ed. Warren W. Wagar (New York: Harper and Row, 1967), 56–88.

32. Hayward R. Alker Jr., *Rediscoveries and Reformulations: Humanistic Methods for International Studies* (Cambridge: Cambridge University Press, 1996), 238–302.

33. Donald J. Puchala, "Harold Lasswell's Legacy and Twenty-first Century International Relations," in Puchala, ed., *Visions*, 142–56.

34. Hayden White, *Tropics of Discourse*, 63–65; see also White, *Metahistory: The Historical Imagination of Nineteenth Century Europe* (Baltimore: Johns Hopkins University Press, 1973), 5–6.

35. William James, *The Meaning of Truth* (Cambridge, Mass.: Harvard University Press, 1975).

36. Rorty, *Philosophy*, 361.

Bibliography

Adorno, Theodor W., Hans Albert, Ralf Dahrendorf, Jürgen Habermas, Harold Pilot, and Karl R. Popper. *The Positivist Dispute in German Sociology*. Aldershot, England: Avebury, Ashgate, 1994.

Ake, Claude. "The New World Order: A View From Africa." In *Whose World Order?*, 19–42. Edited by Hans-Henrik Holm and Georg Sorensen. Boulder, Colo.: Westview Press, 1995.

Alker, Hayward R., Jr. *Rediscoveries and Reformulations: Humanistic Methods for International Studies*. Cambridge: Cambridge University Press, 1996.

Apel, Karl-Otto. *Analytic Philosophy of Language and the Geisteswissenschaften*. Dordrecht: D. Reidel, 1967.

Aron, Raymond. "Conflict and War from the Viewpoint of Historical Sociology." In *Contemporary Theory in International Relations*, 191–208. Edited by Stanley Hoffmann. Englewood Cliffs, NJ: Prentice-Hall, 1960.

———. *Peace and War: A Theory of International Relations*. Translated by Richard Howard and Annette Baker Fox. Garden City, N.Y.: Doubleday, 1966.

———. *Democracy and Totalitarianism*. New York: Praeger, 1969.

Aurelius, Marcus. *Meditations*. Hammondsworth, England: Penguin, 1964.

Avi-Yonah, Michael. *Hellenism and the East: Contacts and Interrelations from Alexander to the Roman Conquest*. Jerusalem: Institute of Languages, Literature and the Arts, The Hebrew University, 1978.

Bagby, Philip. *Culture and History: Prolegomena to the Comparative Study of Civilizations*. Berkeley and Los Angeles: University of California Press, 1959.

Barber, Benjamin. *Jihad vs. McWorld*. New York: Random House, 1994.

Barnett, A. D. "Ten Years after Mao." *Foreign Affairs* 65 (1986): 37–65.

Bartlett, John R. *The First and Second Books of the Maccabees*. Cambridge: Cambridge University Press, 1973.

Barzun, Jacques, Hajo Holborn, Herbert Heaton, Dumas Malone, and George La Piana. *The Interpretation of History*. New York: Peter Smith, 1950.

Becker, Carl G. *The Heavenly City of the Eighteenth Century Philosophers*. New Haven, Conn.: Yale University Press, 1932.

Bell, H. Idris. "Hellenic Culture in Egypt." *Journal of Egyptian Archeology* 8 (1922): 139–155.

———. *Egypt: From Alexander the Great to the Arab Conquest: A Study in the Diffusion and Decay of Hellenism*. Oxford: Oxford University Press, 1966.

Benhabib, Seyla. "Epistemologies of Postmodernism: A Rejoinder to Jean-François Lyotard." *New German Critique* 33 (1984): 103–26.

The Bhagavad Gita. Translated by Eliot Deutsch. New York: Holt, Rinehart and Winston, 1968.

Bickerman, Elias. *The God of the Maccabees: Studies on the Meaning and Origin of the Maccabean Revolt*. Translated by Horst R. Moehring. Leiden: E. J. Brill, 1979.

Binder, Leonard. "The Natural History of Development Theory." *Comparative Studies in Society and History* 28 (1986): 3–33.

Bishop, Donald H., ed. *Thinkers of the Indian Renaissance*. New Delhi: Wiley Eastern, 1982.

Blachman, Morris J., William M. LeoGrande, and Kenneth Sharpe, eds. *Confronting Revolution: Security through Diplomacy in Central America*. London: Thames and Hudson, 1973.

Black, Cyril E. *The Dynamics of Modernization: A Study in Comparative History*. New York: Harper and Row, 1966.

Boulding, Kenneth E. *The Image: Knowledge in Life and Society*. Ann Arbor: University of Michigan Press, 1956.

———. *Conflict and Defense: A General Theory*. New York: Harper Torchbooks, 1962.

Bozeman, Adda B. *Politics and Culture in International History*. Princeton, N.J.: Princeton University Press, 1960.

———. "American Policy and the Illusion of Congruent Values." *Strategic Review* 15 (1987): 11–22.

———. *Strategic Intelligence and Statecraft.* McLean, Va.: Brassey's, 1992.

———. *Politics and Culture in International History.* Revised ed., New Brunswick, N.J.: Transaction Publishers, 1994.

Brady, Thomas Allan. "The Reception of the Egyptian Cults By the Greeks (330–30 B.C.)." *University of Missouri Studies* 10 (1935): 9–41.

Braudel, Fernand. *On History.* Chicago: University of Chicago Press, 1980.

———. *The Perspective of the World: Civilization and Capitalism, Fifteenth–Eighteenth Centuries.* New York: Harper and Row, 1984.

Braybrooke, David. "Through Epistemology to the Depths of Political Illusion." In *Through the Looking Glass: Epistemology and the Conduct of Inquiry,* 52–82. Edited by Maria J. Falco. Washington, D.C.: University Press of America, 1979.

Brinton, Crane. *From Many One: The Process of Political Integration; The Problem of World Government.* Cambridge, Mass.: Harvard University Press, 1948.

Brzezinski, Zbigniew. *The Grand Failure: The Birth and Death of Communism in the Twentieth Century.* New York: Collier, 1989.

———. *The Grand Chessboard: American Primacy and Its Geostrategic Alternatives.* New York: Basic Books, 1997.

Bull, Hedley. "International Theory: The Case for a Classical Approach." In *Contending Approaches to International Politics,* 20–38. Edited by Klaus Knorr and James N. Rosenau. Princeton, N.J.: Princeton University Press, 1969.

———. "New Directions in International Relations Theory." *International Studies* 14 (1975): 277–88.

———. *The Anarchical Society: A Study of Order in World Politics.* London: Macmillan, 1977.

Bull, Hedley and Adam Watson, eds. *The Expansion of International Society.* Oxford: Oxford University Press, 1984.

Burckhardt, Jacob. *The Civilization of the Renaissance in Italy.* New York: The Modern Library, 1954.

Calleo, David P. *Rethinking Europe's Future.* Princeton, N.J.: Princeton University Press, 2001.

Campbell, Joseph. *Creative Mythology: The Masks of God.* New York: Viking Penguin, 1968.

Carr, Edward Harlett. *The Twenty Years' Crisis, 1919–1939: An Introduction to the Study of International Relations.* New York: Harper Torchbooks, 1964.

Cassirer, Ernst. *An Essay on Man: An Introduction to a Philosophy of Human Culture.* New Haven, Conn.: Yale University Press, 1944.

———. *The Myth of the State.* New Haven, Conn.: Yale University Press, 1946.

———. *The Philosophy of Symbolic Forms.* New Haven, Conn.: Yale University Press, 1957.

———. *The Logic of the Humanities.* New Haven, Conn.: Yale University Press, 1960.

Chan, Wing-Tsit. *A Source Book in Chinese Philosophy.* Princeton, N.J.: Princeton University Press, 1963.

Chang, Iris. *The Rape of Nanking: The Forgotten Holocaust of World War II.* New York: Basic Books, 1997.

Chaudhuri, Nirad C. *The Autobiography of an Unknown Indian.* New York: Macmillan, 1951.

Clarke, M. L. *The Roman Mind: Studies in the History of Thought from Cicero to Marcus Aurelius.* New York: W. W. Norton, 1968.

Collingwood, Robin George. *The Idea of History.* Edited by Jan Van Der Dussen. Revised ed. New York: Oxford University Press, 1994.

Comisso, Ellen. "Crisis in Socialism or Crisis of Socialism?" *World Politics* 42 (1990): 563–606.

Condorcet, Jean Antoine Nicolas. *Sketch of a Historical Survey of the Progression of the Human Mind.* New York: Noonday Press, 1955.

Conrad, Joseph. *Heart of Darkness.* New York: W. W. Norton, 1971.

Cook, S. A., F. A. Adcock, and M. P. Charlesworth, eds. *The Cambridge Ancient History,* Volume 7, *The Hellenic Monarchies and the Rise of Rome.* New York: Macmillan, 1928.

Creel, Austin B. *Dharma in Hindu Ethics.* Columbia, Mo.: South Asia Books, 1977.

Dawson, Christopher. *The Dynamics of World History.* London: Sheed and Ward, 1957.

———. *The Movement of World Revolution.* New York: Sheed and Ward, 1959.

Dehio, Ludwig. *The Precarious Balance: Four Centuries of the European Power Struggle.* New York: Vintage Books, 1965.

Der Derian, James, ed. *International Theory: Critical Investigations.* New York: New York University Press, 1995.

Der Darian, James and Michael Shapiro, eds. *International/Intertextual Relations:Post-Modern Readings of World Politics*. New York: Lexington Books, 1989.

Deutsch, Karl W. *Nationalism and Social Communication*. Cambridge: MIT Press, 1953.

Deutsch, Karl W., Sidney A. Burrell, Robert A. Kann, Maurice Lee, Jr., Martin Lichterman, Raymond E. Lindgren, Francis L Loewenheim, and Richard W. Van Wagenen. *Political Community and the North Atlantic Area*. Princeton, N.J.: Princeton University Press, 1957.

Diamond, Jared. *Guns, Germs, and Steel: The Fates of Human Societies*. New York: W. W. Norton, 1999.

Dilthey, Wilhelm. *Selected Writings*. Edited and translated by H. P. Rickman. Cambridge: Cambridge University Press, 1976.

———. *Introduction to the Human Sciences: An Attempt to Lay a Foundation for the Study of Society and History*. Detroit: Wayne State University Press, 1988.

Dorn, Walter L. *Competition for Empire, 1740–1763*. New York: Harper and Brothers, 1940.

Doyle, Michael. *Empires*. Ithaca, N.Y.: Cornell University Press, 1986.

———. "A Liberal View: Preserving and Expanding the Liberal Pacific Union." In *International Order and the Future of World Politics*, 41–66. Edited by T. V. Paul and John A. Hall. New York: Cambridge University Press, 1999.

Doyle, Michael W. *Ways of War and Peace: Realism, Liberalism, and Socialism*. New York: W. W. Norton, 1997.

Durant, Will. *Our Oriental Heritage*. New York: MJF Books, 1935.

Eddy, Samuel K. *The King Is Dead: Studies in the Near Eastern Resistance to Hellenism*. Lincoln: University of Nebraska Press, 1961.

Etzioni, Amitai. "The Epigenesis of Political Communities at the International Level." *American Journal of Sociology* 68 (1966): 407–21.

Euripides. *Medea*. In *Ten Plays By Euripides*, 31–64. Translated by Moses Hadas and John McLean. New York: Bantam, 1960.

———. *The Trojan Women*. In *Ten Plays by Euripides*, 173–204. Translated by Moses Hadas and John McLean. New York: Bantam, 1960.

Faas, Ekbert. *Tragedy and After: Euripides, Shakespeare, and Goethe*. Kingston, Ontario: McGill-Queens University Press, 1984.

Ferguson, Yale H. and Richard W. Mansbach. *The Elusive Quest: Theory and International Politics*. Columbia: University of South Carolina Press, 1984.

———. *Polities: Authority, Identities and Change*. Columbia: University of South Carolina Press, 1996.

———. *The Elusive Quest Continues*. Upper Saddle River, NJ: Prentice-Hall, 2002.

Feyerabend, Paul K. "How to be a Good Empiricist—A Plea for Tolerance in Epistemological Matters." In *Challenges to Empiricism*, 164–93. Edited by Harold Morick. Indianapolis: Hackett, 1980.

———. "Science without Experience." In *Challenges to Empiricism*, 160–64. Edited by Harold Morick. Indianapolis: Hackett, 1980.

Finnis, John. *Aquinas: Moral, Political, and Legal Theory*. Oxford: Oxford University Press, 1998.

Fisch, Eberhard. *Guernica by Picasso: A Study of the Picture and Its Context*. Lewisburg, Penn.: Bucknell University Press, 1988.

FitzGerald, C. P. *The Southern Expansion of the Chinese People*. London: Barrie and Jenkins, 1972.

Foucault, Michel. *The Archaeology of Knowledge*. New York: Pantheon Books, 1972.

———. *The Order of Things: An Archaeology of the Human Sciences*. New York: Vintage Books, 1994.

Franck, Thomas M. and Edward Weisband. *Word Politics: Verbal Strategy among the Superpowers*. New York: Oxford University Press, 1971.

Freud, Sigmund. *Civilization and Its Discontents*. New York: W. W. Norton, 1962.

Friedman, Thomas. *The Lexus and the Olive Tree: Understanding Globalization*. New York: Farrar, Straus and Giroux, 1999.

Frye, Northrop. *The Anatomy of Criticism: Four Essays*. Princeton, N.J.: Princeton University Press, 1957.

Fukuyama, Francis. *The End of History and the Last Man*. New York: The Free Press, 1992.

Gabrieli, Francesco. *Arab Historians of the Crusades*. New York: Dorset Press, 1957.

Gadamer, Hans-Georg. *Truth and Method*. New York: The Seabury Press, 1975.

———. *Truth and Method*. Translated and revised by Joel Weinsheimer and Donald J. Marshall. 2d ed. New York: Continuum, 1994.

Gallie, W. B. *Philosophy and the Historical Understanding*. New York: Schocken Books, 1964.

Garraty, John A. and Peter Gay, eds. *The Columbia History of the World*. New York: Harper and Row, 1972.

Garrett, H. Dean. "Daniel: Ancient Prophet for the Latter Days." In *The Old Testament and the Latter-Day Saints: Proceedings of the Fourteenth Annual Sidney B. Sperry Symposium*, 261–276. Sandy, Utah.: Randall, 1987.

Geertz, Clifford. *The Interpretation of Cultures*. New York: Basic Books, 1973.

Ghirshman, R. *Iran: From the Earliest Times to the Islamic Conquest*. Harmondsworth, England: Penguin, 1954.

Giles, H. A. *The Travels of Fa-hsien*. London: Cambridge University Press, 1923.

Gilpin, Robert. *War and Change in World Politics*. Cambridge: Cambridge University Press, 1981.

Gong, Gerrit. *The Standard of Civilization in International Society*. Oxford: Oxford University Press, 1984.

Goldstein, Joshua S. *Long Cycles: Prosperity and War in the Modern Age*. New Haven, Conn.: Yale University Press, 1988.

Good News Bible: With Deuterocanonicals/Apocrypha. New York: American Bible Society, 1978.

Gordon, David C. *Images of the West: Third World Perspectives*. Savage, Md.: Rowman and Littlefield, 1989.

Gray, John. *Enlightenment's Wake: Politics and Culture at the Close of the Modern Age*. New York: Routledge, 1995.

Green, Peter. *Alexander to Actium: The Historical Evolution of the Hellenistic Age*. Berkeley and Los Angeles: University of California Press, 1993.

Green, Philip. *Deadly Logic: The Theory of Nuclear Deterrence*. Columbus: Ohio State University Press, 1966.

Greider, William. *One World, Ready or Not: The Manic Logic of Global Capitalism*. New York: Simon and Schuster, 1998.

Grimal, Pierre, ed. *Hellenism and the Rise of Rome*. New York: Delacorte Press, 1968.

Grousset, René. *The Empire of the Steps: A History of Central Asia*. New Brunswick, N.J.: Rutgers University Press, 1970.

Gulick, Edward V. *Europe's Classical Balance of Power*. New York: W. W. Norton, 1967.

Haas, Michael. "International Relations Theory." In *Approaches to the Study of Political Science*, 444–76. Edited by Michael Haas and Henry S. Kariel. Scranton, Penn.: Chandler, 1970.

———. "Asian Culture and International Relations." In *Culture and International Relations*, 172–90. Edited by Jongsuk Chay. New York: Praeger, 1990.

Habermas, Jürgen. *Knowledge and Human Interests*. London: Heinemann, 1972.

Hannerz, Ulf. *Cultural Complexity: Studies in the Social Organization of Meaning*. New York: Columbia University Press, 1992.

Held, David, Anthony McGrew, David Goldblatt, and Jonathan Perraton. *Global Transformation: Politics, Economics and Culture*. Stanford, CA: Stanford University Press, 1999.

Hempel, Carl G. *Philosophy and Natural Science*. Englewood Cliffs, NJ: Prentice-Hall, 1966.

Henkin, Louis. *How Nations Behave: Law and Foreign Policy*. New York: Praeger, 1968.

Herz, John H. *International Politics in the Atomic Age*. New York: Columbia University Press, 1959.

Hoffmann, Stanley, ed. *Contemporary Theory in International Relations*. Englewood Cliffs, N.J.: Prentice-Hall, 1960.

———. *The State of War: Essays on the Theory and Practice of International Politics*. New York: Praeger, 1965.

Holborn, Hajo. "Wilhelm Dilthey and the Critique of Historical Reason." In *European Intellectual History since Darwin and Marx*, 56–88. Edited by Warren W. Wagar. New York: Harper and Row, 1967.

Hopkins, Washburn E. *Ethics of India*. Port Washington, N.Y.: Kennikat Press, 1968.

Hoselitz, Bert F. "On Comparative History." *World Politics* 9 (1957): 267–79.

Hourani, Albert. *A History of the Arab Peoples*. New York: Warner Books, 1992.

Howard, Rhoda. "Occidentalism, Human Rights, and the Obligations of Western Scholars." *Canadian Journal of African Studies* 29 (1995): 110–26.

Hsü, Leonard Shihlien. *The Political Philosophy of Confucianism*. New York: E. P. Dutton, 1932.

Hughes, H. Stuart. *Consciousness and Society*. New York: Alfred A. Knopf, 1958.

Hume, David. *A Treatise of Human Nature*. Baltimore: Penguin, 1969.

Huntington, Samuel P. *The Third Wave: Democratization in the Late Twentieth Century.* Norman: University of Oklahoma Press, 1991.
———. "The Clash of Civilizations?" *Foreign Affairs* 72 (1993): 22–49.
———. *The Clash of Civilizations and the Remaking of World Order.* New York: Simon and Schuster, 1996.
Ignatieff, Michael. *The Warrior's Honor: Ethnic War and the Modern Conscience.* New York: Metropolitan, 1998.
Immerman, Richard H. *The CIA in Guatemala: The Foreign Policy of Intervention.* Austin: University of Texas Press, 1982.
International Comission on the Balkans. *Unfinished Peace: Report of the International Commission on the Balkans.* Washington, D.C.: Carnegie Endowment for International Peace, 1996.
Iqbal, Muhammad. *Poems from Iqbal.* London: Murray, 1955.
James, William. *The Meaning of Truth.* Cambridge, Mass.: Harvard University Press, 1975.
———. *Pragmatism.* Buffalo: Prometheus Books, 1991.
Japan Economic Institute. *Japan's Role in Multilateral Aid Organizations.* Washington, D.C.: Japan Economic Institute, 1988.
Jarvis, Darryl S. L. *International Relations and the Challenge of Postmodernism: Defending the Discipline.* Columbia: University of South Carolina Press, 1999.
Jaspers, Karl. *The Origins and Goal of History.* New Haven, Conn.: Yale University Press, 1953.
Jefferson, Thomas. *The Jefferson Bible: The Life and Morals of Jesus of Nazareth.* Boston: Beacon Press, 1989.
Johnson, Paul. *Modern Times: The World from the Twenties to the Eighties.* New York: Harper and Row, 1983.
Jönsson, Christer. "The Ideology of Foreign Policy." In *Foreign Policy: USA/USSR,* 91–110. Edited by Charles W. Kegley Jr. and Patrick McGowan. Beverly Hills: Sage, 1983.
Jouguet, Pierre. "Les Lagides et les Indigènes Égyptiens." In *Révue belge de philosophie et d'histoire* 2 (1923): 419–45.
———. "L'Égypt Ptolémaïque." In *Histoire de la Nation Égyptienne,* vol. 3, 34–188. Edited by Gabriel Hanotaux. Paris: Librarie Plon, 1931.
K'ang, Yu-wei. *Ta T'ung Shu: The One-World Philosophy of K'ang Yu-Wei.* Translated by Laurence G. Thompson. London: George Allen and Unwin, 1958.
Kann, Robert A. *A History of the Habsburg Empire, 1526–1918.* Berkeley and Los Angeles: University of California Press, 1974.
Kant, Immanuel, "Eternal Peace." In *The Philosophy of Kant: Immanuel Kant's Moral and Political Writings,* 430–76. Edited by Carl J. Friedrich. New York: The Modern Library, 1949.
———. "Idea for a Universal History with Cosmopolitan Intent." In *The Philosophy of Kant: Immanuel Kant's Moral and Political Writings,* 116–31. Edited by Carl J. Friedrich. New York: The Modern Library, 1949.
Kaplan, Morton. *System and Process in International Politics.* New York: Columbia University Press, 1957.
Kaplan, Morton. "Problems of Theory Building and Theory Confirmation in International Politics." In *The International System: Theoretical Essays,* 6–24. Edited by Klaus Knorr and Sidney Verba. Princeton, N.J.: Princeton University Press, 1961.
———. "The New Great Debate." In *Contending Approaches to International Politics,* 39–61. Edited by Klaus Knorr and James N. Rosenau. Princeton, N.J.: Princeton University Press, 1969.
Kaplan, Robert D. "The Coming Anarchy." *Atlantic Monthly,* February 1994, 44–76.
———. *The Ends of the Earth: A Journey to the Frontiers of Anarchy.* New York: Vintage, 1997.
———. *Warrior Politics: Why Leadership Demands a Pagan Ethos.* New York: Random House, 2002.
Keegan, John. *War and Our World.* New York: Vintage Books, 2001.
Kegley, Charles W. Jr. "Bridge Building in the Study of International Relations: How 'Kuhn' We Do Better?" In *Visions of International Relations: Assessing an Academic Field,* 62–80. Edited by Donald J. Puchala. Columbia: University of South Carolina Press, 2002.
———, ed. *The Long Postwar Peace: Contending Explanations and Projections.* New York: Harper Collins, 1991.
Kekes, John. *Facing Evil.* Princeton, N.J.: Princeton University Press, 1990.
Kelly, Aileen. *Toward Another Shore: Russian Thinkers between Necessity and Chance.* New Haven, Conn.: Yale University Press, 1998.

————. *Views From Another Shore: Essays on Herzen, Chekhov and Bakhtin.* New Haven, Conn.: Yale University Press, 1999.

Kennedy, Paul. *The Rise and Fall of the Great Powers: Economic Change and Military Conflict from 1500 to 2000.* New York: Random House, 1987.

————. *Preparing for the Twenty-First Century.* New York: Random House, 1993.

Keohane, Robert O. *After Hegemony: Cooperation and Disorder in World Political Economy.* Princeton, N.J.: Princeton University Press, 1984.

————. "Theory and World Politics: Structural Realism and Beyond." In *International Relations Theory,* 126–66. Edited by Paul R. Viotti and Mark V. Kauppi. New York: Macmillan, 1987.

————. "International Liberalism Reconsidered." In *The Economic Limits to Modern Politics,* 165–94. Edited by John Dunn. New York: Cambridge University Press, 1990.

Keohane, Robert O. and Joseph S. Nye Jr. *Power and Interdependence: World Politics in Transition.* Boston: Little, Brown, 1977.

————. *Power and Interdependence.* 3d ed. New York: Longman, 2001.

Kinross, Lord. *The Ottoman Centuries: The Rise and Fall of the Turkish Empire.* New York: Morrow Quill, 1977.

Kipling, Rudyard. "The White Man's Burden." In *Great English Poets: Rudyard Kipling.* Edited by Geoffrey Moore. New York: Clarkson N. Potter, 1992.

Kissinger, Henry. *Report of the National Bipartisan Commission on Central America.* Submitted to the President of the United States January 10, 1984.

Knorr, Klaus and James N. Rosenau, eds. *Contending Approaches to International Politics.* Princeton, N.J.: Princeton University Press, 1969.

Kochan, Lionel and Richard Abraham. *The Making of Modern Russia.* 2d ed. Harmondsworth, England: Penguin Books, 1983.

Kockelman, Joseph J., ed. *Hermeneutic Phenomenology: Lectures and Essays.* Washington, D.C.: Center for Advanced Research in Phenomenology and University Press of America, 1988.

Koebner, Richard. *Empire.* New York: Grosset and Dunlap, 1965.

Kohn, Hans. *The Twentieth Century: A Mid-Way Account of the Western World.* New York: Macmillan, 1949.

Korbin, Stephen. "Back to the Future: Neomedievalism and the Postmodern Digital World Economy," *Journal of International Affairs* 51 (1998): 361–86.

Kostelanetz, Richard, "Contemporary American Esthetics." In *Esthetics Contemporary,* 19–35. Edited by Richard Kostelanetz. Buffalo: Prometheus Books, 1978.

Kott, Jan. *Shakespeare Our Contemporary.* Translated by Boleslaw Taborski. Garden City, N.Y.: Doubleday, 1964.

Krasner, Stephen D., ed. *International Regimes.* Ithaca, N.Y.: Cornell University Press, 1983.

Kuhn, Thomas. *The Structure of Scientific Revolutions.* 2d ed. Chicago: University of Chicago Press, 1974.

Kuhrt, Amélie and Susan Sherwin-White, eds. *Hellenism in the East.* Berkeley and Los Angeles: University of California Press, 1987.

Kurth, James. "Inside the Cave: The Banality of IR Studies." *National Interest* 53 (1998): 29–41.

Langer, Suzanne K. *Mind: An Essay on Human Feeling.* Baltimore: Johns Hopkins University Press, 1972.

————. *Philosophy in a New Key.* Cambridge, Mass.: Harvard University Press, 1972.

Lapid, Yosef. "The Third Debate." *International Studies Quarterly* 33 (1989): 235–54.

Lasswell, Harold D. *World Politics and Personal Insecurity.* New York: The Free Press, 1965.

Leiken, Robert and Barry Rubin, eds. *The Central American Crisis Today: The Essential Guide to the Most Controversial Foreign Policy Issue.* New York: Summit Books, 1987.

Lerner, Daniel. *The Passing of Traditional Society: Modernizing the Middle East.* New York: The Free Press, 1958.

Lin, Yutang. *The Wisdom of Confucius.* New York: The Modern Library, 1938.

Lippmann, Walter. *Men of Destiny.* Seattle and London: University of Washington Press, 1927.

Liska, George. *Imperial America: The International Politics of Primacy.* Baltimore: Johns Hopkins University Press, 1967.

Lloyd, Alan. *Destroy Carthage!* London: Souvenir Press, 1977.

MacIver, Robert M. *The Web of Government.* New York: Macmillan, 1947.

Mahbubani, Kishore. *Can Asians Think?* Singapore: Times Books International, 1999.

Makkreel, Rudolph A. *Dilthey: Philosopher of the Human Studies.* Princeton, N.J.: Princeton University Press, 1975.

Mann, Michael. *The Sources of Social Power 2: The Rise of Classes and Nation-States, 1760–1940.* Cambridge: Cambridge University Press, 1993.

———. "Has Globalization Ended the Rise and Rise of the Nation-State?" In *International Order and the Future of World Politics,* 237–61. Edited by T. V. Paul and John A. Hall. Cambridge: Cambridge University Press, 1999.

Manning, C. A. W. *The Nature of International Society.* London: John Wiley and Sons, 1962.

Mansbach, Richard W. "Deterritorializing Global Politics." In *Visions of International Relations: Assessing an Academic Field,* 101–18. Edited by Donald J. Puchala. Columbia: University of South Carolina Press, 2002.

Manuel, Frank E. *Shapes of Philosophical History.* Stanford, Calif.: Stanford University Press, 1965.

Marcus, George E. and Michael M. J Fisher. *Anthropology As Cultural Critique.* Chicago: University of Chicago Press, 1986.

Marder, Arthur J. *From Dreadnought to Scapa Flow, The Royal Navy in the Fisher Era, 1904–1919.* Vol. 1. London: Oxford University Press, 1961.

Marlow, A. N., ed. *Radharkrishnan: An Anthology.* London: George Allen and Unwin, 1952.

May, Ernest. "The Cold War." In *The Making of America's Soviet Policy,* 209–30. Edited by Joseph S. Nye, Jr. New Haven, Conn.: Yale University Press, 1984.

Mazrui, Ali Amin. *Cultural Forces in World Politics.* London: James Currey, 1990.

———. "Islamic and Western Values." *Foreign Affairs* 76 (1997): 118–32.

McClelland, Charles A. *Theory and the International System.* New York: Macmillan, 1966.

McGowan, Patrick J. and Howard B. Shapiro. *The Comparative Study of Foreign Policy: A Survey of Scientific Findings.* Vol. 4. Beverly Hills: Sage, 1973.

McNeill, William H. *The Rise of the West.* Chicago: University of Chicago Press, 1963.

———. *Mythistory and Other Essays.* Chicago: University of Chicago Press, 1986.

Mei, Y. P. "The Basis of Social, Ethical, and Spiritual Values in Chinese Philosophy." In *The Chinese Mind,* 149–66. Edited by Charles A. Moore. Honolulu: East-West Center Press, 1967.

Messer, Robert L. "World War II and the Coming of the Cold War." In *Modern American Diplomacy,* 107–26. Edited by John M. Carroll and George C. Herring. Wilmington, Del.: Scholarly Resources, 1986.

Milne, J. Grafton. "Egyptian Nationalism under Greek and Roman Rule." *Journal of Egyptian Archeology* 14 (1928): 226–34.

Mitrany, David. *A Working Peace System.* Chicago: Quadrangle Books, 1966.

Mittelman, James H. *The Globalization Syndrome: Transformation and Resistance.* Princeton, N.J.: Princeton University Press, 2000.

Modelski, George and William Thompson. *Leading Sectors and World Politics: The Co-Evolution of Global Economics and Politics.* Columbia: University of South Carolina Press, 1995.

Montagu, M. F. Ashley. *Toynbee and History: Critical Essays and Reviews.* Boston: Porter Sargent, 1956.

Moore, Barrington, Jr. *Social Origins of Dictatorship and Democracy: Lord and Peasant in the Making of the Modern World.* Boston: Beacon Press, 1966.

Moore, Gerald and Ulli Beier, eds. *The Penguin Book of Modern African Poetry.* London: Penguin, 1963.

Morgenthau, Hans J. *Politics among Nations: The Struggle for Power and Peace.* 4th ed. New York: Alfred A. Knopf, 1967.

Morick, Harold, ed. *Challenges to Empiricism.* Indianapolis: Hackett, 1980.

Morse, Edward L. *Modernization and the Transformation of International Relations.* New York: The Free Press, 1976.

Moynihan, Daniel Patrick. *On the Law of Nations.* Cambridge, Mass.: Harvard University Press, 1990.

Musti, Domenico. "Syria and the West." In *The Cambridge Ancient History,* Vol. 7, part 1, 2d ed., 175–220. Edited by F. W. Walbank, A. E. Austin, M. W. Frederiksen and R. M. Ogilvie. Cambridge: Cambridge University Press, 1984.

Neillands, Robin. *The Hundred Years War.* New York: Routledge, 1990.

Newark, Tim. *The Barbarians: Warriors and Wars of the Dark Ages.* Dorset: Blandford Press, 1985.

Ngugi, wa Thiong'o. *Decolonizing the Mind: The Politics of Language in African Literature.* London: James Currey, 1986.

Nichols, Robert S. *Factors Influencing Perception of the US/USSR Military Balance.* Carlisle Barracks, Penn.: Strategic Studies Institute, U.S. Army War College, 1978.

Nisbet, Robert A. *Social Change and History: Aspects of the Western Theory of Development.* New York: Oxford University Press, 1969.

Northrup, F. S. C. *The Meeting of East and West: An Inquiry Concerning World Understanding.* Woodbridge, Conn.: Ox Bow Press, 1946.

Novick, Peter. *That Noble Dream: The "Objectivity Question" and the American Historical Profession.* New York: Cambridge University Press, 1988.

Nussbaum, Martha C. "Human Functioning and Social Justice: In Defense of Aristotelian Essentialism." *Political Theory* 20 (1992): 202–46.

Nye, Joseph S., Jr. *Bound to Lead: The Changing Nature of American Power.* New York: Basic Books, 1990.

Nye, Joseph S., Jr. and Robert O Keohane. "Transnational Relations and World Politics: An Introduction." *International Organization* 25 (1971): 326–50.

O'Neill, Eugene. "Mourning Becomes Electra." In *Three Plays of Eugene O'Neill,* 227–376. New York: Vintage Books, 1959.

Ogata, Sadako. "The Changing Role of Japan in the United Nations." *Journal of International Affairs* 37 (1983): 29–42.

Oneal, John R. and Bruce M. Russett. "The Pacific Benefits of Democracy, Interdependence, and International Organizations, 1885–1992." *World Politics* 52 (1999): 1–37.

Onuf, Nicholas. *World of Our Making: Rules and Rule in Social Theory and International Relations.* Columbia: University of South Carolina Press, 1989.

Organski, A. F. K. "The Power Transition." In *International Politics and Foreign Policy,* 367–75. Edited by James N. Rosenau. New York: The Free Press of Glencoe, 1961.

Ostrogorsky, George. *History of the Byzantine State.* New Brunswick, N.J.: Rutgers University Press, 1969.

Palmer, Richard H. *Tragedy and Tragic Theory.* Westport, Conn.: Greenwood Press, 1992.

Panikkar, K. M. *Asia and Western Dominance: A Survey of the Vasco Da Gama Epoch of Asian History, 1498–1945.* London: George Allen and Unwin, 1959.

Parker, Geoffrey. *The Thirty Years' War.* New York: Military Heritage Press, 1987.

Parkinson, F. *The Philosophy of International Relations: A Study in the History of Thought.* Beverly Hills: Sage, 1977.

Parsons, Talcott. "Evolutionary Universals in Society." *American Sociological Review* 29 (1964): 339–57.

Pfaff, William. *Barbarian Sentiments: How the American Century Ends.* New York: Hill and Wang, 1989.

Pharr, Susan J. "Japan and the World: The Debate in Japan." *Harvard International Review* 10 (1988): 35–38.

Pirenne, Henri. *Mohammed and Charlemagne.* Translated by Bernard Miall. New York: Barnes and Noble, 1992.

Polanyi, Karl. *The Great Transformation: The Political and Economic Origins of Our Time.* Boston: Beacon Press, 1957.

Pollack, Jonathan. "China and the Global Strategic Balance." In *China's Foreign Relations in the 1980s,* 146–76. Edited by Harry Harding. New Haven, Conn.: Yale University Press, 1984.

Polybius. *On Roman Imperialism: The Histories of Polybius Translated from the Text of F. Hultsch.* Translated by Evelyn S. Shuckbaugh. South Bend, Ind.: Regnery/Gateway, 1980.

Pomeroy, Sarah B. *Goddesses, Whores, Wives, and Slaves: Women in Classical Antiquity.* New York: Schocken Books, 1975.

Pond, Elizabeth. *The Rebirth of Europe.* 2d ed. Washington: Brookings, 2002.

Popper, Karl. *The Poverty of Historicism.* New York: Harper and Row, 1961.

Preaux, Claire. "Esquisse d'Une Histoire des Révolutions Égyptiennes sous les Lagides." *Chronique d'Égypte* 22 (1936): 522–52.

———. "Les Égyptiens dans la Civilisation Hellénistique d'Égypte." *Chronique D'Égypt* 35 (1943): 148–60.

Preston, Ronald. "Christian Ethics." In *A Companion to Ethics,* 91–105. Edited by Peter Singer. Oxford: Blackwell, 1991.

Puchala, Donald J. "The Ethics of Globalism," John F. Holmes Memorial Lecture, Academic Council on the United Nations System, New York, June, 1995. Providence, R.I.: Academic Council on the United Nations System, 1995.

———. "World Images, World Orders, and Cold Wars: Mythistory and the United Nations." *International Social Science Review* 144 (1995): 243–59.

———. "Third World Thinking and Contemporary International Relations." In *International Relations and the Third World,* 133–58. Edited by Stephanie G. Neuman. New York: St. Martin's Press, 1998.

———, ed. *Visions of International Relations: Assessing an Academic Discipline.* Columbia: University of South Carolina Press, 2002.

Quigley, Carroll. *The Evolution of Civilization: An Introduction to Historical Analysis.* New York: Macmillan, 1961.

Radhakrishnan, S. *Eastern Religions and Western Thought.* Oxford: Clarendon Press, 1949.

———. *An Idealist View of Life.* London: George Allen and Unwin, 1964.

Randall, John Herman, Jr. *The Making of the Modern Mind: A Survey of the Intellectual Background to the Present Age.* Cambridge, Mass.: Houghton Mifflin, 1940.

Ranke, Leopold von. "The Great Powers." In *The Theory and Practice of History,* 65–101. Edited by Georg Iggers and Konrad von Moltke. New York: Bobbs-Merrill, 1973.

Rapoport, Anatol. *Strategy and Conscience.* New York: Schocken Books, 1969.

Ray, James Lee. *Democracy and International Conflict: An Evaluation of the Democratic Peace Proposition.* Columbia: University of South Carolina Press, 1995.

Reid, Louis Arnaud. *Knowledge and Truth.* London: Macmillan, 1923.

Reischauer, Edwin O. and John K. Fairbank. *East Asia.* Boston: Houghton Mifflin, 1960.

Richardson, Lewis Fry. *Arms and Insecurity: A Mathematical Study of the Causes and Origins of War.* Pittsburgh: Boxwood Press, 1960.

Rorty, Richard. *Philosophy and the Mirror of Nature.* Princeton, N.J.: Princeton University Press, 1979.

Rosenau, James N., ed. *International Politics and Foreign Policy.* New York: The Free Press of Glencoe, 1961.

Rostovzeff, Michael. "Ptolemaic Egypt." In *The Cambridge Ancient History,* vol. 7, 109–54. Edited by S. A. Cook, F. E. Adcock and M. P. Charlesworth. London: Cambridge University Press, 1928.

Ruggie, John Gerard. "Continuity and Transformation in the World Polity: Toward a Neutralist Synthesis." *World Politics* 35 (1983): 261–85.

———. "Territoriality and Beyond: Problematizing Modernity in International Relations." *International Organization* 47 (1993): 139–74.

Russett, Bruce M. *International Regions and the International System: A Study in Political Ecology.* Chicago: Rand McNally, 1967.

Russett, Bruce M., John Oneal, and David R. Davis. "The Third Leg of the Kantian Tripod: International Organization and Militarized Disputes, 1950–1985." *International Organization* 52 (1998): 441–68.

Said, Edward W. *Orientalism: Western Conceptions of the Orient.* London: Penguin, 1991.

———. *Culture and Imperialism.* New York: Alfred A. Knopf, 1993.

Salmon, Wesley C. *The Foundations of Scientific Inference.* Pittsburgh: University of Pittsburgh Press, 1979.

Sanders, Jerry W. *Peddlers of Crisis: The Committee on the Present Danger and the Politics of Containment.* Boston: South End Press, 1983.

Sarup, Madan. *An Introductory Guide to Post-Structuralism and Postmodernism.* 2d ed. Athens, Ga.: University of Georgia Press, 1993.

Schilpp, Paul Arthur, ed. *The Philosophy of Radhakrishnan.* New York: Tudor, 1952.

Schlereth, Thomas J. *The Cosmopolitan Ideal in Enlightenment Thought: Its Form and Function in the Ideas of Franklin, Hume, and Voltaire, 1694–1790.* Notre Dame, Ind.: University of Notre Dame Press, 1977.

Schmidt, Brian. *The Political Discourse of Anarchy: A Disciplinary History of International Relations.* Albany, N.Y.: State University of New York Press, 1998.

Schmookler, Andrew B. *The Parable of the Tribes: The Problem of Power in Social Evolution*. Boston: Houghton Mifflin, 1984.

Schopenhauer, Arthur. *The World As Will and Idea*. Translated by R. B. Haldane and J. Kemp. London: Kegan Paul, Trench, Trubner, 1907.

Schuyler, Robert Livingston. "Indeterminism in Physics and History." *Social Studies* 27 (1936): 507–16.

Schuman, Frederick L. *International Relations, The Western State System and the World Community*. New York: McGraw-Hill, 1958.

Schumpeter, Joseph. *Imperialism and Social Classes*. Cleveland: World, 1955.

Sellars, Wilfrid. *Science, Perception and Reality*. London: Routledge and Kegan Paul, 1963.

Sewall, Richard B. "The Tragic Form." *Essays in Criticism* 4 (1954): 345–58.

———. "The Vision of Tragedy." *Review of Metaphysics* 10 (1956): 193–200.

Shakespeare, William. "The Tragedy of Macbeth." Edited by Eugene M. Waith. Revised ed. New Haven, Conn.: Yale University Press, 1954.

Sharma, I. C. *Ethical Philosophies of India*. Lincoln, Neb.: Johnsen, 1965.

Sherwin-White, Susan. "Seleucid Babylonia: A Case-Study for the Installation and Development of Greek Rule." In *Hellenism in the East: The Interactions of Greek and Non-Greek Civilizations from Syria to Central Asia after Alexander*, 1–31. Edited by Amélie Kuhrt and Susan Sherwin-White. Berkeley and Los Angeles: University of California Press, 1987.

Shulman, Marshall D. "The Superpowers: Dance of the Dinosaurs." *Foreign Affairs* 66 (1987–1988): 494–515.

Simes, Dimitri K. "Soviet Policy toward the United States." In *The Making of America's Soviet Policy*, 291–324. Edited by Joseph S. Nye Jr. New Haven, Conn.: Yale University Press, 1984.

Singer, J. David. "Data-Making in International Relations." *Behavioral Science* 10 (1965): 68–80.

———. "The Incomplete Theorist: Insight Without Evidence." In *Contending Approaches to International Politics*, 62–88. Edited by Klaus Knorr and James N. Rosenau. Princeton, N.J.: Princeton University Press, 1969.

———. *The Correlates of War*. New York: The Free Press, 1979.

———, ed. *Quantitative International Politics*. New York: The Free Press, 1968.

Singh, Durlab. *The Sentinel of the East: A Biographical Study of Rabindra Nath Tagore*. New York: Haskell House, 1974.

Skocpol, Theda. "A Critical Review of Barrington Moore's *Social Origins of Dictatorship and Democracy*." In *Social Revolutions in the Modern World*, 25–54. Edited by Theda Skocpol. New York: Cambridge University Press, 1994.

Smith, Steve. "The Self-Images of a Discipline: A Genealogy of International Relations Theory." In *International Relations Theory Today*, 1–37. Edited by Ken Booth and Steve Smith. University Park: Pennsylvania State University Press, 1995.

Smith, Steve, Ken Booth, and Marysia Zalewski. *International Theory: Positivism and Beyond*. Cambridge: Cambridge University Press, 1996.

Somit, Albert and Joseph Tanenhaus. *American Political Science: A Profile of a Discipline*. New York: Atherton Press, 1964.

Sontag, Raymond J. *Germany and England, Background of Conflict, 1848–1918*. New York: Appleton-Century, 1938.

Sorokin, Pitirim. *Social Philosophies of an Age of Crisis*. Boston: Beacon Press, 1950.

———. *Social and Cultural Dynamics: A Study of Change in Major Systems of Art, Truth, Ethics, Law, and Social Relationships*. New Brunswick, N.J.: Transaction Publishers, 1991.

Soroos, Marvin S. *Beyond Sovereignty: The Challenge of Global Policy*. Columbia: University of South Carolina Press, 1986.

Spanier, John. *American Foreign Policy since World War II*. 11th ed. Washington, D.C.: Congressional Quarterly Press, 1988.

Spengler, Oswald. *The Decline of West*. Abridged ed. New York: Oxford University Press, 1991.

Spuler, Bertold. *History of the Mongols*. New York: Dorset Press, 1988.

Starr, Harvey. "Visions of Global Politics As an Intellectual Exercise: Three Questions without Answers." In *Visions of International Relations: Assessing an Academic Field*, 42–61. Edited by Donald J. Puchala. Columbia: University of South Carolina Press, 2002.

Stillman, Edmund and William Pfaff, *The Politics of Hysteria: The Sources of Twentieth Century Conflict*. New York: Harper and Row, 1964.

Stirling, James Hutchinson. *Text-Book to Kant: The Critique of Pure Reason*. Edinburgh: Oliver and Boyd, 1881.

Strange, Susan. "Cave! Hic Dragones: A Critique of Regime Analysis." In *International Regimes*, 337–54. Edited by Stephen D. Krasner. Ithaca, N.Y.: Cornell University Press, 1983.

Swedberg, Richard. "The New 'Battle of Methods,'" *Challenge* 33 (1990): 33–38.

Tarn, W. W. *The Greeks in Bactria and India*. London: Cambridge University Press, 1951.

Taylor, A. J. P. *The Struggle for Mastery in Europe, 1848–1918*. London: Oxford University Press, 1954.

Teggart, Frederick J. *Theory and Process of History*. Berkeley and Los Angeles: University of California Press, 1977.

Thayer, H. S. *Meaning and Action: A Critical History of Pragmatism*. Indianapolis: Hackett, 1968.

Thompson, Kenneth W. "Toynbee and the Theory of International Politics," *Political Science Quarterly* 71 (1956): 365–86.

Thompson, William R. *On Global War: Historical-Structural Approaches to World Politics*. Columbia: University of South Carolina Press, 1988.

Thucydides. *The History of the Peloponnesian War*. Edited in translation by Sir Richard Livingston. New York: Oxford University Press, 1960.

Tilly, Charles. *The Formation of Nation-States in Western Europe*. Princeton, N.J.: Princeton University Press, 1975.

Todorov, Tzvetan. *The Conquest of America*. New York: Harper Perennial, 1992.

Toynbee, Arnold. *The World and the West*. London: Oxford University Press, 1953.

——— with Jane Caplan. *A Study of History*. Revised and abridged ed. New York: Portland House, 1988.

Treadgold, Donald. *Freedom: A History*. New York: New York University Press, 1990.

Trudeau, Robert and Lars Schoultz. "Guatemala." In *Security through Diplomacy in Central America*, 23–49. Edited by Morris J. Blachman, William M. LeoGrande, and Kenneth Sharpe. New York: Pantheon, 1986.

Tsukamoto, Zenryu. "Chinese Culture Overseas." In *Half of the World: The History and Culture of China and Japan*, 169–94. Edited by Arnold Toynbee. London: Thames and Hudson, 1973.

Tucker, Robert W. and David C. Hendrickson. *The Imperial Temptation: The New World Order and America's Purpose*. New York: Council on Foreign Relations, 1992.

UNESCO. *All Men Are Brothers: Life and Thoughts of Mahatma Gandhi as Told in His Own Words*. Paris: UNESCO, 1958.

Van Alstyne, Richard W. *The Rising American Empire*. New York: W. W. Norton, 1974.

Vernadsky, G. *The Mongols and Russia*. London: Oxford University Press, 1953.

Wagar, W. Warren. *World Views: A Study in Comparative History*. Hinsdale, Ill.: Dryden Press, 1977.

———, ed. *European Intellectual History Since Darwin and Marx* . New York: Harper and Row, 1967.

Walbank, F. W., A. E. Austin, M. W. Frederiksen, and H. M. Ogilvie, eds. *The Cambridge Ancient History*, Vol. 7, pt. 1, 2d. ed. Cambridge: Cambridge University Press, 1984.

Wales, H. G. Quaritch. *The Indianization of China and of South-East Asia*. London: Bernard Quaritch, 1967.

Wallerstein, Immanuel. *The Capitalist World-Economy*. New York: Cambridge University Press, 1979.

———. "Should We Unthink Nineteenth-Century Social Science?" *International Social Science Journal* 118 (1988): 525–31.

Waltz, Kenneth. *Man, the State and War*. New York: Columbia University Press. 1959.

———. *Theory of International Politics*. Reading, Mass.: Addison-Wesley, 1979.

Warner, Fred Neal and Bruce D. Hamlett. "The Never-Never Land of International Relations." *International Studies Quarterly* 13 (1969): 281–305.

Watkins, Frederick M. *The State As a Concept in Political Science*. New York: Harper and Brothers, 1934.

Watson, Adam. *The Evolution of International Society: A Comparative Historical Analysis*. New York: Routledge, 1972.

Weber, Max. "'Objectivity' in Social Science and Social Policy." In *The Methodology of the Social Sciences*, 49–112. Translated and edited by Edward Shils and Henry A. Finch. New York: The Free Press, 1949.

Weber, Max. *The Protestant Ethic and Spirit of Capitalism.* New York: Scribner's, 1958.

Wedgewood, C. V. *The Thirty Years' War.* London: Jonathan Cape, 1938.

Weil, Simone. "The Iliad, or Poem of Force." Translated by Mary McCarthy. *Politics* 2 (1945): 321–31.

Weltman, John. *World Politics and the Evolution of War.* Baltimore: Johns Hopkins University Press, 1995.

Wendt, Alexander E. "The Agent-Structure Problem in International Relations Theory." *International Organization* 31 (1987): 335–70.

———. "Anarchy Is What States Make of It: The Social Construction of State Politics," *International Organization* 46 (1992): 383–425.

Westerfield, H. Bradford. *The Arms Race and Current Soviet Doctrine.* New Haven, Conn.: Yale University Press, 1959.

White, Hayden. *Metahistory: The Historical Imagination of Nineteenth Century Europe.* Baltimore: Johns Hopkins University Press, 1973.

———. "Interpretation in History." In *Tropics of Discourse: Essays in Cultural Criticism,* 51–80. Baltimore: Johns Hopkins University Press, 1978.

———. *Tropics of Discourse: Essays in Cultural Criticism.* Baltimore: Johns Hopkins University Press, 1978.

Whitehead, Alfred North. *Adventures of Ideas.* London: Cambridge University Press, 1933.

Wilkinson, David. *Twelve Articles in Blue Covers.* Unpublished manuscript. University of California at Los Angeles, 1995.

———. *Sixteen Papers in Grey Covers.* Unpublished manuscript. University of California at Los Angeles, 1996.

Wittfogel, Karl A. *Oriental Despotism: A Comparative Study of Total Power.* New Haven, Conn.: Yale University Press, 1957.

Woolhouse, R. S. *The Empiricists.* New York: Oxford University Press, 1988.

Wright, Quincy. *A Study of War.* 2 vols. Chicago: University of Chicago Press, 1942.

Yarshater, Ehsan, ed. *The Cambridge History of Iran.* Vol. 3, part 1, *The Seleucid, Parthian and Sassanian Periods.* London: Cambridge University Press, 1983.

Young, Oran R. "Professor Russett: Industrious Tailor to a Naked Emperor," *World Politics* 21 (1969): 486–511.

———. "Aron and the Whale: A Jonah in Theory." In *Contending Approaches to International Politics,* 129–48. Edited by Klaus Knorr and James N. Rosenau. Princeton, N.J.: Princeton University Press, 1969.

———. *Governance in World Affairs.* Ithaca, N.Y.: Cornell University Press, 1999.

Zacker, Mark W. and Richard A. Matthew. "Liberal International Theory: Common Threads, Divergent Strands." In *Controversies in International Relations Theory: Realism and the Neoliberal Challenge,* 107–50. Edited by Charles W. Kegley Jr. New York: St. Martin's Press, 1995.

Zakaria, Fareed. "Culture Is Destiny: A Conversation with Lee Kwan Yew." *Foreign Affairs* 73 (1994): 109–26.

Index

ABOUT THE AUTHOR

Rosemary Righter is the chief editorial writer of the *Times*, London, specializing in international affairs. Educated at Cambridge University, she worked in historical research before entering journalism in the Far East, where she was assistant editor of the *Far Eastern Economic Review* and worked for *Newsweek*. Her interest in the United Nations is of long standing. As development and then diplomatic correspondent of the *Sunday Times* between 1978 and 1985, she traveled extensively, observing the UN in the field as well as attending international conferences. She is a member of the Royal Institute of International Affairs and of the Council of the Overseas Development Institute, London. This is her third book on international affairs.